DOUGLAS FAIRBANKS
AND THE AMERICAN CENTURY

Other books by coauthors John C. Tibbetts and James M. Welsh

American Classic Screen: Features (2010)
American Classic Screen: Profiles (2010)
American Classic Screen: Interviews (2010)
The Encyclopedia of Novels into Film (2005)
Shakespeare into Film (with Richard Vela) (2002)
The Encyclopedia of Filmmakers (2 vols.) (2002)
The Encyclopedia of Stage Plays into Film (2001)
The Cinema of Tony Richardson: Essays and Interviews (1999)
His Majesty the American (1977)

DOUGLAS FAIRBANKS

AND THE AMERICAN CENTURY

John C. Tibbetts *and* James M. Welsh

Foreword by Kevin Brownlow

University Press of Mississippi / *Jackson*

www.upress.state.ms.us

The University Press of Mississippi is a member
of the Association of American University Presses.

Drawings in Appendix B by Maurice Leloir are courtesy of the authors. Unless otherwise indicated, all other illustrations are courtesy of National Film Society Archives.

First printing 2014
∞
Library of Congress Cataloging-in-Publication Data

Tibbetts, John C.
Douglas Fairbanks and the American century / John C. Tibbetts, James M. Welsh.
pages cm
Includes index.
ISBN 978-1-62846-006-3 (hardback) — ISBN 978-1-62846-007-0 (ebook) 1. Fairbanks, Douglas, 1883–1939—Criticism and interpretation. I. Welsh, James Michael. II. Title.
PN2287.F3T46 2014
791.4302'8092—dc23 2013042775

British Library Cataloging-in-Publication Data available

This book is dedicated to the late James M. Welsh (1938–2013). He was a loyal friend and inspiring colleague for many of us for more than half a century. This book, his final project, stands as a testament to his life's work and enduring presence.

This book is also dedicated to Tracey Goessel, whose enthusiasm, scholarship, and tireless devotion to the Fairbanks story inspires a new generation of Fairbanks scholars.

CONTENTS

Douglas and Vera Fairbanks, 1996 (courtesy Vera Fairbanks).

A PERSONAL GREETING

—Vera Fairbanks (Mrs. Douglas Fairbanks Jr.)

Here are two remarkable men, Douglas Fairbanks and Douglas Fairbanks Jr., father and son, both so different from one another and yet both so accomplished. Included in these pages are the voices that bring both men back to life . . . both men who in the end, although shy of one another, finally come together to form an everlasting bond.

I knew that life would never be the same once I met Douglas Fairbanks Jr. (1909–2000). Never had I met anyone like him, before or since. To this day, others fade by comparison. Looking back, I wonder, was this all a dream? It was as though he had stepped out of the pages of a romantic novel. Once you saw him, you could never forget him. Once you met him, you never wanted to leave him.

All his life he enriched the lives of not only the English-speaking world, but the world as a whole. His credits . . . actor, producer, director, writer, diplomat, war hero, raconteur . . . only skim the surface of the man himself. It is indeed difficult to imagine this man who had it all.

He was six-feet tall, with baby blues, a dazzling, infectious smile to warm the entire room, impossibly handsome and charming, impeccably attired, and with a refreshingly modest demeanor. He was a gentleman's gentleman. He was intelligent and well-informed, witty, fun-loving, and adventurous. He had an insatiable curiosity about everything and anything there was to do and know about life and the world—

And he experienced it all.

When asked to what he attributed his longevity, the reply was always the same: "Never being bored a day in my life." Indeed, I soon found out that he lived the life found only in storybooks.

I first met Douglas in 1965 in Acapulco, Mexico, on the rooftop of the Tropical Hotel. It was at a publicity dinner/dance for Pucci's Vivara perfume, hosted by Harding Lawrence of Braniff Airlines. "Jet-setters" were flown in from all over the world. Douglas was staying with Merle Oberon. I was a merchandiser for QVC, the home shopping network, and I was on holiday with friends. At first, I had no idea who he was. Having met, we soon discovered that we lived seven blocks from one another in New York City! Little did I know then that the trip to Acapulco would forge my destiny. Never would I have believed . . . !

In 1991, Douglas and I married at St. Thomas Church on 5th Avenue. We lived blissfully and happily for ten years until his passing in 2000. To this day, he is the light of my life and my energy. He was a rarity, the likes of which we shall not meet again.

It is only recently that, after much thought, I decided to have an estate sale at Doyle Gallery in New York in his memory. The opening night reception was billed, "Dashing, Daring, Distinguished." Rather than continue to hoard the things Douglas loved, I thought it appropriate to allow the public to enjoy the things that he surrounded himself with during his lifetime, with the proceeds earmarked for a scholarship at the USC School of Cinematic Arts. It was his father, Douglas Sr., whose vision had been the foundation for establishing the school. His father's life-size bronze statue stands in the center courtyard. Today, the school enjoys the reputation as the largest and finest film school in the country. I feel confident that Douglas Jr. would have wholeheartedly approved of my decision. Although the scholarship is yet to be funded, I have decided to invest all auction proceeds myself until which time I have enough to make a meaningful contribution.

If anyone is so inclined, your participation would be gladly welcomed.

I hope that I have piqued your curiosity about Douglas Jr. I am so glad his story is included here in this book. Among other things, it is a testament to the devotion he had for his father all his life. He was not born with a "silver spoon in his mouth," as one might suppose, having such a distinguished father. Against so many odds, he made it on his own, starting out at the age of thirteen of divorced parents, with a scarcity of money. He marched to his own drum and never looked down. He loved life with a passion. His only regret was not being able to go on.

Here is the address for the Vera and Douglas Fairbanks Jr. Scholarship Fund:

Dean Elizabeth Daley,
Professor and Dean
School of Cinematic Arts
University of Southern California 90089-2211
900 West 34th Street
Suite 465
Los Angeles, California 90089-2211
(213-740-2804)

FOREWORD: A FAIRBANKS MEMOIR

He was the kind of man I would have liked to have grown into—as strong as a boxer, as lithe as a dancer, and he never forced his athleticism on you. He used it only when he had to.
—KEVIN BROWNLOW

I am delighted to see this newly revised and expanded edition of *His Majesty the American*, which has long been out of print since it first appeared in 1977. It takes me back to my own lifelong enthusiasm for silent films, which was first sparked by Douglas Fairbanks.

I was just eleven when my parents gave me a hand-cranked 9.5 mm projector and two short films. It was 1949. The streets off Baker Street, near where I lived in London, were lined with little shops which seemed to make no money. One of these was a photographic shop. I walked in and asked if they had any 9.5 mm films. I was thrilled when the shop assistant presented me with a pile of small tins. They were made of heavy black metal, imprinted with the name "PATHE-BABY" and containing 60 feet of film. The assistant wanted 1/6d a tin, the equivalent in those days of a pocketbook, or a lengthy bus journey. When I got the films home I projected them for my mother; the first I put on was entitled *The First Man*. I was immediately struck by the beautiful photographic quality—the film was a joy to watch. I was also very taken with the ebullient personality of the leading man. I had no idea who he was, but when my mother cried, "It's Douglas Fairbanks!" I realized I had heard the name. My mother had loved Fairbanks in her youth. She remembered that in one of his films there was a scene that flashed into her head every time she got up in the morning: Doug had rigged his bed so that it drove automatically to the bathroom, and at the pull of a lever, slid him effortlessly into the warm tub. (It turned out to be a scene from *The Nut* [1920]). The excitement I felt at

Kevin Brownlow, London (courtesy John C. Tibbetts).

having found a film so fascinating in its own right was increased by my mother's delight.

The First Man was set in "Narraport-by-the-Sea," a thin disguise, I learned, for the high-society resort of Newport, Rhode Island. It was a satire on the commercial aristocrats of America, the railroad tycoons and the beef barons. While they spend the week in New York, their womenfolk idle away the summer at Narraport. Life here is so dreary for the girls, so starved of male company until the weekends. One of them, Geraldine (Jewel Carmen), promises to kiss the first man she meets. He turns out to be a startled butterfly hunter, Cassius Lee, (Fairbanks) an authentic FFOV (First Family of Virginia). When the guests arrive at the hotel, one of them, Percy Peck, a malted milk manufacturer, makes a dead set at Geraldine, but fails to impress her. He notices that Cassius is dressed as he is, and has the same build, so he persuades him to pull a few stunts—like flying a hydroplane—while taking the credit himself. Geraldine is at last impressed, but Peck is running weapons to the Mexicans at a time when American troops are pursuing Pancho Villa. As soon as Cassius realizes this he sets off in pursuit. Peck kidnaps Geraldine and her father and Cassius has to seize the hydroplane to rescue them.

An American Aristocracy (1917) first captured Kevin Brownlow's interest in Fairbanks.

The film was handled in a charming and humorous way and gave Doug the chance to demonstrate his athletic skills. I could tell the film was very old, because of the hydroplane. I had never seen such an aircraft before—it looked as though someone had installed an engine in a bare wooden skeleton and sent it aloft. To a boy accustomed to the Spitfires and Messerschmitts of that time, the machine seemed antediluvian and intrigued me as much as the motor cars, whose engines were ten times longer than those I was used to.

Fairbanks appealed to me more than most of the actors I saw at my local cinema. He was both charming and funny, a refreshing contrast to that manufactured, not-quite-human quality of current Hollywood stars I had been seeing, like Rock Hudson or Mario Lanza. Doug was unpredictable—I found out later that he had little talent for the straightforward playing of a scene, so to give it pep he invariably did something unexpected. Encountering an obstacle—a locked gate, a high wire fence—he hops over it. Instead of walking into a scene and talking to his valet, as another actor would do, he expresses his feelings by hurtling into the shot and leaping over him. In *When the Clouds Roll By*, made in 1919 and the best of the pre-costume pictures, he leaves his girl by hitching himself onto a door and swinging out of the room with that irrepressible grin. He was the kind of man I would have liked to have grown into: as strong as a boxer, as lithe as a dancer, he never forced his athleticism on you. He used it only when he had to. Barred from the hotel, he tosses a coin at a doorman, and while the man is on his knees searching for it, he climbs the building, sprints over the balcony and mingles with the guests. I was hopeless at any sort of athletics at school, but when I saw Doug in *Don Q, Son of Zorro* (1926) at the National Film Theatre a couple of years later, I was so exhilarated that I leaped down the stairs at Waterloo Station and twisted an ankle.

Fairbanks had a way of communicating with the audience that was used by very few other screen players. Actors are told that they must never look directly at the lens—to do so is to make eye contact with each person in the audience and thus shatter the illusion. Doug ignored that rule, as he ignored so many others. In 1984, when we presented *The Thief of Bagdad* with live orchestra at the Dominion Theatre in London, the publicity people at Thames Television asked for a tape. When they looked at it, they all thought it paralyzingly boring and forecast complete and embarrassing disaster. At the show, however, the magic of the big screen and live music cast its usual spell. Things invisible on video sprang to life on the big screen. The publicity people were all astounded at the difference. Fairbanks established a rapport with the audience by flashing them looks none of us had noticed. And the audience loved it—you could hear their delighted murmur. It proved among the most popular films we have run. People still remember that show and ask for the film to be repeated.

Thanks to *The First Man*, I fell for Doug much as my mother had done, and I still feel as warm towards him as I did sixty years ago. The little film seemed to me fresher and livelier than the turgid dramas I sat through week after week at the Odeon. The 1950s represented to me the nadir of Hollywood film production, so this was a useful moment to discover the silent cinema. Silents may have lacked dialogue, but, thankfully, they also lacked back projection, the curse of the talkies. When a car drives along a road in a silent, the cameraman is invariably on a platform lashed to the front. Heroism was an essential ingredient of early picture-making, as I was to find out. And I was to learn that Doug was a screen hero to a greater extent than the term usually implies. He was a creative producer in an industry which has seen very few. (His second wife, Mary Pickford, was another.) He encouraged his directors to give more than they thought themselves capable of. Donald Crisp was a routine director, but his best pictures were made for two men who lived and breathed celluloid: Buster Keaton and Douglas Fairbanks. Raoul Walsh was a good director, but compare *The Thief of Bagdad* to *The Wanderer* (1925), the Prodigal Son story made shortly after *The Thief* with some of the same cast—*The Wanderer* conveys all the boredom those publicity people had felt about *Thief.*

Exhilarated by my find—the films that came with the projector included dramas with William S. Hart and Bessie Love—I wanted to discover more about them. There was no Media section in the library in those days. I was directed to the Theatre shelf, where, among books on Bernhardt and Irving was one entitled *The History of the Film* by two Frenchmen, Bardeche and Brasilach. As I took it down, it fell open at a still of Douglas Fairbanks behind the wheel of a motor launch—a scene from my film! In those days, I took this sort of luck for granted, wondering only why the title was different, *American Aristocracy* (1916). (I discovered later that Pathé routinely altered the titles of their home movie releases, perhaps because they had neglected to clear the copyright.) If my film was important enough to be included in a book, then my 1/6d per reel had been well spent.

So, I began to search for more films, preferably with Douglas Fairbanks. I found more—the delightful *Matrimaniac* (1916), with Doug clambering along telephone wires to put an unconventional marriage proposal through to his girl, Constance Talmadge; *The Americano* (1916), in which he takes part in the Mexican revolution; and his very first picture, also set in Mexico, *The Lamb* (1915). And at the National Film Theatre I saw an original nitrate tinted print, loaned by the Museum of Modern Art, of *The Three Musketeers* (1921), a print which has long since decomposed, but which remains in my memory as one of the most satisfying experiences of my early filmgoing. When I see modern dupes, the film looks ordinary and rather dull. It is amazing the difference a fine print can make.

Eventually, I learned of the existence of the British Film Institute, and as a brand new member at age thirteen, I went to their offices at 164 Shaftesbury Avenue. Up the stairs was an office filled with grey filing cabinets, ruled by a Miss Traylen. Intrigued by this skinny schoolboy asking for Douglas Fairbanks, she showed me all the stills they had on his films. I left with a portrait from *The Black Pirate*; she surprised me by saying the film had originally been shown in color. In the basement was a library, and here the helpful staff directed me to a Holy Grail: an index by Seymour Stern to the films produced for Triangle-Fine Arts by D. W. Griffith. (By coincidence, all the films I had bought so far had been produced for Triangle.)

Now I could find the names of the people who made *American Aristocracy,* and they are imprinted on my consciousness: director Lloyd Ingraham, cameraman Victor Fleming, ingenue Jewel Carmen, villain Albert

S. Parker, and Charles Stevens, an important member of many Fairbanks films.[1] The scenario was by Anita Loos, best known for her book *Gentlemen Prefer Blondes.*

My enthusiasm for collecting increased and fostered a passion for film in general. When I was seventeen, I joined the cutting room of a documentary film company. Every so often I heard colleagues refer to an actors' agency called Al Parker Limited. Since I had a one-track mind, I assumed this was owned by the Albert S. Parker who had played the heavy in *American Aristocracy.* I looked the firm up in the phone book and found myself talking to Mr. Parker himself. Reassuringly, he had an American accent.

"Do you know the name Douglas Fairbanks?"

"Sure. I directed him!"

"Directed him? In what?"

"*The Black Pirate.*"

"Good heavens!" (I had never made the connection.) "I have a film you played in 1916 called *American Aristocracy.*"

"Bring it over!"

I went to his flat in Park Lane, set up my portable projector, and showed the film on his wall. Parker watched in silence, but his wife, the actress Margaret Johnston, laughed with delight at the sight of her husband long before she knew him. Parker told me he had been a close friend of Fairbanks's—that Fairbanks's first wife, Beth Sully, came from the kind of Newport high society being kidded in the picture. Many of the extras were the real thing. The picture was shot on location at Beth Sully's home, Watch Hill, Rhode Island. She was present during the production, and the plump little boy selling newspapers was her son, Douglas Fairbanks Jr., making his first screen appearance at the age of six. (A dog had bitten the boy and this was Doug's way of making amends.) The Ocean House Hotel—which is still there—was used extensively. Interiors such as the malted milk factory were also shot on location, although the more routine domestic interiors were shot at the Willat studio in Fort Lee, New Jersey (Eastern Triangle). Parker recalled that Lloyd Ingraham was fond of the bottle. One day he sat in the back of the car. "I'll be with you in a minute," he said. "I'm reading."

"Well, keep on reading!" said Fairbanks. And he and Parker co-directed the scene, ad libbing as they went along.

Parker later directed Fairbanks in *Arizona* (1918), *Knickerbocker Buckaroo* (1919), as well as in *The Black Pirate* (1926); he also directed John Barrymore, Norma Talmadge, Gloria Swanson, and Clara Kimball Young. He and his wife invited me for film shows-cum-dinner many times and introduced me to the actors represented by the agency: James Mason (who eventually spoke the narration for the *Hollywood* series), Trevor Howard, and Clive Brook, another silent-era veteran who became a friend. Most important of all, he introduced me to Douglas Fairbanks Jr., who told me all he knew about his father and proved to be an invaluable source.

I remember Parker organizing one of these dinner party-cum-film shows and when I set up the projector and switched out the light, he announced in the darkness: "Ladies and gentlemen. You are about to witness an animated graveyard. Everyone appearing in this picture is dead—except me."

When I traveled to America for the first time, in 1964, I met collector and silent-era cameraman Don Malkames in New York. He had built a magnificent viewing theatre in his home—complete with projectors of every gauge. When I told him about my interest in Fairbanks—one he shared—he revealed a similar enthusiasm for *American Aristocracy*, but instead of a measly little 9.5 mm version, he had a glorious 28 mm tinted print of the entire film. What a difference! My abridged version had sliced through the story with the ruthlessness of a trailer. Now I could see subtleties I had never been aware of, and, equally important, I could read the witty Anita Loos titles; a dignified lady approaches another on the verandah: "I am Mrs. Budhauser—Budhauser, the brewers."

The other lady looks at her, askance. "Madam, *we* are distillers."

Fairbanks's performance was more effective in this longer version—his athletic tricks were a joy—and the whole thing had much more substance. Some of Victor Fleming's cinematography—shot in backlight in the late afternoon—was exquisite. When I heard it had been copied on to 16 mm, by Blackhawk, I bought a copy and was inevitably disappointed at the way the copying process had introduced a softness alien to both the 9.5 mm and the 28 mm prints. The faces had that maddening blankness of so many postwar 16 mm prints. The Malkames collection went to Eastman House, but the softness reappeared in their 35 mm blowup. I live in hope of a crisp, properly timed restoration produced to the sort of standard Fairbanks would have insisted on. Nevertheless, I still look wistfully at my 9.5 mm print and wonder what my life might have been like had that first film been something less enchanting.

Since those days, Fairbanks films have been rediscovered at a highly satisfactory rate. The Museum of Modern Art had always had three reels of *A Modern Musketeer* (1917), a delicious film which links Fairbanks inseparably to the d'Artagnan legend, but not until the Danish Film Institute revealed a complete print was that outstanding film revived, to the glory of Doug and his director Allan Dwan. Dwan also directed the charming *Mr. Fix-It* (1918), the restoration of which was sponsored by Tracey Goessel, who is currently writing a new biography of Fairbanks. There is an incomplete version with Lobster Films in Paris of *He Comes Up Smiling* (1918), in which Doug plays a bank clerk whose job is to look after the president's canary. Doug is also shown battened each day into his cage. The bird's escape leads to perhaps the most endearing opening of any Fairbanks film.

The authors of this new Fairbanks book, John Tibbetts and Jim Welsh, have championed Fairbanks for more than forty years. This newly revised edition of the original *His Majesty the American* boasts many revisions and additions. I am so pleased to see Vera Fairbanks's contributions to this book. I have always been impressed by her loyalty to her late husband, Douglas Fairbanks Jr. Other additional materials include interviews with Doug Jr. and Fairbanks's cameraman, Glen MacWilliams, a richly deserved tribute to Alistair Cooke, new material on some of the rarest films, and an appendix with an English translation of a book by French designer Maurice Leloir, who worked on Fairbanks's last silent film, *The Iron Mask* (1929). Like Fairbanks himself, Tibbetts and Welsh have provided us with more than we had any right to expect.

—KEVIN BROWNLOW
May 15, 2013

DOUGLAS FAIRBANKS
AND THE AMERICAN CENTURY

The Black Pirate.

INTRODUCTION: THE CHOREOGRAPHY OF HOPE

[He was] an individual standing alone, self- reliant and self-propelling, ready to confront whatever awaited him with the aid of his unique and inherent resources.
—R. W. B. LEWIS, *The American Adam*

At the height of his career in the early 1920s, Douglas Fairbanks was the most popular film star in the world. Since his arrival in Hollywood in 1915, he had quickly vaulted from his former status as a stage star to the power and prestige of a captain of the film industry. Playwright Robert E. Sherwood pronounced his films "the farthest step that the silent drama has ever taken along the highroad of art."[1] His sermons of hope and optimism pulled high fives with the spirit of the young progressive American century and claimed its privileges. His leaps and bounds devoured space and time. "He is boy enough to want to be a boys' hero forever," noted poet Vachel Lindsay.[2]

But that was his tragedy. Puck didn't know how to grow old. By 1930, gravity was nipping at his heels. When his limbs faltered and his pace slowed, Fairbanks had no immunity systems to protect him from the infirmities of age, the strain of a divorce from his beloved Mary Pickford, the challenge of talking pictures, and the growing realization that his son, Douglas Jr. was now a handsome rival for the public's attention. "Jayar," as Senior called him, was already at that time an intelligent, talented, and experienced twenty-year-old actor. He was also an acute observer of his father: "He is a man of great ego but little conceit," he wrote at that time, "a man to whom success comes easily, but failure hard. Success is to him a habit, and he is intolerant of reverses."[3]

Senior's last movie, *The Private Life of Don Juan* (1934), featured a poignant confrontation between the reality of an aging Don Juan and his

Young Fairbanks in pensive mood.

legend, forever young. After that, his acting career finished, Douglas did the only thing he knew how to do: run harder. He traded the arrows of Robin Hood for the golf clubs of the tourist and left Hollywood. Once impatient to be a part of all things, he now lacked the patience to be part of any one thing. "Why should I spend my life in a narrow little village when there's a whole world to amuse myself in?" he said in 1934.[4] He fled the long, mocking reach of his shadow and dodged the youthful images implacably fixed on his films. But he couldn't outrace them, and he died on December 11, 1939, at age fifty-six, his flight come to ground and his image already starting to fade. After that, for more than a decade . . . nothing. It seemed as if the American century, whose quick and energetic spirit he had embodied and promoted so strenuously all his life, forsook him. If the Fairbanks legacy were to be remembered at all, it would have to be through the revival of his films and the actions of that redoubtable keeper of the flame, his son, Douglas Fairbanks Jr. He brought the Fairbanks American century to its close, with his death in 2000. That story is in this book, too.

Those of us who grew up in the 1950s didn't know very much about Douglas Fairbanks Sr. How could we? Only a handful of modest book-length commentaries and biographies had appeared to fill the void. A gossipy, anecdotal little book from 1927 was Allene Talmey's *Doug and*

Mary and Others, which offered a collection of brief Hollywood celebrity profiles. Doug and Mary were already enjoying a mythology of their own, private as well as public, which Talmey gently debunked, writing, "Doug, the king at ease, home from the studio, and Mary, the grave queen, home from a cornerstone laying, slip back their haloes and chew peanut brittle."[5] Far more substantial in its way was another slim volume, Alistair Cooke's *Douglas Fairbanks: The Making of a Screen Character.* It appeared in 1940 under the auspices of the Museum of Modern Art. Although it would prove to be highly influential to future scholars, it had been long out of print; copies were difficult to find until a facsimile edition was published in 2010. Appearing a little more than a decade later, Ralph Hancock's *Douglas Fairbanks: The Fourth Musketeer* (1953) was a chatty and highly entertaining narrative, as long in anecdotes as it was wanting in scholarly detail. "Look, I had to fill those pages in some way," Hancock admitted to future biographer Booten Herndon. "If you have a different version, I'd advise you to go with it!"[6] Not until 1977 did Herndon publish his own volume, *Mary Pickford and Douglas Fairbanks.* It was a far more responsible, albeit informal account. "As the book is directed more to readers than scholars," admitted Herndon, "I have not burdened them with notes."[7] Likewise, Gary Carey's *Doug & Mary,* published that same year, "was not meant as a formal, comprehensive biography," but confined its quick narrative account primarily to the years of the Fairbanks/Pickford romance and marriage.[8]

Fortunately, a number of important volumes began appearing that improved the status of Fairbanks scholarship. Kevin Brownlow's incomparable *The Parade's Gone By* (1968) was a revelation, replete with learned comments and exciting interviews (particularly concerning Fairbanks's 1922 *Robin Hood*). Richard Schickel's examination of American celebrity culture, *His Picture in the Papers* (1974), was a portable study that began as an article for *American Heritage.* It rightly regarded Fairbanks as a transitional figure in an era of change in American media and mass consumption. "It was possible to achieve 'celebrity' through attainments in the realms of play," Schickel wrote. "We have reached a point where most issues, whether political, intellectual, or moral in nature, do not have real status . . . until they have been taken up, dramatized, in the celebrity world."[9] Most recently, three more notable books are essential to any examination of the subject. The first is Gaylyn Studlar's invaluable *This Mad Masquerade: Stardom and Masculinity in the Jazz Age* (1996), which figures prominently among current studies about masculinity constructions in popular

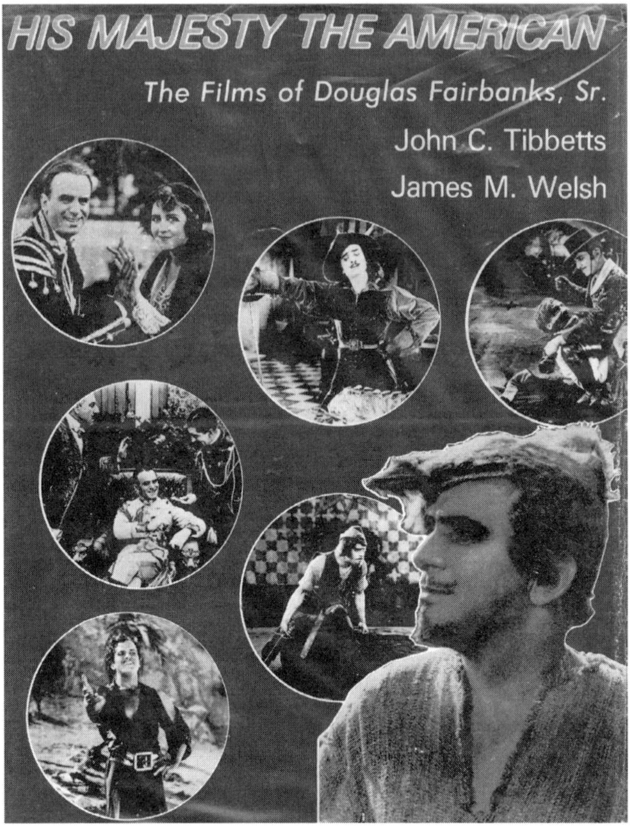

Cover of *His Majesty the American* (1977) (courtesy John C. Tibbetts and James M. Welsh).

culture; moreover, its opening chapter, "Building Mr. Pep: Boy Culture and the Construction of Douglas Fairbanks," is a long and detailed examination of the subject.[10] The second is Jeffrey Vance's *Douglas Fairbanks*, the most pictorially lovely and detailed biographical treatment to date.[11] The third is Frederic Lombardi's *Allan Dwan and the Rise and Decline of the Hollywood Studios*, a first-ever biography of the director with whom Fairbanks made many of his most important films.[12]

When James M. Welsh and I began research on our first book, *His Majesty the American*, in the mid-1960s, we had only old copies of the Cooke and Hancock books at hand and a few memories of a short-lived television series from the late 1950s, *Silents Please!*, which afforded us tantalizing glimpses of highly abridged versions of *The Black Pirate* and *Thief of*

Bagdad. And the pages of Blackhawk Films and Classic Film Collector boasted a few 8 mm films in the public domain.[13] We were determined to actually *see* more films, particularly those elusive and largely forgotten pre-1920 satires. As Kevin Brownlow writes in the foreword to the book presently in your hands, our quest was to be a compound of persistence and luck. Many of these earlier films were especially difficult to locate and screen. A few were thought to be "lost" (and, as we shall see, some still are); and many of those that were extant were unavailable outside of archives and private collections. Of course, this was a time before the easy access of today's proliferation of films on digital formats, YouTube, and streaming channels of transmission. Luckily, the boom in 16 mm film distribution was rapidly changing things. In the mid-1960s, we formed a Film Society at the University of Kansas and booked a handful of Fairbanks films, early and late. Moreover, we availed ourselves of the generosity and patience of historians and collectors like William K. Everson of New York City, Don Malkames of nearby Tuckahoo, and Miles Kreuger of Los Angeles, who allowed us to invade their homes for private screenings. Happy days were spent in Washington, D.C., viewing Fairbanks's rarities in the American Film Institute screening room with archivists Robert Gitt, Anthony Slide, and David Shepard. In 1974, we attended a major retrospective of his films at the American Film Institute, which was introduced by Douglas Jr. Speaking about his father and his father's close friend, Charles Chaplin, he acknowledged that "both felt . . . that the silent screen was their proper medium. They could express themselves in mime and tell the story in action, a purely visual medium."[14]

Meanwhile, we dipped back into contemporary accounts of the Fairbanks story, buried on paper and on microfilm, reviews and stories in *Variety, Motography, Photoplay, Moving Picture World,* etc., consulted the papers of the Triangle Motion Picture Company at the Motion Picture Academy in Los Angeles and gained stack access to the extensive motion picture research archives of the Library of Congress. And, of course, there were those redoubtable early acolytes of the Fairbanks brand to take account of, that Whitmanesque vagabond Vachel Lindsay; the Broadway critic and playwright Robert E. Sherwood; and the young English journalist Alistair Cooke.

Anecdotal material from Fairbanks's living contemporaries and friends was available through our association with the National Film Society's annual celebrity gatherings in Los Angeles and New York and in the pages of its journal, *American Classic Screen* (1976–1985).[15] We shared luncheons and panel discussions with directors Allan Dwan, King Vidor, and Henry King. Cinematographer Glen MacWilliams recalled filming *A Modern Musketeer* (1917) in Arizona. Legendary stunt man Yakima Canutt remembered training sessions with Douglas: "I used to work out with him in the gym. He taught me several things that helped me in my motion picture career—and by the same token I taught him a few tricks." Veteran soundman at Universal, Bernard Brown, reported, "As one of Doug's 'Doug' players, I spent the happiest times of my life in those games on the Pickfair lawn—the competition was every Friday night." Buddy Rogers, then husband of Mary Pickford, took us on tours of Pickfair. Buddy, a fellow alum of Kansas University, remained a staunch supporter of our work until his death in 1999. And, last but not least, Douglas Jr. generously replied to our correspondence with questions about the collaborations he had planned with his father. Our thanks and gratitude go out to them.

As a result of the above, *His Majesty the American* was published in 1977 and presented an informal portrait of Fairbanks and his work that not only filled out some of the gaps in accounts of the early satires, but also amplified the work of the aforementioned Alistair Cooke. Cooke's pioneering insights into Fairbanks's sociocultural significance continue to be of inestimable value. "[Fairbanks] will bear intellectual scrutiny as well as any other artist with a talent of his own," Cooke had prophetically declared.[16] Robert Fairbanks, Doug's brother, was "immensely pleased" with it at the time, and hoped Cooke would eventually write a full biography (which he never did).[17] Published in 1940, this slim little volume remains to this day, as Richard Schickel has attested, "one of the few distinguished studies of movie iconography."[18] The circumstances behind this book and how it came to be written are seldom acknowledged. It is a story that needs to be told.[19]

• • •

The present volume, *Douglas Fairbanks and the American Century*, is more than an expanded revision of our *His Majesty the American*; it is virtually a complete reassessment.

Much has happened during the intervening decades since its publication in 1977. Fairbanks has executed his greatest stunt. Just within the last five years, with the aid of digital technologies, he has made the long jump from the silent film era to today's new generations of viewers. Thanks to the tireless efforts of archivists, preservationists, and historians like Kevin

Laughing at danger in *Bound in Morocco* (1918).

Brownlow, David Shepard, and Tracey Goessel, and packagers like Lobster Films, Kino Films, and Flicker Alley, many of the films have been rescued, preserved, and restored for the first time for new generations.

Douglas Fairbanks and the American Century makes no pretentions of being a biography. Rather, it is a series of essays linked by our contention that Fairbanks was the most vivid and strenuous exponent of what we call the American century, whose dominant mode after 1900 was the mass marketing of a burgeoning democratic optimism, at home and abroad.

We can see more clearly in these pages how Fairbanks helped define what this new American century was all about. During those first crucial decades, his satiric comedies shadowboxed with the illusions of class and custom—at the American duality of eastern experience/pretension and western promise/expansion. As the masculine personification of the Old World aristocrat and the New World self-made man—tied to tradition yet emancipated from history—he had constructed a uniquely *American* aristocrat tumbling into a new age and sensibility.[20] The wonder of it all is that there is no contradiction in this blend of Old and New World aristocracies. Moreover, we see ever more clearly a figure whom we now recognize as a prime architect—choreographer, if you will—of a masculinity that danced a national optimism through speed, agility, and aggressiveness. "There is a parallel between the American man of action, however vulgar his aims, and the old feudal idea of the gentleman with a sword at his side," wrote G. K. Chesterton in his contemporary observations of the American character. "The gentleman may have been proud of being strong or sturdy; he may too often have been proud of being thick-headed; but he was not proud of being thick-skinned. On the contrary, he was proud of being *thin*-skinned . . . that sensitiveness was a part of masculinity."[21]

Alistair Cooke once wrote, "If Douglas Fairbanks did not exist in the person of Douglas Fairbanks off-screen, it was necessary to invent him for that role."[22] But Cooke had forgotten that in a very real sense, he had *always* been around. We can go back, if you will, to the *puer aeternus*, the "divine youth," of folklore, the indestructibly childlike part of the human personality. Claim as his literary forebears Ariel, Peter Pan, and those noble Children of Nature, the high-flying heroes of Edgar Rice Burroughs, Lord Greystoke ("Tarzan of the Apes") and that aristocratic Gentleman from Virginia, "John Carter of Mars." Burroughs's two progenitors of the American superman first appeared in 1912, just at the time Fairbanks was gaining success on the Broadway stage. The kinship on display with Fairbanks is obvious.

To return to Chesterton, we should also acknowledge another immediate literary predecessor of especial note, the character of "Innocent Smith" in Chesterton's novel, *Manalive*. Written in 1911, four years before Fairbanks came to Hollywood, it uncannily, and unerringly, anticipates the first appearance of the tumbling, tree-climbing, upside-down Fairbanks we saw in movies like *American Aristocracy* (1917). Smith is always in full flight, writes Chesterton. He launches himself into the lives of his friends with a "flying wheel of legs," expending his preternatural energies in a choreography of hope and optimism that ruthlessly shakes people out of their morbidity and lethargy. Smith provokes, he pummels, he pounds. And then he's gone, on to the next victim. Moving with the "rattling rapidity" of a silent film, he's always just out of reach, a figure we can only pursue: "He was already up the tree, where, swinging himself from fork to fork with his strong, bent, grasshopper legs . . . [he remains] among the last tossing leaves and the first twinkling stars of evening." Smith rebukes the priest who reminds us that one day we will die; rather, writes Chesterton, "he reminds us that *we are not dead yet*. He refuses to die while he is still alive." He says his method is simple enough: "I do it by having two legs."[23]

Fairbanksians of the National Film Society (from left), John C. Tibbetts, Kevin Brownlow, Jim Welsh, Frank Thompson (courtesy John C. Tibbetts).

Many years later, Merce Cunningham, who knew a thing or two about dance movement, expressed substantially the same thing, in words even more apposite to Fairbanks: "A man is a two-legged creature—more basically and more intimately—than he is anything else. *And his legs speak more than they 'know.'*"[24] (By no means incidentally, we will hear from Chesterton many times in these pages. If his "Innocent Smith" is a literary contemporary of the early Fairbanks, Chesterton's *The Return of Don Quixote* [1925] provides, as we shall see, the literary counterpart of the mature Fairbanks's 1920s costume adventures.)

We hope that *Douglas Fairbanks and the American Century* will likewise stand on its own two legs! Here you will share the happy enthusiasms of many staunch Fairbanksians, like Kevin Brownlow, who, as the dean of film historians—having restored to public viewing many of his films—contributes an affectionate memoir of growing up under the influence of Fairbanks's films. Cameramen Glen MacWilliams and Victor Fleming, and directors Allan Dwan and Joseph Henabery, recall the glory days of making Fairbanks's action comedies. Independent scholar Tracey Goessel shares the fruits of her lifelong accumulation of Fairbanksiana and her own efforts to restore several of his films. (Her ongoing research into a

Fairbanks as the elder d'Artagnan (sketch by Maurice Leloir for *The Iron Mask,* courtesy Tibbetts and Welsh).

Fairbanks biography will one day prove to be definitive, matching Samuel Johnson's admonition: "I would really have his life written with diligence.") Douglas Fairbanks Jr. and his wife Vera talk about keeping alive the flame of the Fairbanks name and their efforts to preserve the films and research materials for future generations. And, of course, there are many "new" films, hitherto "lost" or inaccessible, that are here freshly reconstructed, screened, and re-evaluated—*The Half Breed, The Good Bad Man, The Habit of Happiness, Reggie Mixes In, A Modern Musketeer, He Comes Up Smiling, Say, Young Fellow!, Mr. Fix-It*—and unjustly neglected later films like *The Gaucho, The Taming of the Shrew,* and *The Private Life of Don Juan.* New chapters and interview materials compare and contrast the contemporaneous careers of Mary Pickford and Fairbanks at crucial moments in their forging of the archetypal models of American masculinity and the "growing girl." And, lastly, we are proud to offer three appendices. The first provides hitherto unpublished interviews with Douglas Fairbanks Jr. about his growth from worshipful son to proudly independent artist. The second is the first English translation available of Maurice Leloir's *My Five Months with Douglas Fairbanks,* a charming day-by-day account by the French designer about his work on the set of Fairbanks's last silent film, *The Iron Mask.* And the third presents a brief summary of scholarly investigations into screen masculinity.

Finally, Douglas Fairbanks taught us a lesson that we must learn and relearn again and again, that happiness, opportunity, and hope are not static conditions but dynamic processes. Like religious faith, they are a mystery difficult to rationalize. To slow down is to lose your balance. So he pushed himself as he pushed others. He wasn't kidding when he said, in *The Thief of Bagdad*, that "happiness must be earned." He was aggressive about it in film after film, and woe to those who couldn't keep up. Admittedly, some viewers coming to them today for the first time are likely to fall back in fatigue and consternation. What is this antic relentlessness, they might well wonder, *all about?* Plucked out of the slipstream of time, out of the prevailing contexts of his day, this apostle of an aggressive American optimism and hope may come across today like a gate crasher of lunacy, a jester of *gesture*, an equal opportunity enthusiast. To those new viewers we address this book: Blame your failure to withstand and sustain his strenuous velocity on your cynical and disillusioned lapse of hope and optimism. Hope requires conditioned muscles. And we have all grown soft.

We hope the story is true that up to the very end, as his own strength and spirits began to fail, just hours before his death, Douglas Fairbanks could still summon up his old spirit and exclaim, "I never felt better in my life!"[25] We ourselves admit to an unabashed empathy with the man that borders on bias. We nominate as his epitaph the words of James M. Barrie: "I believe I am rather a fine fellow when I am flying."[26]

Part I

ODYSSEY OF A SPRING LAMB

In youth . . . the prospect seems endless, because we do not know the end of it. We think that life is long, because art is so, and that, because we have much to do, it is well worth doing.

—WILLIAM HAZLITT

Young Fairbanks ready to take on the movies.

Chapter 1

"Windows Are the Only Doors"

The First Films (*The Lamb*, 1915, and *Double Trouble*, 1915)

Power ceases in the instant of repose: it resides in the moment of transition from a past to a new state, in the shooting of the gulf, in the darting to an aim.

—**RALPH WALDO EMERSON,** *Experience*

In the spring of 1915, Douglas Fairbanks left the New York stage and traveled west to the newly formed Triangle Film Corporation in Los Angeles. On the strength of his credentials as a lively and engaging light comedian, Triangle boss Harry E. Aitken promised him the impressive fee of $2,000 per week, with a $500 increase every six months. The leading director of the day, D. W. Griffith, was to personally supervise all of his films (although this promise was not to be fulfilled). The story of how Fairbanks left a successful career as a light juvenile on the New York legitimate and variety stage for the movies in California is yet to be told in detail. What we have so far has suffered too much hearsay. As recently as Jeffrey Vance's biography (2008) we still find the tired, oft-repeated anecdote that Fairbanks was spotted one day in Central Park by a motion picture cameraman and, after some mugging for the camera, was contacted by Aitken with a contract offer.[1] This is difficult to credit. Surely, Fairbanks had already been eyeing the promise of movies for years and was already known for the sorts of roles he would bring to the screen in the middle-teens. "Instead of the classic roles, I played modern young men," he recalled in 1922, "young men about town and alert young reporters . . ." Moreover:

> For five years I went from one play in New York to another. I had had enough of the road. And the lines that I had studied with the hope that I might one day declaim them in the theater have proved very useful to paraphrase for adaptations and titles in the making of my film plays.[2]

Many of the stage producers with whom he had either worked or known, notably William A. Brady, David Belasco, and Klaw & Erlanger, had themselves been dabbling in film production with an eye to bringing prominent Broadway stars to the screen, and it's likely that either he or they would have been considering the possibilities.[3] Writing in December of 1916, George Creel suggests there had been nothing "accidental" about Fairbanks's deserting the stage for the movies.

> Nothing was more natural than that the movies should seek such an actor . . . "Come over to us," they said, "and we'll let you do anything you want. . . . The sky's the limit". . . . The movie magnates got what they wanted, and Fairbanks got what he wanted. For the first time in his life, he was able to "let go" with all the force of his dynamic individuality, and he took full advantage of the opportunity.[4]

We await further research into this crucial period in Fairbanks's career.[5] For our purposes, suffice it to say, that in just two years, Fairbanks would emerge among the stage stars imported to Triangle as one of the few who would go on to rank as an A-list film star.

What does require our immediate attention here are the first hints on film of the aggressive and mobile Fairbanks masculine persona that he had already crafted with much success on the stage. Although *The Lamb* and *Double Trouble* (both 1915) are rarely seen today and languish among his least appreciated efforts, they confront us immediately with what cultural historian Gaylyn Studlar describes as Fairbanks's "transformative masculinity," which reconciles several binaries—the working and upper classes, eastern tradition and western promise, and urban and rural contexts.[6]

The Lamb, directed by Christy Cabanne and "supervised" by D. W. Griffith, was released on September 23, 1915. The precise identity of its source text has proven elusive. The copyright submission of the film declared that its basis was a novel by Granville Warwick (D. W. Griffith) called *The Man and the Test*. Griffith may have written the film's scenario, but it is unlikely, according to the *AFI Catalogue of Feature Films, 1911–1920*, that such a novel was ever published.[7] Meanwhile, to further complicate things, the screen credits pronounced Cabanne, not Griffith, the author of the story. Flying in the face of this is an allegation that was first voiced by biographer Ralph Hancock in 1954 and that has surfaced repeatedly ever since: "[*The Lamb* featured Fairbanks] in the role of Bertie, 'the lamb,' which Douglas Fairbanks had played in *The New Henrietta* on Broadway."[8] Fairbanks did indeed play a character nicknamed "The Lamb" in *The New Henrietta* in 1913, which justifies Hancock's comment. "W. H. Crane, Amelia Bingham, Patricia Collinge and I had played in a modernized version of Bronson Howard's old play, *The Henrietta*," confirmed Fairbanks. "Crane acted his familiar role of the owner of the famous mine, and I was Bertie, 'the lamb.'"[9] When examined, however, the parallels between the play and the film are few.

The New Henrietta's lineage goes back to *The Henrietta by* Bronson Howard (1842–1908), a four-act comedy-drama of family intrigue on Wall Street, which began its successful run at the Union Square Theater on September 26, 1887. Playwright Howard was much admired by theater historian Montrose Moses as a pioneering champion of a new generation of American playwrights—ranking with contemporaries Clyde Fitch and James A. Herne—devoted to what he called a truly "American Dramatic Literature."[10] As reported by *The Bookman*, it was a big success in its day:

> *The Henrietta* was the earliest attempt to exhibit the dramatic elements in American business life, and to this day remains a better drama than any of the host of plays which have been devised in imitation of it. In it, the evils of Wall Street can be seen extending to the household.[11]

The plot revolved around efforts by "Bertie" van Alstyne (Stuart Robson) to thwart the attempt by an unscrupulous older brother to destroy the family wealth. The venerable W. H. Crane portrayed Nicholas van Alstyne, the patriarch of the family.

On December 22, 1913, a new, updated version opened on Broadway, retitled *The New Henrietta*, adapted by Winchell Smith and Victor Mapes. William H. Crane returned to the role of Nicholas van Alstyne, and now Douglas Fairbanks appeared as his son Bertie, "the lamb." The modern version differed from the original in several respects. The soliloquies and asides of the earlier text were cut, and a contemporary setting including telephones and motorcars was incorporated. A new character, Mark Turner, van Alstyne's son-in-law, became the villain, while Bertie retained his status of hero. A quick synopsis of the plot confirms how little of the play is present in *The Lamb*. Nicholas van Alstyne is smitten by the widow Updike. He has a rival, the Reverend Murray Hilton. To get her away from him, he takes her for a cruise on his yacht. Meanwhile, the son-in-law, Turner, tampers with the *Henrietta* stock. Bertie, who had earlier been given a million dollars and turned loose to sink or swim, finds himself in an important position when his father's stock is all but declared worthless. Bertie proves himself a man and gives his father a check for all the money he has left. Van Alstyne saves the day and Bertie makes a pile.[12]

That Bertie's new characterization was a good thing for Fairbanks is evident in a notice in *Theater Magazine* a few months later:

> Fairbanks is whimsical and unctuously humorous. As the son who is equal to the emergency . . . he is so entertaining that criticism must be silenced . . . with all his overcharged vacuity he has the saving grace of infinite comedy.[13]

The phrases "unctuously humorous" and "overcharged vacuity" uncannily predict the naïve and curious energy that Fairbanks would bring to many of his early films. About the only parallel between the play and the film is that Fairbanks's character of "Gerald," like Bertie, is a rich young idler who never had to earn a living but who eventually proves himself to be a man of character and enterprise.[14] Fairbanks himself recalled that during the production of *The New Henrietta*, he had been eyeing the advantages that the film medium held out for his athletic tendencies:

> Oftimes the question of why I deserted the speaking stage for the films has been hurled at me. Because of the possibilities and the outdoor life. Three years ago when I played with W. H. Crane in *The New Henrietta* we often spent our time between shows seeking vivid melodramatic pictures, especially Western subjects. We were amused by the primitive emotions and active life in the West.[15]

At any rate, after two more Broadway successes in 1914, *He Comes up Smiling* and *The Show Shop*, Fairbanks was on his way to Los Angeles to report to Triangle's Fine Arts Studio, supervised by D. W. Griffith. *The Lamb* premiered at the Knickerbocker Theater on September 23, 1915, as part of Triangle's grand plan to unveil its inaugural triple bill, including Thomas Ince's *The Iron Strain* and Mack Sennett's *My Valet*. The occasion was, according to all accounts, quite spectacular and, according to *Motography* magazine, the talk of the entertainment world:

> That something new had reached Broadway was evident as soon as the capacity first-night audience stormed the lobby and were admitted to an auditorium completely altered and redecorated to meet the requirements of the productions of Triangle.[16]

Too often, received opinion from historians has held that *The Lamb* was an "unexpected" hit and that it was a last-minute inclusion in the first program. Gaylyn Studlar, as recently as 1996, reported that "unexpectedly, there was an overwhelming response to *The Lamb* and to its star."[17] Yet advance publicity made it clear that Fairbanks was among Triangle's highest-paid performers, and *The Lamb* was not only regarded as the anchor of the program but also a promising debut for Fairbanks.

For our purposes, as we have suggested, *The Lamb* marks the first time Fairbanks performed on film what he had already specialized in stage in productions like *Hawthorne of the U.S.A.* (1914)—a masculine examination of the uniquely American duality of eastern experience/tradition and western promise/freedom. If the film is little known today and of limited interest, however, one might blame in part its quaint, faintly archaic style of diction in the title-writing, which is quite outmoded today. Too little study has been devoted to title-writing and how titles inflected the visual narrative in the silent film. Here, as we shall see, their identification of situations and characters becomes quickly annoying. For example, consider this opening title:

> *This is the story of a Lovesick Lamb, whose Dad, an Old War Horse, had died, clinching his Teeth in a Wall Street Bear, leaving the Lamb to gambol around on the Long Green.*

Thankfully, in just a few months, as we shall see in the next chapter, the sharp and satiric scenarist Anita Loos will join the Fairbanks team and save his next films from this sort of floridly rhetorical embarrassment. For the moment, however, the unfortunate practice of archaic capitalizations, generic characterizations, and precious tone was routine. D. W. Griffith was himself particularly guilty of this sort of thing: We think of character labels in *Intolerance* as "Brown Eyes," "Princess Beloved," or, simply, "The Girl." Later, in *The Lamb*, we find "Bill Cactus" referred to as "Cactus-Fed Goat from Arizona"; an aviator is introduced as "the Birdman"; the half-caste villainous Mexicans are called, at various times, "Giddy Huns" and "those unpleasant Mexicans." This reckless flinging about of racist labels and stereotypes plagues the film throughout, particularly in their intrusiveness in the action scenes at the end. Even a machine gun is referred to as "the Death Pumper"!

Briefly, the plot revolves around the love between Gerald, a rich idler (Fairbanks), and "Mary, the American Girl" (Seena Owen). At first Mary is reluctant to accept Gerald's marriage proposal because of his effeminate ways. One day at the seashore, a cry of help is heard from the surf. While Gerald stares on, paralyzed, his rival, Bill Cactus, a rancher from Arizona, rushes in to save the drowning man. Now branded as a coward, Gerald decides to build himself up with boxing and jujitsu lessons while Mary is away with friends at a party at the Cactus ranch. Later attempting to rejoin the group in Arizona, he is waylaid and knocked out by two bandits. Worse, a tribe of rampaging Yaqui Indians captures him. Mary, too, falls into their clutches when she is separated from the party. While Bill Cactus and the others rush back to the U.S. Barracks on the American side of the border for help, Gerald and Mary face certain death at the hands of the Indians. In desperation, Gerald breaks loose and manhandles a number of cutthroats and finally rejoins Mary. Together, they defend themselves with a machine gun that the Indians had previously captured from the Mexican army. As they use the last of their ammunition, the American troops gallop to the rescue. The Griffith-style last-minute rescue is accomplished and Gerald proves himself a man at last.

In effect, we see two Geralds. The Gerald we meet in the opening scenes is not the Gerald we see at the end. These two characters within one skin represent polar opposites—how the distance from one to the other is traversed constitutes the chief interest in Fairbanks's acting styles. To the credit of *The Lamb*, this transformation is much more credible than the one in *The Mollycoddle*, made four years later in 1919. In both films, the foppish character finds his strength in the fastnesses of the Arizona desert. In the latter, the change is sudden and arbitrary, whereas in the former it is more reasonable and natural through exercise and application. Indeed, the exercise scenes prefigure the later films in which physical exercise is a key to masculine health and vigor. Suggestions like this "cult of the body" represent a physical fitness craze that was not only sweeping the country but that Fairbanks also further inspired among his fans. As Gaylyn Studlar notes, this counter to "overcivilization" was "the ideal outlet for the healthy expression of masculine instincts . . . the so-called driving force of masculinity."[18]

The Lamb has given us hints of this from the very beginning; and we can follow the process henceforth with doubled interest. There is the title, for instance, that precedes his initial effort to woo Mary:

Mamma wanted to show him off but he longed to jump the Hedge.

Having easily—if unexpectedly—negotiated the hedge, we get our first hint of Gerald's true nature. That such a wholly irrelevant feat is essayed by a man wearing a morning suit with top hat and cane imparts a slightly mad and jaunty air to the whole thing. This is the sort of touch that marked many of Fairbanks's best early pictures. Gerald's athletic potential is also indicated in a scene a short time later when it is Gerald's inclination toward, rather than the achievement of, the virile characteristics of manhood that keys the scene. Cactus Bill has just arrived and been introduced. His handshake has disrupted both Mary and Gerald, and his swaggering Arizona ways eclipse Gerald's mild manner, to say the least. At a party that night, it is not Bill who seems out of place, but Gerald. Mary is highly impressed with Bill and cannot understand why Gerald is not like him. So, scorning him, she attends to Bill while Gerald, now curious, stalks about behind the broad, oblivious back of Bill, coughing, bulging his cheeks prizefighter fashion, squaring his shoulders, and otherwise aping his style. Fairbanks balances opposing traits with some convincing pantomime. It is also a welcome indication of his mute obsequiousness changing to a more aggressive stance.

Gerald's arrival in Arizona is echoed later in many other films. As we shall see in a later chapter, the "elastic soil" of the American West would suit Fairbanks as a proving ground for athletic and moral virtues. It is fitting that Fairbanks's arrival here is a slightly mad affair—after all, we shall find in this, and in later films, that anything can happen on this mythical terrain—for him, it is the Land of Oz. Gerald shows up in the desert country wearing nothing less than alpine togs, with an accompanying title:

Geography meant nothing to Gerald.

But it meant everything to Fairbanks, and in Arizona the whole film begins to move like a heavy machine that finally overcomes its inertia. Not only does the action pick up, but the comedy element also improves. There is a beautiful little routine with an automobile that has arrived to pick him up. Seating himself in the car, he props his cane at a racy angle upon the fender, gripping its stock as if it were a gearshift; the cane moves forward, the car drives off. He misses his train, and in a long sequence, gets taken in by some Indian bead sellers. He tries to proffer the Indians a huge wad of bills to buy their blanket and a piece of fool's gold. Nearby, two crooks just happen to see this exchange and, sensing a wealthy target, offer to drive him to the train. These rough, tobacco-chewing scoundrels knock him out and find nothing but the piece of fool's gold. They leave him lying in the dust of the desert.

At last Gerald is alone. The situation we have impatiently awaited is finally at hand. Even if the humor in the next scenes does not quite come off, it is nonetheless fascinating to watch the immaculately dressed Gerald steadily becoming more and more disheveled. As he gets dirtier the character becomes more interesting. It is an oddity with Fairbanks that the dirtier he gets the better he looks. In rapid succession, he battles a jawbone, a rattlesnake, and a puma. In his first real burst of defiance he states:

> *No lion lies down with this Lamb.*

Much of the interest in a Fairbanks movie resides in our waiting for the moment when he suddenly switches off gravity and jumps over a house or something—when he is going to discard his former self like an old skin and emerge with a kick into a new daylight. We know that this point has arrived with the next title, which displays the none-too-subtle racism lamentably present in many films of this era:

> *All of a sudden a half-caste Mexican Tribe indulged in a little rebellion. They captured a band of Mexican soldiers, and a machine gun, the latter in their eyes was mere junk.*

The only inkling we had gotten of this moment, at this point, was a shot of several disreputable Indians pushing soldiers around and tearing the clothes off a girl. At any rate, after the menace has been established and we have been prepared for the future involvement with the rebellious Indians, we are back with Gerald waking up in the desert:

> *Gerald still kept his regular Hours and Rose at Noon.*

At which point he and Mary are promptly surrounded and captured by the Indians.

We savor Gerald's physical transformation. His shoulders seem to set squarer now, and those nervous, flighty mannerisms of the early Gerald are gone. He stands defiantly within the circle of the Indians. The shorter length of the shots quickens the story's pace and we know we are in for some exciting footage. Nor are we disappointed. The Mexican troops return to recapture the renegade Indians, and in the resulting battle Gerald manages, unseen, to loosen his bonds. He works his way free—

> *and—realizing that his father had died with his boots on he determined to follow in his footsteps.*

Fairbanks is off and running. He fells several rascals, leaps out the doorway, and hurtles down between the grass huts toward the camera. He turns and clambers nimbly up a house front—

> *Such a playful giddy Lamb.*

Even after spectacular fistfights, more titles persist in this awkward tone, as in Gerald's aside to Mary:

> *"I say . . . deuced uncomfortable people these Indians."*

And a bit later he declares,

> *"I say, old girl. . . . We're in a deuced tight corner now, and I'm going to get you out!"*

Thankfully, such arch rhetoric would never thereafter appear in a Fairbanks film.

Meanwhile, the Mexican troops are beaten back. The Indians fall upon Gerald and Mary. They hold them off with the machine gun (remember "the death pumper"?). But ammunition is getting low. The Indians are creeping closer. Finally Gerald is out of bullets. He's saved the last one for her. The Indians close in for the kill:

> *When the chief learned it was the last of the Bullets he coveted the Brave Lamb's Living Heart.*

It is at this point that director Christy Cabanne comes into his own. A skillful manipulation of aerial shots of the battlefield alternating with close shots of Gerald, Mary, and the approaching Indians yields up a dramatic montage. There is a reptilian suggestiveness to the Indians' creeping bodies slithering toward and encircling the machine gun emplacement. And, of course, all the time the cavalry is roaring to the last-minute, Griffith-style rescue.

When the smoke clears, there is a compliant Mary, in close-up, nestling in Gerald's arms, a relaxed smile on her face.

It is the end now and Gerald is back in his expensive home. But now he stands straighter, shoulders well back, his movements full of quiet ease and grace. He regards his father's picture with a slight smile. An explanation for his Arizona transformation arrives in a title that could have been used verbatim for many of his later westerns, such as *The Mollycoddle*, four years later:

> *Blood will speak—though Society may drown the Conversation.*

Moments with the "early" Gerald, the weakling, have given us the best opportunity to assess Fairbanks the *film actor*. To be sure, the dashing, reckless bravado of the more "masculine" Gerald is a persona that Fairbanks essays with little trouble. However, with the "other" Gerald, he exaggerates the silly posturing and is unable to bring much sympathy to such a potentially repellent character. Fairbanks at this point is unable to reduce the role down to the telling nuances required by the camera. He will improve on this later in his career. His foppish Don Diego in *The Mark of Zorro* five years later will mark a considerable improvement.

Even if we view *The Lamb* today with some reservations, we should confirm that, as Triangle had predicted, its audiences loved it. One week after the premiere on September 23, 1915, *Variety* reported:

> After viewing *The Lamb* it is no wonder the Triangle people signed up Fairbanks for a period of three years [*sic*] at any salary within reason. They would even have been justified in stretching a point to secure Douglas. He "registers" on the screen as well as any regular film actor that has ever appeared in pictures and more strongly than most of them.[19]

Fairbanks's second film, *Double Trouble*, appeared in another of the "Triangle Weeks" in November 1915. It was based on a 1906 novel by Herbert Quick. Also on the bill was another Thomas Ince production, *The*

Golden Claw, with Bessie Barriscale. *Double Trouble* remains today one of the least seen, least remarked, and least available of all Fairbanks's films. Heretofore, only our earlier book, *His Majesty the American* (1977), and Gaylyn Studlar's *This Mad Masquerade* (1996) have considered it in some detail. We revisit it here. In contrast to *The Lamb* (and most of the subsequent films) it is a light chamber comedy that has scarcely a "thrill" in it. It is firmly anchored in the type of light comedies he was known for on the stage. Yet it has a charm and intimacy less forced than in *The Lamb*. And it spins a variation on the identity duality already hinted at earlier. As per the title, there are again *two* Fairbankses here, which is to say, there are two conflicting identities.

Fairbanks has two alter egos. Florian Amidon is a sedentary bank clerk, a Sunday-school type with mincing, fluttery mannerisms and speech, his hair carefully curled around his eyes. By contrast, Eugene Brassfield is a brash, fast-talking politician with a way for the ladies. The "Florian" personality is completely altered when he is injured by a blow to the head:

> *For five years after this unfortunate occurrence, Florian's life was a blank to him. When he came back to his senses he was in a Pullman, traveling to New York.*

The "Eugene" personality has taken over. During the intervening five years his devilishly clever personality and knowing ways have made him a wealthy candidate for city mayor. When the "Florian" personality finally revives, he is puzzled at the new surroundings and circumstances. He consults a medium, Madame Leclaire. Through her psychic manipulations, a series of identity shifts begin, from one personality to the other—the question being which of the two will ultimately dominate. As Eugene, Fairbanks wins the mayoral election; as Florian, he ditches Eugene's shady associates.

In Quick's novel, the persona of Florian Amidon is not a fop, but "the most attractive unmarried man in Hazelhurst," a banker described as "a galley slave chained to the sweep of interest tables, cash balances, and lines of credit, to whom there came daily the vision of a native Arcadia of art, letters, and travel." Moreover, he is "the most attractive unmarried man in Hazelhurst." Although this nicely describes a Fairbanks persona that will appear on screen in the later comedies, a title card reveals a more timid character:

> *The swish of a skirt would send his heart into a flutter of fear.*

As president of the Sabbath Day Society, Fairbanks works this to the hilt with quick, nervous gestures, limp handshakes, and nervous smiles. By contrast, his Eugene Brassfield is coarse and aggressive. He wears loud clothes, puffs enormous cigars, and furtively lifts up milady's dress for a quick scan of her ankles. Yet Brassfield's traits are precisely those needed to win the mayoral election. For example, one of the most arresting scenes in the film is the political rally, a chaotic situation quite beyond Florian's capacities to control. With the help of one of Madame Leclair's induced trances, Florian changes into Eugene and takes complete charge. (His speech to the crowds on Main Street oddly reminds us of newsreel footage of Fairbanks selling war bonds in New York a few years later.) At the same time, Florian's personality saves the day when he prevents the wife of a man (whom Brassfield had had framed for a crime) from committing suicide. Significantly, the conflation of the two personalities is what is needed to consummate the romantic interest with the girl.

Parenthetically, a German film made two years earlier bears a striking resemblance not only to this plot but also to other Fairbanks's identity dualities to come, particularly the bizarre story of *When the Clouds Roll By* (1919). *Der Andere* ("The Other") was a dramatization of a Jekyll-and-Hyde situation. The "Jekyll" here is an enlightened Berlin lawyer, a Dr. Hallers, who smiles skeptically at the idea of the split personality. But later, when the overworked lawyer suffers a fall from a horse, he sinks into a deep sleep, from which he emerges as "the other." This other self is a rogue who joins a burglar in an attempt to break into his own flat. Later, he falls asleep again and awakens as Dr. Hallers, completely unconscious of the crime. Upon subsequent questioning, he collapses after being forced to identify himself as the other burglar. The story has a happy ending as Hallers regains his health and gets married—"the prototype of a citizen immune to all psychological disturbances."[20]

Double Trouble reveals some interesting parallels with this plot. In each, the ending reveals a synthesis of the two personalities that points up the construction of a healthy masculine identity. This is made clear in a concluding intertitle:

> *As Amidon he remembers nothing of the Brassfield life, but in time the two will gradually become merged. . . . You must understand that a little Brassfield stays on to harden the softness of Amidon; while the fineness of Amidon kills the evil of Brassfield.*

As Gaylyn Studlar notes, "*Double Trouble* illustrates . . . the need to balance moral goodness with impulsive, overtly dangerous masculine instincts. . . . In different forms this same duality of identity would become a film convention that Fairbanks (and many other male stars of the period) returned to again and again."[21] Indeed, the Fairbanks of the pre-1920 films will always expound this philosophy of integration and balance, promoting clean living and a sunny disposition even while flying over the rooftops and chasing cattle rustlers across the prairie.

Double Trouble is essentially a chamber satire, exhibiting none of the athletic antics of *The Lamb,* save for a brief sequence involving Brassfield's barroom brawl. Director Cabanne is again at the helm. He eschews the long shots and crowded compositions that mark the latter half of the earlier film and tones things down here to medium and close shots, to nuances of gesture, and the avoidance of complex parallel editing strategies. This enables the quietly wacky events to unfold in their own quiet pace. *Double Trouble* has been neglected unjustly by Fairbanks enthusiasts. Nevertheless, its thematic importance recommends it, and its restraint and charm greatly improve on *The Lamb.* Certainly, it represents the farthest pole from the flamboyance and action of the later films. More of *that* barbed wit and flashing action would begin to surface in his third film, *His Picture in the Papers.* For now, *Double Trouble* is a pleasant reminder of his Broadway days and his growing assurance in front of the camera.

Chapter 2

"The Leap to Greatness"

The Years at Triangle, Artcraft, United Artists, 1916–1919

. . . and thus we shall be quack-ridden and folly-ridden until mobocracy comes to its inescapable debacle, and the common people are relieved of their present oppressive duty of deciding what is wrong with their tummies, and what doctor is safest for them to consult, and which of his pills is most apt to cure them.

—H. L. MENCKEN

From 1916–1919, Douglas Fairbanks rose from the ranks of tyro film actor to a major player in the American film industry. Only Mary Pickford and Charles Chaplin rivaled him in power and popularity. Among his other contemporaries in screen comedy in the mid-teens, only Roscoe "Fatty" Arbuckle and Mabel Normand rivaled him in physicality and clownish sweetness. The other great physical clowns, Harold Lloyd, Buster Keaton, and Charlie Chase, did not reach maturity until the late teens and early twenties. By all accounts it was an especially happy and vigorous time for Fairbanks. "During my career, I worked with many fine people [D. W. Griffith, Valentino, Thomas Ince, Roscoe Arbuckle]," wrote director Joseph Henabery in his autobiography, "but Doug topped them all. He was the kind of fellow who 'came across strong,' both on the screen and in his everyday life. . . ."

> I found that most of those who first met him off the screen expected to meet a much larger and taller man. He was only about five feet, nine inches, but very strong and muscular. He was dynamic in real life and on the screen. Like most big stars, he had great determination and will power. . . . He was a capable, experienced actor."[1]

The Popular Philosopher (drawing courtesy John C. Tibbetts).

Unfortunately, many of the films Fairbanks made during this period have remained relatively unseen over the years, due to a combination of obscurity, neglect, and scarcity of available materials. A handful that are "lost," including a few of the reputably finest westerns and comedies released by the Artcraft Pictures Corporation in 1917–1919, remain only in the form of stills and a few faded pressbooks. But recent restorations in video and digital formats of surviving titles are bringing to new generations of viewers and scholars the action, charm, and, at times wickedly satiric humor that attracted enthusiastic audiences in their day.[7] Indeed, they need not shrink in the shadow of their bigger brothers, the costume films of the 1920s. They can stand on their own and deserve special consideration and appreciation.

Having already examined Fairbanks's first two films, *The Lamb* and *Double Trouble*, we now turn here to the later titles from Triangle-Fine Arts, Artcraft Pictures Corporation, and finally, the first year of United Artists. Four writers and directors, so crucial to the Fairbanks brand at this time—scenarist Anita Loos, director John Emerson, writer-director Allan Dwan, and writer-director Joseph Henabery—are singled out for particular mention.

Topical Satires: *His Picture in the Papers, In Again—Out Again, The Matrimaniac*

The light, topical satires examined here skewed the new American century's optimistic mania for speed, publicity, patriotism, "bean-can" nobility, and vegetarian fads; juggled the geographical referents of "East" and "West"; and straddled with energetic masculinity class and economic differences in "Old World" traditions and "New World" opportunities.

Recent material gains in electrical energy and automatic machinery, coupled with industrial growth and social reform, were grist for these films. Just two decades earlier, historian Henry Adams had noted, "The period from 1900 to 1930 is in full swing, and, gee-whacky! How it is going! It will break its damned neck long before it gets through, if it tries to keep up the speed."[3] How prescient that prophecy would turn out to be! Personally choreographing it all was the bounding Fairbanks himself, "a vigorous young man as uncompromising as his splendid physique," wrote Alistair Cooke, "unfazed by tricky problems of taste and class behavior, gallant to women, with an affection for the American scene tempered by a wink."[4] As commentator Gaylyn Studlar writes, this was "an optimistic, performative masculinity that promoted "character-building ideals" in the "revitalization of American masculinity."[5] No one exemplified this more—and influenced Fairbanks more—than those transformative figures of the American century, Fairbanks's great heroes, Theodore Roosevelt and Billy Sunday.

The team of scenarist Anita Loos and director John Emerson either wrote and adapted, or in some respect participated in, in chronological order, *His Picture in the Papers, The Half-Breed, Mystery of the Leaping Fish, American Aristocracy, The Matrimaniac, The Americano, In Again—Out Again, Wild and Woolly, Down to Earth,* and *Reaching for the Moon.*

Allan Dwan either wrote, directed, or supervised eleven Fairbanks films, of which only *The Habit of Happiness, Manhattan Madness* (with Loos's contributions in the titles), and *Mr. Fix-It* will be discussed here (the others, including the westerns and the costume films, are examined later in these pages).

We begin with the team of Anita Loos and her future husband, John Emerson (who married in 1919). The diminutive Loos (1888–1981) was a veritable *wunderkind* of the American cinema. "Anita Loos, the demitasse librettist, is a great help to our hero," enthused *Photoplay* in 1917. "Her frolicsome scenarios are not only immense entertainment, but they are satires more subtle than our contemporary vocal dramatists [of the stage]."[6] It is not too much of a stretch to claim that her comic visions, to apply the words of philosopher Henri Bergson, were able "to throw light for us on the way the human imagination works, and more particularly social, collective, and popular imagination."[7]

While barely out of her teens, Loos sold her first scenario to the Lubin Company, an opus entitled, *The Earl and the Tomboy.* Apparently this was never filmed.[8] A month later, in April 1912, she made her first sale to Biograph with a story called *The Road to Plaindale,* which was not filmed until 1914. It was with her third sale, however, that Loos scored her first popular success. Biograph bought *The New York Hat* for $25 and produced it with director D. W. Griffith and principal players Mary Pickford and Lionel Barrymore. Loos followed Griffith from Biograph to Mutual and finally to Triangle in 1915, where along the way she contributed to the titles of *Intolerance.* This precocious girl had written by then something like 105 scripts, of which, she claims, four were never sold. By 1915, however, the scenario department for Fine-Arts, according to Loos, was not that advanced: "I worked in the scenario department. I *was* the scenario department. There was nobody else on the lot who was writing. Fine-Arts used to buy scenarios, and I think there were two or three writers who sent things in rather regularly."[9]

Loos's method for writing her scripts for Fairbanks was a bit unorthodox, perhaps, compared to today's high-speed assembly-line writing. Written in longhand, her scripts averaged forty pages. Her account of this effort is worth quoting in its entirety:

> Seeing that typewriter desks and chairs are designed for full-grown people, I was never a typist; it was more pleasant to curl up on a chaise lounge in my room at the Hollywood Hotel and scribble my plots on a big yellow pad. The only thing that required serious thought was a basic theme; once I hit on it, the rest was child's play. After finishing an outline, I would be driven to the studio in one of the company limousines, the elegance of which I never got used to. We held our conferences in Doug's dressing room. It was equipped with a punching bag, electric horse, and boxing gloves and looked like a gymnasium. Interrupted by Doug's boisterous clowning . . . I would read my script aloud.[10]

True or not—and we must take many of the reported incidents in the Loos autobiography with the requisite helping of salt—this is certainly the way one would have supposed the Fairbanks/Loos films were conceived. Her account captures all the disarming freshness and lack of pretension that mark the films themselves.

Of a limited educational background and experience, she had an intuitive feel for the national pulse, wrote Alistair Cooke. Does this mean that Loos spoke from an "average" temperament and point of view? G. K. Chesterton, in his masterful study of Charles Dickens, touches upon the issue with words that readily apply here:

> Dickens was an immoderate jester, but a moderate thinker. He was an immoderate jester because he was a moderate thinker. What we moderns call the wildness of his imagination was actually created by what we moderns call the tameness of his thought. I mean that he felt the full insanity of all extreme tendencies, because he was in the centre. We are always, in these days, asking our violent prophets to write violent satires; but violent prophets can never possibly write violent satires. In order to write satire like that of Rabelais—satire that juggles with the stars and kicks the world about like a football—it is necessary to be one's self temperate, and even mild.[11]

That Anita Loos herself valued this gentle whimsy inherent in moderation is apparent. She once disparaged its loss in American letters when subjects like sex were treated with a pretentiousness that was by turns morbid and dour:

> . . . out of this trend there developed a school of writing that reduced the American scene to the status of a bowl of worms and then reported their convolutions from the viewpoint of one of the worms.[12]

Probably her most famous character, Lorelei Lee in the novel *Gentlemen Prefer Blondes* (1925), virtually makes an institution of normalcy, which Loos has some fun with:

> Besides being a sound thinker, Lorelei is so normal that when, in Vienna, she undergoes analysis at the hands of Freud, the learned professor can only advise her to try to cultivate a few inhibitions.[13]

Her work brought her in contact with some of the sharpest wits of the day. She was a good friend of poet Vachel Lindsay, journalist H. L. Mencken, and theater critic George Jean Nathan, and she occasionally joined the famed Round Table set at the Algonquin (some of her films with Fairbanks took her and the crew to New York where they stayed at the famous hotel). She was the first to point out that someone like the terrible Mencken is at heart a believer in human instincts—"what makes New York so dreadful," she quotes him as saying, "is the fact that its people have been forced to rid themselves of the oldest and most powerful human instinct—the love of home."[14] Nathan perfectly described the concerns a satirist like her shared with the contemporary theater:

> Fashionable society . . . American advertising, American newspapers, American politics, American municipal administration, American hypocrisy, American money-madness, American business—such subjects have been the food of American farce and as a consequence the latter has frequently proved to be the most stimulating, corrective and derisorily tonic page in the native dramatic catalogue. . . . In it there has been a keener and more recognizably pointed appraisal and criticism of American life, enterprise and manners than in all the more serious plays which that theatre has shown.[15]

Loos herself stated her objectives with characteristic snap and verve:

> Forget the symbolism and fairy stuff. Go out in the kitchen and write the history of the cook, and you will probably have a much more interesting story than any tiresome allegorical abstractions about humanity. . . . Write about real life even if you have to wade through the mud to do it.[16]

With a twist, she would take an essentially commonplace situation and character and turn them topsy-turvy. She envisioned a sanitarium full of hypochondriacs in *Down to Earth*; a marriage ceremony performed via a three-way telephone hookup in *The Matrimaniac*; a jail cell with the comforts of home in *In Again—Out Again*; and a button salesman on the throne of a European kingdom in *Reaching for the Moon*. If this lunacy is to work, again turning to G. K. Chesterton, the real and the fanciful must be inextricably combined:

> The streets and shops and door-knockers of the harlequinade, which to the vulgar aesthete make it seem common-place, are in truth the very essence of the aesthetic departure. It must be an actual modern door which opens and shuts, constantly disclosing different interiors; it must be a real baker whose loaves fly up into the air without his touching them, or else the whole internal

excitement of this elvish invasion of civilization, this abrupt entrance of Puck into Pimlico is lost.[17]

Thus, in *His Picture in the Papers* Douglas is a carnivorous creature in a world of vegetarians; in *American Aristocracy,* he is a go-getter in the staid, snobbish society of Rhode Island; in *Reaching for the Moon,* he is a naïve young American suddenly thrust into the political ferment of a Balkan monarchy. Moreover, Loos's gift for striking visual metaphors is everywhere in evidence. When the hapless brewer's wife in *An American Aristocracy* finds herself snubbed by the other industrialists' wives, she is told—

"Madame, we are distillers!"

And she is left alone in a screened-in porch full of empty (but still tilting) rocking chairs. This unusual visual metaphor for the empty and mechanical operations of class-bound society is typical of Loos's ability to reveal with a deft touch the "human condition" beneath it.

What also strikes us are several innovations in the act—and artistry—of title writing. Too little attention in silent film scholarship has been paid to the presence and function of titles in silent films. In the following Fairbanks/Loos films, we will frequently quote them and pay close attention to how they propel, embellish, and comment on the action. Indeed, Loos's literate, witty, and punchy dialogue titles, expository intertitles, and ironic asides and meta-commentaries on the action invest her stories with a mocking playfulness that is frequently fantastic and absurdly exaggerated.[18] It's no exaggeration that she brought to the screen the "sound" of a quick and progressive new American century, just as her dialogue on the soundtracks of later talking pictures such as *Red-Headed Woman* (1932) and *San Francisco* (1935) performed the same function in the Depression years. Brought up on the Barbary Coast, she captured a quick and blunt rhetorical topicality and detail. One of Loos's early heroes on the Barbary Coast, Wilson Mizner, was famous for his cultivation of American slang, and she later characterized him as "Blackie" for Gable's role in *San Francisco.*

Just as Loos was about to revolutionize silent film title writing, Mencken was publishing in 1913 in *The Smart Set* a series of articles on the American character, including "The American: His Language." "America is now so rich in new words, new phrases and old words transferred to new objects," he wrote, with some exasperation, "that it is utterly unintelligible to an educated Englishman." He could have been describing Loos's pungent rhetoric and slang when he noted that "[the American's] one desire is to make speech lucid, lively, dramatic, staccato, arresting, clear."[19]

This was her language and she knew it was her audience's also. Yet, at first, translating this verbal humor to the screen presented some problems. The potential was not grasped even by someone as innovative as D. W. Griffith. Griffith himself was not above inserting a completely superfluous title upon the action, and he would frequently interrupt a dramatic rescue scene to inform us in an annoying, superfluous title what was going to happen. But the fact remains that he was cold to her kind of diction and style. As commentator Gary Carey explains, much of her humor was contained in the turn of a phrase, a witty description, even a wisecracking line or so of dialogue—all of which, maintained Griffith, would be lost on the silent screen.[20] One has only to take a look at the forced and precious rhetoric of the early Fairbanks titles *not* by Loos—the aforementioned *The Lamb*, for example—to appreciate her own contributions.[21]

The Loosian subtitle was a relatively novel addition to screen grammar in 1916. Of course, there were titles for opening and closing credits, titles to identify a scene or character, titles for dialogue, and so on, but the Loosian subtitle, as one commentator at the time put it,

> . . . has only been in vogue a few years. It differs from the title—the wording between scenes which describes the action of the picture that is to come—in that it need not attend to business. It is meant only for the audience, and though at times in the supposed speeches of the characters in the film, it may be a mere comment outside the picture and addressed to the audience like the aside of our fathers' theatre.[22]

In her book, *How to Write Photoplays*, Loos takes her task quite seriously:

> The only place where the photodramatist may "spread himself in clever verbiage and literary style" is in the sub-titles, the inserts of printed matter flashed on the screen between photographed scenes. It is this matter of subtitling which is winning the continuity specialist his place as an artist.[23]

She insisted that an expository title, for instance, should be in the same mood as the scene it introduces, and, most importantly, that "the shades of meaning in the title must correspond so perfectly to the shades of the meaning of the scene in which it is inserted that the audience feels no shock at the change from a picture from the written words."[24] Fairbanks himself knew her worth: "Time and again I have sat through plays with Miss Loos and have heard the audience applaud her subtitles as heartily as the liveliest scenes. This has convinced me of the great value of the kind of work she does."[25]

Meanwhile, a third figure has been waiting in the wings. It was he who brought Loos and Fairbanks together. John Emerson (1874–1956) was a participant in the great influx of stage stars that came from New York to Los Angeles between 1914–1915. His career on Broadway had begun with small parts in the company of Minnie Maddern Fiske ("Mrs. Fiske"), the distinguished star of high comedy at the time. Later, he joined up with Charles Frohman, then the most important of the Broadway producers. In Hollywood, he was approached by Griffith about the possibility of making a film from one of his stage hits. Emerson took cinema seriously, unlike many of the newly imported stage celebrities. Meanwhile, he had formed a friendship with Fairbanks in New York, where they were both members of the Lamb's Club. After making a few films in Los Angeles, Emerson decided to direct one with Fairbanks and persuaded Griffith to let him handle the film. He betook himself to the file of scripts in Frank Woods's Scenario Department. He ran across a number of stories that seemed perfect for Fairbanks. They were lightly satiric, peppy, and abounded in wisecracks.

They were written by somebody named Anita Loos.

Emerson thought them great material for Fairbanks and told Griffith so. The Great Man remained unimpressed. "All the laughs are in the lines," he said, "you can't print lines on the screen—people don't go to the movies to read." Bewildered, Emerson wanted to know why Griffith had bought so many of the stories.

"I like to read them myself" was Griffith's famous rejoinder. "They make me laugh."[26]

Emerson prevailed and soon he, Loos, and Fairbanks—"The Great Triple Alliance," declared *Variety*[27]—quickly crafted in the next few months two of the most idiosyncratic and successful pictures of this stage in Fairbanks's career: *His Picture in the Papers* and *The Matrimaniac*. Along with a later collaboration, *In Again—Out Again*, these topical satires captured a nation's current preoccupations about, respectively, advertising, the technology of speed, and, in the latter example, wartime preparedness.[28] If things got a little crazy in these films—as they assuredly do—that's all part of the deal. As *Photoplay* reported,

His Picture in the Papers (1916) satirized America's obsession with celebrity.

> America is a large neighborhood of hustle and bustle, good nature and dogged persistence, fine animal spirits and outrageous optimism, much physical magnetism and a few esoteric ingredients. . . . The good-bad loveable chap Douglas Fairbanks always plays *does* represent America.[29]

His Picture in the Papers

Loos, Emerson, and Fairbanks sprint out of the blocks with *His Picture in the Papers.* The frenetic action is sprinkled with slangy expository and dialogue titles, with a few puns and knowing winks at the viewer thrown in. Emerson's direction keeps the story freewheeling along. And there's no question that the bounding Fairbanks himself is having the time of his life. A detailed synopsis provides at least a hint of this richly textured comedy.

The gloves are off immediately with the introductory title:

> *Publicity at any price has become the predominant passion of the American People.*

And here's Pete Prindle (Fairbanks), the "nonconformist" member of the Prindle family, whose patriarch, Proteus (Clarence Handyside), presides over Prindle's "27 Vegetarian Varieties." Loos has great fun with these products, which include "Prindl's Pressed Prunes," "Life Preserving Lentils," "Toasted Tooties," "Dessicated Delights," and "Puffed Peanuts." For his part, Emerson, er, *relishes* shots of the Prindle clan furtively disposing their food when their father is not looking. As for Father Prindle, he not only manufactures his products, relates an intertitle—

> *But he* eats *them.*

Pete, by contrast, hates this tepid stuff and prefers his own daily regimen of morning exercise and a hearty meal of steaks and cocktails—

> *Pete prefers pugilism to pushing Prindle's Products.*

Pete dutifully appears at the family table, but—

> *Having banqueted at home, Pete sneaks off to get something to eat.*

Pete finds an ally at the restaurant, Christine Cadwallader (Loretta Blake). It's love at first bite—

> *Flying to Christine's side, he asks her to join him for life on a good, strong meat diet.*

Meantime, Proteus asks, "What have you ever done for Prindle's Products?" Pete decides if he is going to inherit a partnership in the family business and gain permission to marry pretty Christine from his future father-in-law ("another vegetarian nut"), he must get publicity for the company by getting "his picture in the papers." So he embarks on a series of publicity stunts, exclaiming to the press:

> *"I was raised on Prindle's Products, and here is my autograph!"*

First, he fakes a car crash, which rates only a few lines in the back pages of the paper. Next, he races to the local boxing club, where he bests "Battling Burke" in a brutal series of fisticuffs. But the police raid the club and seize the photographs. Frustrated, he seeks advice from a clairvoyant, "Madame Vera Carewes." But his buddies mistake his request, thinking he wants to go to *Vera Cruz* (typical of Loos's punning). So they pack him off to a steamer bound for you-know-where. When Pete wakes up, literally all at sea, he dives off the boat and swims to shore, clad only in pajamas. The ship's captain advises his mates to let him go—

> *"His empty head will keep him afloat!"*

Pete washes ashore—

> *"I refuse to be arrested. These are perfectly respectable pajamas!"*

By now, any sense of story logic is up for grabs. The police drag him to headquarters. A photographer appears, and Pete repeats his mantra:

> *"I'm Pete Prindle, raised on Prindle's Products, and I've just beat up two cops.* Please *take my picture for your papers!"*

But the subsequent newspaper story fails to cite his name, out of "respect" for his family name.

Poor Pete. He's failed at every hand. However, there's a gang of railroad thieves who are bent on wrecking a train carrying Pete's prospective fiancée and her family. Released from jail, Pete finds himself on the tracks (never mind how *that* happened!), and he foils the plot after beating up the villains and averting the wreck at the last minute. A few well-aimed bottles of "Prindle's Prohibition Punch" dispatch the bad guys—

> *"At last, a use for Prindle Products!"*

Pete is a hero at last and finally succeeds in getting his picture—and lots of headlines—in the papers.

> *"Ain't he the REEL hero?"*

winks an intertitle. And the newspaper headlines promptly exaggerate Pete's exploits by inflating by the thousands the number of rescued victims.

A charming epilogue discloses a group of people clutching newspapers that conceal their faces. Two newspapers are lowered to reveal Pete and Christine in a clinch.

Our Triple Alliance pulls off a small miracle here. The delightfully bizarre succession of wacky episodes jumps from place to place—from

New York City, to Grand Central Station, to Atlantic City, to ships at sea, to railroad trains—and imparts a delightfully surreal quality to the story. Most importantly, Fairbanks's Pete Prindle is first in a succession of roles in which he embodies the Rooseveltian self-made man of the new American century: On the one hand, he manages to work—and promote—the system; he can admire the industrial titans like Andrew Carnegie. However, at the same time, he is restless in their office spaces and discontented at being just a cog in the organization. As historian Lary May points out, Fairbanks "shows manufacturers how to capitalize on the needs of the new generation. . . . Men continued to achieve in the world of production; but they now strove equally hard for the money to purchase goods and leisure pursuits to compensate for boredom on the job . . . As leisure now supplied a new frontier for male energy, mass-produced but high-class consumer goods became a reward for tolerating the modern economy."[30]

Variety greeted the film ecstatically, pronouncing, "Douglas Fairbanks again forcibly brings to mind that he is destined to be one of the greatest favorites with the film-seeing public."[31]

(By no means incidentally, the cinematographer on that film [uncredited in the title cards] was a young man who would become another important member of the Fairbanks team. He would not only photograph more Fairbanks films, but he would make his directorial debut with two more of his comedies, *When the Clouds Roll By* and *The Mollycoddle* [both 1919]. His name was Victor Fleming, and he will figure prominently in the next chapter on the Fairbanks westerns.)

In Again—Out Again

Loos and Emerson underpin the romantic antics of *In Again—Out Again* with contemporary political concerns. It was Fairbanks's first picture to be released by the newly formed Artcraft Pictures Corporation, a distributor for Paramount. Artcraft also released the films of Mary Pickford. At this time, late April 1917, America was entering the Great War after two and a half years of Woodrow Wilson's attempts to keep the country neutral. America's attitude had been divided into "preparedness" and "pacifist" camps. D. W. Griffith and Mary Pickford were promoting patriotic sentiments in films such as, respectively, *Hearts of the World* and *The Little American*. By contrast, Henry Ford had been vehemently opposing war and was harshly critical of those who financed it. He had just funded a so-called "Peace Ship" to war-torn Europe. Garnering little more than ridicule, he abandoned the project. Attitudes like this drew Fairbanks's ire. At thirty-four, he was too old for active service, but he was vocal in promoting preparedness efforts by the Red Cross and, later, the Liberty Bond rallies and the War Relief Organization.

In Again—Out Again indicts such organizations as the "Athenium Massage Cream" factory, which, unknown to the pacifists, secretly produces boxes of explosives; and there is "Carter's Little Liver Pills," which manufactures mines. At a meeting of a group of New Jersey Pacifists ("Bless their hearts," a title sneers), we see messages adorning the walls and podium proclaiming,

> *We are too comfortable to fight!*

And—

> *Blessed are the peacemakers* [which hangs below a portrait of William Jennings Bryan]

And finally—

> *No one can insult us but ourselves—and we won't.*

The story introduces young Teddy Rutherford (Fairbanks), an exuberant advocate of American "preparedness," who is unhappily engaged to a pallid creature aptly named "Pacifice" (Helen Green). She more than lives up to her name:

> *Pacifice Jennings—a female of the species, though not as deadly as the male.*

When the frustrated Teddy is thrown into jail after a drunken spree, he meets the pretty jailer's daughter, Janie (Arline Pretty), who is more sympathetic to his views. Aware now that his stay in the cooler has its advantages, he greets the judge's sentence of thirty days with a broad smile and a vigorous handshake. At the same time a title states:

> *At the end of a perfect trial.*

Once inside, he transforms his cold and bleak cell into a cozy nook with curtains, quaint pictures on the walls, flowers, and a couch upon which he reclines with a pipe and ukulele, serenading his beloved beside him. What more telling image of the middle-class dream than this: paradise recaptured in domestic bliss. However, when he is released from jail, he resorts to all manner of strenuous tactics to get himself *back* behind bars. (This plot device is vaguely reminiscent of O. Henry's short story, "The Cop and the Anthem.") He gets arrested for speeding, only to find himself thrown into the *wrong* jail. Finally, he impersonates a saboteur, only to find himself confronting the real thing. After a whirlwind scuffle and capture of the villain, he succeeds in marrying the sheriff's daughter at last. Our hero exerts every ounce of athletic and technological resource to wed his lady love—and in the process, preach a none-too-subtle sermon promoting athletic preparedness.

The Matrimaniac

An energy of a different sort fuels the high-flying *The Matrimaniac*. Two runaway lovers, Jimmie Conroy and Marna Lewis (Fairbanks and Constance Talmadge) outrace Marna's irate father, a rival suitor, and assorted detectives and policemen on their way to a most unusual altar. Again, Loos and Emerson cut Fairbanks loose, tracking the swift trajectory not just of a man in love, but of a nation in motion. Loos's predilection with the currents of American life that George Santayana called the "vast modern mechanical momentum" and the "rushing tide of instrumentalities"—is everywhere apparent. *The Matrimaniac* is a little gem linking everyday life with the machine muscle of America.

Deciding that eloping via high window and a rope ladder is too inconvenient, Jimmie and Marna decide on a simpler route:

> *Outraging all rules of romance—a daylight front-door elopement.*

Just ahead of her pursuing father, they clamber aboard a moving train. Momentarily at peace on the train, Jimmie's romantic ardor elicits this peroration:

> *"I love you so much I feel rotten."*

During a brief stop, Jimmie disembarks to fetch Reverend Tubbs, a local minister. But the train leaves before they can return to the train. Thereafter, Jimmie drags the hapless minister aboard every available mode of transportation to catch up, including a motor railcar, a switch engine, the brake rods of a freight train, three brands of autos, and a recalcitrant mule! Meanwhile, Marna's father is pursing *him* and catches up with him and the minister.

> *"They're a pair of escaped lunatics!"*

He tells the conductor,

> *"Wire ahead for an officer and I'll pay their fare."*

Dad then proceeds to lock up his daughter in a hotel room. He explains that Jimmie and the minister have been detained:

> *"They're safe in jail on three counts—stopping the Limited, abduction, and lunacy!"*

Meanwhile, after a series of narrow escapes, involving some of Fairbanks's most nimble tree climbing, wall vaulting, and rooftop flying, he finds himself aloft in a forest of telephone wires. Perched amid the crossarms and wires, he has the lineman put through a multiple hookup to his fiancée in her hotel room, where she is being kept a virtual prisoner by her father, and to a minister who is being likewise detained in a jail cell. The wedding is thus a "long distance" affair while the lineman, a maid, and a deputy sheriff are witnesses. The furiously gesticulating father at the foot of the pool elicits Jimmie's retort—

> *"Shut up, down there! Don't you see I'm getting married?"*

To paraphrase Walt Whitman, "They sing the marriage electric." Or, to quote another poet, Alexander Pope:

> *Ye gods!*
> *Annihilate but space and time*
> *And make two lovers happy.*

It seems that holy matrimony in a progressive America is simply a matter of completing an electrical circuit. *Variety* singled out this most unusual sequence for praise: "The road that leads to this point is a rough one for Fairbanks and the accommodating minister; i.e., runaway railroad cars, a contrary donkey, the rods of a train, an impressed auto were some of the means of location employed by this modern Don Quixote in pursuit of his Dulcinea."[32]

The story ends with Jimmie distributing cash to a parade of helpful people he had met along the way and to whom he had pledged a string of IOUs. And there, last in line, none the worse for wear, is poor Reverend Tubbs. Bless him, he had shared in all of Jimmie's travails. His IOU is the biggest of all.

There is a delicious, anarchic sense of bodily abandon and disorder in these films. The city was Fairbanks's gymnasium. To quote G. K. Chesterton again (who else could have captured this energy in words better than he?), we have here a bouncing character in a harlequinade:

> [He] had indeed a great and fundamental affinity with the landscape, or rather house-scape, of the harlequinade. He liked high houses, and sloping roofs, and deep areas. But he would have been really happy if some good fairy of the eternal pantomime had given him the power of flying off the roofs and pitching harmlessly down the height of the houses and bounding out of the areas like an indiarubber ball.[33]

The special pleasures of this form of comedy, explains cultural commentator Henry Jenkins, comes with the "desire to break free from restraint, to enjoy an abundance of energy and spontaneity, to challenge authorities who restrain our creative potential, and to negate the logical order." It didn't matter so much where Fairbanks was heading in these crazy trajectories, what really mattered was *how he would get there*. To be sure, the emphasis at the conclusion on Fairbanks's return to social order, matrimony, and the job was as much a part of the meaning and pleasure. "Order must be demolished for a liberating disorder," continues Jenkins. "Disorder must be constrained within a more satisfying order."[34]

Gymnastic Sermons: *The Habit of Happiness, Reggie Mixes In, Down to Earth, Mr. Fix-It, He Comes Up Smiling, Say Young Fellow*

The Habit of Happiness

"Well, all right, what's your fine high purpose in becoming a Man of God, Brother Gantry?"

"Well, I—Rats, it's perfectly clear. Preacher can do a lot of good—
give help and—And explain religion."

The Habit of Happiness (1916), co-starring Dorothy West, brought a sermon of hope to the downtrodden.

"Yea! It certainly must make the common people feel awfully common to hear Brother Gantry spiel about the errors of supralapsarianism!"

"I never preach about any such doggone thing!" Elmer protested. "I just give 'em a good helpful sermon, with some jokes sprinkled in to make it interesting and some stuff about the theater or something that'll startle 'em a little and wake 'em up and help 'em to lead better and fuller daily lives."

—**SINCLAIR LEWIS**, *Elmer Gantry*

The Habit of Happiness was Fairbanks's fourth film for Triangle and the first in a series of what are best described as "gymnastic sermons," including *Reggie Mixes In*, *Down to Earth*, and *Mr. Fix-It*. Of the many sources of virtue Fairbanks would delineate and advocate in his films—certainly what we call his "choreography of Hope"—it presented a positive blend of gymnastics and optimism. Here is Fairbanks in the role of what Alistair Cooke called the "popular philosopher," a kind of gymnastic preacher, or Boy Scout, pledging health and physical fitness against all manner of social ills and medical neuroses, pretensions, stale ideas, and the other ills of an expanding America: "Fairbanks had the feel of the popular pulse," wrote Cooke; "—he knew to a degree the median limits of romance, prejudice, social conservatism; he knew them instinctively because they were his own."[35] Thus, if in *Picture* we encountered a generally breezy attitude toward strength, health, and vigor, in *Habit* we find a much more consolidated and insistent attitude toward defining the good life and the means to obtain it. If *Picture* was satirical, *Habit* was a sermon. Fairbanks comes across as a blend of Teddy Roosevelt, Horatio Alger, and Billy Sunday. Not only were societal ills exposed but so were practical solutions proposed.

Habit of Happiness also marks the Canadian writer-director Allan Dwan's (1885–1981) first project for Fairbanks. This new "musketeer" of the Fairbanks team is completely in tune with the Loos-Emerson formula. At the same time, he invested in his pictures his own unique stamp of sentiment and toughness. Even counting John Emerson and, later, Victor Fleming, no other director was to be more important to Fairbanks's subsequent career. Despite an active directorial career spanning 1911–1961, little of substance has been written about him until interviews appearing in Kevin Brownlow's *The Parade's Gone By* (1968) and Peter Bogdanovich's *The Last Pioneer* (1971). A long-awaited major biography, Frederic Lombardi's splendid *Allan Dwan and the Rise and Decline of the Hollywood Studios* (2013), is particularly welcome. Dwan himself has been the subject of several recent retrospectives of his work, including a festival in Bologna, Italy, in the summer of 2013.

Upon completion of *His Picture in the Papers*, director John Emerson left the Triangle studios for two months on loan to Famous Players Company in their eastern studios. Directorial chores to *The Habit of Happiness* were instead given to Dwan. He had taken over as studio general in the East for Triangle in Yonkers, New York, by March 1916. Among his films for Triangle had been *Jordan Is a Hard Road*, with Frank Campeau, and *Soldiers of Fortune*. He directed several Mary Pickford features later on, among them *The Foundling* and *Girl of Yesterday*. Dwan's working methods reveal him as the perfect director for a man in motion like Fairbanks. His was the necessary practical approach to Doug's freebooting style:

> One of the most important things was economy of gesture, which to me is a very important portion of the art of acting. To do a great deal with very little in terms of motion. The broad gestures, the scene-eating type of acting has never appealed to me. I like the little gesture. I think in anything you can give too much and if you do, you can lose all.[36]

On the other hand, he never lost sight of the innate sweetness and sentiment of his characters:

> I believe only in the art which expresses and arouses human emotions and to which people react with the heart rather than the mind. I believe that the great mass of people want to live in the characters they see on the screen . . . feeling vicariously the human and the pathos of the story woven around them. Only the critics care about taking a picture apart to see what makes the wheels go around, and they are the only ones who derive enjoyment solely from artistic workmanship. . . . There was a time when I had the artistic ideal but I was young then. . . . Later I got a job and went back and redeemed my overcoat with cold cash . . . when in later years I turned out some scripts for a motion picture company, I did it for so much a week in an office and when I got into the production of the business, I did it for so much a week too. No more masterpieces! No more art for art's sake! That first experience made a realist of me and I've kept my feet on the ground ever since.[37]

Practical and efficient, Dwan was the perfect man for the fledgling Triangle to have around. Unlike many idealistic directors who had no interest or capacity for economics, Dwan knew the business end of the industry:

> The director is the man who has control of the money. The director is the man who can make or break a picture financially and artistically. Most directors are not business men. Therefore the films have had to arrange for business managers, for men who, when the director had laid out the thing artistically and outlined the results he could achieve, will find out it can be done at the lowest cost. These men contract for material, set salaries, tend to all the commercial delay.[38]

What is more, Dwan turned them out fast and efficiently:

> Pictures must be made fast. If you muddle around with them, you've lost your clear vision. You cannot hurry art, of course, but you can hurry commercial production. Get your art in hand before you start to produce and you'll save a lot of time and trouble.[39]

Moreover, he shared with Doug a tough and rambunctious physicality and possessed an eye for the sorts of choreographed stunts that became the star's trademark. "Mr. Dwan is probably the ideal director for the star," wrote Peter Milne in *Motion Picture News*. "The tempo of the action, the arrangement of the scenes, the evident spontaneity of every bit of business are always mindful of his genius as a director of the Fairbanks type of picture."[40]

The Habit of Happiness anticipates the pictures of Frank Capra in its populist concerns with the redistribution of wealth. It was shot in Fort Lee, New Jersey, and in the studios at Riverdale. Dwan's title-writing strongly reveals the influence of Anita Loos. "Sunny" Wiggins (Fairbanks) is the scion of a wealthy, social-climbing family. As a title tells us, they have

> *. . . risen in society to the point that they are snubbed by the best people in town.*

Unlike his grasping father, he pursues his "Brotherhood of Man" theories, dispensing cash and food and housing to the Bowery derelicts he picks up in the breadlines. In the first scene, Sunny wakes up to a houseful of bums, in his bed, in the bathroom, all over the house. After hosing them down, he troops them downstairs, to the bewilderment of his stuffy sister and her friends. He tries to explain to his father his intentions to redistribute wealth to the poor. This dialogue is intercut with striking contrasts between the poor and the wealthy: a shot of the wealthy set dining at the table is intercut with bums huddling in the cold on the breadline; a close-up shot of women's hands having a manicure is intercut with gnarled men's hands twisting a rope; and a third shot of society women feeding their dogs is intercut with a mother at a shabby table feeding her baby.

Mr. Wiggins greets this, saying:

> *"You don't know what you're talking about. Go down there and live for awhile without money, and you'll see for yourself what a worthless lot they are."*

Off goes Sunny, his pockets empty, to a flophouse where we find, as a title tells us:

> *A Sargasso Sea of humanity, where the derelicts of life are drawn to await the Potter's Field.*

Seeing the group, Sunny exclaims:

> *"They need cheering up. I wonder if I can make them laugh."*

Immediately, he demonstrates with arm-waving and calisthenics the healthy spirit of laughter.

The scene abruptly shifts to the gloomy home of a Wall Street tycoon, Jonathan Pepper (George Fawcett). Mr. Pepper has dyspepsia, appropriately enough, and has "lost his pep." It's a hilarious moment when we see the mournful old man glooming in the foreground, while in the background an aging cellist grinds out Chopin's Funeral March. The butler and the housemaid look as if they strayed out of Castle Dracula. Sunny is dispatched there to cure Fawcett of "the grouch." Sunny says,

> *"A man with as much money as old Pep has no right to be happy."*

His attempts at jokes fail, until he gets the cellist to "rag" up the music. Soon, the butler and maid break out into a dance. Fawcett is dispatched to his room, where he's denied food to the point that, starving, he launches into a big steak.

The plot thickens as a gang of men, recruited by Fawcett's rival, break in to kidnap the old guy. Sunny leaps to his defense and tackles several of the thugs. In a surprising moment, Sunny is shot and collapses. As some rescuers arrive, the old man takes one look at the recumbent, semi-conscious Sunny—and *laughs*. For the first time. This may be the best gag in the whole film.

Variety reported:

> As long as [Fairbanks] appears in comedies of this sort there will be no need of his organizing a "one, two, three-laugh" club anywhere in the neighborhood where his pictures are shown . . . This picture will undoubtedly start the happiness habit the country over . . ."[41]

And the *New York Times* cheered:

> "Laugh and the world laughs with you. Don't and you're a darned old grouch" would seem to be the fable in film taught by *The Habit of Happiness*, the latest Triangle-Fine Arts feature production in which Douglas Fairbanks is being starred. This picture will undoubtedly start the happiness habit the country over, for it is one of the best comedy-dramas that has been seen on the screen in many a day. Of course the inimitable Duggy [*sic*] Fairbanks does a lot to make the picture go, but even at that there are certainly a host of situations created for the young comedian and he

does make the best of them in a manner that would even make the veriest "grouch" in the world laugh.[42]

Reggie Mixes In

Reggie Mixes In was Fairbanks's sixth film for Triangle. This time neither Dwan nor Loos-Emerson is involved—Christy Cabanne directed the story by Roy Somerville—but the formula is by now solidly in place. If anything, the amiable gymnastic sermons we saw in *Habit* are more strenuous than ever. The story cast Bessie Love as "Agnes" in a Cinderella fable of a poor girl from the wrong side of the tracks whose reputation and poverty-stricken family is saved by the dashing Reggie Van Deuzen (Fairbanks). Reggie is "just *fresh* out of college" and, dissatisfied with his "diet" of upper-class living, he find himself "slumming" down town. He is immediately struck by poor Agnes's impoverished living conditions, winsome beauty, and demure manner:

> *She is a new sort of girl in Reggie's experience.*

Indeed, she is quite a contrast to Reggie's uptown fiancée, Lemona (Alma Reubens), whose ambitions are quite clear—

> *Lemona has one eye on Reggie and the other on his bank account.*

In order to look after Agnes, Reggie takes a room in the neighborhood and becomes a bouncer at Gallagher's Bar, a low New York dive, where innocent Agnes is working as a dancer. Some of Doug's best scenes have him relinquishing his evening dress and high-class diction and manners and rehearsing his newly acquired "tough guy" manner: He hitches his shoulders, practices his swagger, pulls a rude cloth cap over his eyes, and tucks his tie into a rude work shirt. He saunters through the bar, just evading an occasional swipe from a local tough, turning about, glaring defiantly, then moving on. Reggie saves the girl from a group of toughs by besting them in several combats. This involves a challenge from the lead bad guy, Tony (W. A. Lowery)—

> *"You and me will go into that room and lock the door. Whoever comes out gets the girl!"*

With Bessie Love in *Reggie Mixes In* (1916).

Fairbanks is all seriousness as he grits his teeth and launches into the fray. They batter and pummel each other until, after a series of falls, leaps, and wrestling moves, Reggie emerges from the room in half darkness, his face puffy and bloodied and shirt torn to the waist. In its brutality, the fight anticipates the tone and graphic realism of the fight scenes in Buster Keaton's *The Battling Butler* and Lloyd's *The Kid Brother* (both 1926).

The story hurries to its climax as Reggie reveals his wealthy station to the delighted Agnes.

The fights immediately drew praise from the critics. "Never was such a fight seen on the screen," gushed the *New York Times*: "The audience fairly gasped at some of the falls, which were not confined to the star's opponent, for Fairbanks himself took his share of the drubbing . . . When it was all over, Fairbanks was just able to stagger out of the room, which may have been acting, but more probably was not."[43] Likewise, *Variety* praised the "physical prowess of Douglas Fairbanks in his latest. . . . [There are] comedy, captions, fine production, good acting and, once more, some scrapper that Doug . . . Jess Willard has nothin' on him."[44] And *Motion Picture Classic* quotes Fairbanks's account of watching the finished film with a theater audience: "One of the big fight scenes came along and, as the big bruisers in the saloon jumped down on me, I lived again through the wild hard tussles and pounding blows that were struck in the studio during the days that scene was taken and re-taken. We were black and blue by the time the director was satisfied the fight looked real . . . Then suddenly, to destroy the illusion, came the remark of a woman in front of me, They suttinly fake that grand!"[45]

The sermon is clear: only Fairbanks's tough, aggressive attitude, driven by a superbly trained militant masculinity can spring the trap of poverty and defeat the doldrums of despair.

Down to Earth

We are back to Loos and Emerson in this purest of Fairbanks's gymnastic sermons. He is Billy Gaynor, "lusty, strong, and brave," proclaims an intertitle. While he is busily winning the big football game, galloping across the prairies, and climbing icy mountain slopes, his girlfriend, Ethel Forsythe (Eileen Percy), who has refused his marriage proposal, falls under the influence of the slimy Charlie Riddle (Charles Gerrard), who leads her into a life of parties, dancing, and drinking. As an intertitle informs us,

> *Ethel and Billy go their separate ways—Bill trying to forget, and Ethel forgetting to try.*

Upon learning of Ethel's internment in the sanitarium of the quack "Dr. Jollyem," Billy races to the institution to find Ethel has joined a group of lazy, self-indulgent hypochondriacs, all victims of "overcivilization." The good doctor tells Bill:

> *"Ethel is in the condition of over half of our wealthy city-bred women. There's no cure for them, because they won't help cure themselves."*

Bill purchases the sanitarium and presumes to literally exercise his own cures. He takes them on a yachting trip and intentionally strands them on what they think is a desert island (actually just off the coast of Catalina). He announces to the bewildered group:

Gymnastic sermons of health and happiness in *Down to Earth* (1917).

> *"Some people are born healthy, others achieve health, but you're going to have health thrust upon you!"*

Ever on the move, he urges, gesticulates, harasses, and humiliates his "patients."

> *"What shall we do to be saved?"*

—they all wail. Bill directs the fat woman to roll on the ground, the dyspeptic to laugh and slap his arms, the man with the liver ailment to gather firewood, the alcoholic (pursued by a lavender elephant) to drink two quarts of water between meals, and the others to climb trees and turn handsprings. Doug moves from one "patient" to another, swiftly prescribing, gesturing, grinning, slamming one fist into his palm, rocking back from the hips, thrusting forward his forearms, describing arcs in the air with his hands. He teaches them outdoor skills, like woodcraft and living off the land. In short, he literally choreographs a physical regimen that will restore them to health and sanity. Life on the "island" becomes a summer camp for grown-up Boy and Girl Scouts. "In getting his patients onto the royal road to health," observes Gaylyn Studlar, "Billy's cure fulfills the era's idealized conception of outdoor exercise as instinctive play that would make children into adults and adults into children."[46] Thus begins Fairbanks's own plans to promote character-building through physical fitness in a series of ghostwritten books in the 'teens bearing titles like *Laugh and Live*, *Making Life Worthwhile*, and *Whistle and Hoe—Sing as We Go.*

A Restoration and Two Fragments

For many years, several Artcraft productions in this category, *Mr. Fix-It* (1918), *He Comes Up Smiling* (1918), and *Say, Young Fellow* (1918) existed only in fragmentary form. Now, thanks to the untiring efforts of Dr. Tracey Goessel, longtime Fairbanks enthusiast and researcher, the former is now available in relatively complete state. *He Comes Up Smiling*, alas, is still incomplete. (*Say Young Fellow* is discussed in a later chapter, "On an Odd Note.") Although only the first two reels have come to light—come up *smiling*, as it were—they reveal a fascinating glimpse into a "might-have-been." (Other "lost" Artcrafts, *Headin' South*, *Arizona*, *Bound in Morocco*, and *Knickerbocker Buckaroo*, are considered elsewhere in these pages).[47]

Mr. Fix-It is an Artcraft production and once again features Allan Dwan as writer and director.[48] Because of Fairbanks's participation in the Third Liberty Loan Drive, he was hard-pressed to work the film into his busy schedule. Ever the practical artist, Dwan came up with a scenario that required mostly interiors and a day-and-night shooting schedule. Reginald Burroughs (Leslie Stuart) is the scion of a wealthy American family who has been living and studying in England for 15 years. They sent him there because they fear America is "too democratic." His studies at Oxford are interrupted when he learns his aunts wish him to return to New York and take charge of his property and meet the woman they have "selected" for his fiancée, Olive Van Tassell (Margaret Landis). Failure to appear may forfeit a substantial portion of his inheritance. Reluctant to leave England, he persuades his roommate, Fred Remington (Fairbanks) to take his place in America. Remington finds a very stuffy and staid household, dominated by a stuffed-shirt uncle (Frank Campeau) and three aunts. His "sister" is unhappy, since she's supposed to marry a man she doesn't love.

His "fiancée" is also unhappy, since she's really in love with a war veteran. Remington immediately sets out to "fix-it," to rearrange the relationships so the two women can be with their loving partners.

Meantime, one day he rescues a little girl from a street accident. There's a charming scene at the hospital where surgeons repair the girl's damaged doll. The girl leads him to a house where her older sister, hapless Mary (Wanda Hawley) and her other young siblings live. Next door is a saloon operated by the landlord, a wicked man named Flannigan. Flannigan tells her she can stay in the rooms as long as she "cooperates" with the men downstairs. Remington comes to the rescue and promptly invites them to live with him in the Burroughs mansion. He greets his aunts' resistance:

> *"Now listen to me, these children need help. They're my guests now. Besides, this is my house. And you're my guests, too. Feel free to stay as long as you wish."*

In moments reminiscent of *The Habit of Happiness,* the scruffy kids invade the precincts of the elaborately appointed dinner table. Fairbanks is irresistible in these scenes. He and the kids romp all over the house. He roughhouses with them, literally mops up the floor with them, leads them in tumbles and handstands down the staircase, and shares their games in the playroom. For their part, the kids ingratiate themselves with the aunts and uncle. Everybody rouses from their lethargy. Barriers of class and station fall away. Remington surveys the happy scene:

> *"God bless you all!"*

And he writes back to Reginald in England:

> *"Don't worry if I bring a little havoc to your family; it will do them good."*

But when Mary is mistakenly led to believe that Fairbanks is engaged, she is disconsolate and prepares the leave with the kids. Discovering the empty playroom, Fairbanks sets out to find her. What ensues is a sudden burst of action. He goes to Flannigan's where he takes on a whole roomful of thugs in the place. Thinking he is pursuing a woman (who turns out to be a stranger), he scales house fronts, tightropes across rooftops, and slides down to the street on a makeshift clothesline. But Mary is gone.

Back at the mansion, Mary is discovered where she's been hiding all along with the kids. During the joyful reunion, who should arrive but the real Reginald Burroughs and his wife. He finds a very different household. Mary turns away from Fairbanks, angry at his deception. He wails now that he's been fixing everything except his own life:

> *"Isn't that strange? I fixed it for everyone but myself!"*

It's now up to one of the children to "fix" things. The child takes him by the hand back to Mary. She melts into his arms and everything is all right.

Mr. Fix-It is a thoroughly enjoyable light comedy that capitalizes on Fairbanks's gifts for intimate comedy. His antics, to a great degree, are confined to horseplay with the children and a series of mischievous parlor pranks—he even booby-traps the dining table in one scene. "*Mr. Fix-It* looks more like a Mary Pickford film," writes Dwan biographer Frederic Lombardi. "But even more than in *Habit of Happiness* Doug's gentle side is wrung from the essence of his screen persona."[49] It's not until the climax that he suddenly bursts at the seams and charges into the search for Mary. "How [Fairbanks] 'clowns' his way through five reels of almost Keystone comedy," writes *Variety*, "with cleverly written titles and 'fixes' things for everybody but himself . . . makes a diverting feature for the hordes of Fairbanks's fans."[50]

He Comes Up Smiling

Adapted from one of his last Broadway successes in 1914, *He Comes Up Smiling*, like *Mr. Fix-It*, is something of a change of pace for Fairbanks and director Allan Dwan. The scenario was provided by Francis Marion (Mary Pickford's favorite scenarist). Premiering in September 1918, there is a breezy, outdoor quality to the story that is relatively light on knockabout acrobatics and long on intimate charm. Actor and director have gone on holiday. Unfortunately, only a little more than a reel survives today.

Fairbanks is Jerry Martin, a lowly bank teller who is literally "caged up" in his teller's position. Aside from the daily grind, he has been told to take special care of the boss's pet canary, Agamemnon.

> *"If you are guilty of neglect, you'll be fired!"*

One day the bird escapes and Fairbanks sets out in hot pursuit. For a glorious few minutes, Jerry embarks on a wonderful pursuit trajectory: The bird just out of reach, Jerry swings up awnings to a second-story window, clambers inside, leaps back out again, climbs a series of fire escapes and flag poles, leaps from rooftop to rooftop, crosses a city street via telegraph wires, executes a series of maneuvers on a high ladder, and finally hitches a ride on a cart out into the country. Finally, he dives into the underbrush and comes up with the bird. He also makes a new friend, "the richest man in the world, the philosopher Mike," who advises Jerry,

> *"Freedom is our greatest gift on this earth, let it fly away."*

The bird is released, and Jerry watches blissfully as it flies away.

Mike is indeed quite the philosopher:

> *"Surely you have been a slave, just like this bird. Why would you go back to your cage?"*

Jerry is convinced. Falling in with Mike and some other tramps, he doffs his clothes and makes himself at home in the woodland glade. Clad only in a towel, he bathes Mike's dog and dives into the water for a swim. It's a wonderful summer's day—

> *"Tempted by the beauty of the landscape and by the fresh water"*—

He enjoys his woodland idyll. However, a horde of bees complicates the pastoral serenity, forcing Jerry to seek momentary refuge high up in a tree, from which he swings from branch to branch. He dives back into the water. . . .

The rest of the plot can be gleaned from the *AFI Catalogue of Motion Pictures, 1911–1920*: During his watery escape from the bees, Jerry's clothes are stolen. He dons a new suit with the permission of a passerby, Mr. Batchellor, a Wall Street tycoon. They concoct a ruse whereby Jerry will assume Batchellor's identity and live for a few weeks at the home of a wealthy businessman named Mr. Bartlett. There just happens to be a pretty daughter, Billy, in the house, for whom Jerry forms an instant attachment. Complications ensue when Jerry learns Mr. Bartlett is the target of a scheme to ruin him. Jerry comes to the rescue and wins both a partnership in the business and the affections of Billy.

Noting the film's Broadway origins, the *New York Times* critic notes that many liberties have been taken with the plot, including a climax replete with "the physical fireworks without which a Fairbanks picture is not considered complete." More to the point, however, is the critic's praise for Fairbanks's quieter and subtler comedy for most of the film's length:

> The distinctly minor part which physical action plays in the picture, however, leads to the hope that the star may finally leave the field behind him and devote himself to more subtle comedy. Like Chaplin, he has something of a genius for small comedy touches, and now that he is established high in popular favor, he should be able to hold his public easily—even to find an additional public—by the selection of subjects which call for treatment more delicate than a blow with an axe. "He Comes Up Smiling," at all events, makes a beginning and should be encouraged.[51]

Again, we are struck with Fairbanks's abilities to invest his customary athletic style with a charming light touch. Director Dwan will again exploit that quality later in the two costume films he made with Fairbanks in the 1920s, *Robin Hood* and *The Iron Mask*.

A Sunday Punch

A further word is needed to contextualize these gymnastic sermons. They find their precedent and example in two of Fairbanks's heroes and contemporaries, the politician Theodore Roosevelt, whom we have already met, and the "Baseball Evangelist" Billy Sunday. Since the 1880s Roosevelt had been accusing America's "gilded" youth of growing "soft" because of the "over-civilization" of an increasingly industrialized, bureaucratic and sedentary culture. Only the strenuous life and a renewed masculine toughness could save the country.[52]

"As athletics became popular among the urban masses," observes historian Lary May, "Fairbanks saw a way to perpetuate the American character. Sport was more than mere play; it offered an arena for restoring the virtues of an expanding [America] . . . It provided a place where all men begin as equals and win prizes according to merit. No hierarchy or class order got in the way." And offscreen he extolled those same virtues. "Rather than denying the physical self, Fairbanks delighted in it," continues May:

> Often photographed with a bare torso, he took on part of the primitive being he was always so eager to conquer, showing it to be wholesome and

> healthy. . . . As fans watched his perfect body on the screen and read his success tracts, they absorbed his religion of health and beauty. Now men could delight in their bodies—something that might make one strong, attractive to women, and above all happy. . . . Every photographic device accentuated his muscular physique. Making the most of the movie medium, viewers really *saw* Fairbanks, literally, in the flesh.[53]

"Energy—the power to force himself into action!" Fairbanks urged America's youth. "For him there is no hope unless he will take up physical training in some form that will put him in normal physical condition—after that, everything simplifies itself."[54]

Fairbanks's generation was listening. While he was chasing stardom on the American stage in the first decade of the century, Roosevelt had been enjoying his tumultuous term as president of the United States. Within a year of leaving the White House in 1909, he was pronouncing a "New Nationalism" of progressive social and political reform.[55] His energetic platform held out a particular appeal and, in the opinion of William Allen White, represented "the gaiety and optimism that belong to youth . . . which men keep so long as they have not smudged their ideals and trifled with their consciences."[56] He challenged America's youth, explains Henry F. May, "to maintain high standards of morality and conduct," and, at the same time, "to keep our ideals within range of realization. We should not, for instance, scorn material wealth, but use it for ideal ends."[57] There was nothing subtle about this message, admitted Roosevelt himself: "I think that the command or entreaty to clean living and decent politics should no more be subtle than a command in battle should be subtle.[58] The "moral regeneration" of America was at stake:

> . . . it was just plain wrong for some people, by tricks and wiles, to get a stranglehold on business and politics, while others were cheated out of opportunity. This was the kind of talk that millions of Americans of all walks of life—people allergic to ideologies, impatient of economic theory, but highly susceptible to moral evangelism and devoted to the idea of a fair chance for all—could understand and respond to.[59]

Fairbanks enthusiastically endorsed this. "You lawyers and businessmen can't exactly see leaping up steps and jumping fences and climbing trees. Well, Theodore Roosevelt managed to be President of the United States and to plant himself firmly in history, and to do all of these things because he knew they were worth more than this thing we call 'dignity.' That's the accelerator of age."[60]

Another contemporary who shared Fairbanks's gymnastic morality was his friend, the evangelist Billy Sunday. "I am burning up to do you good and keep you out of hell," roared the former baseball player, sliding across the revival platform, spikes upraised, into the "home base" of redemption.[61] Roosevelt himself applauded Sunday's zeal. Speaking from Sunday's tabernacle platform, he once referred to him as "the most wide-awake militant preacher of Christianity I know."[62] And H. L. Mencken aptly dubbed him "The Calliope of Zion." An athlete and a savvy showman, he fine-tuned a platform style that was its own message. He got to know Fairbanks and, on some occasions, as we shall see, shared the same platform with him. They resembled each other in appearance, dress, and manner. Both were just under six feet, both sported trim business suits, and both had athletic backgrounds, in sports and gymnastics. To paraphrase Booth Tarkington's memorable description, first applied to Fairbanks: *They were fauns who had been to Sunday School.*[63]

Sunday was born in Ames, Iowa, in 1862. For four years, from 1883 to 1887, he was a professional baseball player for "Pop" Anson's Chicago White Stockings. His "conversion" occurred in a Chicago rescue mission in 1887, and he finally gave up baseball in 1891 for preaching. No matter that he was never ordained—the Chicago Presbytery waived the examination on the grounds that he "had already made more converts than all his examiners."[64] By 1905 he was already gaining a name for himself on the Chautaqua and evangelical circuits. His peak years, 1908–1918, correspond roughly with Fairbanks's stage and burgeoning film career. Together, their militant masculinity fueled a message that was essentially the same. As Richard Hofstadter has noted:

> Sunday wanted to kill the idea that "being a Christian takes a man out of the busy whirl of the world's life and activity and makes him a spineless, effeminate proposition." Rather, he struck a Rooseveltian note in his assertion: "Moral warfare makes a man hard. Superficial peace makes a man mushy."[65]

In a variation of what became known at the time as the "Social Gospel," they preached that a tough-minded brotherhood, service, and goodwill were the essence of Christ's teachings. This "social theology" taught that an immanent God worked through society toward the steady improvement of both human nature and social relations.[66] To many people he was as important a crusader for reform as Theodore Roosevelt or William Jennings Bryan, both of whom publicly acknowledged him as their friend. Sunday's services assumed the form of "entertainments." He imitated the oratory style of Bryan and Robert Ingersoll, and his words assumed the tone and diction of an Anita Loos title card: "Christ was a go-getter!"

Long before he came to Hollywood, Sunday's revivals were pure showbiz. His week-long road shows, with a tabernacle like a Grauman's theater, where the suckers came to pray. His platforms, like Fairbanks's sets, were converted into gymnasiums. The attention-catching manipulations of Sunday's voice and the gestures and gyrations of his body led his authorized biographer to call him a "gymnast for Jesus." He learned to construct his sermons along the lines of a popular melodrama that would build slowly from climax to climax and move his auditors in rapid succession from guilt to fear, to laughter, to anger, to tears, to hate, to grim determination. He learned to use the tricks of the actor and the demagogue. Doubtless, novelist Sinclair Lewis had Sunday in mind when he penned *Elmer Gantry* in 1927. Gantry likewise resorted to theatrical tactics:

> Every Sunday evening now people were turned from the door of Elmer's church. If they did not always have a sermon about vice, at least they enjoyed the saxophone solos, and singing "There'll be a Hot Time in the Old Town Tonight." And once they were entertained by a professional juggler who wore (it was Elmer's own idea) a placard proclaiming that he stood for "God's Word" and who showed how easy it was to pick up weights symbolically labeled "Sin" and "Sorrow" and "Ignorance" and "Papistry."[67]

Sunday's performance style brought his athletic tendencies to the fore. It was pure Fairbanks:

> He raced up and down the green-carpeted platform . . . waving his hands, kicking up one knee now and again, like a park walking horse, brandishing a chair, standing with one foot on the chair and another on the pulpit, bending over backwards like a springy sword blade, bobbing back and forth, and waving a handkerchief between his legs as he reeled off one of his amazing long lists of vituperative epithets and displaying as much energy, determination, and virtuous enthusiasm as Douglas Fairbanks.[68]

It was estimated that he walked a mile back and forth across the thirty-foot platform in every sermon—one hundred and fifty miles in every campaign. This was not merely walking, but sliding, jumping, falling, staggering, whirling, and throwing himself about the platform.

Mixing theater and baseball, he would often act out several parts in skits, scenes taken from the Bible ("The Prodigal Son," for instance), or from his life as a professional baseball player:

> A characteristic movement of extreme emphasis [said one observer], involves the entire body and suggests a pitcher in the act of throwing the ball. At the conclusion of his sermon to men only he always parodied the famous comic poem "Slide, Kelly, Slide" and made a running dive across the full length of the platform on his stomach. Then he would jump to his feet to imitate "the Great Umpire of the Universe" and yell, "You're out, Kelly!" This scene climaxed his account of a former teammate named Kelly who had taken to booze and thus failed to get home to heaven.[69]

Indeed, Sunday was an outstanding athlete:

> Sunday was fast all right; his baseball years were marked by a dare-devil speed on the base paths. He was the acknowledged champion sprinter of the National League. His slides and stolen bases were adventures beloved of the fans. He was the first man in the history of baseball to circle the bases in fourteen seconds. He could run a hundred yards from a standing start in ten seconds flat. Speed had always been his one distinction.[70]

He knew that people understood with their eyes as well as with their ears—and he appealed to both:

> The intensity of his physical exertions—gestures is hardly an adequate word—certainly enhanced the effect of the preacher's earnestness. No actor on the dramatic stage worked so hard. Such passion as dominated Sunday cannot be simulated; it was the soul pouring itself out through every pore of the body.[71]

Inevitably, Sunday came to Hollywood in 1915 at precisely the same time as Fairbanks and director Allan Dwan. He appeared in a one-reel subject produced by the Columbia Film Company and a feature from the Lubin Studios, *The Evangelist*, with Arthur V. Johnson in a Sunday-type role. For Allan Dwan's religious drama, *Jordan Is a Hard Road*, starring Fairbanks's friend and colleague, Frank Campeau, he was a technical advisor. Dwan describes their collaboration:

> I got . . . Billy Sunday . . . as my technical adviser. We put up a huge tent over in Hollywood across from the studio and filled it full of extras—not professional ones—just people off the streets. Now, in the story, Frank Campeau is supposed to harangue them about religion and make them come to God, but I got Billy Sunday up there and he let them have one of his best hot lectures, and I had about three cameras filming only the audience. And pretty soon these people began to feel it, and the first thing you know, they were crawling up the aisles on their knees, coming up to Billy Sunday to be saved hollering "Hallelujah" and going into hysteria. A terrific scene. No bunch of million-dollar actors could have done it. You could see the frenzy in their faces. And after we cut, he actually went on with a religious revival right there. Then I was able to put Campeau up there and let him go through the gestures of talking, cutting back all the time to these people I'd already shot.[72]

Sunday even influenced a new satiric play by George M. Cohan, *Hit-the-Trail Holliday*, wherein America's favorite "Yankee Doodle Boy" portrayed a Sunday-esque evangelist, "Billy Holliday." The drama critic of the New York *Tribune*, Heywood Broun, remarked:

> George Cohan has forced a comparison between himself and his greatest rival [Sunday] in the use of dramatic slang, and strange as it may seem, it is George and not Billy who cracks under the strain . . . Cohan has neither the punch nor the pace of Billy Sunday. . . . It is true that Cohan waved the flag first, but Billy Sunday has waved it harder. . . . It is in language that the superiority of Sunday is most evident. . . . All in all, we believe that Sunday has more of the dramatic instinct than Cohan.[73]

Undaunted, Cohan produced and appeared in a 1918 film version written by—not surprisingly—Anita Loos and John Emerson!

That same year, Sunday and Fairbanks appeared together in baseball uniforms at a benefit to raise funds for sports equipment for American soldiers in France. A photo exists of them at this game, standing together, arms thrust out in identically flamboyant gestures.

Neither men, as Allan Dwan has suggested, flinched from viewing "art" as a business. Practical idealism did not preclude shrewd business sense—it demanded it. Sunday, in the best tradition of the American businessman (not to mention the Hollywood entrepreneur) maintained a financially sound operation. He may have been dealing with spiritual values, but they were material wares as well. With the help of a permanent staff, he developed in the years before World War I what one professor of economics ranked as one of the five most successful businesses in the country, right up there with Standard Oil Co., U.S. Steel, and National Cash Register![74]

How closely in touch with the realities of life was this message? It's worth noting that when Fairbanks attempted its practical application during the making of *Habit of Happiness*, things didn't work out as planned. He had gone to New Jersey to test it out. Allan Dwan has left us this account:

> [Doug] tried it out on a millionaire to good effect but he wanted to work it on the lower echelon so he went down to skid row and into a flophouse to see what he could do about brightening the lives of those fellows. We built a set over in our New Jersey studio and went down with some buses and brought back these bums from the real flophouses. They didn't know where they were going—half of them were all booze-soaked old winos. We put them in our flophouse and they all wanted to sleep. It got pretty discouraging. So I said to him, "try a little off-color story—see if that'll work." It was a silent picture so anything he said couldn't be heard. Well, he tried an off-color thing and one guy got a slight quirk on the side of his face—very small—it wouldn't even photograph. I said, "Well, let's go a little further," and we tried a real seamy one and got several grins and some teeth—or lack of teeth—appeared. Open mouths. So we came up with jokes as raw as we could find and finally we got so low-down that they really were roaring, and we had what we wanted. When we cut it, the title would say simple humorous things and then howls of laughter would come. But when we released the picture, I began to get letters by the hundreds and finally censorship appeared in the form of a couple of executives who said, "You've got to do something about that picture." They were scared stiff because all the deaf-and-dumb people all over the place had read Doug's lips and were horrified at the awful things he was saying to these fellows to get them to laugh! We had to call the picture back and make different shots of Doug. And that's how I learned to be very careful about what actors said even in silent pictures.[75]

Likewise, the theatrical maneuverings behind Sunday's carefully staged revivals parallel this. It is a kind of politics that does not eschew theatrical artifice as long as the result is effective. To those who do not scorn material wealth and keep ideals within sighting distance, as Roosevelt advocated, such methods are entirely appropriate. Content and form meet and each informs the other.

In the final analysis, we must ask ourselves, does all this back-slapping, torso-twisting, grinning, aphorism-quoting antics of the Sunday and Fairbanks style tend to fatigue their "congregations"? *Photoplay* wondered the same thing:

> Douglas Fairbanks . . . suffers from over-exploitation of a unique personality. "Habit [of Happiness]" which starts out with the thunderingly good idea of right-side-uping a floundering grouchy old world by grinning at grief, hammers so long on the single major key that before the play's finished a bit of minor would have been high and welcome relief.[76]

Perhaps anyone reading the foregoing pages would guess that there were to be black days ahead for relentless optimists like Sunday and Fairbanks. Both Sunday and Fairbanks would be plagued in later days by restlessness and melancholy. The passing years would leave them facing the visible and inevitable refutation of age. It was a hard rebuff to persons of such manic energy. Sunday turned to hardened conservative beliefs about what constituted Americanism, propounding doctrines that left out virtually everybody. During the war he preached the madness and necessary extermination of the German race as a whole. Fairbanks's restlessness, as we shall see, compelled incessant globe-trotting; life became for him, as he put it, a slide downhill, an endless wandering through the thin ranks of café society. When Sunday said that he was burning up to keep people good and out of hell, he was speaking not only of himself but also of Fairbanks. They both positively flared with a flame that, left untended, consumed them totally.

But if some of the sharper critics carped in 1916, the public seemed to love it all, finding no quibbles with the philosophy expressed. We mustn't forget that. Fairbanks's mass appeal, linked as it was to the runaway express train of his body and to the larger currents in the public temper, was firmly consolidated. For the moment. Consider, for example, this little ditty composed for *Photoplay* in 1916 by one Helen Joyce:

> Dietician Doug
> Laughing, they say,
> Takes excess flesh away;
> If you're thin, it will help you gain weight.
> I've found Douglas' mission—
> He's a 'Laugh Dietician'—
> A first-rate physician, I'll state!

The New American Aristocrat: *An American Aristocracy, The Americano, Reaching for the Moon, His Majesty the American, Bound in Morocco*

"The *New York Rowdy Journal*, sir," resumed the colonel, "is, as I expect you know, the organ of our aristocracy in this city."

"Oh! there *is* an aristocracy here, then?" said Martin. "Of what is it composed?"

"Of intelligence, sir," replied the colonel; "of intelligence and virtue. And of their necessary consequences in this republic. Dollars, sir."

—**CHARLES DICKENS,** *Martin Chuzzlewit* (1844)

It is the hard fate of new aristocracies that . . . the best society, everywhere has grown in all sorts of ways, in spite of itself . . . trying, trying its very hardest, to grow, not yet knowing (by so many indications) what to grow *on*.

—**HENRY JAMES,** *American Scene* (1907)

I think this young fellow is just what you want—an all-around chap, just a regular American.

—***THE AMERICANO*** (1917)

An American Aristocracy

An American Aristocracy introduces a peculiarly *American* "aristocracy" into our discussion. Examined here are two kinds of aristocracy, if you will—one founded on the notion of American "first families," itself adapted from the European brand of lineage; and one that has already been hinted at in *His Picture in the Papers,* i.e., of the formation of an American class structure that is founded on individual enterprise and stratified by money. This will be elaborated and carried further in what we call the "imperialist reach" of later pre-1920 films, notably the Loos-Emerson *The Americano* (1917) and *Reaching for the Moon* (1917); the Allan Dwan *Bound in* Morocco (1918); and Fairbanks's first film for United Artists, *His Majesty the American* (1919, cowritten by director Joseph Henabery and Fairbanks). Fairbanks's personification of the New World self-made man begins to succumb to the rituals, forms, and pretensions of the Old World aristocrat. Or were they both there all the time? Indeed, we see a duality that strikes deeply into Fairbanks's American century.

An American Aristocracy was directed by Lloyd Ingraham from an Anita Loos script. It plunges our hero into the pretensions and hypocrisies of the American industrial nouveau riche. (It was this film, by the way, that would later fire the ambitions of a young Kevin Brownlow—see his memoir at the beginning of this book—to pursue what was to be an abiding interest in Fairbanks and his work.)

And so we take up the question, is there—can there—be an aristocracy in America? The question brings us squarely against one of the major dialectic pairings in American thought, one that we will revisit shortly in the chapter on Fairbanks's westerns. There is the traditional man tied to the past, a member of the party of Memory; and there is the so-called American Adam, a newborn member of the party of Hope. Must they be mutually exclusive?

At the beginning of *An American Aristocracy*, we are greeted by Anita Loos's title card:

> *Has America an aristocracy? We say yes! And to prove it we take you to Narraport-by-the-Sea, where we find some of our finest families whose patents of nobility are founded on such deeds of daring as the canning of soup, the floating of soap and the borating of talcum.*

In 1808 John Adams had said essentially the same thing: "We have one material which actually constitutes an aristocracy that governs the nation. That material is wealth. Talents, birth, virtues, services, sacrifices, are of little consideration with us."[77] This indicates a difference between an intrinsically American version of aristocracy based upon money and what we automatically think of as Old World aristocracy—that is, one based upon monarchs and the traditions of class and fealty grounded upon inherited blood lines. Both kinds of aristocracy have had their place in American history and certainly in American culture.

For the record, the word "aristocracy" comes from the Greek *aristos* (best) and *kratia* (rule) and originally meant "government by the best citizens." Of course, all the trouble comes from defining the "best" citizens. Old World aristocracy sets its standards by bloodlines. However, in Crevecoeur's famous letter "What Is an American?" the existence of a monarchical kind of aristocracy in America is denied vehemently:

> Here are no aristocratic families, no courts, no kings, no bishops, no ecclesiastical dominion, no invisible power giving to a few a very visible one . . . We have no princes, for whom we toil, starve and bleed: We are the most perfect society now existing in the world.[78]

This democratic ideal is counterbalanced by William Dean Howells's comment that society is intrinsically exclusive: "Inequality is as dear to the American heart as liberty itself."[79] Nothing fed that inequality more than money. The center of American society was the Eastern Industrial Establishment. This establishment embraced two kinds of "societies"—the preindustrial eastern upper class, and the "new rich" who owed their status to industrial wealth. Henry James called the preindustrial classes "professional"; the "new rich" "commercial." They all lived "in high comfort and respectability," and, "in their small provincial way, doubtless had pretensions to be exclusive."[80] The Ivy League university, the college club, the metropolitan men's club, *The Social Register* had all been formed in the last quarter of the century or had altered their shape to conform to industrialism's demands. Merchants, lawyers, and men of letters were success models. This class preserved its status by helping to maintain a system of "artificial but exclusive standards through which individuals were evaluated on a social basis, and they also consolidated power in the hands of a relatively small number of individuals and families by equating social success with occupational success."[81]

By contrast, in the first decades of an industrial affluent America, wealth and power came to many Americans who, in general, were not of old family, had often not attended college, and in some instances avoided public office. The apologists of these men concluded that "a rudimentary education was sufficient unto success," that college training "was positively harmful in that it made men unfit for business," and that the political arena was "unpredictable, unsound, and even immoral," which just about says it all.[82] It is not hard to see the seeds of the anti-intellectualism or at least a distrust of the intellectual elite that would mark the later broad middle class that Billy Sunday reached early in the twentieth century.

The incursion of the "new rich" into the ranks of the preindustrial upper class can be seen in microcosm, in that mainspring American standard of society, *The Social Register*. The *Register* was founded by, oddly enough, an ex-gunsmith, Louis Keller. In the post-Civil War East, the *Register* had informally based its selection of candidates for admission into the ranks of society on two grounds: "descent" and "social standing." The appearance of the "new rich," however, created a standard of measure cryptically called "other qualifications." This is particularly interesting since it recognized *economic achievement*. Clearly, money was becoming an increasingly important aspect of society. If, as James says, America was having a hard time in finding traditions for its own aristocracy, it was at least substituting its own standards. The result was a reverence for status acquired if not through blood, then at least through money.

Now let's turn back to Fairbanks and *An American Aristocracy*. "It was a satire on the big names of United Industry," Anita Loos recalls,

> such as the Fords, the Heinzes, so important to the world of pickles, and the Chalmerses, who were touchingly proud of the underwear they manufactured. Eventually every experience became grist to my movie mill . . . I even began to make fun of the rich who had so overawed me on first acquaintance.[83]

We find ourselves in Narraport-by-the-Sea, a posh resort where the upper crust of the American nouveau riche gather. The people dwell upon their own peculiar brand of social snobbery. We meet a young swain named Percy Peck (Albert Parker), a malted-milk manufacturer. Another is Mr. Hicks, "The Hat Pin King," whose success in producing a non-sliding hat pin has earned him millions. His daughter, Geraldine (Jewel Carmen), is the object of the affections of Peck. Unimpressed, Geraldine is so bored with the female society at Narraport-by-the-Sea that she vows to kiss the first man she meets. So one day while driving, she hops out of the car and kisses one Cassius Lee, who turns out to be the scion of a "first family" of Virginia, but who spends his time as an enthusiastic and penniless entomologist. Because Percy lacks the manly attributes Geraldine prefers, he hires Cassius to assist him in winning her admiration by doubling for him in some difficult stunts, involving flying seaplanes and driving fast cars. The penniless Cassius needs the money and when he sees who the girl is he is most willing to take on the proposal.

Meanwhile, there are sinister doings at the resort. It develops that a mysterious porter is in league with Percy Peck concerning that "malted milk." He passes a note to Cassius (still dressed as Peck) indicating that a ship is in the harbor waiting to deliver the malted milk to Mexico—a highly irregular missive under any circumstances. Suspicious, Cassius investigates Percy's nearby factory. The "malted milk" turns out to be gunpowder. Percy learns of the misdirected note and has Cassius disabled and imprisoned in the factory along with the Hicks, who has also been alerted to the nefarious situation. Percy cannot let well enough alone and takes Geraldine with him when he makes his escape aboard the Mexico-bound ship. Cassius's escape from the warehouse after a terrific fight into the country, down a cliff, out into the seaplane, and after the boat, is all fast-paced action benefiting from much location shooting. He clambers aboard the runaway ship and swings about disabling everybody single-handedly until the U.S. Navy torpedo boat arrives.

Fairbanks invests the role of that preindustrial aristocrat, Cassius Lee, with all the attributes of some kind of Child of Nature, or American Adam. His first appearance follows a title announcing:

> *Cassius Lee of Virginia, amateur entomologist, who has arrived in these parts on the trail of the migratory caterpillar.*

He suddenly appears from behind a rock, sits astride it, hurls himself into a front somersault down the hill and comes up with a butterfly in his grasp. He then climbs a tree, jumps from branch to branch, hangs by his knees, and in general, establishes the simian characteristics of primitive man. (A little later a visual pun is perpetrated when he hangs the same way from a telephone wire after clambering onto it from the hood of a speeding automobile.) That a scion of one of America's first families should find himself flying around the treetops and city streets with equal ease reminds us of the contemporaneous *Tarzan* books written by Edgar Rice Burroughs.

Now let's go to Narraport-by-the-Sea and meet the principal characters in the play. After some shots of white-clad, parasol- carrying matrons parading in front of a beautiful white mansion, we meet the appropriately named Mrs. Greene-Rivers—

> *—one of the leading spirits of the alcoholic set—*

and her societal rival, Mrs. Budhauser,

> *whose husband has done so much to make Milwaukee famous.*

Mrs. Budhauser's efforts to befriend Mrs. Greene-Rivers are met with the chilling snub:

> *"Madam,* we *are distillers."*

Immediately after this interchange Mrs. Greene-Rivers limply shakes fingers with a friend and confides,

> *"These climbers are ruining Narraport."*

The pretensions and class distinctions present even within the ranks of the "new rich" are cleverly visualized here. In a startlingly cogent image, Mrs. Budhauser flutters around the screened-in porch trying to engage these snobs in conversation. They only depart in disgust, leaving her alone on a porch of tilting rocking chairs. Not only does a distiller assume class superiority to a brewer, but they both disdain the preindustrial classes. At the same time they assume their own titles of distinction:

> *Saturday the men began to arrive at Narraport, among them the Barons of Beans, Starch, Razors, Pickles, Corn Plasters, Glue, Rubberheels, Tooth-Paste, Garters, and Chewing Gum.*

Mr. Hicks, whose daughter Geraldine provides the romantic interest, is called "The Hat Pin King," and has made his fortune by manufacturing the "Hat Pin with the Hump"—an ingenious little device, which, by virtue of a wrinkle halfway down the pin, prevents m'lady's hat from slipping off her head. "What is your business," demands Mr. Hicks, of the would-be suitor Cassius. He responds,

> *"Why, our family never went into trade."*

"Young man," sniffs Hicks,

> *"this hotel is for aristocrats. We ain't got any time for upstarts."*

The conflict between Cassius and Percy Peck—which is to say, natural aristocracy versus industrial aristocracy—is at the heart of the story. As the nominal villain, Percy is, significantly, only half a man, in that he has to hire Cassius as a substitute for his deeds of daring. Percy, for instance, persists in driving his sporty car too cautiously for Geraldine's taste—a nicely ambivalent view of the conservatism of the "new rich." Cassius, by contrast, tears around in the car as if he were Barney Oldfield (a friend of Fairbanks, incidentally). Cassius also uses Percy's seaplane to rescue Geraldine. This picture of the industrialist victimized by his own product is neatly done. Percy's product, the malted milk, is also a counterfeit. It is really gunpowder—an ominous kind of image for a representative of an industrial society. There are overtones here of potential conflagration that clearly imply the potentially destructive nature of the institutions of industry. Whether this implication is intentional or not is quite beside the point; it is there, nonetheless. It is worth recalling Henry Adams's prediction that someday the human race will commit suicide by blowing up the world.

Alongside this sort of consequence, Cassius Lee stands in a favorable light indeed. If "natural aristocracy" wins out over the industrial brand, then it is only in keeping with the Fairbanksian version of an *American* aristocracy.

Cassius consolidates his position by marrying Geraldine, surely the oldest solution for containing opposites. This sort of maneuver was an obsession for Fairbanks in all of his films. Here, he mirrors his real-life marriage to Beth Sully, daughter of the "Cotton King" of Wall Street. The marriage offered Douglas distinct advantages both socially and economically—Daniel J. Sully had millions and a vivacious daughter (one suspects in that order). Fairbanks had to agree to quit a promising stage career and go into his father-in-law's soap business in New York to get his consent for Beth's hand. The business failed, however, and soon the enterprise was bankrupt (or should we say, *all washed up*?), forcing Fairbanks to return to the theater. Certainly the prestige of the marriage stood him in good stead in gaining a foothold in New York's club society—a fact particularly interesting since Fairbanks was partly Jewish and on those grounds alone could have been excluded from said clubs. At any rate, in *American Aristocracy* Cassius invents a new kind of hatpin and immediately thereafter marries Geraldine. The last shot is most disturbing since it shows his smiling face plastered all over an advertisement for the product. Cassius actually ends up like all the other industrialists so skillfully parodied earlier. The difference is that he embodies additionally those other aristocratic virtues in line with the American Adam. It is a truly American resolution: victory through consolidation.

Variety hailed the film as "mad, improbable, and highly amusing. . . . Yesterday the exhibition of *An American Aristocracy* was punctuated with bursts of spontaneous laughter. It is full of humorous touches characteristic of the star. More than any other actor, Mr. Fairbanks's magnetism defies the odd elements of celluloid, electricity and canvas and communicates itself to the audience."[84]

The Americano

We turn now to three films that further develop a uniquely American kind of aristocracy, *The Americano*, *Reaching for the Moon*, and *His Majesty the American*.

First in order of chronology is *The Americano*. The Loos-Emerson story is based on a novel by E. P. Lyle, *Blaze Derringer*. The irrepressible humor and hijinks of *An American Aristocracy* and *The Matrimaniac* are here replaced with a relatively serious melodrama. Plot takes over and the customary Fairbanks humor and acrobatics are subordinated to it. The story opens

> *in the days before the Great War, when little wars were of some importance, hidden away in a bend of the Caribbean Sea the little republic of Paragonia—"A Jewel set in the girdle of the Earth, a land of sunshine and music, adventure and romance."*

We quickly meet the characters, Alberto de Castille the premier (Tote Du Crow), his daughter Juana (Alma Rubens), Salso Espada (Carl Stockdale), the wicked minister of war, and the beloved popular presidente, Hernande de Valdez (Spottiswood Aitken). Espada is marked from the beginning as the villain:

> *. . . cruel and ambitions, with his own idea of who should rule Paragonia.*

It seems that the American mining concession is up for renewal, but the conniving Espada opposes working with the "American pigs." The presidente objects to Espada:

> *"Without American capital and engineers, our mines would be useless!"*

Back in America, a letter is sent to the American Mining Company requesting help from its best mining engineer:

> *"—a young live wire who could go up against a lot of difficulties with the temperamental Paragonians.*

To which the Mining Company recommends Blaze Derringer (Fairbanks):

> *"I think this young fellow is just what you want—an all-around chap, just a regular American."*

While the premier and his daughter come to America to work out an arrangement, Espada plots a coup.

Enter Blaze Derringer, who can't find Paragonia on the map. He concludes:

> *"It's too far from Brooklyn!"*

He meets the presidente:

> *"Glad to know you, Señor de Castille, I use your soap!"*

And he looks at some photos of Paragonia, but only says,

> *"Your views are great, but the scenery hurts my eyes."*

But one look at Juana strikes his fancy. The office boy tells him:

> *"She's a Spanish chicken—came with the gink in the old man's office."*

He decides now to take the job:

> *"I've been looking at some other views of Paragonia, and my eyes feel better."*

The premiere and his daughter are abruptly called home. Jauna leaves a note begging Blaze not to follow them. So, of course, he immediately takes the next boat. After arriving in Paragonia, his every request to find the home of the presidente is mysteriously rebuffed. Armed guards refuse his entry at the gate, whereupon he vaults over the wall. He finds a note thrown down from a high window begging him to return at midnight. Then, at the Mining Office, he finds the signs defaced and the rooms a shambles. Only an agent of the company, a shambling black man remains. He explains what has happened in some dialogue fraught with unfortunate racist language:

> *"A rebolution, boss, rebolution! Dey done put de President in de jug!"*

Blaze enlists the black man in his cause. General Espada usurps Presidente Valdez and confines him to a cell high up on a cliff, closes the mines, reduces the workers' wages, and keeps Juana prisoner in her home where she is forced to receive unwelcome attentions from his lieutenant.

"If you do not marry me, I can have your father put to death."

Blaze follows a beggar to a convent, only to see the man remove his disguise to reveal himself to be Castille, who tells him:

> *"The usurper is unable to operate the mines and the workers are idle and hungry. They are ready to restore the President if we can release him."*

Blaze finds notes tossed down from the presidente's cell at the top of the cliff. They lead him to the discovery of a tunnel connecting the presidente's jail cell with the floor of the cliff. But before he can do anything else, he is arrested and brought before Espada.

> *"Sit down, Señor, we wish to discuss your activities in bringing aid to our enemies."*

He wants Blaze to join him and work the mines. He throws down several sacks of gold:

> *"This is what you call our 'rake-off'—for one month, from the Army alone. And again, as you say in America, we 'split it three ways.'"*

Blaze pretends to accede to the proposition and agrees to appear supportive of Espada on the balcony the day of Juana's wedding and the reopening of the mines. On his own, he races to the foot of the cliff and, using a soldier's head for a battering ram, hammers his way through the blocked tunnel entrance. He frees the presidente and races to the palace. A henchman says,

> *"You don't get on that balcony, you dirty American dog!"*

But Blaze dispatches the soldiers and reaches Espada on the balcony. Blaze addresses the crowd and assures the populace the mines will be opened and the country governed wisely for the good of the people—at which point, Presidente Valdez appears, Blaze by his side.

In the epilogue, we see Blaze and his bride. As the newly appointed general of the army, he is decked out in a splendid military uniform and helmet, with many appropriate spangles and braid.

Reaching for the Moon

Although *The Americano* is the last of the Triangle collaborations of the Great Triple Alliance, Fairbanks will retain Loos and Emerson and bring them over to his newly formed Douglas Fairbanks Pictures, which will release through Paramount's Artcraft releasing company. The resulting Loos-Emerson *Reaching for the Moon* casts Fairbanks as Alexis Caesar Napoleon Brown, a lowly clerk in a New York button factory:

> *Our hero—Alexis Caesar Napoleon Brown—a young man of boundless enthusiasm whose physical self is chained to a desk in a button factory, but whose spirit, led vaulting ambition, walks with the kings of the earth—and sometimes stubs his toes.*

He is fired from his job because he has been spending too much time daydreaming about claiming the throne of a European monarchy called Vulgaria. His late mother, he imagines, had had royal connections there:

> *[She] was a refugee from the little kingdom of Vulgaria during the fierce conflict for the throne, which followed the death of the good King Alexis the Great.*

If he *concentrates* enough, so the "New Thought" of the positive-thinking philosophy of the day assures him, he will attain his own royal status:

> *How often do you wish for something and want it very,* very *badly? The next time you do, make a mental picture of the object of your desire and hold it—concentrate!*

And he does: Not only does he dream that he is consorting with his pal the Vulgarian King, but he converts his apartment into a shrine to the kingly heroes and emperors of history. Then, as if in answer to his wishes, something extraordinary happens. A Vulgarian diplomat appears and declares that now that the king is dead, Alexis is the sole heir:

> *"Long live Alexis, the King of Vulgaria!"*

Kneeling, he kisses Alexis's hand. They are to leave for Vulgaria immediately. However, the diplomat warns, agents of the wicked pretender to the throne, Black Boris, are bent on preventing Alexis's arrival. Thus ensues a chain of events at sea as Alexis eludes several assassins and exercises caution against eating poisoned food. So irksome does this constant danger become that Alexis declares, bitterly,

"I'm a helluva king!"

At last Alexis reaches Vulgaria, where he is greeted with much pageantry and more assassination attempts. At every repetition of the mantra, "Long live the King," at every parade and every fete, a fresh peril presents itself. Even his introduction to his intended bride, Princess Valentina, confronts him with a perfect horror of a tall stick of creature with a pointed chin and bad teeth. After the festivities, he slouches into a chair and growls,

"For the love of Mike, somebody give me a cigarette!"

But even that turns out to be an explosive device. He angrily confronts Black Boris (Frank Campeau), rival for the princess's hand:

"Look here, Boris, if you want that comic valentine of a princess, you can have her, and the Kingdom goes with her. I'm done!"

Affronted, Boris issues a challenge. A duel at dawn ensues. Backed against a cliff edge by Boris's blade, Alexis tumbles backward down a steep mountain side. . .

. . . and falls out of bed! Alexis has been "concentrating" so hard, he's dreamed the whole thing! Relieved, and now disabused of his royal presumptions, he salutes the picture of his mother:

"Mother, whatever you were, I hope you were never *a Princess!"*

He places a blanket over his shrine, throws away the "New Thought" book (declaring it "bunk!"), races back to reclaim his job in the button factory, and proposes to his girlfriend. She has been pleading with him all along to give up "reaching for the moon" and accept family life in a little cottage. Sure enough, in the concluding scene we find Alexis dandling his little boy on his knee.

"No, I've had enough of the moon,"

he declares,

> *"I am more interested in the* son!"

Having dispatched that awful pun, *Reaching for the Moon* finally runs aground.

With the release three years before from Paramount-Famous Players of *The Prisoner of Zenda* (1913), starring the venerable James K. Hackett duplicating his popular stage production, the so-called "Ruritanian Romance" tradition was ripe for a sendup.[85] The source novel by Anthony Hope was published in 1894 and had resulted in several popular sequels. "Ruritanian" became the descriptive adjective for swashbuckling adventures of intrigue and mistaken identities set in imaginary kingdoms somewhere between Germany and the Balkans.

As we watch *Reaching for the Moon*, we tick off all the clichéd tropes. For example, it seemed so simple—and so very typically Fairbanksian—for Alexis to think gaining a kingdom and a royal title was merely a matter of *will*. How easily, he thinks, presuming the American democratic ideal—the self-made man—to cut through the Gordion Knot of centuries of European monarchical traditions. Witness the quote from Carlyle cited at the beginning of the film:

> *"The King is the man who* can."

The impatient Alexis thinks he can be a king *immediately*:

> *"We can be anything in this world we want to be! I am going to make a place for myself!"*

And so we see Alexis's dream vision come to life: He's decked out in kingly garb, with its preposterous assortment of braid, sashes, epaulettes, polished boots, plumed hats, and numerous other medals and doodads—as he sashays around the canals, balconies, and streets of spy-infested Vulgaria, evading assassins at every hand (they all have beards, of course). His mounting disgust at each "Long live the King" is perfectly counterpointed with his angry exclamation—

> *"Can that hokum and get me out of here!"*

Bound in Morocco.

The prospect of a beautiful princess that we would expect from such romances is dashed by the harridan that is Princess Valentina. Even the climactic sword duel, so necessary to all Ruritanian romances, is botched, with Alexis fumbling and waving his sword all over the place, endangering everybody but his opponent.

Yes, Alexis's foolish dream of royalty—and his Shrine of Kings—must be literally abandoned. He will accept the admonition of his wife-to-be and his boss:

> *"Now keep your feet on the earth and stop reaching for the moon."*

He ultimately settles for the domestic ideal of home and family and a chicken in every pot.

Bound in Morocco

The third film, in chronological order, is *Bound in Morocco.* Released on July 28, 1918, it was one more of that memorable series of action films Fairbanks made with Allan Dwan. Unfortunately, it is a "lost" film, and among Fairbanks specialists it has long enjoyed a kind of "holy grail" status. We relish the prospect of a Fairbanks bringing his brash American aristocrat to the burning desert sands, mixing it up with desert chieftains, and participating in harem intrigues. Add a *soupcon* of spectacular stunts and we should have a special entertainment, indeed. Alas, we may never know. We can only draw upon a few contemporary reviews that hint at its nature. According to the *AFI Catalogue of Feature Films, 1911–1920* and other sources, the story begins *in medias res*: Fairbanks is bound arms and feet to a prison wall. Two ferocious Moroccan villains have just hurled a bomb, with lighted fuse, at his feet. And then . . . well, we flashback to the beginning: Fairbanks is racing an American car across the sandy desert pursued by several villains. He makes his way to a small desert town where he finds an American girl (Pauline Curley) in distress. He rescues her and her mother (Edythe Chapman) from the clutches of Basha El Harib (Frank Campeau), who wants to add them to his harem. He does this by gaining entry into the harem's quarters by disguising himself as a woman. He finds the girl and fights off hordes of villains in the escape, executing the requisite swings, jumps, and vaults.

Dwan historian Frederic Lombardi dismisses its "thin" plot, and a poor review in *Motion Picture News* complained it was "the poorest picture in which up to date Fairbanks has appeared."[86] Other reviews, however, strongly disagree. Here is Fairbanks "in all of his athletic glory, and a little more," gushed the *New York Tribune*. "*Bound in Morocco* is closer to perfect nonsense than most of even the Fairbanks films, but this is one of its virtues." Critic Walter K. Hill, in *Moving Picture World*, predicts fabulous box office: "Hail to Fairbanks! He is going to achieve the greatest of Americans amusement records."

What is clear is that this is the sort of a fantasy celluloid Arabia that historian Jack G. Shaheen, in his *Reel Bad Arabs* (2001), complains about. "Seen through Hollywood's distorted lenses," he writes, "filmmakers have collectively indicted all Arabs as Public Enemy No. 1—brutal, heartless, uncivilized religious fanatics and money-mad cultural 'others' bent on terrorizing civilized Westerners, especially Christians and Jews." Its farcical humor and fantasy notwithstanding, he singles out *Bound in Morocco* and pronounces "guilty." [87] The reviews at the time, however, praise these faults. Critic Walter Hill calls the indigenous population "morocs." About the setting, he writes, "Whatever the town is in Morocco . . . it was built for Fairbanks, and when 'Doug' had finished with it, there was every indication at hand that [Arabs] had retreated from the immediate vicinity." The

Tribune critic says the film is supplied with "a plentiful supply of people who look like Arabs." And Fairbanks "stops once to converse with a camel, but makes no attempt to ride the beast, as it was obviously too slow for him."

All of which points to the fact that it is not the Arab hordes that are menacing Fairbanks, but the other way around. Fairbanks carries his blithe American arrogance around with him, no matter where he goes, regardless of the ethnic identity of his destination. Morocco can do little except to submit to the process.

His Majesty the American

The fourth of the films to be considered here, *His Majesty the American*, is another spin on the Ruritanian formula, but with some key differences. The trappings of royalty are not satirized, but taken seriously. No longer a fantastic dream, this story is all too real. It is by far Fairbanks's most extravagant and expensive production to date, clocking in at eight reels. Not only was it the inaugural release from United Artists—a company formed in 1919 for the release and distribution of his partners Mary Pickford, Charles Chaplin, and D. W. Griffith—it was also the first to be made at his new studios on the W. H. Clune studio lot in Hollywood. The film's debut on September 1, 1919, at the Capitol Theater in New York elicited an enthusiastic reception and praise from *Variety*, which described it as "a sort of Fairbanksian *Prisoner of Zenda*." *Photoplay* pronounced it "a good-humored diversion in which no one, including the star, seems to take things or himself too seriously."[88]

By way of introduction to the United Artists brand, Fairbanks tumbles through a wall-sized screen and announces to the camera:

> *"Listen folks—they made me start the ball rolling. So here's the first picture. Gee whiz, I hope you like it."*

The story begins with a series of titles, very much in the Loosian spirit:

> *William Brooks chased excitement and thrills from one end of the world to the other. In his New York apartment we see—*

—as the camera pans across a room chock full of every kind of sporting gear—

> *he has a complete equipment in his apartment for his favorite sports—fires and police raids. In the words of one of his friends—"Bill is a fire-eating, speed-loving, space-annihilating thrill hound."*

He hears the fire bell, checks the ticker-tape, puts on his fire hat, slides down his own fire pole, and speeds out of his garage in a fast car.

> *Unusual? Yes, but Bill's position in life* is *unusual. He comes from a good family but knows nothing about them. He has pots of money and doesn't know whence it comes. . . . Every blaze is a thrill for Bill; but a big tenement fire—Oh boy!*

He races to the fire and finds that a blaze is keeping the firemen from reaching the third floor and rescuing the occupants. Undaunted, he seizes a rope, scales the side of the building, swings across to the burning building, and carries the mother and her children to safety. One last swing is required to save the cat!

From whence this mysterious zeal?, his friends ask. He replies,

> *"Mystery? You're right. I can't solve it myself. But I want you to know there's a reason for all the unreasonable things I do."*

The revelation of that mystery will have to wait. For now, the thrills continue as he joins the police in a raid on a local saloon. The action is nicely choreographed in an open, two-story set, as Bill races from room to room, eventually tussling the villain to the ground and into the hands of the police.

> *Bill speeds on as months fly by—but eventually receives a crushing blow. A reforming District Attorney cleans up New York—over, under, around and through.*

Now the policemen idly fan themselves in the sun, and the very, very fat firemen have nothing to do but play croquet.

> *"There's nothing stirring. Nothing to do. I tell you—New York's on the BUM!"*

So Bill decides to go west in search of more adventure. But now another story line is introduced. A title card explains:

While Bill journeys toward the West, let us turn our faces to the rising sun, and journey to a little European kingdom tucked away in a little corner of the picturesque Alps. Alaine the beautiful—with the treasure of peaceful centuries in her history. . . . But agitating demagogues have changed a peace-loving people into a rioting succession of mobs. . . . Whipped into frenzy by leaders doing a lying traitor's secret bidding—the mob forgets their sovereign's age-long benefactions—and in their new-born rage shout—"Down with the King!"

Philip IV (Sam Sothern) is the King of Alaine, and he is very worried. His next proclamation will give the people self-government. But he fears stronger hands will be needed than he can muster. He suspects that he is surrounded by a gang of villains "sowing discord" among the populace. They include the minister of war, Grand Duke Sarzeau (Frank Campeau), and Prince Brizac. Sarzeau says,

"Mobs are playthings if you know the trick of handling them. Pick some grievance and make it look big. They never stop to reason. If they did, they'd get on to us. But they never do—see?"

The king watches in despair as his loyal chancellor is assassinated. Without an heir it may mean the end of the blood line.

"No, there is no hope. Our foes will continue their secret, underhanded lying. And then—our ancient family—no more.

Crosscut back to Bill's story. He is heading for Murdero, Mexico—

—with its alluring promise of the wild and woolly.

No matter that the train stops short of Murdero. From the sounds of gunfire, Bill supposes the little town of "Peace Vale" might provide plenty of thrills.

"Sounds like Hell's Hinges. Good enough for me!"

But he finds only a bunch of kids celebrating the 4th of July with cap pistols. Disgusted, Bill gallops the rest of the way to Murdero:

Presenting MURDERO, MEXICO (where Bill expects to find) reptiles, bullets, bandits featuring FRANCISCO VILLA.

He gestures expansively toward the region and plunges down a hill—

—rushing eagerly to sample Murdero's brand of blood-curdling lawlessness.

When he inquires of the citizens where the "live ones" are, he's told:

"DEAD."

But Bill perks up when suddenly Villa and a hundred horsemen storm into the town. And there's Bill, shouting and leaping exultantly as they ride by in a cloud of dust . . . on their way *out* of town. Disappointed again, all Bill can do is ask a peasant:

"Got a fire department?"

But when he's told there is a jail, he hot-foots it to the hoosegow, where he digs a tunnel to release a prisoner. But Villa learns of this and vows to put him *back* in jail. Bill takes his new friend back to the man's mother. Here, suddenly, the mood takes on a somber note. Witnessing the mother-son reunion, he realizes how much of a void the lack of his own mother has created:

"I've tried all ways to fill that void, but they're all counterfeit."

Crosscut back to Alaine. The king receives a mysterious collection of documents left behind by the dead chancellor. In it is an admission of guilt about an indiscretion years ago about the life of someone "long lost." Sarzeau warns the king the natives are getting restless:

"—they demand new blood within the reigning house."

He demands an alliance between the king's ward and de Brizac. The king rejects this. He hopes that this "long lost" missing person will appear:

"There is one, young and strong—one of the blood—but wait, you'll see!"

He has deduced the bloodline will continue in the person of the Prince of Mont St. Lazaire. An accommodating title card spells out the preposterously titled prince:

Henri Jean Paul Louis Francois Louis de Frontenac, Count of Froissaire, Duc de Renaud, Duc de Riopelle—Prince de Mont St. Lazaire and Heir Apparent to the Throne of Alaine.

Cut to the "heir apparent." It's Bill! And he's covered with mud and tussling with Pancho Villa in a watery ditch. Interrupting the fight is a letter . . . from King Phillipe, ordering him to come to Alaine. Bill loses no time:

"Here, Pete, turn [Villa] over to Carranza, or put him in the movies, I don't care which. I'm off to Europe!"

From here on in, the plot gets even more convoluted. . . . Upon Bill's arrival, there's a mix-up at the train station and a paper is furtively slipped into his pocket. (Keep your eye on this paper. It reveals a plot against the king!) Not realizing that the minister of war is in on it, Bill goes to see him about the plot. Bill is promptly surrounded by the villains, and he executes some nice moves around the room to escape them. But the men keep searching for him, fearing that the incriminating paper will reach the king.

Interrupting all this is a lengthy comic digression at Bill's hotel. It seems at first an irritating distraction from the action, but then we gradually realize we are getting a rare glimpse of some amusing Fairbanksian sight gags: He performs some parlor tricks for the maids; he mugs into a revolving mirror; and he pantomimes "playing" a chest-of-drawers" as if it were a piano. He places a bank note atop it and then says he'll try to hit "the high note."

But the melodramatic machinery picks up again. Bill sits down to read the mysterious note from the king. It warns him that his mother is in danger and to be wary. An emissary will meet him.

The villains show up and corner Bill. In some very nice acrobatics, he clambers in and out of rooms, leaps from roof to roof, swings from a flagpole into a window, continues on horseback, by car, ever eluding his pursuers and disappears.

Despite his distress, the king dares not delay reading his proclamation to the people:

"My countrymen: Our people having reached that degree of enlightenment which assures successful self-government, we hereby assign to them their new duties. And these changes will benefit both of high and low degree."

All the while Sarzeau's incitement of a mob is causing a riot. They are bearing down on the palace. Bill reaches the soldiers' barracks and leads the troops out with him back toward the city. They arrive in time to disperse the mob. Bill races into the palace and climbs over the backs of the crowd to rescue the king and the girl from the menacing Sarzeau.

> *"There's going to be a big clean up start right here!"*

As his first order, he trains his pistol on Sarzeau:

> *"Straighten up that rug."*

The king gives Bill a paper revealing his true parentage. Stunned, Bill declares:

> *"I can't believe it all! I, a Prince? Then—my mother is—*

Indeed, the king's daughter standing there at his side is his mother (as per the "indiscretion" from her earlier affair with the late chancellor). Bill turns to the king's ward, Felice, and declares his love.

They all gather on the balcony of the palace, where the king declares to the crowd:

> *"To this boy from America we owe everything. Strange as it may seem, he is none other than the heir apparent to the throne of Alaine. Abdications are very popular these days. Perhaps our young benefactor has some new ideas of government."*

Bill steps forward:

> *"My friends. A countryman of mine once said, 'A government of the people, by the people, and for the people shall not perish from the earth'—And believe me, that's some dope!"*

Applause. Handholding. Fade out.

When we take a breath and step back from the flurry of last-minute chases and intrigues, we see Bill, now Prince What's-His-Name, the heir to the throne, a newly appointed minister of war, and wearer of the royal costume and braid, proclaiming "a government of the people." This is no longer Bill, the New Adam, the *"fire-eating, speed-loving, space-annihilating thrill hound,"* committed to the "joys of bodily abandon and the pleasures of social disorder"; nor is he just a "gymnastic evangelist" preaching moral and physical health. This is a new American aristocrat. He belongs to a new century that by the mid-teens had shifted away from a nation hopeful of an acceptable exceptionalism to an America that was becoming politically and economically a world power, a status that was, ironically, more pretentious and imperialistic, more Old World than New. It answered to an abiding hunger that G. K. Chesterton observed in his notes on American institutions, *What I Saw in America*: "Democracy must have a heraldry, it must have a proud and highly coloured pageantry, if it is to keep always before its own mind its own sublime mission."[89] He could be speaking on behalf of Fairbanks.

In America, as we have already seen, the aristocratic *idea* had always been present. For instance, in 1789 a large group of admitted "aristocrats" of their day—including James Madison and Richard Henry Lee from Virginia and Thomas McKean and William Bingham of Philadelphia—met to propose a title for George Washington. Merely "President" did not seem enough. Titles proposed were "Most Serene Highness," among others. Washington himself supposedly favored "High Mightiness." At long last, of course, the simple title of "President" was decided upon; a title so bereft of respect, it is recorded, that "on at least one occasion Washington was refused lodgings at a village inn upon the assumption that he was the president of Rhode Island College."[90]

Perhaps the most typical representation of the ambivalence of early American leanings is the character of Alexander Hamilton. Elegant, impassioned, ingratiating, he could have fit into the Versailles of Louis XV. Yet he was the illegitimate son of a relatively unsuccessful Scottish merchant and a daughter of the French Huguenots. From such a man, born the lowliest of the low, as they say, came the highest expression of aristocracy that America was ever to know. This kind of nobility was not the mysteriously transmitted genetic trait of generations, but arose spontaneously from the combustion of character and circumstances. While Hamilton represents an American aristocrat, he also represents the self-made man, or "American Adam," someone representative of life and history just beginning.

And so, unlikely as it may seem, Douglas Fairbanks, who, when he stands still long enough, inherits the Hamiltonian mantle. *Reaching for the Moon*, *The Americano*, and *His Majesty the American*, writes historian Lary May, reveal Fairbanks carrying "capital" and democracy into Latin

America and on into Europe: "[Fairbanks] mastered tyrants from above and revolutionaries from below who endangered foreign leaders sympathetic to the expansion of American interests."[91] Thus, in *The Americano*, he defeats the usurper Valdez, restores the presidente to the applause of "the people," and as the new head of the army will be an *active participant* in that government. If, in *Reaching for the Moon*, his presumptions to a Kingship turn out to be a fantastic dream, in *His Majesty the American* he gets the prize, as it were, a real kingly crown.

Fairbanks's "imperial reach" is a reciprocal dynamic. He not only seeks and dreams, but he now "appropriates" Old World traditions and, as a result, "Americanizes" them in the process. In this Fairbanks is prophetic of another force to come in American popular culture, Walt Disney, who was, in the beginning, indeed self-made and self-propelled, but who with success and power would seize upon European models of storytelling and make them over in his own image.[92] Fairbanks's own "reach" will continue, as we will see in later chapters on the costume historical films of the 1920s. For example, in his review of *The Three Musketeers* (1921), the *New York Evening Post* critic will observe that Fairbanks's Paris looks as though it were "made in America," and Fairbanks himself comes across "with the dashing assurance of a good American salesman . . . One buys, and willingly."[93]

Perhaps *His Majesty the American* is signaling Fairbanks's realization that the contemporary action pictures and western adventures he has made in the 1916–1919 period no longer will do. His character of Bill had been disappointed at the lack of adventure in modern urban life; he was likewise bored in the West. Significantly, it is only when he reaches the Kingdom of Alaine, safely tucked away in the European Alps, that he can slake his thirst for adventure. Henceforth, with the exception of three more releases from Artcraft in 1919–1920—*The Mollycoddle*, *When the Clouds Roll By*, and *The Nut* (to be considered in a later chapter)—all his films in the 1920s will follow the lead of *His Majesty* and locate their costume adventures in exotic locations in the mythical regions of the past.

The "revolution" pictures we've been talking about so far have depicted revolutionary agitation in *contemporary* terms. But it is striking that a few years later Fairbanks's costume films of the 1920s will showcase our hero toppling dictatorial regimes *in the past*. Writing in the late 1920s, cultural commentator Siegfried Kracauer had a theory about why this was happening.

> The further back the story is situated historically, the more audacious film-makers become. They will risk depicting a successful revolution in historical costumes in order to induce people to forget modern revolutions, and they are happy to satisfy the theoretical sense of justice by filming struggles for freedom that are long past.

Thus, continues Kracauer, *The Mark of Zorro* (1920), *Robin Hood* (1922), and *Don Q* (1925) are in striking contrast to productions like Eisenstein's *Potemkin* (made the same year as *Don Q*), which depicted a revolution in the past (1905) but did so in terms *of the present*, eliciting a much more incendiary call to arms. Thus, "Douglas Fairbanks, the gallant champion of the oppressed, goes to battle in a previous century against a despotic power whose survival is of no consequence to any American today.[94]

Happily, through it all, we can count on at least one constant: Wherever he goes, *whenever* he goes, Fairbanks is ever ready at the drop of a hat—or crown—to redress tyrannical wrongs. What kind of aristocratic implication resides in this militant masculinity? Again we turn to Chesterton's observations about the American character:

> There is a kind of sense of honour, like that of a duelist, in his readiness to be provoked. Indeed, there is some parallel between the American man of action, however vulgar his aims, and the old feudal idea of the gentleman with a sword at his side. The gentleman may have been proud of being strong or sturdy; he may too often have been proud of being thick-headed; but he was not proud of being thick-skinned. On the contrary, he was proud of being thin-skinned. He also seriously thought that sensitiveness was a part of masculinity."[95]

Chapter 3

"Arizona Jim"

The Fairbanks Westerns, 1916–1920

—By John C. Tibbetts

Exertion and action [are] as natural to him as respiration: A more completely healthy mortal had never trod the elastic soil of Great States of his option. . . . [H]e had defied example and precedent and probability.
—**HENRY JAMES,** *The American*

"Well, I'm afraid Arizona will either kill or cure you!"
—***THE MOLLYCODDLE*** (1920)

And there is that famous moment in a Douglas Fairbanks western when our hero reigns in his steed and addresses the vast amphitheater of the Arizona canyons below:

"Hurrah for God!"

It's more than a salute. It's more than a sentiment. It's a sermon.

The Arizona canyons and mesas, the Wyoming grasslands, the forested slopes of northern California constitute a vital geography for Fairbanks. This "elastic soil" is, on the one hand, a westward advancing frontier that has no past, only a present, a promise, and a future; on the other, a territory perpetually retreating before encroaching communities and industrial development. Arizona, in particular, plays an important part in most of his western films, with its spectacular cliffs to climb, mesas to

The Westerner (drawing courtesy John C. Tibbetts).

traverse, and endless deserts to track. And it is here, as we shall see, that Fairbanks became an honorary tribal chief of the Hopi and the Navajo. Indeed, Arizona's growth toward statehood paralleled his own advance toward stardom: It was still a territory when he was a boy; and it was the last coterminous state to gain admission to the Union in 1912 when he was a rising young stage star.

Fairbanks is the First Citizen of the very *idea* of Arizona. He is the godfather, the progenitor, if you will, of that later incarnation of western romance, "Arizona Jim," in Jean Renoir's *The Crime of M.* Lange (1937).[1]

Fairbanks's romantic predilection for outdoor life and rugged athleticism would seem to point to a western upbringing fraught with wild horses, blazing six-guns, and boundless horizons. Surely, only a person who had lived such a life could bring it so zestfully to the screen. Paradoxically, however, like his contemporary William S. Hart—and like so many other western characters, notably Roy Rogers—he was just as much a product of the East as the West. He deftly juggled both geographical referents: Although his boyhood years were spent in Denver in the 1880s, a talent for acting led to his engagement with the Fredric Warde Theater Troupe, and subsequently to a highly successful stint as a Broadway stage juvenile. His years on the stage, moreover, were interleaved with an active social and club life and several business ventures, such as his partnership in a Wall Street firm and the vice-presidency of a soap company. However, like the restless character of Jeff in one of his best westerns, *Wild and Woolly* (1917), he began to chafe at city life and grew hopelessly infatuated with an easterner's fantasy of the West. Jeff's words are apt:

> *"Hang the office! I'm sick of this life! I want to be out in the West, where there's room to breathe—where the blood runs red in one's veins—and where a six-shooter is a man's best friend!"*

And, like Jeff, as we will see presently, he was able to make that dream come true. When he left the stage and headed west for the movies, he arrived at the closest equivalent to Jeff's vision of rip-roarin' Bitter Creek: Hollywood. And here he found a tool chest of scenarios, sets, cameras, and costumes with which to construct that fantasy. Prefiguring Jeff's words, he wrote in *Motion Picture Classic*, "Of course, it would be a hardship for me to go back to the stage . . ."

> I've the wanderlust . . . [and] the movies have developed it until I'm eternally restless for the open country and new scenes. The pictures satisfy my wanderlust. The element of adventure is always present. . . . Nowadays, I shudder to think of the stage with its routine, its artificiality and its unhealthy back-stage atmosphere.[2]

Our survey of Fairbanks's western films extends from 1916 to 1920. For the Triangle Studios he is "Passin' Through," a western Robin Hood in *The Good Bad Man* (1916); "Lo Dorman," the son of a Native American woman in *The Half-Breed* (1916); cattle man "Steve O'Dare," come to town in *Manhattan Madness* (1916). For the newly formed Artcraft company, from 1917 to 1918, he is "Jeff Hillington," heading west to build a railroad in *Wild and Woolly*; Detective "Fancy Jim" Sherwood in pursuit of rustlers in *The Man from Painted Post*; "Ned Thacker," a Kansan in search of adventure in Arizona's Grand Canyon in *A Modern Musketeer*; a Northwest Mounted Policeman disguised as an outlaw in *Headin' South* (1918); "Lt. Denton," a cavalryman turned ranch foreman in *Arizona* (1918); "Teddy Drake," a New York clubman turned cowboy battling Mexican bandits in *The Knickerbocker Buckaroo*; and "Richard Marshall," besting foreign smugglers in *The Mollycoddle* (1920). Unfortunately, not all of these westerns are available for examination here. At this writing, alas, a few are "lost," including *Arizona, Headin' South,* and *Knickerbocker Buckaroo*. They can only be assessed through surviving reviews and some speculation. Thanks to recent restorations, *The Half-Breed* and *The Good Bad Man* can now be seen in their near-complete state. All these westerners embody, as we shall see, a combination of New Adam and American aristocrat, who is always glancing backward while advancing forward.

Complaining of their unfortunate and unwarranted neglect by historians in favor of Fairbanks's later costume swashbucklers, western specialist William K. Everson described them as "some of the best action pictures ever made":

> They were also some of the most diverting, with their rollicking sense of fun, and the implicit demand made on the audience to take them any way but seriously . . . One can only assume that many critics and historians of the cinema have either forgotten, or are totally unaware of his earlier and livelier work.[3]

Even in an important volume of western mythic history, Richard Slotkin's *Gunfighter Nation,* Fairbanks is conspicuously absent in favor of his humorless cowboy contemporary, William S. Hart. This omission is downright unfortunate. It is our contention that these westerns deserve more scrutiny in their constructions of Progressive Era masculinity during rapid social and economic change. They would influence Hollywood westerns' representations of a new century's masculinity for decades to come.

Elastic Soil

Fairbanks brought his idiosyncratic cowboys to the screen at a propitious time. Aware that the figure of the real cowboy was vanishing as the new American century dawned, his own characters came bustin' out of the Garden and into a New World of his own devising. The frontier was expanding and imploding at the same time. Industrial growth was rapidly transforming the raw west into a progressive territory, and nostalgia was busily reimagining and transforming the vanishing past into a dream-like fantasy. The challenge for a filmmaker like Fairbanks was the same as that faced by the nation itself, as extolled by historians, artists, and cultural leaders like Theodore Roosevelt, Frederic Jackson Turner, novelist Owen Wister, and painter Frederic Remington: how to preserve and develop a territory of individualism and masculine virility necessary to "win the West" into a new American nation-state lacking the conflicts of wilderness and Indian wars.[4] As a result, Richard Slotkin has observed, the frontier west was becoming "no longer a geographical place and a set of facts requiring a historical explanation. . . . [I]t was becoming a set of symbols . . . a *mythic space* that began to outweigh its importance as a real place."[5]

Thus, the Fairbanksian westerner derives from a wholly American tradition of the West as a *philosophical concept* and a *process* rather than a fixed cultural and geographical referent. G. Edward White points out that a "Western centered" study would examine the spread of democratic institutions and the role of individualism, states' rights, and the frontier. By contrast—as we see with Fairbanks—a more "*American* centered" study would deal with the development of *imaginative* and *philosophical* constructs of "the West."[6] In intellectual history the "idea" of the West has always meant more than its value as a geographical indicator. As the westward movement reached the Pacific, all those areas west of the Mississippi Valley, formerly designated as the "West," underwent a new shift. Now these lands were two distinct "Wests." There was the commonplace domesticated area within the agricultural frontier with a social strata; and the Wild West beyond it, with its more anarchic society. The shifting boundary between them was, of course, the frontier. Edwin Fussell, in his famous study of the frontier's effect upon American literary culture, deals extensively with some of the confusing ramifications of "frontier," "border," "space," and other dialectic pairings. "The American West," he says, "is almost by definition indefinite and indefinable, or at least changing, pluralistic, and ambiguous in signification."[7]

As far as defining "frontier," Frederick Jackson Turner, writing just twenty years before Fairbanks began making westerns, famously called attention to the way "frontier" had come to mean for America the edge of settlement rather than, as in Europe, a fixed political and geographical boundary. The frontier was the imaginary line between American civilization and nature, or the uncreated future, and everything that came to depend upon that line was ironically reversible. In his classic study, *Virgin Land: The American West as Symbol and Myth*, Henry Nash Smith elaborates on this:

> The process of westward expansion would create three main divisions of the society: a remote fringe of backwoods settlements, a central region of comfortable farms, and, to the East, a region of growing wealth, cities, and social

> stratification. Crevecoeur believed that both the beginning and the end of the process brought about undesirable social conditions. But the middle condition offered a unique opportunity for human virtue and happiness.[8]

Accordingly, the shifting frontier determines that the character of the westerner becomes, variously, trailblazer, cowboy, outlaw, and homesteader. At once, he or she could be seen as a "good" and a "bad" person, respectively, inhabiting a land of promise and virtue, or languishing in a regressive territory. The ambivalent figure of Daniel Boone can be considered either as standard bearer of civilization—with all the more ominous and destructive aspects of civilization that entails—or as a fugitive child of nature, retreating from that encroachment. As exciting as the West might seem to be metaphorically, a promotional tract in the early 1800s conceded that in the actual West "the very atmosphere of society is averse to mental culture."[9] Thus, it is not surprising that at the heart of the American language radically divergent conceptions of the national destiny were seen in conflicting notions of "back" ("backwoodsman") and "front" (frontiersman").

Fairbanks's famous apostrophe—"Hurrah for God!"—implies that the cowboy hero confirms the "natural" western landscape's virtues of goodness, instinctive nobility, and untutored piety. However, he is not above satirizing such moments. "Golly, what a Gully!" he declares after executing a handstand on the canyon rim in *A Modern Musketeer* (1917), after which he cautiously retreats to safety on hands and knees. But his zest for populating his stories with black-hearted villains and degenerate Indians—not to mention the duality of his own characters as equal parts detective and bandit—implies that the opposite could be true, when untrammeled space arouses the anarchic, possibly demonic spirit. America's first great novelist, Charles Brockden Brown, writing late in the eighteenth century, located absolute evil in the forested wilds of Pennsylvania in *Edgar Huntley* (1799). Leslie Fiedler points out that Nathaniel Hawthorne cannot conceive of an "innocent" westerner, and that even James Fenimore Cooper cannot be free of ignoble Indians and is forced to admit that even in the wilderness there was violence and terror. In his spiritual descendants we can see some of the same contradictions. Thus, the westerner progresses from the anarchic freedom of Boone to the standard bearers of a "dubious civilization"—empire builders like the buffalo hunter, scout, cowboy, and lawman—populated by men who risked losing contact with nature.[10]

Gradually, the Western Man, with each westward surge in America, and with the establishment of each new community, became identified with these communities: the range rider with barbed wire territories, the trail herder with the cattle drives, the rancher and sheep man with their respective domains, the frontier scout with the advancing wagon trains, and the lawman with the need for social order. Obviously, as Fairbanks knew, it was time to retool the mundane, historical reality into modernist fantasy. He didn't have to look very far for models. The famous "dime novels" of Erastus Beadle and Ned Buntline idealized figures like the cowboy, the range rider, the bandit, and the lawman. In 1882, Buffalo Bill prefigured the western movies to come when he presided over an "Old Glory Blowout" in North Platte, Nebraska. His brightest cowboy star was the celebrated Buck Taylor, ancestor of Fairbanks and his later imitators Tom Mix, Ken Maynard, and Fred Thomson, "who could ride the worst bucking horse, throw a steer by the horns or tail, and pick up a neckerchief from the ground at full speed." "We lead a wild life," boasted Taylor, "get hard knocks, rough usage and our lives are in constant peril, and the settling of a difficulty is an appeal to revolver or knife."[11]

Embellishing this were circus tricks of horsemanship, feats of sharpshooting, an array of bizarre costumes, and an almost sadistic dramatization of acts of violence. This kind of circus atmosphere, very much a part of the wild and fanciful fun of conscious myth-making, incurred much derision from various quarters, just as Fairbanks's aggressive violence, humor, and stunts elicited similar cavils from some quarters. Does the following criticism of Buffalo Bill by Joe Frantz and Julian Choate seem apposite to Fairbanks's characters?

> Cody, or Buffalo Bill, has come to be a symbol for the Wild West, proving again that there is considerable value and significance to any liar-promoter provided he can perform his dubious services in a grandiloquent manner. Buffalo Bill could do just that.[12]

So, for most Americans the West was a landscape known and identified by the fictions created about it late in the century, namely the competing Wild West shows, the dime novels, and—most importantly—the fledgling motion picture industry. For better or worse, the motion-picture cowboy to come inherited three basic tropes from the circus cowboy. First, he is rarely seen in his routine workday; second, his activities lay in rather melodramatic directions not especially intrinsic to the West; third, his costume and technique were stylizations enforced upon the subject matter. Readers would not be bored with the tedium of range life when they could be titillated by the thrills of desperadoes, fainting heroines, and the sequined saddles and buckskins of cowboys. "Whatever may be the merits of the dime-novel cowboy," Smith explains,

> . . . he apparently has nothing to do with cattle . . . most cowboy tales are hardly distinguishable from the Deadwood Dick and Buffalo Bill series. The professional duty of Beadle cowboys is to fight Indians, Mexicans, and outlaws. And the atmosphere created by wronged women seeking vengeance upon their false lovers, Mexican girls in men's clothing, and Army officers detailed for secret service is thoroughly typical of the decadent phase of Beadle fiction.[13]

Fairbanks frequently satirized the preposterous costumes worn by the circus cowboys. In the series of dime novels written by Prentiss Ingraham, Buffalo Bill was lifted entirely out of any kind of prosaic activity. His pursuits were devoted to Indian fighting, hunting, and derring-do; the splendor of his costume, accordingly, was flamboyant, even exotic. Henry Nash Smith views him at various stages in his career, both in the novels and in real-life; we see him, variously, in a red velvet jacket and white corduroy pants, embroidered silk shirt and gauntlet gloves, black velvet slashed with scarlet, and trimmed with silver buttons and lace, etc. His protégé, incidentally, the redoubtable Buck Taylor went him one better, wearing a miniature lariat about his dove-colored sombrero. All this, in real life, and in novels, shows how conscious myth-making prevailed, that Buffalo Bill and others seemed literally to wear their hearts on their highly embroidered sleeves. We see their like not just in the western satires of Douglas Fairbanks, but in the Tom Mix films of the 1920s and in the musical westerns of Gene Autrey and Roy Rogers in the 1940s.

Arizona Jim

As we know, when the newly formed Triangle Film Corporation beckoned in early 1915, the thirty-two-year-old Fairbanks was one of a host of Broadway players who came west in what amounted to a second Gold Rush. In a special sense, "the *stage* went West." Few survived more than a few pictures, but the exuberant Fairbanks, as we have seen with his first film, *The Lamb*, shot in 1915 on location in the San Fernando Valley, quickly caught on. Already, we see his character demonstrating the duality of the preciousness of a bumbling society sophisticate contrasted with the hardy

"Arizona Jim."

toughness of a rootin-tootin westerner, who tussles with rattlesnakes and mountain lions, grapples with a horde of Yaquis Indians, and blazes away with a machine gun in the rousing climax. "For the first time in his life," enthused George Creel at the time in *Everybody's Magazine*, "he was able to 'let go' [of the stage's limitations] with all the force of his dynamic individuality, and he took full advantage of the opportunity."[14]

The Lamb came hot on the heels—or spurs—of the first boom in "cowboy" and "cowgirl" pictures, as they were known then, in the years from 1907–1912. Produced by Essanay, Selig, Kalem, Pathé, and Bison studios, and frequently exploiting western locations, these relatively crude one-reelers presented, in the words of *Motion Picture News* and the *New York Dramatic Mirror*, a new "sensibility of action" that characterized the "life, snap, and vigor" of a distinctively "American" temper—the beginnings of what historian Richard Abel has called a truly "national cinema" emerging from what had been the hegemony of Old World styles, subjects, and tropes. Since 1907 the first big western star, Broncho Billy Anderson, had established himself as a brand name. However, near the end of this period, viewers were beginning to complain they were "utterly sick and tired . . . of Wild West Pictures." An upswing in quality and a renewal of popularity began in 1913 when Thomas Ince at the New York Motion Picture Company and Cecil B. De Mille at the Jesse Lasky Company, began making longer, multi-reel westerns exploiting bigger budgets, a more gritty realism, and a greater relish for the spectacle of authentic outdoor locations.[15] Tough, sternly laconic William S. Hart teamed up with Ince; quietly noble Harry Carey Sr. rode the range as "Cheyenne Harry" at Universal; and Tom Mix was getting his start with Selig. Even D. W. Griffith was producing some "quality" westerns.

But, as Fairbanks would soon demonstrate, the public was hungering for a different kind of westerner, someone as much at ease in the saddle of an expanding west as in the office spaces of the busy modern big city. As spokespersons for this new American spirit, they are too busy to hang around the bunkhouse for very long, or do routine ranch work. We can recall only one scene in his westerns—in *The Man from Painted Post*—where he gets down to the daily chore of punching cattle. Otherwise, his westerners busily deploy the tools of the cowboy—the lariat, the horse, the spurs—to bring a wry, satiric touch to action fantasies of cowboy life. He never just mounts or dismounts a horse when he can leap, flip, and somersault into and out of the saddle. Frequently he satirizes his prowess. There's a delicious scene in *The Man from Painted Post* (1917) when, as a tough detective pursuing rustlers, he disguises himself as a city dude in formal dress clothes and a preposterous cowboy hat. To the hilarity and scorn of the cowhands, who have presented him with a "tame" horse to ride, he feigns ignorance of stirrup and saddle and clumsily fails to negotiate both ends of the bucking beast.

Figures in a Landscape: *The Half-Breed, The Man from Painted Post, A Modern Musketeer, Headin' South, The Mollycoddle*

Many of these westerns are written and directed by John Emerson, Anita Loos, and Allan Dwan, that "great triple alliance" discussed in the preceding chapter. Another figure, writer-director Joseph Henabery, now joins the group with *The Man from Painted Post.* About the westerns, Loos later remembered in her memoirs, "The action always had to conform to 'the strenuous life,' and my heroes always had to be on the move . . . even my most seductive love scenes had to be interrupted by an abrupt and sometimes unaccountable bit of action, requiring Doug to jump onto a chandelier or swim upstream over a waterfall."[16]

Now, two cinematographers leap into the frame, Fairbanks's great friend and roistering buddy, cinematographer Victor Fleming (whom we met with *Down to Earth*), and Fleming's young protégé, cameraman Glen MacWilliams. Both began work with Fairbanks during the Triangle and Artcraft years and both went on to distinguished careers. After photographing Fairbanks's westerns *The Half-Breed, The Good Bad Man, Wild and Woolly,* and *The Man from Painted Post,* Fleming directed Fairbanks's last western, *The Mollycoddle,* before embarking on his spectacular career in the 1930s and 1940s as MGM's top director (*Captain's Courageous, The Wizard of Oz, Gone with the Wind,* etc.). In his recent study of Fleming, Michael Sragow points out that "Fleming got his biggest professional break when he began working the camera for Douglas Fairbanks, Sr."[17] Sharing Fairbanks's athleticism and prankish humor, he was "a photographer nimble enough to follow this actor-acrobat wherever he might roll—and daring enough to inspire some amazing stunts of his own." He insisted on shooting Fairbanks's "full body" in stunts on horseback "in compositions that emphasize athletics *and* character traits like impatience and ebullience."[18]

After his own association with Fairbanks, Glen MacWilliams became a top cameraman in England for the Jessie Matthews musicals and, later in the 1940s for Alfred Hitchcock, Lewis Milestone, Henry Hathaway, and others. His early years with Fairbanks were, he said in an interview, "my apprenticeship."[19] By 1917 he was assisting Fleming and another cameraman, Hugh C. McClung, on a number of Fairbanks westerns.

The Half-Breed

The Half-Breed was released on July 30, 1916, and was adapted by Anita Loos from Bret Harte's story, *In the Carquinez Woods* (1883). Allan Dwan directed and Victor Fleming photographed the scenic locales in the Sequoia National Park and Yosemite Valley near Santa Cruz in a series of breathtaking, deep-focus shots. Fairbanks's portrayal of the titular hero, Lo Dorman, as we will see, perfectly matches that species of American aristocrat we see so often in Fairbanks's characters. Lo's status in nature and society owes little to bloodlines or wealth or property, but arises from superior natural instincts, intelligence, and physical prowess. Like the forest itself, which "admits no inferior trees," in the words of Bret Harte, he exists purely on a superior level of taste and grace. Moreover, in what is perhaps the most unusual of the Fairbanks westerns, it eschews antic humor and gratuitous athletic embellishment for a more somber, sympathetic and relatively serious portrait of a man who belongs wholly neither to a Native American or Anglo-Saxon lineage. His attraction to two white women create the tensions that drive the story.

Because prints of *The Half-Breed* have been subjected to a variety of different releases, formats, and reconstructions over the years, it has been difficult hitherto to locate an original, complete version. Formerly, the only materials available were abbreviated fragments from Grapevine Video that radically altered the storyline with titles rewritten by Raymond Rohauer. (That travesty has to be avoided at all costs!)[20] Thanks to the resourcefulness of the Goessel Family Foundation and restorer Robert Bryne, the film has been presented intact for the first time for its "premiere" at the San Francisco Film Festival in July 2013. According to Dr. Goessel, the process of restoration has utilized 16 mm and 35 mm materials from the Library of Congress and the Cinematheque Francaise. I will cite only the original surviving titles. Other titles that were rewritten for a later release are omitted here.

The story begins with an explanatory title:

> *A chapter from the picturesque days of early California, in the country of "the big trees."*

A beautiful panning shot reveals a scenic vista of forests and streams. An Indian woman, a baby strapped to her back, toils up a slope:

> *Betrayed by a white man, cast out by her own people, the Cherokee squaw wanders among the Sierra forests.*

She comes to the hut of a hermit naturalist, "her only friend," and tenderly holds out the child.

> *"I give him back to his father's people. Make of him a white man."*

She leaves. In an extreme long shot, we see her standing at the top of a mountain . . . and she disappears.

We now flash forward twenty years to the child, grown into manhood. He is known as "Lo Dorman" ("Sleeping Water"). We first see him, partially nude, emerging from the forest stream. He scrambles on top of a rock and stands a moment, shaking off the water before donning his fringed buckskins and coonskin cap. He salutes the landscape in one of those apostrophes Fairbanks was prone to deliver to the West. But his idyll is cruelly interrupted when his foster father dies.

> *He is left alone to face a world of ruthless white men.*

After burying him, Lo returns to the cabin to find several men ransacking the hut. He tries to fight them off but is subdued.

> *"An Indian can't hold land in this country. You've got to get out."*

He is forced at gunpoint deeper into the forest.

Cut to the nearby mining camp of Excelsior,

> *where the superior white man is paramount.*

Here is the center of the "social and political life" of the town, where we meet Sheriff Dunn (Sam De Grasse), who is introduced by a title identifying him as the "betrayer" of Lo's mother; and the town pastor, Winslow Wynn (Frank Brown Lee), "who perhaps did the best he could." Wynn glad-hands his way through the saloon, exhorting everyone to attend Sabbath that day, pausing to take a nip himself. He refuses to donate to a charitable cause, protesting the poor unfortunate is not a member of his congregation. And we meet Wynn's foolish daughter, Nellie (Jewel Carmen):

> *Expensively educated she was profoundly ignorant in two languages, with a trained misunderstanding of music and painting, and a faultless taste in dress.*

Indeed, our first view of her face is obscured by a preposterous hat, adorned with numerous ribbons and bows. She pauses in close-up, adjusting her hat and hair in obvious self-satisfaction, before attending church, where her father delivers his sermon on "intolerance."

In a beautifully composed deep-focus shot, Lo is seen in the distance through the church doorway, framed in the foreground by the pastor and his pulpit. He is ushered inside by Wynn and seated beside Nellie. Near him is Sheriff Dunn, although neither recognizes the other. The service completed, the flirtatious Nellie sidles up to Lo and invites him to walk with her, earning the nearby discomfiture of her admirer (and Lo's rival), the sheriff. During their stroll, Nellie submits to Lo's impulsive kiss. Reports of the kiss reach town and Pastor Wynn, incensed at the audacity of the "Cherokee half-breed," rebukes Lo, reminding him he is "only an Indian." The sheriff accosts him in the following exchange:

> *"She's a white woman, you're an Indian. You know what that means here."*

Lo replies,

> *"My father was a white man."*

Dunn answers haughtily—

> *"That may be true, but there are all kinds of white men."*

Lo slowly walks away. He pauses and holds up his hand, gazing at the skin. Face wrinkled in pain, he turns away. . . . A title editorializes the moment, as if privy to Lo's thoughts:

> *No matter how drunken and sottish you be, so long as you are a white man!*

At this point another "specimen of the superior race" enters the scene, one Dick Curson (Tom Wilson), an itinerant "medicine man,"

> *who lived chiefly on the credulity of the ignorant Indians.*

Banjo in hand, he entertains the townspeople. By his side is his daughter, Teresa (Alma Reubens)—

> *just human drift but far too good for him.*

That night during the revels at the Palka Saloon, Curson's drunken Indians dance for the amusement of the crowd. Angrily, Lo appears and breaks it up, displaying

> *the pride that would not let them jeer at his mother's people.*

He hustles them out into the street. Back in the saloon he turns on Dunn, threatening to make *him* dance. But Teresa, clearly impressed with Lo, intervenes and leads him away in a dance of their own.

The next morning, Teresa confronts Curson, who has been dallying with the dancehall girls. In the furious interchange, Teresa stabs him. She jumps aboard a buckboard and flees the town with Dunn and his men in hot pursuit. Dunn catches up with her but Teresa, her knife once more at the ready, stabs him. Now alone amid the vast big trees, with the other men still on her trail, her plight seems hopeless. But Lo arrives, hides her inside the bole of an enormous tree, which is serving as his hideout, and sets out to forestall the pursuers. He scampers about the trees and rocks with the abandon typical of the Fairbanks audiences had come to see.

Inside the tree, Teresa finds safety at last—

> *In this Sanctuary under the green leaves, Teresa breathed with a sense of freedom.*

Gallantly, Lo, too naïve to understand Teresa's fears that he might take advantage of her, volunteers to sleep outside.

Cut to the town hospital, where Sheriff Dunn nurses his wounds and vows to hang Teresa and marry Nellie. Lo, in the meantime, goes in to town to find a dress for Teresa. Nellie, ever the flirt, questions why he hasn't come to see her. He replies,

> *"I don't think any good can come from that, Miss Wynn."*

Undaunted, she hints she might track him down to his "lair." She contrives to leave town in her search.

Meanwhile, Lo and Teresa are enjoying their own forest idyll, rather like Peter and Wendy in a Neverland of their own.

But the irrepressible Nellie soon arrives on the scene. Hopelessly lost among the big trees, she is found by Lo. She does all she can to make a play for him, but he resists. It is clear by now that it is Teresa who has won his heart. He later tells her that he will look after her "like a brother." She looks at the matter quite differently:

> *She, the daring, fighting, restless Teresa, subdued by the first noble love of her life.*

But Sheriff Dunn, convinced that Lo has been seeing Nellie, leaves his sick bed, bound to kill him. But he finds Teresa instead in the tree house and learns from her the true identity of Lo. Realizing he is Lo's father, he collapses and dies. Back in town, Nellie, suddenly aware of the gossip about her and Lo, writes him a note, hypocritically rationalizing her visits to him as "religious instruction."

Fate takes a hand when several of the drunken Indians set fire to the Carquinez Woods. What follows is a superbly photographed conflagration sequence. Roaring flames silhouette the rioting Indians, trees and limbs crash and burn amidst roiling clouds of smoke. In the midst of the confusion, Lo arrives and rescues Teresa. The next morning, we see them, in long shot, framed by the arch of a fallen tree. He declares they must part their ways. She protests her love. But he refuses and walks away. In the final moments, as his figure fades from view, she takes a few tentative steps to follow him.

For its time, *The Half-Breed* is an unusually sober and thoughtful critique of racism, abetted by Bret Harte's source material, Fairbanks's quietly sensitive characterization, Anita Loos's acidly satiric titles, and Victor Fleming's superbly photographed deep frames of forested landscapes. Nature, not civilization, is the source of virtue. Corruption resides in the authority figures of the sheriff and the minister. Nellie is quite simply a foolish hypocrite, oblivious to the dangers of her flirtation with Lo. "Dwan and Fairbanks clearly tried for something daring and different," declares Frederic Lombardi in his biography of Dwan. "[It] was definitely the most original and risky of Fairbanks's Triangle features."[21] Critics at the time were generally enthusiastic about its departure from the usual Fairbanksian antics. Louis Reeves Harrison, for example, praised the emphasis upon story values: "At last we have a picture in which the intense personality of Fairbanks does not bulge out of the story, one in which the characterization is difficult and where it is not made dominant to story interest. The result is not only an artistic achievement, but a stronger proof of his ability."[22]

What at first seems an odd choice for both Fairbanks and scenarist Anita Loos makes more sense upon examination of Bret Harte's original story. Here we find the character of "Low Dorman," prefiguring some of the distinctly "Fairbanksian" qualities Loos has been busily constructing on screen. Low lives in perfect harmony in a forest environment that is described as if it were a cathedral:

> The straight, tall, colossal trunks rose dimly like columns of upward smoke. The few fallen trees stretched their huge length into obscurity and seemed to lie on shadowy trestles. The strange breath that filled these mysterious vaults had neither coldness nor moisture; a dry, fragrant dust arose from the noiseless foot that trod their bark-strewn floor."[23]

His hollowed-out tree dwelling has all the domestic comforts of home. He is preternaturally agile and can freely scamper about the treetops. His is a "sublime paganism," a "crystallized personification of the sedate and hospitable woods." (76). Indeed, writes Harte, "he was of a grace so unusual and unconventional that he might have passed for a faun who was quitting his ancestral home . . . With him was the picturesque and unstudied relaxation of perfect symmetry." (6)

Into his world comes a city girl, Teresa, a saloon dancer, on the run from the local sheriff. The authorities are after her, so Low gallantly protects her in his tree dwelling. At the same time, Low has been seeing the virtuous Nellie, the daughter of Reverend Wynn. This is a spiritual passion for "an unapproachable divinity, as inaccessible and cold as her father was impulsive and familiar." (21) She had met Low in the settlement church, and now she comes to see him in secret, nursing a secret passion for him. He gives her a ring, pledging his love.

Intrigues grow out of these situations: Low, who has comported himself like a perfect gentleman towards these women, finds himself falling out of love with the shallow Nellie and nursing a growing affection for Teresa. But we know any consummation of these amorous intrigues is doomed. "There should be a law, sir, against the mingling of races," declares one of the townspeople. "There are men, sir, who violate the laws of the Most High by living with Indian women—squaw men, sir, as they are called." (80).

In the end, after the revelation that Sheriff Dunn is his biological father and after Nellie ultimately spurns him, a great forest fire sweeps the area. The flames ultimately engulf Teresa and Low, and they both die in the blaze. Their remains are found in the charred forest.

It is Teresa, not Nellie, who understands him and sees past his hybrid ethnicity to divine in him a deeper kind of humanity: "[He's not an Indian] unless being born of a mother who scarcely knew him, of a father who never even saw him, and being brought up among white men and wild beasts less cruel than they were, could make him one!" (95)

Topsy-turvy western action in *The Man From Painted Post* (1917).

The Man from Painted Post

The Man from Painted Post was adapted by Fairbanks and director Joseph Henabery from Jackson Gregory's 1916 short story, "Silver Slippers." Victor Fleming was again the cinematographer. This picture brings into focus the work of Henabery, who had been working for more than a year with Fairbanks at Artcraft at the Jesse Lasky Studio in Hollywood. For more than a year he had assisted as location scout and script adviser on a number of films, including *Wild and Woolly* (see later in this chapter).

Henabery reports that Loos and Emerson were having difficulties with the story for *Painted Post* and that Loos invited him to come into the project. "The idea of shooting a Western in the real West appealed to me," he writes. "I told her I would be happy to make the picture." Almost immediately the cast (including a few authentic cowboys from the Cheyenne

Rodeo), staff, and horses and props took the train to Laramie, Wyoming—more specifically, a 25,000-acre spread in Long Valley, near the Laramie River, bordered on the far west by the Medicine Bow Mountains. "All the movie people were to sleep on straw in the loft of a massive barn made of logs," remembers Henabery. "Our meals, prepared by our own cook, were to be cooked and served in the ranch chuck house. The horses and equipment would be housed in the barn." The living conditions were truly "western," including horrendous mosquito attacks. All this time, reports Henabery, Loos and Emerson had vacated the project, leaving Henabery to write the titles. There was general agreement that Fleming's location photography was exceptional and the story a fine vehicle for Fairbanks.[24]

The conflict here pits the cattlemen of Wyoming against the growing threat of rustlers. Fairbanks portrays a range detective, "Fancy Jim" Sherwood, who is hired to protect the stockmen against their losses. The situation points to a problem that, by the late 1880s, was a serious concern, writes western historian David Dary: "Evidence [against rustlers] was not easy to obtain. In Wyoming, some cowboys had quit their jobs on the big ranches, filed homestead claims, and built their own herds allegedly at the expense of their former employers." The big ranchers, in turn, brought rustling charges against the new cowmen. "By the late 1880s rustling had become such a problem in eastern Wyoming that several of the large ranchers, including some of the absentee-owners, organized and hired detectives to eliminate the rustlers."[25]

The Man from Painted Post echoes in many respects Owen Wister's seminal novel of the American West, *The Virginian*, which was published fourteen years earlier. The novel, which grew out of seven short pieces between 1893 and 1902, became the most widely read and influential western novel of its generation. Wister himself prepared a popular stage version in 1904, which, in turn, spawned numerous film adaptations. The first, directed by Cecil B. DeMille, appeared just two years before the Fairbanks film (the 1929 version would be directed by Victor Fleming).[26] The parallels are significant: The film also takes place in the Medicine Bow area near the Big and Little Laramie. The central action concerns the depredations of rustlers against the cattle ranchers. And its moral center concerns the ambiguity of law and order in a territory relying solely on a crude brand of frontier justice. "Fancy Jim" Sherwood, like Wister's Virginian, maintains that justice on the frontier is not served by "civilized" norms. Opposing him is the schoolma'am, who, like Molly in Wister's story, clings to her eastern heritage of the rule of law.

"Fancy Jim" Sherwood is a range detective, a character common to the dime novels of the day, particularly those of Allen Pinkerton, who comes west to apply standards of justice outside the bounds of civilized order. A title card introduces us to the type:

> *A little known but very important factor in the development of our great West is the detective employed by the stockmen's associations to wipe out cattle thieves, commonly called "rustlers." Playing a lone hand against organized bands of such marauders, these detectives have been called on to display an unequalled degree of shrewdness, courage and endurance in rounding up their quarry.*

Aside from an occasional wink to the viewer, and a few stunts on horseback, Fairbanks plays the role in a relatively straightforward manner. His customarily antic physicality is subordinated to the story. And his scenes with the schoolma'am are played down and nicely nuanced; likewise his scenes with the boy possess considerable charm. Even in the badly deteriorated print materials available, Victor Fleming's photography effectively steals the show. He effectively captures the spacious level grasslands, the spectacular natural architecture of the looming mountains, and the vast cloudscapes. At times, the action and characters are reduced to mere tiny specks against the expansive vistas.

Our first view of Jim has him running toward a barn and climbing up to the roof, where he takes target practice with two six-guns.

> *A detective, yes! Fearless, surefire; the relentless foe of the "bad man" and the "rustler." Fate played a part in casting him in this role. We find Sherwood, a young man, educated in the East. Into his life came a stranger who was identified as the notorious "bad man" "30-30 Smith," so-called because his intended victims always received a warning note accompanied by a "30-30" bullet.*

Yes, Sherwood has a past. His sister was shot dead by "30-30 Smith." We flashback to the scene . . .

> *"30-30 Smith" got away. The shot that killed Jim's sister glanced and struck his arm. A reminder of this tragic event was his scarred arm.*

The story proper begins with spectacular shots of the Wyoming landscape . . .

—set between the Big and the Little Laramie, where the far-reaching plains reach the foothills of the Medicine Bow range.

Angered by the activities of the rustlers, namely, one "Bull" Madden (Frank Campeau), rancher Warren Bronson (Herbert Standing) calls together the Big Hollow Cattlemen's Association.

"Bull Madden's got us all buffaloed. Get the goods on him and you'll have the man who's at the bottom of all this."

He suggests they call on a detective from the Horn Basin Cattlemen's Association. Another rancher objects that a former detective, "Longhorn Thompson," had already been killed by the notorious "30-30" killer.

"But this man from Painted Post is different. They say he's the best shot, with either hand, west of the Rockies—and that ain't all. Did you ever hear how he cleaned out the Burns' Brothers Gang—?"

We flashback again to a demonstration of Sherwood's prowess: Jim is hanging out with buddies in the saloon, when two desperadoes arrive through the swinging doors. One look at them and Jim knows trouble is ahead. With crossed hands, he shoots his pistols in opposite directions, dispatching them in an instant. He then swings up into the rafters, where he straddles a beam. He looks down at the other bad men entering the doors.

"Hands down!"

he orders;

"Belly the wall, you lizards!"

Bronson sends for Jim. A letter arrives explaining that because Sherwood is unavailable, but an eastern dude named Rogers is interested in buying the V-Bar Ranch and will appear momentarily. In actuality, the "dude" is Jim Sherwood in disguise.

Cut to the Triple O Ranch, where none other than "Bull" Madden lives with his "squaw" wife and "half-breed" son. He's a brutal character, who frequently beats both wife and son. Flinging the woman to the ground, he growls,

> *"I'm going to town to see a white woman."*

The "white woman" is Jane Forbes (Eileen Percy), the "schoolma'am" of District 29, just arrived from the East. Madden's intention is to force her into marrying him (never mind that he already has a wife).

And now "Rogers" arrives. He is quite a sight, attired in city clothes and carrying golf clubs.

> *And so, when the new owner showed up at the V-Bar, the boys got just what they were looking for—and then some.*

The cowboys barely conceal their mirth at the foppish apparition they see before them. Unfazed, Rogers/Sherwood gets down to business and consults a map to locate his neighbors. His foreman suggests the owner of the Triple O might know something about the missing cattle:

> *"I'm thinkin' a party by the name of 'Bull' Madden could tell where a lot of our cows have strayed to."*

Sherwood smiles sweetly and declares,

> *"Well, I'm going to stop this rustling and drop a note to Mr. Madden."*

The foreman chuckles,

> *"If you send that note, you'd better learn to shoot."*

Meanwhile, the corral is full of cowboys hurling lariats and riding bucking broncos. Sherwood appears in immaculate boots and riding attire, looking for a "tame" horse. But what he's presented with is so skittish that it eludes his attempts to saddle up. In an amusing sequence, Sherwood feigns difficulty negotiating both ends of the fierce bronc. After some false starts (and a knowing wink at the camera), he's finally into the saddle—and promptly bucked off. Timidly, he mounts another horse and clumsily trots away, leaving behind a corral full of laughing cowboys.

Sherwood visits the schoolma'am and immediately takes a shine to her. He befriends one of her students, none other than Madden's "half-breed" son. The scenes between Sherwood and the boy convey a great deal of gentle charm and establish their growing bond. A nice moment, in particular, shows the two of them in the corral, roughhousing and practicing roping a calf and wrestling it to the ground. Sherwood smiles at the boy:

> *"You and me both, ev'ry jump in the road!"*

Meanwhile, angry at the note he's received from Sherwood, Madden shows up during Jim's woeful attempts at target practice. Rogers "inadvertently" shoots off his hat. Madden threatens Rogers, but only elicits Sherwood's casual response:

> *"We have tea at 5 o'clock, won't you stay?"*

We cut away to learn that Madden has been using an abandoned cabin where he hides the stolen cattle and alters their brands. A nearby tunnel takes the cattle into the next valley. Sherwood follows and climbs the rock face above the shack and lowers himself into the cabin, where he witnesses the illicit branding.

Later, he visits Jane. He learns she's also from the East. Their cozy conversation grows more somber when the topic turns to punishing rustlers like Madden. She insists that the rule of law should prevail:

> *"People in the East uphold law and order. In the West violence is common; men take into their own hands matters the law should settle."*

He replies:

> *"Eastern methods don't always work in the West. As far as Madden is concerned, he'll soon be driven out."*

He flashbacks to the film's opening moments, when he killed members of a gang of desperadoes. How to explain this brand of frontier justice?

> *Something that was good for the community: could he make her understand?*

The action cranks up when the Madden gang makes one last raid on the V-Bar herd. Madden himself kidnaps Jane and threatens Sherwood with a "calling card" of a 30-30 shell. Now Sherwood realizes Madden is none other that the man who killed his sister years before. While the V-Bar cowboys try to head off the rustlers, Sherwood rushes out and takes a *long* leap off the porch into the saddle of his horse. He gallops across the grasslands and gains Madden's hideout. After dispatching some of the rustlers, he places the 30-30 bullet into his rifle and gives it to Jane:

> *Madden's 30-30 bullet. A shot for her protection should he lose.*

He gets the drop on Madden and shows him his scarred arm:

> *"For years I've waited to get the drop on you. But I've changed my mind about killing you. You're going to Rawlins to spend twenty years of regrets in an iron-barred corral."*

And so, saved by Sherwood's latent mode of eastern justice, Madden exits. Sherwood shouts after him:

> *"I'm dead stuck on your kid. From now on, he's got a new dad!"*

The beautiful epilogue sets the scene:

> *And so, between the Big and Little Laramie, where the far-reaching plains meet the foot hills of the Medicine Bow range, our story ends.*

The final shot shows the two lovers on horseback, silhouetted against a spectacular clouded sky.

Jim Sherwood's decision to send Madden to jail instead of killing him points to the central ambivalence of his character, as is the case with many of Fairbanks's roles, On the one hand, as a westerner, he would condone killing him, just as Wister's Virginian had justified the hanging of the rustlers (including his best friend, Steve). We recall a key moment in Wister's novel when Judge Henry explains to the Virginian's girlfriend, Molly, the code of frontier justice. "The courts, or rather the juries, into whose hands we have put the law," says the judge, "are not dealing the law . . . [and] they cannot hold a cattle-thief. . . ."

> And so, when your ordinary citizen sees this, and sees he has placed justice in a dead hand, he just takes the justice back into his own hands where it was at the beginning of things. Call this primitive, if you will. But so far from being a *defiance* of the law, it is an *assertion* of it—the fundamental assertion of self-governing men, upon whom our whole social fabric is based.[27]

Thus, as Richard Slotkin points out, "In punishing the rustlers, the Virginian acts in the name 'of the people,' who (through him) take back the power that once they gave the state."[28]

On the other hand, because Sherwood is a detective, a duly appointed upholder of the laws of a civilized nation, he ultimately must enforce those laws. So it is that, at the end of the film, he opposes a lynching. Moreover, it's apparent that he will marry the girl, work his new ranch, and settle down to another kind of civilized order: the domestic hearth and home. In that way, he resembles characters we have seen in other Fairbanks films, such as *His Picture in the Papers, Reaching for the Moon*, and *The Matrimaniac*: Despite their willful ways, they ultimately temper their "self-propelled" instincts and accept the conventional responsibilities of marriage, business, and community.

A Modern Musketeer

A Modern Musketeer infuses the lawless American West with the gallantries of Alexandre Dumas's swashbuckling stories about d'Artagnan and his musketeers. It premiered in New York on December 31, 1917. This time Glen MacWilliams is behind the camera. The redoubtable Allan Dwan directs. Exterior locations included the Grand Canyon and the Canyon de Chelly in New Mexico. The story, adapted from E. P. Lyle's 1912 novel, *D'Artagnan of Kansas*, cleverly demonstrates the "imperial reach" we examined in the last chapter. Fairbanks has co-opted the rituals and traditions of the French ruling orders and reconfigured them into his own—and America's—western image. It's as if in order to extend his "reach" and renew his virility, he must now go beyond the continental frontier and take up Old World cultural products.

In the first half of the story, our hero, Ned Thatcher, imposes his manic fantasies of seventeenth-century France upon the bewildered citizens of his native Kansas town. The action is as fast, funny, and rambunctious as anything Fairbanks ever put on the screen. The second half, by contrast, finds Ned moving west and, in the process, settling down into a more

At cliff's edge in *A Modern Musketeer* (1917).

moderate melodrama played out against the spectacular scenic vistas of Arizona's Grand Canyon. The dream of chivalry in the first half is realized in the actuality of real-life adventure in the second.

For the sake of the uninitiated viewer in 1917, the opening title card asks:

> *Do you remember D'Artagnan of France? Can you recall the thrills you got from the adventures of that famous swashbuckling gallant of three centuries ago?*

A costumed swordsman gallops into the frame, approaches in close shot, and smiles as he gestures toward his hair and mustache. He winks. Except for the wink, it's a virtually unrecognizable Fairbanks. For the first time we see him with a mustache, hair down to his shoulders, equipped with cape and sword. He gestures us to follow him into a nearby inn. He strides around the place, all smiles and arm-waving. His attempt to retrieve Milady's fallen handkerchief immediately plunges him into duels with the entire male company. He vaults tables, climbs the walls, traverses the ceiling, and bests his opponents one by one. Finally, triumphant, he bows and presents the kerchief to the lady. He leaps to the window, onto his horse, and gallops off.

Has D'Artagnan gone forever?—Maybe not. Perhaps it is his spirit that actuates Ned Thacker of Kansas.

The image of d'Artagnan gradually dissolves into a brisk modern young man in a business suit. He rolls up his coat sleeves and advances toward the camera. Recognizably "Doug," he breaks into the famous smile and wink.

A lady in distress was a fly in Ned's ointment—and his ointment was usually full of flies.

Gazing out his second-story window he sees a woman accosted by a thug. He leaps out the window to a conveniently placed pole, slides down it, and follows the man into a tough saloon. In a duplication of d'Artagnan's furious choreography, he attacks a room full of villains, demolishes the furniture, careers around the walls and across the ceiling, and, of course, bestows a kiss on the wronged lady. She slaps him furiously and pushes him out of the room. So much for chivalry! Outside, a passerby explains his error:

"Listen, son—you've got the wrong idea. Women want equal rights. *If you want their* love, *give them* lefts *too."*

The woman back in the saloon comforts the wounds of her bad-boy lover:

"Did that big brute hurt mama's little Spikie?"

Back in his room, Ned ruefully lowers his window shade, upon which is emblazoned:

Society for the Prevention of Cruelty to Women

Believe it or not, there are reasons for Ned's mad behavior. We flashback to Ned's youth—

Kansas must have known he was coming.

A tornado is tearing through the town. House fronts collapse, trees uproot, people tumble about, debris flies everywhere (shades of another Kansan, Buster Keaton). Meanwhile, inside, Ned's pregnant mother is unfazed. She's praying for a son. She's in bed reading *The Three Musketeers*, an edition illustrated by Maurice Leloir (a harbinger of the musketeers' stories to come, when that same Leloir will come to Hollywood as Fairbanks's technical adviser for *The Iron Mask* [1928]).

> *"If I am blessed with a son, I pray he may be like D'Artagnan."*

And then this title:

> *Cyclone + D'Artagnan = SPEED!!!*

As the twig is bent . . .

> *Mrs. Thacker's wish came true. Ned grew up—like D'Artagnan—always chivalrous—always misunderstood. He finished four years of college in six months—by request.*

But by this time—

> *Kansas was getting on Ned's nerves—and Ned was getting on Kansas' nerves. It was almost time for them to part.*

And Ned, unusually frenetic and frustrated, says,

> *"I can't stand it. I've got to get out of Kansas!"*

And so Ned jumps up and down, vaults the gate, hurdles the mule, and finally climbs up to the very top of the steepled church—and waves. His mother looks on and approves:

> *"I'm glad! He will always be a boy!"*

A series of shots compares Ned's departure to d'Artagnan's leave-taking of his father. The old car bestowed on him by his father is likewise compared to d'Artagnan's nag.

Motoring through the Arizona desert, Ned realizes he's not in Kansas anymore. He encounters Elsie Dodge (Marjorie Daw), her mother, and her would-be suitor, Forrest Vandeteer ("the richest man in Yonkers"). Their car is out of gas. Ned cleverly manages to jack up his car onto the railroad tracks and drives them along to the El Tovar Hotel at the Grand Canyon. Crosscut to the base of a tributary canyon (*vide* a long vertical pan down the cliff face), where we get an ominous glimpse of the villain of the piece, a Native American named one Chin-de-dah (Frank Campeau), the local guide and the self-appointed ruler of the outcasts of the area.

Meanwhile, after dinner the guests are treated to a Hopi Dance. Ned pursues Elsie, despite the opposition of Vandeteer. They stroll along the edge of the Grand Canyon, eliciting Ned's majestic flight of purple prose:

> *"What is God's purpose to so rend the earth under this majestically fretted dome as to horribly shake our dispositions with thoughts far beyond the reach of our souls?"*

Then, for no apparent reason, Ned does a handstand on the cliff edge. Seconds later, realizing the peril, he sheepishly crawls away to safety on hands and knees.

Chin-de-dah shows up and takes an instant liking for Elsie. He salutes Ned, "How." To which Ned replies:

> *"Scrambled."*

Vandeteer hires Chin-de-dah to take him and Elsie down into the Canyon. Ned, meanwhile, wins over Elsie's scheming mother (who wants to marry off her daughter to Vandeteer for his wealth), and warns her against her plan:

> *"Do you really want your only child to sacrifice everything beautiful in life—just to . . . well, you know what I mean . . . !"*

Ned is encouraged now. But one of Chin's gang shows up to warn him that Vandeteer has a villainous past (he has killed his former "wives") and that Chin intends to kill Vandeteer and make off with the girl. If Ned is going to go after them, his only recourse is to descend the canyon from above. He lowers himself down by a rope, penetrates the adobe dwellings and finds Chin's cave. In hiding he spies on Chin, Vandeteer, and Elsie, and he overhears Chin telling Vandeteer:

> *"You buy what you want, me take what I want . . . and I want her!"*

Ned intervenes and gets the drop on Chin. Chin demands to know where he's come from—

> *"From Kansas, the home of the really great cyclones!"*

There's a tussle with all three Indians. . . . Ned gets them all in a wrestling hold:

> *"Aren't we cozy, laying here!"*

Ned's accomplice uses the opportunity to confront Vandeteer and reveal that years ago Vandeteer destroyed his reputation in a shady business deal. He lassoes Vandeteer and dangles him over the cliff edge. Ned arrives and forces a confession out of Vandeteer. Chin is then killed by one of his own men. And Ned, Elsie, and Vandeteer are raised by rope back to safety to the cliff edge. At the end Ned and Elsie are on horseback admiring the canyon backdrop:

> *Ned learns that chivalry, like virtue, receives its award*

D'Artagnan appears here for the first time in a Fairbanks film. He's been barely concealed all along in the garb of Fairbanks's urban and Ruritanian characters. But he emerges now, instantly recognizable, a prophecy of the characters and adventures of films to come.

Cameraman Glen MacWilliams recalls his experiences on the location of *A Modern Musketeer* with particular affection. The location shooting in Arizona reveals Fairbanks's zest for "natural" and "untouched" western locations, no matter how logistically difficult they were. "By 1917 Doug was nuts on cowboy stuff," explains MacWilliams.

> His idea of life was to make western pictures. He wanted to go on location among the Indians. He had a very good friend by the name of Hubbell who was one of the biggest Indian traders in New Mexico. Doug contacted him to take us to an unknown location where no other motion picture company had ever been. Now, that wasn't hard in those days, especially in Arizona. Hubbell decided to take us to the Canyon de Chelly. That's in the northeastern corner of Arizona.

The logistics of getting there proved to be complicated.

> We went first to Gallop, New Mexico and loaded up in Pierce Arrow automobiles and started on the trails to Chinle, Arizona, a trading post. We made sixty miles the first day, stopping at Fort Defiance for the night. The next morning we switched to horses and wagons. We rode all day across the desert, and very late that afternoon Doug was out in front with his binoculars and spotted Chinle. We established camp on the floor of the canyon, with granite walls 600 feet high surrounding us.

Several miles further up the Canyon were a tribe of 250 Hopi Indians, who were contacted to participate in the film (they can be seen in several tribal dance sequences, with Fairbanks among them).

> We were all set for a big scene with them, and we fed them lunch from our chuck wagon. Comes the big day, however, and no Indians. We finally got word that they were all sick with diarrhea. Doug dispatched my brother to check it out. He had a hunch and checked the first-aid tent. Sure enough, a whole case of Feen-a-Mint chewing gum was missing! The Indians had taken it and . . . well. . . .

MacWilliams describes the difficulties shooting with cumbersome cameras the big concluding fight scene.

> We shot it some 500 feet high up on the canyon. Doug wanted to stage a fight there with the Canyon clearly visible below. There was a little trail that could be used to get the cast up there, but it was tough to transport the equipment. So they decided to put a boom out and lower a cable down to the platform holding the camera and haul it up with a windlass. So I went up with the equipment. It was very slow going up on that thing, swaying in the wind all the while. And every once in a while the cable would pile up and when they'd fix it, there'd be a drop and a big jerk—all I could do was sit there and hope for the best.

Looking back over the years—our interview was conducted in 1979—MacWilliams sifted through a scrapbook filled with photographs of him and Fairbanks on locations for *A Modern Musketeer* and *Man from Painted Post*. "When [Fairbanks] was making westerns, he was in his glory. . . ."

> He was like a little boy playing cowboy. A lot of people don't believe this, but the whole time I was with him, he never had a stunt man. He kept real

East meets West in *The Mollycoddle* (1920).

> cowboys around him all the time. And he never sat still. He was always rehearsing, building up stunts, practicing, working. He'd figure out a stunt and we'd build the whole picture around it.

Alas, concluded MacWilliams, that area now is greatly changed. The entire area that had been virtually uninhabited is now paved and boasts of several food-chain restaurants!

Director Allan Dwan, who would direct his own version of *The Three Musketeers* in 1938, regarded *A Modern Musketeer* as one of Doug's (and his) finest films. According to his biographer Frederic Lombardi, Dwan won praise for the wonderful titles quoted above. He may also be credited, in part, for the stunts. Pound for pound, the first half contains more nonstop acrobatic thrills than any of his other collaborations with Doug. "I had learned to do a little scrapping in college," recalled Dwan, "as well as having done some wresting and played football. I told Fairbanks I could teach him how to do the stunts which have since made him famous, and he was willing."[29]

The Mollycoddle

The Mollycoddle introduces us to a "first family"—an aristocracy of sorts—of the American West, four generations of rough and tough "Richard Marshalls" who have been in the vanguard of settling the region. Unlike his forebears, however, the present-day Richard Marshall (Fairbanks) has grown soft and suffers from "overcivilization." He has forgotten his heritage of blood and buried his primal instincts. But by going to Arizona, as we shall see, Marshall will recover his true values. We've seen characters like this before: "By recovering the martial discipline and mission of the frontiersmen," writes Richard Slotkin, "they also regain . . . their model of family government, their energy as 'fighters and breeders.'"[30] Thus, *The Mollycoddle* will trace Marshall's "education," and his rebirth as an American.

The film begins with this unfortunately patronizing title card:

> *FOREWORD: Thanks are expressed to the government officials, tribal chiefs, and to the hundreds of picturesque Hopi Indians in their reservation near the Painted Desert of Arizona, who, in their savage way, heartily welcomed us to their prehistoric village and with primitive cheerfulness played an import part in this picture.*

Which is followed by a succession of introductory titles:

> *A Mollycoddle is a body of man entirely surrounded by super-civilization.*

A montage of images of Indian dwellings are compared to the posh buildings of Monte Carlo:

> *Fundamentally, they are just the same-just rock. One is highly polished—that's all.*

We are introduced to those four generations of Arizonans, the Richard Marshall dynasty:

> *For many generations back the RICHARD MARSHALLS have been found in the vanguard of civilization—God-fearing, hell-bustin,' fighting adventurers—tireless and two-fisted pioneers.*

The first Marshall is a soldier who receives a medallion from George Washington in 1779. The next Marshall is an Indian fighter—*"a leathernecked, shag-gutted buckaroo"*—who, in 1853, is killed in an Indian attack. Still later, in 1880, a "chivalrous Richard Marshall" rescues a wronged woman from a gang of saloon ruffians.

And finally we come to the last Richard Marshall: The camera pulls back from what seems to be the man on horseback, only to reveal he's merely astride a carousel pony. The location is Monte Carlo, and Marshall is appropriately decked out in city-dude attire; he is an exact look alike to Theodore Roosevelt, with monocle, mustache, gloves, cane, cigarette holder, the works. When the wind blows off his hat, several young American bystanders give chase.

> *"Thanks, awfully—"*

he says. They mistake him for an Englishman and are astonished when he tells them he was born in Arizona and that his father had moved here after making "a pot of money."

> *"All my people were cow persons in Arizona."*

Astonished, they laugh among themselves:

> *"Nobody would ever take him for an American. That fellow is contrary to the Constitution of the United States. Something ought to be done about it."*

Another American, Virginia Hale (Ruth Renick), is instantly attracted to him and starts her crash course in "educating" him to be an American, which consists of losing the monocle and learning how to roll a cigarette. As a prank, her friends kidnap him and stow him away on the yacht of Van Holkar (Wallace Beery). Van Holkar is a diamond smuggler who steals rough diamonds from an Indian reservation and sends them to Amsterdam to be cut. When he is warned that there is a Secret Service agent on his trail, he immediately suspects Marshall, who as a stowaway has been put to work stoking coal. Virginia takes pity on him:

> *"Well, I'm afraid Arizona will either kill or cure you."*

Which is where they all end up. And it is there that Marshall gets involved in many adventures with Indians and smugglers. He borrows cowboy clothes from an Indian and throws himself into the saddle:

> *The blood of his forefathers seemed to respond. Primitive cunning, born of instinct, now guides his every move.*

After joining the Hopis in a dance, he sets out to help Virginia get evidence against the smugglers. While exploring the terrain, there is this title:

> *Years before, young Marshall's grandfather came abruptly on this very spot and reining in his horse, exclaimed: "Hurrah for God."*

In a dizzying chain of events, Marshall rescues everybody from Van Holkar's plan to dynamite the area and start an avalanche to destroy the mines and the Indian settlements. Van Holkar escapes and Marshall pursues him on horseback. In a terrific action trajectory, Marshall leaps from the cliff edge to a tree, where he and Van Holkar struggle as they descend from branch to branch, sliding down a rocky slope, tumbling through a rooftop, through a wall, down *another* slope, into a rushing stream, over a waterfall, to the shallows.

In the epilogue, a bruised and battered Marshall sits beside Virginia, gazing at the magnificent canyon spread out before them. To Virginia's approval, Richard deftly rolls a cigarette—the final confirmation of his manhood.

Perhaps cameraman Victor Fleming's greatest contribution to the film, beyond the superbly captured towering cliffs and plunging gorges, came in planning and directing the landslide at the climax of *The Mollycoddle*. A reviewer for the *New York Times* reported:

> [It] outdoes anything of the kind in the memory of the writer. Half a mountain, it seems, moves down the steep slope, through an Indian village, and over half a dozen people protected by a thin ledge. [Fairbanks] even challenges the landslide to beat him at its own game and demonstrates that he and Wallace Beery, the villain of his story, can roll and tumble, and fall and slide, down a steep mountain with quite as much concentration on getting to the bottom as any rock that was ever started anywhere by the single-purposed force of gravity. . . . Camera tricks? Some of it, but none that can be noticed and more that must have been performed exactly as it is seen.[31]

Fleming's eulogy of his longtime friend and colleague in 1939 summed up the whole experience: "He was a stanch [*sic*] friend and a fine influence. . . . the man who put motion into motion pictures. He lived and breathed action."[32]

East to West . . . and West to East: *Manhattan Madness* and *Wild and Woolly*

And now we come to two of Fairbanks's greatest westerns, *Manhattan Madness* (1916) and *Wild and Woolly* (1917). They are paired here because, more than any of the others, they most explicitly ponder the variable geographical referents of the American "East" and "West."

Western historian William K. Everson regards *Manhattan Madness* (1916) as the best of Fairbanks's Triangle-Fine Arts westerns. It "cast him as the irrepressible modern youth, happily unconcerned with making a living, existing only for adventure" (124).

Fairbanks is Steve O'Dare, a gilded Manhattan youth who has gone west to pursue the cattle business. As the film opens, he has returned to New York with a freight of cattle and horses destined to be shipped to Russia. While waiting for the final details of the transaction, he thoroughly annoys everyone at his gentleman's club with his roughhousing and backslapping. Only in Wyoming, he proselytizes, can life be *really lived*. Everybody wrestles him to the floor to shut him up.

What follows is a wonderful montage, a series of crosscuts that compare and contrast the "thrills" of urban city life with those of the Wild West—juxtaposing street fights with western gunfights; bus rides with stagecoach chases; lunch at the club with chow at the roundup; and city slickers with western toughs like "Black Burke" (the latter illustrated with a montage of shots of Burke's holdups and chases).

But then—when one look at the lovely Jewel Carmen is contrasted with a shot of arid and empty sage brush—Steve muses:

> *"I wonder if I'd rather stay here and see her smile or go back home to the sting of the cactus and the swing of my bronc."*

Well, we know the answer to *that*. So when his friends bet him $5,000 that he will find thrills while in New York, he readily accepts the bet. Steve is summoned to the home of a Russian agent to conclude the business deal. Upon arrival, he is promptly assaulted and robbed. Moreover, he witnesses the murder of two men and learns that his girlfriend is mysteriously held prisoner. Bewildered by these unexpected hazards, he promptly leaps into the fray and there's a terrific scuffle as he races around the house, out the windows, on the rooftop—and is finally knocked out and bound and gagged. But, inexplicably, a maid arrives and releases him from his bonds. He finds a telephone and sends out an urgent call for his clubmen and his cowboys to come to his aid. After a pause, he gradually realizes that the bad guys have vanished. The house is empty.

> *"Where is everybody?"*

He explores the rooms. Hearing sounds of laughter from behind a door, he bursts in. He finds a room full of his club friends and several stage actors. Confused for a moment, he suddenly realizes he's been hoaxed.

> *"So, it's a joke, is it? Now, I'll play* my *cards."*

His cowboys arrive and get the drop on the group. Steve trains two six-guns on them and confesses that "Black Burke" was really *him*. (Cut to shot of Burke dropping his mask to reveal Fairbanks.) Steve hoists the girl into his arms and carries her out. He asks her if she'll go along with *his* joke:

> *"You've heard of Young Lochinvar?—Well, I'm out of the West, too!"*

While his cowboys keep guard on the group, they depart.

Cut to shipboard, where Steve and the girl stand together by the porthole. He looks into her eyes and smiles:

> *"After all, it isn't where you are that counts—it's who you're with that counts!"*

Less than a year later, *Wild and Woolly* was released, Fairbanks's second film for the newly formed Artcraft Pictures Corporation. Loos and Emerson wrote and directed, and Victor Fleming photographed. Critics were delighted. "[In] *Wild and Woolly*," wrote critic Paul Grant, "you laugh at the eastern American's idealization of western melodramatic existence" (49). "To say that the picture is entertaining," enthused the critic for *Variety*, "is putting it mildly; but it is difficult to find words in which to fittingly describe Fairbanks' performance. . . . The picture is undoubtedly the best thing he has ever done."[33] Recent biographer Jeffrey Vance echoes the opinion, nominating it as the finest of the surviving collaborations with director John Emerson and screenwriter Anita Loos.[34] A recent viewing confirms its reputation as one of the fastest-paced action films of the day.

After an opening montage of nostalgic views of the rowdy Old West contrasted with the urban realities of the modern West—wagon trains contrasted with locomotives; a stage coach with a trolley car; horsemen on the dusty street with automobiles on paved city streets—we are greeted with this title card:

> *Has this march of progress killed all the romance—all the thrills? Well, we shall see . . .*

And here is Jeff Hillington (Fairbanks), son of a railroad tycoon. His naïve fantasies of the Wild West inflame his ambitions. Kneeling beside a campfire, wearing chaps and ten-gallon hat, he's turning the pages of a book about the rip-roaring Old West:

> *"The thunderous roll of hoofs, echoing and re-echoing through the narrow gully drowned the noise made by the scout's faithful bronco . . ."*

The camera pulls back to reveal an unexpected scene: His "camp site" in actuality is located inside a room in the family mansion. He's furnished it with Indian blankets and Frederic Remington paintings. He skips around the room, slapping his thighs and lassoes the family butler.

> *"Ah, that's the life!"*

He eyes the Remington painting on the wall of a horseman and imagines it coming to life with himself *inside* the picture, mounting and galloping the mustang around the corral. Downstairs, disturbed by the ruckus, his father exclaims to the butler:

> *"Tell that Comanche Indian that we are due at the office in ten minutes."*

But Jeff lassoes the butler and shouts:

> *"Hang the office, Judson! I'm sick of this life! I want to be out in the West, where there's room to breathe—where the blood runs red in one's veins—and where a six-shooter is a man's best friend!"*

Whereupon he ties up the hapless butler, executes a perfect front flip into a chair while simultaneously firing his six-gun at two mechanical toy snakes, and rides the poor man piggyback down the stairs. On the way, he encounters the maid carrying some flowers for his sister. He scoffs:

> *"That's the way the effete easterner woos his woman. When I find my mate, I'll carry her off with my two bare arms!"*

Outside he spurs his horse through Central Park—

> *Only on Sundays is Jeff's imagination free to turn New York into the Wild and Woolly.*

—and attends the "picture-play West" of the local bijou. Here, appropriately enough,

> *There are places where Jeff's dreams come true.*

We have described this opening sequence in detail because, although it transpires in a matter of minutes, it beautifully encapsulates the whole film. We are prepared for whatever will come, no matter how preposterous, how "wild and woolly," it will be. In its own modest way, Jeff's "ritual reenactments of the frontier experience" echo the theatrical stagings of Buffalo Bill's Wild West entertainments.[35]

Jeff is off to the "daily grind," where his office is decorated with more Indian blankets, Indian paintings, and a Frederic Remington sculpture of a bucking horse (the same sculpture that, along with other Remington sculptures and paintings, will later adorn the Fairbanks home, Pickfair, in Hollywood). Imagine his joy when his father decides to run a spur from the railroad through the little Arizona town of Bitter Creek. He shouts with glee:

> *"Yip, yip, Arizona!"*

The city fathers of Bitter Creek very much desire the railroad spur. Aware of Jeff's Western fantasies, they concoct a plan:

"Young Hillington is a nut on the West. He expects to find this country the same as it was in the eighties. Don't you think we ought to give him what he's waiting for?"

They give the town, in the parlance of today, a "makeover." They transform their tiny, forward-looking town into the rip-roaring counterpart of his dreams. They put up clumsily spelled "authentic" signs for the saloon and hotel, plan a fake railroad holdup and an Indian raid, stage fights on the city streets, etc. When Jeff arrives, he's clad in a New York tailor's wildest fantasy of what a Western outfit should look like. The joke, of course, is that he fits right in. The moment, perhaps, can be likened to the experience of so many other tenderfoots who strayed westward:

> . . . the range came to expect and recognize the "mail-order" cowboy" who arrived already fitted in cowboy wear as he knew it from his reading and the assurances of some Middle Western store-keeper—round, soft hat, blue silk shirt, leather knee-leggings over laced boots, short straight spurs, and a glistening pistol in a "closed scabbard."[36]

As we already know, scenarist Anita Loos always enjoyed peppering her dialogue and expository titles with slang words and expressions. Here, she sends up the sort of rootin-tootin rhetoric of the dime novels of the day. For example, when Jeff meets Nell, The Girl of His Dreams (Eileen Percy), it's love at first sight, of course—and one of the "cowpokes" advises him:

"Take keer of our Nell, pard—she ain't had much book larnin' an' she's had to use alkali for face powder, but her heart's as big as all outdoors."

And of course, there's the inevitable barroom confrontation with one of the "Dirty Ditch" gang, who challenges Jeff:

"There's a train leavin' here at 8 o'clock tonight. You be on it, or I'm a-gunnin' for you!"

Look closely at the sign behind the bar, and you'll find these words:

"Gents will do their killing in the bar and not muss up the parlor."

And when Jeff is advised to steer clear of one "Wild Bill," he's warned:

"He ain't like us, pard. We may take our whiskey straight but we're squar with our women. He ain't."

It's all in good fun, of course, the townspeople satirizing their own western myths. And Jeff, blessed fool, takes it all in with a beatific smile.

Towns like Bitter Creek must have seen their share of exotic transplanted easterners like Jeff. Boom times in the 1870s had brought speculation and an influx of cattlemen and their herds. Unknown to everyone, however, two villains (played by Fairbanks veterans Sam de Grasse and Charles Stevens), who have been selling government supplies stolen from the Indians, exploit the situation to pull off a real train robbery. The farce turns ugly. The mythic Wild West is a reality, after all. Pistols are now loaded with live ammunition instead of blanks. "Real Indians" are employed to keep Jeff and the townspeople trapped in the saloon during the thieves' getaway. Jeff's fantasies have now come to life. Galvanized, he quickly swings into action. In one of Fairbanks's finest trajectories, he escapes the saloon by battering his way through the ceiling with his feet, regains his room, loads his six-guns, climbs out onto the roof, drops to the ground, and jumps onto his horse. In a whirlwind climax, he does some nifty trick riding, thwarts the train robbery, lassoes the villains, rounds up the marauding Indians, and rescues his girlfriend, Nell. He's everywhere at once. And the townspeople, as well as we viewers, are astonished:

"Boy, I don't know whether it's something you learned at school, or if you just happened to pick up the right kind of grandfather, but your equal I've never seen in this territory, and I've been here since seventy-six!"

Jeff is momentarily abashed:

"I know I've been a fool, and I've brought a lot of trouble on you boys, but there's no harm done and I've learned my lesson. So I guess I'd better go back east to my dad's office where I belong! Goodbye!"

One could argue that Jeff's fantasy is really a wish, an expectation for a West that perhaps never was and certainly can never be again, but which now can be fantasy alternative to the stifling push of the industrial East. This is no memory of the past, merely an innocent hope for "a clear conscience unsullied by the past," in the words of R. W. B. Lewis.[37] According to this creed, Lewis explains, Americans have no past, only a present and future, only expectation and vision. Thus, in its own way, *Wild and Woolly* is a film that pursues—and enacts—a vision of innocence and a claim of newness. It is the imagination hungering for freedom, a basic element in the formation of the American experience.

An amusing anecdote beautifully demonstrates how the town of Bitter Creek was itself the nexus of East and West for the enterprising Fairbanks production company. Production assistant Joseph Henabery searched for a location that could, by turns, serve as *both* a modern industrial town and a mythic western cow town. Such a town turned out to be, of all places, Burbank! "Such a place could not be too far from Hollywood," he explains. "I looked at an area map carefully and decided that the city of Burbank, which I knew fairly well was the best located." After persuading the Burbank authorities to turn the town over to the movie company for a week, Henabery hatched his plan:

> I planned to erect the Western effect over the existing modern fronts. To cover the modern oil pavement, I would have to bring in truckloads of earth. Then, when we reverted to the modern town effect, there would be a big job of removing this earth. . . . We intended to employ 100 townspeople as general extras at five dollars each per day.[38]

That's exactly what happened. And so it was that the thriving little town of Burbank, nestled in the San Fernando Valley, switched identities in the twinkling of an eye. It's never been the same since. Never was the frontier between East and West, the boundaries of reality and imagination more provisional, even porous.

In contrast to *Wild and Woolly*, we have seen that *Manhattan Madness* is a film of "memory," where Steve manages to bring the West of his memory and experience back to New York, purging the Big Town of corruption and transforming it into a region of adventure and daring deeds. In a clever turn, the "West" that Steve brings to New York ultimately resembles the "West" that Jeff takes to Arizona in *Wild and Woolly*. Both construct a vital geography, untrammeled, based upon *both* hope and memory, yet heavily laced with irony. Certainly, they seldom remain exclusive territories for very long; rather, they "claim-jump" each other and are transplanted in a series of clever reversals, collisions, and conflations. Wonderful concluding images from both films vividly make the point: Mixing it up at the end of *Manhattan Madness* are Steve's rough-and-ready cowboys and his city sophisticates—their top hats and Stetsons flying through the air. A similar reconciliation of East and West concludes *Wild and Woolly.* A title card asks us:

> *But wait a minute, this will never do! We can't end a Western romance without a wedding. Yet, after they're married, where shall they live?*

And so the last shot of the film answers this question:

> *If Nell likes the East*
> *And Jeff likes the West,*
> *So where will the twain meet?*

Framed in the open doorway of a luxurious mansion, two footmen stand aside as Jeff and Nell, dressed in riding clothes, run outside to greet the cowboys and horses that await them.

The Lost Ones: *The Good Bad Man, Headin' South, Arizona, Knickerbocker Buckaroo*

Four of Fairbanks's westerns are now either totally "lost," survive in only fragmentary form, or hitherto have been generally inaccessible in archives. We can only speculate on what they were like from limited evidence. Two of them belong to the "good bad man" type of stories that Fairbanks would further develop in the costume films of the 1920s, notably *The Mark of Zorro* (1920), *The Thief of Bagdad* (1924), and *The Gaucho* (1927). The first, in order of chronology, is Fairbanks's first western and fourth Triangle release, *The Good Bad Man,* released on May 7, 1916. It was directed by Allan Dwan, photographed by Victor Fleming, and written by Fairbanks himself. Location exteriors included Tucson, Arizona and the Mojave Desert.

Although at this writing efforts are underway to restore *The Good Bad Man* for public viewing, it is still unavailable commercially. In 1923 it was edited, shortened, and rereleased with altered titles. Several versions survive in the Library of Congress and the Cinematheque Francaise. Like many of Fairbanks's films, eastern or western, the story concerns a young man's search for his father. We are reminded that when Douglas was five years old, his father, Charles Ulman, deserted the family. He and his older brother, Robert, were brought up by their mother, who took on the family name of Fairbanks, after her first husband. (Ulman died in 1915, before the release of *The Good Bad Man.*) The theme of a search for a "lost" father is thus especially pertinent to Fairbanks; and we see it again and again, providing him with characters who, on the one hand, are self-starting, forward-looking men yet, on the other, are linked to a mysterious past. Indeed, it's the story of Fairbanks's American century—the search for "legitimacy," weighing the promise of the New World against the experience of the Old.

We are indebted to notes by Dwan's biographer, Frederic Lombardi, for a sense of the action. The story begins with a flurry of hints and flashbacks about a mysterious, black-clad figure known only as "Passin' Through" (Fairbanks), whose "crimes" are in reality a series of pranks to extract money for orphaned children. One old cowboy observes,

> *"Yeah, he's an odd one—always helping kids born in shame."*

At once, a playful tone is established.

We get our first actual glimpse of Passin' when he arrives at Maverick City, a frontier settlement. He promptly rescues Amy (Bessie Love) from the advances of a bandit chief named "The Wolf." Passin' and Amy hit it off, but when she asks about his past, he drops his playful demeanor and says, gravely,

> *"I like to keep two jumps ahead of the law. It helps me to forget. To forget there's no decent way I can make a livin' 'cause I had no father."*

This is our first indication that a darker tone will occasionally color the action.

Actually, Passin' has reason to suspect that his father may be a man named "Bud Fraser" (Sam DeGrasse). If Passin' ever catches up with him, he says—

> *"I'll kill him with my bare hands!"*

Sure enough, Passin' meets a U.S. marshall, Bob Evans, who reveals (in a flashback) that Passin's mother had been rescued from Fraser's advances by a stranger who then married her. A child was born. Fraser returned and killed the father. Back in the present, Passin' tells Amy he is happy to learn that the rascal Fraser is *not* his father:

> *"I just found out I had a regular father! I'm all through being an outlaw."*

A pause for romance in *Headin' South* (1918).

At this point the man known as Wolf returns and kidnaps Amy. In pursuit, Passin' comes across Wolf's abandoned cabin and finds evidence revealing Wolf is actually Bud Fraser. In a series of subsequent skirmishes, Fraser is killed by Sheriff Evans, and Passin', who has rescued Amy, fights off Fraser's gang. A new life now awaits Passin' and Amy. But when she asks him to reveal his real name, his answer is obscured by a concluding shot of the two riding away from the camera.

Enthusiastic views greeted *The Good Bad Man*. The *New York Dramatic Mirror* acknowledged that another Triangle star of westerns, William S. Hart, had found a new rival: "We had supposed that Douglas Fairbanks would be satisfied with his well-earned laurels as a first class screen comedian, but lo and behold, he must now set out and endeavor to take those of William S. Hart." And *Motion Picture World* applauded the vivid Wyoming locations of Dwan and Fleming: "Allan Dwan's direction is first rate, and is nowhere more successful than in his capturing the wide sweep of Western mountain and plain scenery as backgrounds for fights, furious riding, and other thrills." To which Allan Dwan authority Frederic Lombardi adds that

"Fairbanks's frolicsome image," combined with "a more somber drama," permits Fairbanks "to make uninhibited and direct remarks about the sources of his maladjustments without sounding pretentious. The humor notwithstanding, the film remains an early psychological Western."[39]

The second "good bad man" story, *Headin' South*, also made by writer-director Allan Dwan, was released by Artcraft on February 25, 1918. Glen MacWilliams assisted in the photography. The film was dubbed "A Tale of Two Borders" and was filmed on location in Tucson, Arizona. This synopsis is based on a scrap of film that surfaced in an anthology film, *The House that Shadows Built* (1931) and on available newspaper accounts.[40] The story begins when a gambler from the Far North (Frank Campeau) has killed a Canadian Mountie and has fled to Mexico. Now known as "Spanish Joe," he organizes an outlaw band. On his trail is a mysterious stranger known only as "Headin' South" (Fairbanks), who infiltrates the gang. Both Headin' and Spanish Joe are rivals for the favors of a pretty girl (Katherine MacDonald). When the gang decides to raid a nearby town, Headin' reveals himself as an officer of the Northwest Mounted Police. With the aid of a bunch of Texas Rangers, he defends the town and defeats Spanish Joe. He returns to Canada with the girl.

The third "lost" western is *Arizona*, which was released on December 8, 1918. Again, there is little known today about this Artcraft release. Historian Frederic Lombardi disputes that the sole directorial credit should go to Albert Parker, who is listed in contemporary notices. Lombardi cites the December 1918 issue of *Photoplay* magazine that Allan Dwan began the picture but departed when it was half-completed. Lombardi also disproves some allegations that Fairbanks himself played a role in the direction.[41] In any event, Ted Reed adapted the scenario from an 1899 four-act play of the same name by Augustus Thomas (1859–1934). Thomas was one of the most respected dramatists in a transitional period in American drama. *Arizona* was his most popular work, a melodrama set against a southwestern backdrop. It is generally credited with initiating the rage for westerns in the American theatre, leading to such productions as *The Virginian* (1904), *The Girl of the Golden West* (1905), and *Rose of the Rancho* (1906), all of which were adapted to the movies before 1915.

According to contemporary accounts, the screen version of *Arizona* tells the story of attempts by cavalry officer Lieutenant Denton (Fairbanks) to win the love of Bonita Canby (Marjorie Daw), the daughter of a prosperous Arizona rancher. When Denton overhears plans by the wife of the regiment's commander to run away with a fortune hunter, he tries to break up the arrangement. In the process, the regiment commander mistakenly assumes Denton to be the culprit. Rather than reveal the wife's culpability, Denton resigns in disgrace to accept a position as foreman of the Canby ranch. But his "disgrace" follows him and poisons his courtship of Bonita. Meanwhile, the local Indians are inflamed into attacking the ranch, but with the aid of those cavalrymen still loyal to Denton, they are beaten back. Finally, Denton's reputation is restored and he weds Bonita.

We know more about *The Knickerbocker Buckaroo,* the fourth "lost film." It was released in 1919, directed by Albert Parker, cowritten by Joseph Henabery and Ted Reed, and photographed by Glen MacWilliams. It may be the most regrettable loss of all, for a variety of reasons. We are indebted to film historian Frank Thompson, whose research into the film provides us with the most complete account of the film. It was Fairbanks's last release for Artcraft Pictures before turning to United Artists for the remainder of his pictures. By all accounts, *The Knickerbocker Buckaroo* was elaborately mounted with a budget of more than $250,000, far in excess of the average film of 1919. Making his acting debut was William A. Wellman, soon to establish himself as one of Hollywood's top directors (*Wings*, 1928; *Heroes for Sale*, 1933; *Beau Geste*, 1939; The *Oxbow Incident*, 1943; *The Story of G.I. Joe*, 1945). "It's a real rip-snorter," wrote R. W. Baremore in the *Exhibitors' Trade Review* on June 7, 1919; "packed to overflowing with the Fairbanks brand of good humor, stunts, and rapid-fire action, this is a thoroughly worthwhile picture in every way, clean, snappy fun and thrills."

Thompson reconstructs the film, based upon a surviving scenario and some of the film's original subtitles. Fairbanks again essays the familiar role of a wealthy young New York clubman, Teddy Drake, who goes west to redeem himself from charges of being indulgent and self-centered. To put a fine point on it, he is expelled:

> *TEDDY: "Judge! What is the matter with me?"*
> *FATHER: "You are inconsiderate of others."*
> *TITLE CARD: And that starts Teddy Drake thinking and wanting to do something for somebody.*

Teddy determines to better himself:

> *"I've got a hunch, Mother, that if I hurl myself out into the seething world, swim with the current, pick myself up where I land, and go to it—all will be Jake."*

He purchases a Pullman ticket:

> *"Measure off eighty-eight dollars and sixteen cents worth of railroad ticket going west."*

Off he goes on the train, where he unsuccessfully attempts a few good deeds. He helps an old lady off the train, for example, but mistakenly returns to the wrong train. He asks the African-American porter if this is the "Limited." The man's response is couched in the racist rhetoric typical of the day:

> *"No, sah, it's de limit. Dis train hesitates at every li'l place between heah and de Mexican bawdah."*

His luggage gone, Teddy acquires clothing from a Mexican, Manuel Lopez (Albert McQuarrie), not realizing the man is a wanted fugitive from the law. At a stop in Sonora, Teddy is mistaken for the bandit and thrown into jail by a dishonest sheriff (Frank Campeau). There he meets a young lady, Rita (in some accounts referred to as "Mercedes"), who is being robbed by the sheriff. It's love at first sight:

> *"I've been looking for a girl like you for years, but I never thought of looking in jails."*

Teddy escapes and leads his pursuers in a wild chase over the rooftops and down the streets of the town. Finally captured by the sheriff, Teddy is back in jail. *Again*, however, he escapes, and this time is saved from lynching by none other than Lopez. Immediately, Teddy heads for an old Spanish mission, where Rita has hidden her money. He finds it surrounded by the sheriff and his gang. In a furious battle, he holds them off until a U.S. marshall arrives and apprehends the villains. All is well in the end, and Teddy and the girl are united. He tells her, ironically:

> *"I've been trying my doggondest to be unselfish and see what it brought me—* you, *you wonderful girl!"*

Researcher Thompson writes: "Fairbanks's existing action comedies during the last years of [the teens] look better and better all the time. The odds seem excellent that *The Knickerbocker Buckaroo* and other lost Fairbanks films . . . would be just as funny and exciting and memorable as Doug meant them to be—if we could only get one more look at them."[42]

Amen.

A "Western" Aristocracy

As we have seen, all of Fairbanks's western characters, like the urban heroes of his contemporary comedies, triumph through moral values, rugged individualism, and physical fitness. His westerners succeed because they are *good at what they do*. They display extraordinary, even preternatural energies and accomplishments. To clarify what this means, we turn again to Owen Wister's *The Virginian*: The character of Judge Henry is a spokesperson for the new western aristocracy. "If you go to try a thing on in this Western country," he explains, "you've got to do it *well*. You've got to deal cyards [*sic*] *well* . . . And if you claim to be quick with your gun, you must be quick, for you're a public temptation, and some man will not resist trying to prove he is the quicker. You must break all the Commandments *well* in this Western country."[43] This upholds, the judge continues, nothing less than the Declaration of Independence, which in actuality "acknowledged the *eternal inequality* of man." He explains:

> "We decreed that every man should thenceforth have equal liberty to find his own level. By this very decree we acknowledged and gave freedom to true aristocracy, saying, 'Let the best man win, whoever he is.' Let the best man win! That is America's word. That is true democracy."

Thus, the judge concludes, our "true democracy" is one and the same with "true aristocracy": "If anybody cannot see this, so much the worse for his eyesight."[44]

The Open Door

Fairbanks never really stopped making westerns. The great costume swashbucklers of the 1920s, especially the two "Zorro" films of 1920 and 1925 and *The Gaucho* of 1927, display many of the same tropes and energies, even if they are epic-scale costume productions rooted in the past in Old World historical settings. (See the later chapters on the "Costume Films."[45])

The territorial, social, and cultural ambivalence Fairbanks maintained in all his films is very much his own shifting "frontier." At his home in Beverly Hills, "Pickfair," he presided with Mary Pickford over his own Hollywood aristocracy, transplanting eastern Old World style to western shores. European royalty and American cowboys—many of whom had ridden with Wild West shows and rodeos—came together to take tea and ride horseback, to doff top hats and don Stetsons. At dawn his guests would follow him on horseback to Coyote Canyon, where they traded tall tales, hunkered down at the campfire, and munched chuck wagon vittles.

Indeed, the doors of that royal seat, Pickfair, like those at the conclusion of *Wild and Woolly*, opened out onto the Wild West of his dreams.[46]

Chapter 4

"*Her* Picture in the Papers"

Mary Pickford's "Growing Girl"

I'd never really known what it meant to be a child. I sometimes feel that my only real childhood was lived through the many children's roles I played, even into adulthood.
—**MARY PICKFORD**

Between 1914–1918, Douglas Fairbanks and Mary Pickford became the first major stage stars to score international success in the movies. Coming from Broadway, they had both brought the prestigious aura of the stage to a new medium with global appeal. Working individually and collectively as part of the Artcraft Pictures Corporation—and later as partners in United Artists—they personified a new American century bursting with youth, energy, and enterprise. Unlike many of their older screen contemporaries, writes cultural historian Lary May, these "extremely talented figures," so full of "cosmopolitan fun and healthy beauty replaced the spiritual symbolism connected to [William S.] Hart or [D. W.] Griffith characters."[1]

Just as Fairbanks was constructing the masculinity of a new American century, May continues, "Pickford questioned the female role at work and in the family. Over and over again she portrayed women striving to be economically free and morally emancipated. . . . She pioneered new trails for women into the domains of men . . . and made the Horatio Alger aspiration viable for women." Like Fairbanks, she was also "a model of vitality, and a boundless force that could not be confined to one place or social station." Again, like Fairbanks, she was joyous and spontaneous "who brought into her personality that which Victorians had repressed: the playfulness of childhood." And "with a 'girl' like Pickford, men such as Fairbanks could

Mary Pickford.

find an emancipated woman whose brief years of freedom gave her an alluring veneer that promised to revitalize his life."[2]

Pickford's "playfulness of childhood" commands our attention at this point. Her screen image provides a vivid counterpoint and complement to the man who soon would be her husband.

"I always study a part very carefully and try to get into the spirit of the child I am to portray," commented Mary Pickford in a July 1918 interview in *Motion Picture Classic*. "The costume, dressing the character, means a lot. You know, when I'm dressed as a child, I never walk. I always skip or run. Funny how one feels a character when . . . dressed for the part. You just naturally lose your own identity."

Within the last two years, the twenty-six-year-old Mary Pickford had achieved international celebrity, appearing in screen adaptations of several classic children's novels and stories: Eleanor Gates's *The Poor Little Rich Girl* (1912), Kate Douglas Wiggin's *Rebecca of Sunnybrook Farm* (1903), Frances Hodgson Burnett's *A Little Princess* (1903), William J. Locke's *Stella Maris* (1913), Belle K. Maniates's *Amarilly of Clothes-Line Alley* (1915), and Bret Harte's *M'liss* (1868). In the next two years, she would consolidate that fame with film adaptations of Jean Webster's *Daddy Long Legs* (1912) and Eleanor H. Porter's *Pollyanna* (1913). They instantly eclipsed the popularity of her earlier films, most of which had featured her in adult roles.[3] Audiences (if not the critics), notes biographer Robert Windeler, were delighted to discover the "Little Mary" of the long, backlighted blonde curls, "in Tattered-Tom clothes, a sometimes smudged face, and with no visible breasts."[4] Now, at the zenith of her career, Pickford's little-girl roles were making her the highest paid, most recognized, most idolized, and most powerful female in the entertainment business.

Pickford's own girlhood was anything but normal. Gladys Smith (as she was then known) was only five when her father died, leaving her and her mother and two siblings penniless. Her beauty, precocity, and determination soon led her to the stage, where as a mere child she quickly found herself the family's breadwinner. "A determination was born in me . . . that nothing could crush," she remembered in her autobiography, *Sunshine and Shadow* (1955). "I must try to take my father's place in some mysterious way and prevent anything from breaking up my family."[5] Dozens of stage plays—including her definitive portrayal at age nine of "Little Eva" in *Uncle Tom's Cabin*[6]—and hundreds of motion pictures later, and after graduating from the tutelage of stage impresario David Belasco and film director D. W. Griffith, she found herself in her mid-twenties acclaimed for doing what she had by now learned to do only too well. "I'd never really known what it meant to be a child," she recalled. "I sometimes feel that my only real childhood was lived through the many children's roles I played, even into adulthood."[7]

The Poor Little Rich Girl was released by Artcraft/ Paramount on March 5, 1917, just a month before Fairbanks released his first Artcraft film, *In Again—Out Again*. It was, as biographer Scott Eyman declares, "a landmark film for Mary, one that exercised a major influence over the rest of her career."[8] Her eleven-year-old Gwendolyn marked her first attempt on screen to portray a girl so young.[9] This "was an entirely new Mary Pickford," noted the *Exhibitor's Trade Review*;[10] and in *Photoplay Journal* for April 1917, commentator Bert D. Essex wrote, "It is pretty well agreed among the erudite that this is the best part she ever created before the camera." (33)[11] Whereas hitherto a character like Little Eva had been the exemplar of Victorian sentimentality—the child whose greatest act, according to cultural historian Ann Douglas in *The Feminization of American Culture*, was to die a saint—the hyper-sensitive, sickly Gwendolyn had the good sense to develop into a normal, healthy child.[12] Gwendolyn, along with the titular characters in the aforementioned books and films, was the epitome of the American "growing girl." She epitomized the child in transition from the relative brevity and innocence of girlhood to the complications of adolescence. She was practical, high-spirited, independent, and, above all, an imaginative creature determined not to become a victim of the adult world's miseries and inequities, but, in the best pragmatic spirit, to confront them on her own terms.

Audiences loved Pickford and they loved Gwendolyn. However, to Pickford's growing dismay, they began to confuse the two. "Every now and then," she said in her autobiography, *Sunshine and Shadow*, "as the years went by and I continued to play children's roles, it would worry me that I was becoming a personality instead of an actress. I would suddenly resent the fact that I had allowed myself to be hypnotized by the public into remaining a little girl."[13] However, practical businesswoman that she was—producer Adolph Zukor referred to her as "The Bank of America's Sweetheart"—Mary knew she had to cater to her fans. As will be noted later in this book, she continued to play little-girl roles well into her maturity, even when it meant artificially diminishing her mature figure by trussing her chest, creating oversized props and sets, and casting tall actors opposite her.

Unfortunately, it has become fashionable among many commentators and scholars—most of whom seemingly have not had the opportunity to see her pictures—to dismiss Pickford's "growing girl" films as disposable relics of a vanished popular culture.[14] Their whimsies, frivolities, sentiments, even their very popularity—not to mention the possibly perverse fact that an adult woman is portraying little girls—served only to hasten their lapse into obscurity upon Mary's retirement from the screen in 1934. Nothing was left, it seemed, but the ghost—or was it only a memory?—of her dimpled, Cheshire-cat smile. In her last years, Pickford herself regarded her films as hopelessly old-fashioned and was restrained only at the last minute from burning the negatives.[15]

Recently, however, the arrival of several new book-length studies of Pickford and her contemporaries—including Eyman's book; Cari Beauchamp's biography of Pickford's scenarist, Frances Marion, *Without Lying Down* (1997); Eileen Whitfield's *Pickford: The Woman Who Made Hollywood* (1998); Kevin Brownlow's *Mary Pickford Rediscovered* (1999); and Jeanine Basinger's *Silent Film Actors* (1999)—and the restoration and release of selected features on film and video formats by Milestone Films in New York City, in association with the Mary Pickford Foundation, demands a reconsideration of her "growing girl" films.

The process begins first by locating these films within their original cultural contexts. Just as little serious inquiry has been made into Pickford's "growing girl" films, a comparable lack of critical attention has been directed toward the emergence of the "growing girl" image in the second half of the nineteenth century that gave birth to them. Lynne Vallone in *Disciplines of Virtue: Girls' Culture in the Eighteenth and Nineteenth Centuries*, argues "that the study of girls' culture and girls' reading is crucial to our understanding of femininity, women's history and literature, and ideologies of domesticity, conduct, and class."[16] Yet many cultural historians and feminist scholars seem to have failed to examine this phenomenon. As Beverly Lyons Clark says in her survey of the subject, "Fairy Godmothers or Wicked Stepmothers?": "Feminists who theorize marginality have paid virtually no attention to the position of children. Such feminist and culture critics often address race, gender, and class. But not age, not children."[17] Along with the much-needed proliferation of books and articles treating topics like postcolonialism and queer theory, there should also be, as Vallone suggests, "youth studies within the model set up by cultural studies wherein we examine literary, cultural, and ideological practices of childhood and adolescence."[18] Graham Greene acknowledges particularly the need for a serious examination of the books that were being written for and about children: "Perhaps it is only in childhood that books have any deep influence on our lives. But in childhood all books are books of divination, telling us about the future, and like the fortune teller who sees a long journey in the cards or death by water, they influence the future."[19]

The "growing girl" paradigm does not appear in American popular culture until after 1840. The social roles previously assigned females in general, notes Alfred Habegger in his book, *Gender, Fantasy, and Realism in American Literature*, had "led them to assume responsibility for the care of others, embody the finer feelings and discriminations, function as vicars of Christ in a coarse, ungodly world, and aspire to a high, self-sacrificial way of living." Indeed, this so-called "Cult of the True Woman" offered little distinction between the girl and the woman.[20] The point in cultural history where childhood and adulthood assumed separate and opposed distinctions began late in the eighteenth century with the post-revolutionary social, political, and philosophical shifts that counterposed the presumed natural innocence of childhood to the corrupt experience of adulthood.[21] The child, especially the girl, was no longer regarded as a diminutive adult but a self-active soul endowed with natural tendencies to virtue which needed careful nourishment.

Thus, the sentimental domestic novels—written by women for women—that had been dominating the middle-class literary market began to be supplemented by growing numbers of conduct books and juvenile literature targeted specifically for children. Wielded by those moral conscience keepers, women, and clergymen, these instruction guides demonstrated a national desire for stability and stasis in the social order. While titles like Catherine Maria Sedgwick's *Means and Ends; or, Self-Training* (1839) and *Morals of Manners; or, Hints for Our Young People* (1846), as well as the anonymous *Young Girl's Book of Healthful Amusements and Exercises* (1840), were duly filled with images of order, cooperation, and sober attention to duty and conscience, they also introduced a new pragmatism in the socialization of young women.[22] Out of the passivity of the Cult of True Womanhood was emerging the activism of the Ideal of *Real* Womanhood—or, more pertinent to my study, the "Ideal of the *Real* Girl" (a term used by Lynne Vallone throughout her book, *Disciplines of Virtue*, and which I shall use interchangeably with the term "growing girl").

Young females were encouraged to be practical, productive, and physically fit. This popular, middle-of-the-road image addressed in a "feminine" way the social inequities being protested by early feminists. The domestic ideal held out to young women, notes Vallone, no longer meant that she was to be sequestered from the world in her palace; her influence could now reach past the front door. Putting it another way, her domestic authority would take the home out into the world, and "everybody was to be placed in the home, and hence home and the world would become one."[23] Physical culture, as it would soon be playing a part in the preachments of Roosevelt and the strenuous sermons of Fairbanks and Billy Sunday, was playing a role in this process. The Angel of the House was going outside for a good, long walk, as it were. For example, *The Young Girls' Book of Healthful Amusements and Exercises* contained drawings of young women performing calisthenics, prefiguring the formation in 1912 of the Girl Scouts of America, whose avowed aim was to bring girls out of their cloistered home environments to serve in their communities and experience the open air. "For the girls who were to become pillars of their home, maintaining a healthy body and mind was considered a moral duty."[24]

American novelists, mostly female, in the second half of the nineteenth century quickly took up the Real Girl as a character type. In her study of such works, "Popular Culture and the Romantic Heroine," Beatrice K. Hofstadter cites a number of modest "underground rebellions" by a succession of orphaned, or disadvantaged girls against the sentimental ideal of Sacred Womanhood in the works of Susan B. Warner—particularly *The Wide, Wide World* (1850) and the novels of Augusta Evans Wilson, like *St.*

Elmo (1867). "Despite [their] seeming conventionality," writes Hofstadter, "[these books] made a subtle but far-reaching change in the accepted view of the tension between love and duty, between individual inclination and parental authority."[25] And, of course, there is the model of Jo March, the quintessential "tomboy" of post-Civil War American literature in Louisa Mae Alcott's *Little Women* (1868).[26]

The "growing girl" books that Mary Pickford adapted to the screen in 1917–1920 were authored by her direct contemporaries, a younger generation of social, cultural, and educational reformers, most of whom were women. Kate Douglas Wiggin, Jean Webster, Frances Hodgson Burnett, William J. Locke, Eleanor H. Porter, Belle K. Maniates, and Eleanor Gates packaged their fables of cultural, social, and educational interrogation in a clear, accessible, and vivid prose targeted especially for girls and adolescents. Their young protagonists, most of whom were orphans or, at the very least, products of dysfunctional family situations, all sought to find and establish the "home" they had never known from the wreckage of an unjust or uncaring society into which they had been thrust. Their success depended upon channeling their imagination, aggression, humor, self-sufficiency, and physical energies into a productive and valuable—yet womanly—conduct.[27]

Kate Douglas Wiggin's delineation of the titular *Rebecca of Sunnybrook Farm* (1903), and its sequel, *The New Chronicles of Rebecca* (1907), was, in the words of contemporary commentator Grant Overton, a "triumph of naturalness, a perfect fidelity to the life of the child."[28] Ten-year-old Rebecca Rowena Randall was "generous, romantic, resourceful, and brighter than her surroundings—a person it does us all good to know."[29] Wiggin, herself a suffragette and progressive educator, invested this tale of "the makin' of Rebecca" (as several characters phrase it) with her own ideas of educational reform.[30] The field of education was regarded at the time as the most productive area for feminine influence. "Classroom control of America's primary-school system was as surely the divine prerogative of their sex as absolute sway over their children's unformed souls," writes Ann Douglas. "Over the course of the nineteenth century, women gradually came to constitute the overwhelming majority of grade-school teachers in America's public and private schools, a feat they accomplished in no other country."[31] Wiggin makes it clear that early instruction is necessary for Rebecca: "the soul grows into lovely habits as easily as into ugly ones, and the moment a life begins to blossom into beautiful words and deeds, that moment a new standard of conduct is established" (184).

Thus, as Rebecca moves from school to school, she gradually realizes her talents for art and literature and envisions a future for herself as a teacher and writer. The death of family members, however, alters her plans. At seventeen, she relinquishes her dreams and returns home. But this is no happy reversion to the ideal of True Womanhood. Author Wiggin has already pointedly noted that Rebecca had "no aspirations toward being an angel of the house" (5). The novel ends on a wistfully elegiac note: "How brief, how fleeting, had been those splendid visions when the universe seemed open for her young strength to battle and triumph in! How soon they had faded into the light of common day!" (269–70).

The character of Judy Abbott, in Jean Webster's *Daddy-Long-Legs* and its sequel, *Dear Enemy* (1915), shares many affinities with Rebecca.[32] Although older at the story's outset—she is seventeen—she is an athletic, self-willed person who must employ a sturdy, creative imagination to survive hard times (she has grown up as a foundling in a strictly disciplined orphanage) and to realize her most cherished ambition: to become a published author. The story is told in the form of Judy's letters to her anonymous benefactor, "Daddy-Long-Legs," which are filled with references to her ongoing education and, in particular, to the many books she is reading (many of which feature strong female heroines, as in *Jane Eyre* and *Portrait of a Lady*). At the story's conclusion, as she stands poised on the brink of fulfilled love with her benefactor, she writes, in typical Real Girl spirit: "When I first came to college, I felt quite resentful because I'd been robbed of the normal kind of childhood that the other girls had had; but now, I don't feel that way in the least. I regard it as a very unusual adventure. It gives me a sort of vantage point from which to stand aside and look at life. Emerging full-grown, I get a perspective on the world that other people who have been brought up in the thick of things entirely lack."[33]

Like Rebecca and Judy, young Sara Crewe in Frances Hodgson Burnett's *A Little Princess* (1903) is gifted with a wild, precocious imagination. In the words of wicked Miss Minchin, the schoolmistress, "she is always dreaming and thinking of odd things . . . as if she had lived a long, long time."[34] Burnett's book is intensely autobiographical. As Marian E. Brown notes, "Sara's loss of her father; her triumph over adversity through her wits, imagination, and storytelling abilities; and her ability to remain as unembittered by hardship as she is unspoilt by wealth all reflect Burnett's own travails and victories."[35] Thus, Burnett is able to regard Sara with a mixture of sentiment and clinical detachment. "Mrs. Burnett's child heroes and heroines act and think like *children* [italics mine]," writes

Rosemary Threadgold, "rather than scaled-down adults. . . . They are not always approved of by adults, are sometimes not liked by other children, and are by no means always attractive physically. . . . Generally, the children have some failing with which a child reader might identify, as well as some good qualities that might inspire emulation."[36]

Bret Harte's character of "M'liss" appeared on the literary scene in 1868 at the same time as that other famous tomboy, Jo March. Perhaps because Harte was an educator and the father of daughters, and scornful that so many children's stories gave all the heroic enterprises to boys, he cast strong women and girls in many of his stories, notably "Miggles" and "M'liss."[37] A wild, unkempt orphan of the Sierra Nevada mountains, M'liss is distinguished by "great black eyes, her coarse, uncombed, lustreless black hair falling over her sunburned face, her red arms and feet streaked with the red soil."[38] She bests the boys in fights and follows trails with a woodsman's craft. But above all, she hungers for an education, and she impresses the local schoolmaster with her innate precocity: "She knew neither the hesitancy nor the doubts of childhood. . . . Her courage and daring in passing beyond her own depth and that of the floundering little swimmers around her . . . outweighed all errors of judgment" (92). In the end, after the passing of several years, now matured and transformed into an educated young woman, she marries the schoolmaster.

M'liss is the Real Girl going through a tomboy phase on the way to womanhood. As Alfred Habegger notes in *Gender, Fantasy, and Realism in American Literature,* the tomboy figure offered to writers the saving grace of humor and physicality otherwise denied to their True Woman characters. Indeed, writers like Grace Greenwood, Fanny Fern, Elizabeth Stuart Phelps, Mary Jane Holmes, and Louisa May Alcott reserved their best humor for tomboy stories. Laughter was associated with the naturalness of the young. "Girlhood, often seen as the golden age before long dresses or corsets, was the free time."[39] In many of these books the girls are orphans who must affect masculine dress and behavior in order to survive in a man's world.

Pollyanna Whittier in Eleanor H. Porter's *Pollyanna* (1913) and its sequel, *Pollyanna Grows Up* (1915), embodied the belief that life holds up pleasures enough to offset the worst misfortunes.[40] The indomitable spirit of this orphaned and friendless eleven-year-old child changes and brightens the lives of those around her, even if her now-infamous "Glad Game"—the hunt for happiness and beauty in the face of misery and ugliness—has aroused critical controversy ever since. Whereas one editorial of the day applauded the Glad Game, noting that "it is probably not putting the case too strongly when we state that it is the greatest game ever discovered since the foundation of the world," another, more recent assessment complained that "Pollyanna Whittier is possibly the most exasperating heroine in fiction. . . . She seems the epitome of everything that is priggish and sentimental."[41] Author Porter herself defended the little girl's buoyant optimism: "I have never believed we ought to deny discomfort and pain and evil; I have merely thought it is far better to 'greet the unknown with a cheer.'"[42]

But perhaps the most perceptive analysis of the Glad Game came from Grace Isabel Colbron in a 1915 issue of *The Bookman*, describing Pollyanna as "the supreme nonconformist" and "one of the most cunning tricksters to appear in American children's books since Tom Sawyer."[43] Indeed, Pollyanna is something of a con artist. Like the characters to come in Fairbanks's *The Matrimaniac* and *The Habit of Happiness*, she resembles "Innocent Smith" in Chesterton's novel, *Manalive*, written just three years before, in that she ruthlessly bends everyone toward her own strenuous rediscoveries of life's smiling aspects.

These "glad games" of Pickford and Fairbanks are actually a canny blend *en miniature* of two prevailing attitudes in the new American century just before the Great War, the "practical idealism" of Herbert Spencer's Social Darwinism, and the advocacy of social change in Lester Frank Ward's Reform Darwinism. Pollyanna is, if nothing else, very pragmatic. She doesn't look past the sordid world to a brighter sphere to find consolation for her miserable state; she merely looks around her. She keeps her ideals accessible. She measures her values in relative terms. Experience, not fine-spun theory, is the best proof that the universe is moral. Moreover, acceptance of the good and bad in life is only a brief rest stop on the way to *change*. Thus, Pollyanna strikes the sort of balance that, according to Henry May in *The End of American Innocence*, perfectly strikes the modern temper of men and women of the day: "Certainly the average American of 1912 considered himself an idealist, and meant by this [someone] who believed in unseen goals and standards. He also considered himself a realist, which meant to him a practical man who took account of difficulties."[44]

William J. Locke's *Stella Maris* (1913) is the most unusual entry in this catalogue. It presents not one but two Real Girls.[45] It reminds us that Pickford—and Fairbanks, too, for that matter—frequently portrayed dual characters who were polar opposites. Here, the "cockney slavey" Unity Blake and the rich, aristocratic Stella Maris are two sides of the same coin.

Whereas ugly, deformed Unity—"this fatalistic child of circumstance"[46]—has endured too much of the sordid, real world (she has survived the loss of both parents to alcohol and prison, grown up in a squalid orphanage, and been brutally abused in the home of her employer), beautiful young Stella Maris, because of an infirmity that has left her bedridden, has been shielded from the miserable realities of the world. "Stella's room was sacrosanct. An invisible spirit guarded the threshold and forbade entrance to anything evil or mean or sordid or even sorrowful" (5). As a result of a string of circumstances that bring Unity and Stella together, each will grow and change in distinctively different ways. Over the next several years, Stella's regaining of the ability to walk confronts her with experiences that are disillusioning. "But a cloud hung heavy for a long time over her spirits," writes Locke in his characteristically overripe prose, "and a stain soiled the beauty of the garden, so that it never more was the perfect paradise" (178). Consequently, her lover, John Risca, can no longer idealize her as a "child of cloud and mystery" but must recognize her as a mature young woman, a "sweet and palpitating wonder in a marvel of flesh and blood" (179). And Unity's stoic inability to act or think for herself—"the possibility of revolt, of assertion of her own individuality, was undreamed of in her narrow philosophy" (92)—is transformed by her association with Stella Maris into a quest for justice against the woman who had abused her—a quest that ends in murder and suicide.

The story of Amarilly Jenkins in Belle K. Maniates's *Amarilly of Clothes-Line Alley* (1915) is both a variant of *Pollyanna* and a backwater version of the Pygmalion fable.[47] Leaning against her mop and bucket while scrubbing floors, she sighs, "Oh, I wonder if I couldn't rise!"[48] Even if she never achieves her ambition to be a great stage actress, she profits from the tutelage of several adults around her, including a society matron, a minister, and a painter. Just as she loses her street vernacular and rough manners, so she gains friends with her sturdy pragmatism: "I'm glad [things are] so dirty. It's more interestin' to clean a dirty place. Then what you do shows up, and you feel you earnt your money" (87). Ironically, as she loses her gamin-like ways, her painter friend realizes he must require her to "act the part" of a scrub girl. "Now try and put your whole mind on the memory of the horror you felt at the accumulation of dirt on that first day, and begin to scrub" (179). Amarilly is an actress, after all. How apt this is! It is coincidentally a commentary on an actress like Mary Pickford, who would make a career out of acting the part of the miserable, exploited, impoverished child she once was.

It is uncanny, by the way, how these protagonists seem to prefigure the archetypal Pickford screen image to come. They convey the characteristic pose, expression, hairstyle, even the style of lighting she had developed with her cameramen Walter Stradling and Charles Rosher (backlighting to bring out highlights in her curls and the use of baby spotlights to enhance points of light in her blue eyes). Just a few examples of this "look" will suffice: in *Rebecca of Sunnybrook Farm*, we are told that "under her delicately etched brows [her eyes] glowed like two stars, their dancing light half hidden in lustrous darkness" (10); in *Stella Maris*, Stella is "a slip of pale girlhood, startling black and white, with her mass of soft hair beneath the plain, black hat and her great pools of eyes. . . aglow with remote flames" (337); and in *Amarilly*, the painter Derry Phillips sets up Amarilly's pose with instructions that sound for all the world like a movie director placing Pickford before the camera—"You shall stand at this window with your hair as it is now. . . . I will get a filmy, white dress for you to pose in. . . . and as you half turn your head toward the window, you must have a dreamy, reflective expression. You must think of something sad, something that might have been a tragedy." (180). These words are veritable stage directions for the Mary Pickford films to come.

Stage adaptations of these and other related stories appeared early in the twentieth century and bring us closer to Pickford's screen incarnations.[49] At precisely the same time Eleanor Gates was writing her own dramatization of *Poor Little Rich Girl* in 1913, a flood of "growing girl" plays—melodramas, fairy tales, musicals, pantomimes—were attracting popular and critical attention. Clayton Hamilton in *Everybody's Magazine* reported:

> Although we have had many plays for children in the past, most of them have been produced singly and have been regarded as unusual events; but in this season, for the first time, a concerted effort has been made by several different managers to develop in the rising generation a habit of going regularly to the theater.[50]

Burnett's *A Little Princess* was enjoying yet another revival—the latest of many since its first theatrical incarnation in 1901—and her *Racketty-Packetty House* (1906) was playing under the auspices of George C. Tyler's Children's Theatre. Youngsters were treated to Winthrop Ames's production of *Snow White and the Seven Dwarfs* (soon to be made into a movie starring Marguerite Clark); David Belasco's production of *A Good Little Devil* (starring Mary Pickford); and Arthur Hopkins's presentation of Eleanor Gates's own adaptation of *Poor Little Rich Girl.* "A new opportunity will be afforded to writers for the stage," opined Hamilton prophetically, "and, if the vein is not overworked, the juvenile drama should become as important an item in the annual commerce of the theatre as juvenile literature has always been in the annual lists of the leading publishers."[51]

This prophecy was borne out in the subsequent "growing girl" films of Mary Pickford. Since space does not permit a detailed study of all the titles heretofore mentioned, *The Poor Little Rich Girl* has been selected as their best representative. It will be necessary to track it through its successive incarnations of novel, stage play, and, finally, film.

The original novel version of *The Poor Little Rich Girl,* is, by any standard, a remarkable achievement, and its neglect today is unfortunate. It is a passionately felt cautionary tale of the consequences of adult and parental neglect of children, told entirely through the viewpoint of seven-year-old Gwendolyn. As a study in restricted viewpoint, the original novel resembles, in its own modest way, Henry James's *What Maisie Knew,* written fifteen years earlier. Leon Edel's observations about *Maisie* are especially pertinent here:

> [*What Maisie Knew*] dramatised not only the responsibilities of adults for the children they bring into the world by showing instances of gross irresponsibility; they reveal a highly modern insight into the dilemma of children deprived of common affection, turned into pawns, exposed to sensations and impressions which most adults have forgotten. No writer, in all the history of the novel, was more attuned to the particular "awareness" of children; and few writers have been as actively concerned . . . with the question of what a child "learns."[52]

Structured like *Maisie, Poor Little Rich Girl* is a series of scenes in which the reader's view of the situations and the characters is limited to the parameters of Gwendolyn's own perceptions and understanding. The miracle is that the reader, while cognizant only of what Gwendolyn sees and hears, is able to construct a reality that is quite beyond the child's understanding. Again, Edel's description of Maisie is apt:

> She lives in a fragmented world and all of her developing intelligence and her need for emotional stability are directed to putting the fragments together in some reasonable order: the reasonableness being that of an alert little

> girl confronted with an unusual degree of adult instability and adult folly. [Maisie's curiosity and imagination] endow her shabby, tawdry world with the magic of a story in *The Arabian Nights*—or the discontinuity of the magic lantern.[53]

The "trick," as James himself noted in describing this method of narrative viewpoint, is to maintain the innocence of the child while making the reader aware of the surrounding evil: "Make my point of view, my *line*, the consciousness, the dim, sweet, scared, wondering, clinging perception of the child."[54] Elsewhere, he noted, "Small children have many more perceptions than they have terms to translate them. Their vision is at any moment much richer, their apprehension even constantly stronger, than their prompt, their all producible vocabulary."[55]

Little Gwendolyn is impatient with her young life. She's just turned seven, and she's not grown a fraction of an inch since she last measured herself. She lives in a gilded cage, an upper room kept well away from her parents and from the adult activities downstairs. Her view of the outside world is restricted to what she can see through her window—a vague collection of houses across the way with their peek-a-boo windows, a passing policeman, and an organ grinder. She's not allowed to attend public school, but is instead tutored at home by a retinue of private teachers. Her mother is always involved in her own social functions, and her father is buried downtown in his business deals. They don't even allow her to dine with them on the occasion of her birthday. Instead, she's trotted downstairs and exhibited to the guests like a museum display. After lisping a brief "hello" and executing a polite curtsey to each guest, she steals a moment to whisper a pathetic request to her mother: "Would you come up to the nursery soon?"[56]

The servants offer little solace or company. Miss Royle, the governess, is bossy and cold; Thomas the butler is preoccupied with his love life; and Jane the nurse would rather go shopping. They refuse her every wish—to wear plain, plaid dresses instead of fussy white muslin, to go outdoors barefoot, and to have second helpings of food. They confine her to the shuttered limousine during outings. "The limousine meant a long, tiresome run at good speed through streets that she longed to travel afoot, slowly, with a stop here and a stop there, and a poke into things in general" (16). To warn her further against venturing outdoors on her own, they fill her head with bloodcurdling tales of kidnappers waiting in ambush for rich kids, and fearsome bears that roam the downtown streets. These restrictions are not for Gwendolyn's own good so much as they allow the servants more time for their own activities. When Gwendolyn protests that she wants to be allowed to go to day school, the governess replies, "So me and Thomas are to be thrown out of our jobs, are we?" (31)

What the child perceives is a mysterious code-speak among the adults, intended to deflect her own proper understanding of things. "As a rule, when gossip or criticism was talked in her hearing, it was insured against being understood by the use of strange terms, spellings, winks, nods, shrugs, or sudden stops at the most important point" (48–49). For example, in one of the book's most striking scenes, Gwendolyn accidentally overhears a conversation among her mother's society guests whose meanings, while beyond her understanding, are perfectly comprehensible to the reader—that her mother "has got the society bee in her bonnet" and that her father is "in harness" to his business and "burns the candle at both ends." Worse, "a little bird" has told these gossipers that her father is on the edge of a financial "crash." "It's the usual story," clucks one woman, "with these *nouveaux riches*" (50–51). At this point, Gwendolyn's presence is discovered and the guests not so subtly suggest that she not repeat the conversation to her parents.

One day the nurse mistakenly gives Gwendolyn a double-dose of medicine. She lapses into a state of semi-consciousness. And she dreams. . . . Well, it is a remarkable dream, and it occupies fully half the novel. A series of puns and slang expressions overheard by Gwendolyn come to fantastic life. In this protracted sequence author Gates deploys many of the effects of a motion picture. For example, the prose describes events "coming to pass in a pleasantly instantaneous fashion" (188), and when Gwendolyn awakens out of her dream world near the end of the story, the effect is like a lap dissolve: "the glow that filled the Land now seemed suddenly to soften. The clustered tapers had lessened—to a single chandelier of four globes. Next, the forest trees began to flatten and take on the appearance of a conventional pattern. The grass became ruglike in smoothness. The sky squared itself to the proportions of a ceiling" (227).

Meanwhile, all the things Gwendolyn had overheard—but not understood—come to literal life in her dream, metaphors clothed in shape and substance—such as Jane having "eyes in the back of her head," of the policeman being "head over heels" in love with Jane, of her mother's bee in the bonnet," of her father's "burning the candle at both ends," of the organ grinder's "making faces," and of Miss Royle being a "snake in the grass." Gwendolyn greets this strange new landscape with joy: "[It] brought the realization of all her new good fortune—the being out of doors and plainly clad; free from the espionage of a governess; away from the tyranny of a motorcar; barefoot; and—chief blessing of all! *nurseless*!" (116)

Now, barefoot and clad in her favorite, plain gingham dress, and accompanied by the friendly organ grinder—"The Man Who Makes Faces" (he puts a "stiff upper lip" in her handbag for those moments when she is speechless)—she sets out in search of her parents. Along the way, they meet exotic caricatures of all the people in poor Gwendolyn's restricted life—including the two-faced Jane, the snake-like Royle, the "head-over-heels" tumbling policeman, and, ultimately her parents (with a bee buzzing in her mother's bonnet and candles burning at both ends surround her father). One by one, Gwendolyn bests her enemies, including the deceitful, selfish servants. "You want to tell the real truth about those three servants [your parents] are hiring," advises the organ grinder. "Unless I'm *much* mistaken, your parents have never taken one good square look at those three" (127).

Finally, Gwendolyn awakens to the ministrations of her anxious parents and the family doctor. Through her ravings, the doctor understands that she has been a victim of the servant's abuse and parental neglect. "'Too often, I find,' says the doctor, 'where there's an automobile and the beck and call of a nurse, the child in her charge is utterly cut off-and in the period of quickest growth—from a normal supply of plain walking. Every boy and girl has a right . . . to the great world out of doors.'" (230) Gwendolyn's father agrees, shamefacedly. He soothes his agitated wife: "You thought you were doing the best thing for our little girl—*I* know that, dear. You had her future in mind. And it's natural—and *right*—for a mother to think of making friends—the right kind, too—and a place in the social world for her daughter. And I've been shortsighted, and neglectful." (234).

The doctor's prescription is a model of pragmatic advice, a recipe, if you will, promoting the health and physical culture of the "real girl." We find similar prescriptions in Fairbanks's ministrations to the dyspeptic "patients" in *Down to Earth*. "'Take two pairs of sandals,' orders the doctor, 'and a dozen cheap gingham dresses with plenty of pockets and extra pieces for patches, and a bottle of something good for wild blackberry scratches. Mix all together with one strong medium-sized garden hoe. . . . And wade in the creek'" (237–38).

With the assurance that the wicked servants will be banished, the father pledges to put the family business aside long enough to take them all on a long trip to the country. Gwendolyn happily sinks back to sleep.

When Eleanor Gates adapted *The Poor Little Rich Girl* into a three-act stage play, subtitled *A Play of Fact and Fancy*, she conflated the book's events into the hours just before, during, and after Gwendolyn's birthday dinner. Fifteen-year-old Viola Dana portrayed Gwendolyn. It premiered at the Hudson Theatre in New York on January 21, 1913, just a year after the publication of the novel. Up to that time Gates had been principally known as the writer of the novel, *A Biography of a Prairie Girl* (1902), and a series of juvenile narratives.[57] "All the more remarkable, in consequence," reported Clayton Hamilton, "is the technical skill with which she has projected her story over the footlights."[58] At the end of the dream sequence, Gwendolyn is given a speech in which she articulates to her mother more clearly than she had done in the novel the consequences of not being allowed to grow up:

> "And, now I know what terrible things it's done to me. It makes me ride in the motor, and keeps me from going to school with other girls and boys, and it won't let me sit at the grown-up table, or see father every day, or have you sing me to sleep, and oh, that doesn't matter so much, but look at my father. It keeps him in harness, and he'll never get rid of the harness till you give up the bee."[59]

Critics were unanimous in their praise, some noting the play's imaginative blend of fact and fantasy—"[Eleanor Gates] calls it a whimsical fantasy, a title that is sufficiently indefinite to cover all the elements of comedy, tragedy, allegory, morality play and satire which it contains"[60]—while others grappled with how to properly classify it—"We are not sure that, properly speaking, this play falls under the classification of drama, for it is more a sermon in the guise of a fairy tale. . . . For more than two acts we see on the stage visualized what takes place in the subconscious mind of a little girl who takes things very literally."[61] The dream sequence, which occupied the entire second act and which would be the highlight of Pickford's later adaptation, was singled out for particular mention: "This psychological idea, which is at once surprisingly original and profoundly true, is developed by the author in innumerable fanciful details. It would be impossible to praise this second act too highly; for it is the greatest contribution to the literature of dreams that has been effected since Rudyard Kipling wrote 'The Brushwood Boy.'"[62]

Reasons for Mary Pickford's decision to film *The Poor Little Rich Girl* are many and varied. Although she had probably not read the novel (she

Mary Pickford and her favorite scenarist, Frances Marion.

was not a great reader), she must have seen the stage production on Broadway in 1912 at the same time she was appearing on stage in David Belasco's production of *The Good Little Devil*, and she must have also been struck by the healthy contrast little Gwendolyn presented in comparison with her own current role as the saintly little blind girl, Juliet, in *The Good Little Devil*. Indeed, there was nothing in the least saintly, even spiritual, about Gwendolyn. She was a tough little girl whose imaginative gifts enabled her to cope with, rather than escape from, the complexities, cruelties, and betrayals of the adult world. Moreover, ever sensitive to the predicament of victimized children—doubtless an empathy derived from a childhood spent on stage working under miserable conditions to support her family with her earnings—Pickford saw in Gwendolyn the opportunity to make a social statement accessible to children and parents alike. Finally, *The Poor Little Rich Girl* is a definitive statement on a subject common to the literature of the Real Girl and to Mary's and Douglas's films in general—what historian Richard Corliss describes as the theme of "the restoration of family—or, rather, the establishing of a true family where only the counterfeit of one existed."[63]

Pickford's choice of twenty-eight-year-old Frances Marion to adapt Gates's novel and play to the screen was most fortuitous.[64] Just as Douglas Fairbanks at precisely this same time had found in the precocious Anita Loos a sympathetic partner in the writing of many of his early comedies, Pickford now saw in the witty, savvy Marion a partnership that aided immeasurably, as we shall see, in the establishment of her own screen characters. Both women particularly excelled in the art of pungent intertitle and dialogue titles that peppered the scenes with pungent humor.

Like Loos, Marion was beginning a career as a writer at precisely the time when fully one-quarter of all screenwriters in the movie industry were women. One is tempted to compare this formidable work force of literate, well-read women with the legions of female writers forging the way for the New Woman and Real Girl novels of the preceding century. Marion, Anita Loos, June Mathis, Bess Meredyth, Clara Beranger, and Gene Gauntier—to name just a few—took to the new medium of the movies with the same avidity that Susan B. Warner and Augusta Evans Wilson had embraced the novel a half century earlier. "For these women," noted pioneering woman director Alice Guy Blaché, "the arts-oriented professions were the most accessible, and cinema, the newest art form, seemed to provide them with a multitude of opportunities."[65] To an admittedly limited degree, they were in a position to wield their considerable influence in the crafting of films with proto-feminist subjects and viewpoints.

Mary Pickford and Frances Marion had first worked together in 1915 on a now-forgotten (and lost) film called *The Foundling*. It was based on Marion's original scenario (perhaps more than coincidentally derived from Burnett's *A Little Princess*), wherein Mary portrayed (in flashback) a twelve-year-old orphan girl who escapes the miserable orphanage and in later years goes to work for the man she does not know is her own father. Mawkish as the story was, Marion's screenplay gave Mary the opportunity to utilize her comedic skills and sturdy demeanor as a counterpoint against the expected sentimental grain of the character. According to Marion's biographer, Cari Beauchamp, Mary thereafter knew "that Frances's scenario gave her a breadth of opportunities to display her comedic and dramatic skills."[66]

Indeed, although Marion's name was overshadowed by Pickford's stardom and glamour, it was she, almost as much as Mary, who helped define Mary's "growing girl" persona on screen. Separated by only four years, they were very much alike. Like Mary, Frances had been tough, self-reliant, fiercely ambitious, and self-supportive since childhood; in addition,

Mary and co-star Zasu Pitts in *A Little Princess* (1917).

she had sacrificed a "normal" home life to a burning ambition to make good in the movie business (at the peak of her career, in the mid-to-late 1920s, she was the highest paid screenwriter in Hollywood). Unlike Mary, however, she was literate and well-read. She knew the classics of literature and the popular stories of the day. Her feminist sensibilities enabled her to see in the works of Frances Hodgson Burnett, Kate Douglas Wiggin, Eleanor Gates, Eleanor H. Porter, and William J. Locke not only story properties with proven audience appeal but protagonists who were Real Girls of unusual intelligence, vivacity, and self reliance.[67] In just two years, she and Mary would transform *The Poor Little Rich Girl, Rebecca of Sunnybrook Farm, Stella Maris, A Little Princess, M'Liss,* and *Amarilly of Clothes-Line Alley* into some of the most successful films of their day.

Their method of collaboration, according to biographer Beauchamp, was cozily simple: "In the evenings [Frances] often read out loud as Mary spent the obligatory hour washing and setting her hair; always sensitive to her lack of education, Mary was comfortable having Frances read to her without fear of being condescended or judged" (81).

Poor Little Rich Girl was filmed in Fort Lee, New Jersey, under the direction of Maurice Tourneur. The story goes that when it was privately screened for Paramount producers Adolph Zukor and Jesse Lasky, they declared it "putrid" and threatened, according to Beauchamp, not to release it, fearing it would jeopardize Mary's career (68). However, because it had been presold to theaters, and inasmuch as there was no other Pickford film to replace it, it was released anyway. To everyone's astonishment, it opened at the Strand in New York City to enthusiastic audiences. As a result, Famous Players promptly signed Frances Marion to a $50,000 per year contract to write more films for Mary.

Marion's scenario aged Gwendolyn by four years (doubtless a concession to Mary) and lost no time in deploying an admirably concise series of title cards and establishing shots to introduce the novel's main themes and characters. Views of the family mansion are prefaced with a title card—

> *In the Home of Everything—except the Love she longed for, dwells Gwendolyn, the Poor Little Rich Girl.*

In the charge of two tall footmen—

> *The tyrants of Modern Civilization—by Position, Servants, by disposition, Masters.*

Her desire to gaze out a window is thwarted by an intervening hand closing the shutters. Her father (Charles Wellesley) is introduced as a man

> *whose money-making schemes left little time for tenderness.*

and her mother is described as a woman

> *whose social duties seem of more importance than the happiness of her child.*

And the grim-faced governess and teacher are referred to as "Grim Wisdom's teachers." During the dreaded "Four o'clock Drive" in the shuttered limousine, Gwendolyn stoutly declares:

> *"I don't want to be shut up in that old car! I hate riding! I hate the chauffeur! I want to walk on my feet!"*

To which the wicked Jane slyly replies,

> *"Don't blame Jane if the kidnapers [*sic*] get you . . . bad little rich girls who walk will be bitten by big dogs."*

Reinforcing the child's "low-angle" narrative viewpoint in Gates's novel, the film casts tall children and even taller adults alongside the diminutive Mary; and ace set designer Ben Carré—whose contributions to the picture have been examined by historian Kevin Brownlow[68]—surrounded her with a few oversized sets and props. Here is a world that, in Gwendolyn's eyes at least, is outsized and strange. To her view—and ours—the stately rooms and corridors look enormous—and empty. Framed in long shot, flanked by tall doors, she plays alone with her toys on the floor, and a title card proclaims:

> *Empty hearts. Empty lives. Empty homes. Poor little rich girl.*

Similarly, the cares and woes of that world are presented in ways that show that she only imperfectly apprehends what is happening. For example, after a title card informs us that Father has been caught in a stock market collapse, Gwendolyn is puzzled to learn from the ensuing conversation that Wall Street is "full of bears." She promptly visualizes a scene of her father being attacked by huge, bear-like creatures. She moves forward to comfort him. "Please talk to me, daddy," she appeals, taking his hand. He smiles when she asks him if the bears frightened him. But when she asks him if he has time to love her a little, the nurse abruptly intervenes and takes her away.

To an extent, Marion's scenario and Maurice Tourneur's staging and direction are a blend of elements borrowed from both novel and play. As in the play, the Plumber and the Organ Grinder play more important roles, and the Wall Street woes of the father are depicted in greater detail. The metaphors sprinkled throughout the novel—the "snake-in-the-grass" governess, the "two-faced" nurse, the "bee-in-the-bonnet mother," the Wall Street "bears," etc.—lose the subtlety they enjoyed on the printed page; they appear on screen exactly as they appeared on stage—as frankly phony costumes and props. Yet it must be argued that in the process, at least the literal nature of Gwendolyn's imagination is preserved.

The dream sequence fully realizes the proto-cinematic effects we have noted in Gates's novel. In its surreal imagination and detail, it prefigures the bizarre dream sequences two years later in Fairbanks's *When the Clouds Roll By*. For example, after accidentally imbibing the sleeping drug, Gwendolyn staggers out of bed and down a stairway, collapsing on the floor. The camera captures the action from several skewed angles, providing a visual correlative to her hallucinatory state of mind. The house interior dissolves into a flight of steps. Two title cards introduce the subsequent fantasy action. The first reads, "The Child's Mind Wanders," while the second advises:

> *Real voices faintly come and go whilst every character in her actual life is borne into her delirium.*

The Plumber appears and, kneeling over her body, informs her that she has come to the Garden of Lonely Children where "things appear as they really are." He continues,

> *"Take you, for instance, you think you have everything. In fact you have nothing at all."*

In an elaborate crosscutting strategy that is carried out through the entire second half of the film, the ensuing scenes alternate between Gwendolyn's sick bed and the Garden of Lonely Children, reinforcing the connections between real-life events and the materialized metaphors of her dream.

In a striking departure from both the book and play, Gwendolyn ventures beyond the dark forest to the huge gates of Wall Street, where she finds her father grinding out money from a machine-like contraption (prefiguring the "Moloch" of Fritz Lang's *Metropolis*, made ten years later). At this moment, the film crosscuts back to the sickroom, where Gwendolyn recovers for just a moment and mumbles to her father, "They say you're made of money." Back in her dream, the figure of a woman approaches her and says,

> *"You'll never find Happiness until your mother forgets the Society Bee and your father ceases to Grind out Money."*

In another added incident, Gwendolyn, nearing death, meets a shrouded figure in a cemetery who offers her "eternal sleep." But, after a moment's hesitation, she refuses the invitation, turning instead toward the sunlit image of a young girl dancing across a verdant meadow and sings:

> *"I come to light/ Your deep distress/ And show The Road/ To Happiness."*

The two girls join hands and dance. Meanwhile, back in the nursery, Gwendolyn slowly revives to the joy of her tearful—and repentant—parents. Amid quick shots that flash-forward to a vision of their life together in the country, her father declares to his financier that he is leaving his business:

> *"There's enough [money] left for the life we are going to lead."*

The film's biggest alteration to Gates's original story lies in the conception of the character of Gwendolyn. In an attempt to invest a more "masculine" spunk and vigor into the essentially passive child, scenarist Marion has added some striking touches of her own: a snotty little playmate called "Susie May" arrives to provide a welcome foil to Gwendolyn. The two girls take one look at each other and declare war. Susie May knocks Gwendolyn down, and Gwendolyn, in retaliation, smears her face with a wedge of pie. As punishment, Gwendolyn is ordered by her mother to give Susie May one of her new frocks. Enraged, Gwendolyn tosses her entire wardrobe out the window, to the delight of the children below, who gather up the spoils and race away. In another comic mix-up, Gwendolyn single-handedly confronts a gang of boys who invade her garden in a spectacular mud fight. When the gardener arrives to break up the combat, she angrily declares,

> *"Now you've spoiled the best fight I've ever had!"*

And in the film's final scene, a note of humor prevails when the reviving Gwendolyn greets the doctor's prescription of rest in the country with the words,

> *"Oh, I love mud!"*

For a twenty-five-year-old woman to transform herself into an eleven-year-old child was no mean achievement. In facial expression and physical posture, Pickford is utterly convincing. For example, there is an early scene in which Gwendolyn's father punishes her by dressing her as a boy. Sulkily, Gwendolyn regards her masculine attire in the mirror. Surprised by the agreeable image, she tosses her curls, poses and struts, adjusts her hat, and enjoys the luxury of trouser's pockets (in Gates's novel, Gwendolyn demanded that pockets be sewn into her dresses). This delicious piece of cross-dressing humor, coupled with Pickford's delightful pantomiming of childish mannerisms, is more incisively satiric and convincing than all ten reels of her later, more inflated production of *Little Lord Fauntleroy* (1921). At the time of the film's release, Pickford explained her technique, one derived from careful observation of children. It is worth quoting at length:

> There are certain changes in the contour of the face that come with maturity. The face of a child is full and without the depressions that appear in the face of an adult. The adult who portrays a child role must resort to some method of concealing these depressions. Wearing the hair in long curls which fall over part of the cheek is one way of solving the problem. . . . There are many things to remember in impersonating a child role. For instance, the facial muscles of the grown-ups are controlled, while those of a child spontaneously reflect passing moods. A child pouts when it is displeased. When children are awed, or surprised, or frightened, their eyes open wide and their mouths droop, but their foreheads remain unwrinkled—and just there is another difficulty, for when we older people are under the influence of similar emotions, our brows have a tendency to become lined. Then there are the muscles about the mouth; those of the child's, unlike the grown-ups, are relaxed. Another technical problem that is difficult to solve is that of carriage. You see, the child moves about freely, its arms swinging carelessly, its shoulders droop very slightly, the knee joints are loose, and the toes point inward. An actress can't be too careful in noting and copying such movements as these in the case of a child. It all takes time and study—more than my audiences have imagined.[69]

Pickford's artistry notwithstanding, her work on the set did not always meet with director Tourneur's approval. He was a man of self-conscious artistic intent, who once said, "I am a dignified director, and my pictures should be dignified."[70] According to Frances Marion's autobiography, *Off With Their Heads!*, he objected that moments of humor and improvisation on the set would ruin his carefully calculated moments of whimsy:

> All of us entered earnest into the job of turning out another success for Mary, and during the shooting of the scenes, carried away by our own brand of humor, Mary and I often ganged up on poor serious Mr. Tourneur and either sweet-talked or fast-talked him into letting us include some wild comedy scenes which were not in the play or the script. These could have been called spontaneous combustions, and Mr. Tourneur went home many a night with an aching head![71]

Rebecca of Sunnybrook Farm (1917) was a "growing girl" story.

It would be a mistake to claim that *The Poor Little Rich Girl* and the other "growing girl" films of Mary Pickford are overtly feminist in intent and result. It is enough that they, like their literary counterparts, are records of transition and change in the lives of the quintessential American Real Girl. To complain of their relative lack of true depth of character and their lack of plot probability, argue Phyllis Bixler and Lucien Agosta, may be valid criteria for "realist fiction," but "they are not valid expectations, however, for fiction which has a very different function and form." Essentially, Bixler and Agosta conclude, the "growing girl" fiction for both children and adult audiences has a social as well as aesthetic function similar to that of the folk tale, especially in earlier, primarily oral cultures—"to pass accepted values from one generation to another and to help society accommodate change." Moreover, "the assurance provided by adherence to these formulas often allows new ideas or social realities to be cautiously explored, limited injections of the new and controlled touches of realism being typical variations of familiar formulas in popular fiction. . . . As society absorbs

Pollyanna was Mary's first film for United Artists.

'new' ideas or social realities, these ideas or realities may be incorporated in revised or new formulas the audience comes to expect."[72]

Ironically—even sadly—later attempts by Mary Pickford (who had so successfully established herself as the on-screen epitome of the "growing girl") to move into more mature roles of her own failed at the box office. Portrayals of older women in her last films, particularly in *Coquette* (1928), *The Taming of the Shrew* (1929), *Kiki* (1932), and *Secrets* (1933), were ignored by her fans. Unable to look forward, she was forced to negotiate a strategic retreat to little-girl roles, a move she had predicted in a May 1926 interview in *Everybody's Magazine*: "I was forced to live beyond my years when just a child; now I have reversed the order and I intend to remain young indefinitely."[73] She investigated acquiring the dialogue rights to *The Poor Little Rich Girl, Rebecca of Sunnybrook Farm, Daddy-Long-Legs,* and *Pollyanna.* In a telegram dated November 3, 1931, the L. C. Page and Company publishers, who held the rights to *Pollyanna,* encouraged the idea:

> BOSTON PAPERS REPORT YOU PLAN TO RETURN TO JUVENILE PARTS CONGRATULATIONS IF TRUE GLAD TO OFFER YOU TALKING PICTURE RIGHTS TO POLLYANNA WHICH WOULD PROVE EXCELLENT MEDIUM FOR YOUR RETURN.

But in an unsigned response to Page on the Pickford letterhead, written some time in 1932, Pickford obviously decided to shelve the project: "[The producers] seem to think that entertainment based upon the type of story of 'Pollyanna' is not in vogue at the present time."[74] Moreover, Pickford looked into the mirror, and the truth was unkind. The "now-unputoffable challenge of age," writes Richard Corliss, was too daunting:

> To reproduce *Rebecca* . . . as a talkie would be to acquiesce in a documentary of her naked maturity. It would, she knew, amount to an unconscionable assault on the make believe world she had so careful [*sic*] nurtured and for which silent film—that dear, instantly dead medium—was perfectly designed."[75]

Fate was cruel to "Little Mary." While the "growing girls" in her films were permitted to develop and mature and move on with their lives, she was forced to grow old in the cruel and dubious solace of seclusion and alcohol.[76]

Meanwhile, in the public consciousness at least, Mary Pickford was the little girl who would never be permitted to grow up. As we shall see, Douglas Fairbanks faced the same dilemma regarding his boyish persona in his costume films of the 1920s and early 1930s.

Chapter 5

"On an Odd Note"

Say, Young Fellow! (1918), *The Nut* (1920), and *When the Clouds Roll By* (1919)

We have forgotten our own meaning, and we are all wandering about the streets without keepers.

—G. K. CHESTERTON[1]

At the outset, let us make this perfectly clear: Douglas Fairbanks was always Douglas Fairbanks . . . only sometimes *more so*. This trio of pre-costume films demonstrates the point.

Say, Young Fellow (1918), *When the Clouds Roll By* (1919), and *The Nut* (1921) mark a transition between Fairbanks's early satiric comedies and the extravagant fantasies of the later costume films. Here are mad worlds where nightmares reign, waxworks walk, and a gigantic lobster comes to call. They hold a uniquely bizarre place in his oeuvre and deserve special consideration on their own. Of less interest there is another Fairbanks outing, a twenty-five-minute Triangle release from 1916, *The Mystery of the Leaping Fish*. Decked out in a loud, checkered suit, Fairbanks as a madcap detective cavorted shamelessly in what Jeffrey Vance describes as "a hallucinogenic odyssey into the absurd."[2] Historian Kevin Brownlow has treated this repellent burlesque on cocaine addiction in the Mack Sennett mode in *Behind the Mask of Innocence* (1990), and that's where we will leave it.[3]

We have already seen that Fairbanks's contemporary man was always grappling with the disruptions and occasional lunacies of the ever-changing

Say Young Fellow (1918) features Fairbanks at his breezy best.

American century. He always seemed to be the one man in a million who registered the exact norm from which most of us vary more or less. Despite his superhuman physical capabilities and his occasional manic susceptibility to fads and foibles of the time, his audience never mistook him for a freak, fool, or superman. Paradoxically, if he behaved *ab*normally, it was only because it was the only *normal* way to react to mad circumstances. "If Fairbanks had any neuroses, they, then, were the chronic ones of the average man who will never become pathological," wrote Alistair Cooke.[4]

Say, Young Fellow, released on June 16, 1918, is, alas, one of those "lost" Artcraft releases that haunt the Fairbanks historian and enthusiast. All evidence points to an unusual story that is a cross between a study of psychological aberration and a social satire in the vein of the early Loos-Emerson comedies. Released on June 16, 1918, it was written and directed by Joseph Henabery, and photographed by Glen MacWilliams and Hugh McClung. All that is left today are some fine reviews and a valuable memoir by Henabery. According to a plot synopsis in the *AFI Catalogue of Feature Films, 1911–1920,* our hero, known only as "The Young Fellow" (Fairbanks), has a sort of "hunch," as it is personified, a "mini-me," that attends him. This miniature version of himself perches on his shoulder and confides common-sense advice and encouragement during times of stress and confusion. Consequently, when The Young Fellow, recently hired as a cub reporter for the *New York Herald,* is assigned to interview a noted financier who earlier had refused to admit a star reporter, he calls upon his "hunch," screws up his courage, scales the millionaire's wall and forces the interview from him at the point of a gun. The editor, much impressed, then asks the young man to unearth the facts concerning a scheme to defraud a group of minor stockholders in the town of Melford. Unless certain papers in the possession of an old bachelor are delivered to a board meeting, the villainous financier will win complete control of a local company, and the stockholders will lose their investments. With the aid of his Hunch, the aging bachelor's attractive secretary (Marjorie Daw), and The Young Fellow's spinster landlady, the determined reporter thwarts the millionaire and his gang of thugs, delivers the papers on time and obtains a sensational story. In the process, he captures the secretary's heart, while the spinster wins the kindly bachelor.

"My story concerned the power of the subconscious," explains Henabery in his memoirs. "To me, the subconscious mind is a storage place for all observations, experiences, teachings, ideas of self-preservation . . . I didn't want to use a term like *subconscious* or *conscience,* so I chose a more common, slang-like name, *Hunch.*" Photographic double-exposures achieved the effects of a miniature Doug climbing all over the place and perching on Fairbanks's shoulder. "*Hunch* would yell instructions in Doug's ear about what action to take," says Henabery. "After *Hunch* spoke his piece, he would slide down Doug's shoulder and disappear into the upper pocket of Doug's jacket." By means of this device, Henabery "satisfied my desire to lambaste some of the phony 'success' slogans and ideas prevalent in that period." Notwithstanding the distinctly odd implications of a man who carries his alternate identity around in his pocket, Henabery declares it was a happy project: "We had fun making the picture. I was completely relaxed, and everyone was in tune with the others on the set. Doug was as happy as I've ever seen him."[5]

Reviews confirm this. *Photoplay* reported, "The well-known Fairbanks smile and the equally well-known Fairbanks prowess are utilized for both comedy and thrill in his latest picture." *Moving Picture World* cited the "hunch" device for particular praise: "One of the best features of the plot is the 'hunch' that appears to the hero at the decisive moments in his career . . . giving him sound advice."[6]

When the Clouds Roll By was the second release from United Artists, in 1919. *The Nut* came two years later, hard on the heels of his first costume swashbuckler, *The Mark of Zorro*. It would be his last contemporary satire before his sound feature, *Reaching for the Moon* a decade later. Both films take *Say, Young Fellow!*'s psychological "doubling" into more fantastic, even troubling directions. They present a Fairbanksian character whose essential sanity is severely tested by a world that has been turned upside down. Such strains upon the tethers of normalcy are perhaps clear evidence that a major shift in Fairbanks's style of filmmaking was underway, which would soon result in the extravagant costume fantasies to come. Their renting of the fabric of appearances would seem to have been necessary before the fantastic and the bizarre could issue forth full strength from the cracks and fissures. Moreover, as Jeffrey Vance suggests in his biography, "The man and [these films] suffer from an identity crisis. Fairbanks had become disengaged from his screen character; his supple sermons belonged in the past, along with his idealistic heroes Theodore Roosevelt and Billy Sunday."[7] However, we must disagree with Vance's assessment that *The Nut* is nothing more than a "chaotic funhouse" that reveals only a "half-hearted commitment to the project"; and which "comes to life only in fits and starts."[8] Chaotic funhouse it may be, but it nicely sustains a quietly, madly comic tone that makes it well worth watching.

The opening scenes of *The Nut* and *When the Clouds Roll By* display, respectively, the dehumanizing consequences of an increasingly mechanized society and the loss of sanity in a world of nightmare and paranoia. In *The Nut*, for example, Charlie Jackson is an inventor who is the passive victim of his own creations:

> *Our lover is an inventor. He invents ways of pleasing his girl and then he invents ways of getting out of trouble caused by his inventions. . . . He's just different and eccentric.*

He arises in the morning to a mechanical "wake-up call." Ropes lift off his bedcovers, the bed tilts him down into a pool where a revolving brush spins him clean, and a towel brushes him dry. Robot-like, he walks onto a treadmill that takes him to a closet where hooks thrust out his shirt, pants, coat, and neckerchief. No—not the first handkerchief that appears (he rejects that)—but the *second* one. This kind of sequence would be used by Buster Keaton later in films like *The Electric House* and the opening reel of *The Navigator.* Later Pierre Etaix would pay it tribute in the opening of *Yo Yo* (1965).

In *When the Clouds Roll By*, Daniel Boone Brown—"an average young man"—succumbs to the evil machinations of a Mephistophelian hypnotist. An opening title says,

> *Guinea pigs and rabbits are often sacrificed for scientific purposes. But here is a new one . . .*

The following shot discloses the back of a lecturer, one "Dr. Metz," addressing a medical convention with his "theory of evil design."

> *"I mean to take a human life in the cause of science—"*

he says, continuing,

> *"The power of suggestion can destroy both mind and body. But first I weaken the power of resistance in my subject by implanting psychic germs of fear, worry, superstition and kindred annoyances."*

Metz and his assistants, unbeknownst to Brown, insinuate themselves into his daily life. Thus, Brown becomes the helpless object of a perverse world of scientific experimentation, the counterpart of the man on the treadmill in *The Nut.*

After these preliminary scenes, both films assume different trajectories. The similarity remains, however, that in both, our hero must cope with a world that seems to have gone mad. In *The Nut*, the conflict is hilarious and fanciful. In *Clouds*, the confrontation is more disturbing, even frightening.

In *The Nut*, Fairbanks's girlfriend, Estrell Wynn (Marguerite de la Motte), has a theory about social reform, one that Fairbanks himself, as we have seen, promoted in early films like *The Habit of Happiness* and *Mr. Fix-It*:

> *[She] believes a group of slum children brought into a refined home for an hour each day will become good citizens—just like that.*

Again, the emphasis is that "normal" circumstances are all that is needed for a person to grow up healthy and socially adjusted. In promoting her cause, Charlie, who is anything at this point but normal himself, gives a party for prospective patrons of Estrell's plan. He will try to sell them on the idea of opening their homes to unfortunate children. So far so good, but what results is the first of a quick succession of whimsical disguises and visual puns that dominate the entire film. Before the assembled people, Charlie puts on a series of impersonations. He comes and goes behind a screen, successively appearing as Napoleon, General Grant, Lincoln, Tom Thumb, and finally as Charlie Chaplin. The gag is that Fairbanks is obviously not any of them—the changes are so fast, the impersonators so obviously unlike him that no one is surprised when he accidentally knocks down the screen to reveal all five accomplices crouching behind it. The Chaplin character, moreover, is himself an impersonator, albeit a convincing one.[9] Fairbanks cheerfully kicks him off the little stage. The masquerades are just beginning.

The party is disrupted when the bumbling Charlie unleashes fireworks in the house and the guests run for cover, diving out windows while their pants go up in smoke. Charlie's own suit is now a pile of ashes and he flees down the night streets of the city clad only in his underwear. Greatly embarrassed, he dons his own "disguise"—he tears the number "23" off a poster, pastes it on the back of his tee shirt, and blithely jogs through the streets like a track star. Seconds later he is forced to adopt another disguise. This time he cuts out a pasteboard billboard figure, cuts off the head, inserts his own into the opening, and, with it held in front of him, saunters about, always careful to keep his front toward any passersby. In this way he safely returns to his house.

Trying to reach the distraught Estrell in order to placate her, he has to resort to more ruses. Someone who has fainted at the disastrous party has been carried out on a stretcher supine under a sheet. Charlie rigs up a similar effect by holding his hands and shoes out in front of him while the draped sheet conceals the rest of his body. By rocking back his head and keeping the shoes thrust out before him, he is able to fool a squad of policemen who have been alerted by the townspeople that a naked maniac is running through the streets. Still unable to see Estrell, he finally takes refuge in a truck parked outside. Of course the truck turns out to be a police wagon and Charlie's despairing face is seen through the rear window as the truck drives away.

This whole sequence of events happens so fast that it is easy to let it go by without noticing the really clever ways in which the gags are developed. The artifice of magic—the stage- managed illusion in broad daylight—stands at the core of *The Nut.* For the hapless Charlie, however, he's his own worst enemy. He ruefully admits to the distraught Estrell:

> *"Every castle I build for you I seem to kick over."*

Later in the jail, Charlie strikes up an acquaintance with a dapper, affluent-looking fellow who sympathizes with his cause. The man agrees to enlist his society friends in the effort to find good homes for Estrell's scheme. Charlie, in turn, will donate $2,500 for any charity of the gentleman's choice. Of course this is another charade, as the gentleman in question is really one "Gentleman George," a con man who senses an easy mark in Charlie.

Gentleman George joins forces with one Mr. Feeney, himself a rascal with designs of his own on Estrell. Feeney and George plan another masquerade to fool Charlie. Charlie visits the "society gentleman" George has promised to provide. Of course, these social lions are really only George and Feeney's accomplices. Charlie discovers the ruse and leaves in anger. Still desperately trying to placate Estrell, Charlie hits upon another idea. More false faces. He visits Warren's Wax Works, where in a state of confusion he stumbles here and there into the lifelike wax figures. Near closing time, Charlie freezes into a position so that the caretaker mistakes him for one of the figures. It's a quietly eerie effect to see the stiff and immobile Charlie suddenly "coming to life" among the waxworks. The viewer by this time is quite prepared for *all* the figures to walk about—a device used later, incidentally, in the marvelous short story by John Collier, "Evening Primrose."

Bustling about, Charlie swipes two of the wax figures and appropriates a policeman mannequin. While carrying the mannequins across the night streets, he holds the "policeman" in front of him in a simulation of directing traffic. A passing policeman, a *real* policeman, notices the charade—

> *"Say, Clancy, I saw a mysterious man—all dressed up—carrying a body through the street—"*

A call is sent out to the police station that another maniac is loose. A newspaper editor picks up the story and advises his reporter:

> *"Say . . . a man with a silk hat has been seen carrying bodies through the streets down Greenwich Village way. See if you can get the story."*

Back home Charlie positions his dummies in the parlor. He intends to pass them off to Estrell as three prominent social personages who have come to listen to her ideas. He carefully sets up the illusion, seating the dummies and placing a cigarette in the hand of one. Estrell arrives and Charlie pretends to chat with the dummies about her idea. The effect is successful and she is fooled—until the burning cigarette sets one of the dummies on fire. Furious at the deception, Estrell leaves in a huff.

"I'll do anything—"

Charlie pleads to the long-suffering Estrell,

"—I'll go to a reform school or an insane asylum—anywhere—if you'll only see me again."

Before Estrell can recommend the latter option, she is assaulted by a wicked gambler, an accomplice of Gentleman Joe, who, believe it or not, is passing himself off as a society banker. Charlie rescues her by another ruse: He dons the waxwork policeman's clothes and brashly invades Feeney's den and defeats him and his cronies after a furious struggle. The story ends with one last disguise: Charlie and Estrell are hauled into a police court, but the "trial" turns out to be a marriage ceremony, and the two lovers are sentenced to "a lifetime of happiness."

This striking succession of masquerades, this dance of masks, lends *The Nut* a zany, quicksilver quality that not only spotlights Fairbanks's considerable talents as a comedian, but places *The Nut* in a unique position among all his films. In no other film, save *When the Clouds Roll By*, is there such a brittle, mirror-like surface that undermines any secure sense of identity.

When the Clouds Roll By creates a world that is even darker and more troubling. We already know that Daniel Boone Brown is the object of the sinister researches of Dr. Metz. Capitalizing on Brown's susceptibility to superstition, he intends to subject Brown's will to the power of suggestion in order to drive him to madness and suicide. First he will make Brown jealous of the attentions of another man toward his girlfriend; and next he will implicate Brown in a plot to cheat the girl's father of some valuable real estate.

At first, Brown's superstitious nature is the occasion for some scenes of great charm. Brown meets his girlfriend-to-be, Lucette, in the park; their meeting is accompanied by little rituals. They circle each other warily, waving their hands to ward off evil spirits. Later they both crouch over a Ouija board. She drops a letter and the board says,

What falls to the floor
Comes to the door.

Sure enough, a postman arrives with a letter. Startled, she drops a paper knife. The board responds,

A falling knife is a dead sure hunch
That some young man will come to lunch.

Of course, Brown is only too glad to oblige *that* one.

But Dr. Metz's efforts are about to make daily life a hell for Brown. His infernal machinations disrupt his eating, getting up in the morning, going to work, making love to his girlfriend. This is best conveyed in two highlight sequences. In the first, one of Metz's accomplices goes to work as Brown's servant. He persuades the hapless Brown to imbibe enormous quantities of food, such as onions, lobster, Welsh rarebit, and mince pie just before retiring one evening. Not surprisingly Brown goes into convulsions and begins to dream. What follows emerges as one of the single most imaginative sequences in any of Fairbanks's films.

Helpless before a violent onslaught of indigestion (a dissolve reveals the various foodstuffs tumbling around in his stomach), he sits up in bed. Is he dreaming, or is he awake? A distorted, tall, wraith-like figure materializes beside the bed and glowers menacingly at him. He pushes it away. It falls to the floor like a stiff piece of cardboard, but it springs right back up again. Elongated pale hands swarm all over the room and reach for him. Terror-stricken, Brown leaps out of bed and dives *through* the wall. Now he's in the midst of some sort of gathering of society ladies. Tugging at his falling pajamas, he leaps through the crowd toward a painting of a seascape on the wall. He dives through it and falls with a splash into a pool of water. Suddenly, giant vegetables appear. They race toward him in an oddly accelerated motion. Brown flees, his own movements now shifting into slow motion. Outside now, he jumps some timber fences, clears another fence with a front somersault and tuck, leaps onto a waiting horse, and tumbles through yet another wall.

Now he's in a strange room. It's like a dollhouse interior, its front wall cut away. In an uncut medium shot, Brown crosses the floor to frame right, walks *up* the wall, crawls across the ceiling, back down the left wall, and runs across the floor and back up the right wall again. The door opens and the pursuing foods tumble in. Retreating, Brown "stands" on his hands from the ceiling. Back "on his feet," he grips the banister and descends down the staircase. After circling around the ceiling again, he escapes out of the room.

In the next shot, Brown runs toward the camera, again in slow motion. He hurdles a number of barriers as he runs toward a chimney. He leaps into the air, descends through the chimney opening, plunges down the long shaft, and lands in a large metal cylinder or drum at the bottom. Strangers are banging upon it—

At this point Brown wakes up.

The banging is coming from another of Dr. Metz's aides who is standing outside Brown's room.

This remarkable sequence startled viewers at the time. Devised by director Victor Fleming and assisted by cameramen William McGann and Harris Thorpe and art director Edward M. Langley, the stunt was explained in a magazine at the time:

> They built at his studio a set showing a room open at one side and revolving on an axis like a squirrel cage. As Doug walked over to the side wall and placed his foot on it for the first step, the camera, also set with special equipment so that it would revolve, likewise turned, and so on as he walked up one side, over the ceiling, and down the other side. To the turned camera he appeared always to be walking along the floor, head up, but in the picture registered on the film, always vertical, the star had his head out horizontally or downward, as the case happened to be. The pursuers rushing into the room were introduced by double exposure.[10]

The challenge, of course, was to get the mechanism of the revolving room calibrated to the camera to such a mathematical nicety that the illusion was convincing. Certainly there would be nothing this fantastic in any of Fairbanks's costume films to come, including *The Thief of Bagdad*, which looks stodgy and clumsy by comparison. Decades later, similar effects were deployed in Fred Astaire's *The Royal Wedding* (1951) and Stanley Kubrick's *2001*.

Indeed, the sequence foreshadows the many camera tricks, time and space dislocations, and causal disconnects that will typify the European avant-garde cinema of the later 1920s. We think immediately of the comic absurdities of René Clair's silent films. Claire was an avowed enthusiast of Fairbanks. There can be little doubt that the farcical chases, the erotic fetishism, the camera tricks, and the deployment of dream sequences in Clair's *Paris qui dort* (*The Crazy Ray*, 1923), *le voyage imaginaire* (*The Imaginary Voyage*, 1925), and *un chapeau de paille d'Italie* (*The Italian Straw Hat*, 1927) owe something to Fairbanks's example.

But we are leaving poor Brown in desperate straits. He is increasingly vulnerable to his superstitious paranoia. A shaving mirror breaks, the servant opens an umbrella in the apartment, the bathroom is flooded by one of Metz's agents. Meanwhile Dr. Metz furthers his scheme by bringing Brown, his new girlfriend (Lucette), her father, and Brown's uncle together at a party. Metz stands back and seems to pull invisible strings while disaster breaks out. It seems Lucette's father owns some property that, unbeknownst to him, contains oil. Lucette's former boyfriend is a swindler bent on getting Brown's firm to buy the property for a pittance. The secret comes out and the swindler, in trying to protect himself, implicates the innocent Brown in the fraud. In the midst of all this, both Lucette and Brown's uncle walk out in a rage. Unfairly blamed, Brown tries to explain. But the police show up to arrest him. The police, of course, are also accomplices of the good doctor, providing the crowning touch to Metz's whole charade. No matter where Brown runs, he is met by a "policeman" who pops up behind windows and doors, blocking his every move. Dissolve to a curious tableau inside Brown's head: A woman designated as "Reason" sits atop a throne; a figure dressed in motley attire as "Sense of Humor" cringes at her feet; and two more figures, "Worry" and "Discord," appear and abduct Lady "Reason" from her throne.

A confused and distraught Brown stumbles out of the closet. The lights are out (Metz has conveniently turned them off). He staggers aimlessly through the gloom, barred shadows across his face. There's Dr. Metz in the corridor. The good doctor furtively slips a revolver into Brown's pocket. The plot is almost consummated.

This sequence is quite frightening. Brown is now close to ending it all with a bullet . . . but in the nick of time he sees the evil Doctor Metz being carried away by attendants from the local insane asylum. Aha!—one more charlatan is unmasked. Brown's brain clears. The "Sense of Humor" appears again to restore "Reason" to the throne. "Have you heard the one about the old maid in the sleeping car . . . ?" jokes "Reason."

Miraculously restored, Brown dashes away to rejoin Lucette.

One is prepared for anything by this time. And we are not disappointed. A *real* nightmare is waiting in the wings. It's a finale as bizarre in its own way as anything we've yet seen. A hurricane and flood sweep over the countryside. Brown and Lucette are carried away. Lucette is stranded on the roof of her house. But here is Fairbanks, floating by, hanging from the branches of a tree. He dives into the water, swims toward Lucette, and clambers onto the roof. By this time, Brown may have recovered, he may have cleared his name, and he may have regained his "Reason" and "Sense of Humor"—but he still is hungry. What could be more normal than to raid the refrigerator? The fact that the house is half submerged in a flood seems not to matter at all. So he cheerfully dives off the roof, swims down through a window, paddles along a watery stairway, and enters into the kitchen for a snack. (Perhaps this was the origination of the "submarine" sandwich.)

The finishing stroke occurs when a preacher comes floating by atop the church steeple and marries them.

In *Say, Young Fellow!, When the Clouds Roll By*, and *The Nut* comedy and terror, reality and illusion, disguise and revelation come and go at the snap of the prestidigitator's fingers. If normalcy is finally restored, it is at best provisional. Monsters may walk, little men live in shirt pockets, darkness falls, but—and this is final miracle—we continue to laugh. "To laugh is to dream," wrote René Clair, that most amiable of surrealists. "To laugh is to be free, to laugh is to take a revenge, to laugh is to possess everything we lack in reality."[11]

Part II

"The Imperial Reach"

Democracy must have a heraldry, it must have a proud and highly coloured pageantry, if it is to keep always before its own mind its own sublime mission.

—G. K. CHESTERTON

Mr. Fairbanks flashes through brawls and dangers and court assemblies with the assurance of a good American salesman.

—P. F. RENIERS, the *New York Evening Post*, 1921

Spoofing Ruritanian romance in *Reaching for the Moon* (1917).

Chapter 6

Prologue

As chronicled in detail in our earlier volume, *His Majesty the American* (1977), the founding of United Artists in 1919 marked an important development in the history of Hollywood and in the trajectory of Fairbanks's screen career.[1] The story of United Artists is too complex to repeat here, but it is enough to note that when he tumbled through the title credits in the prologue to United Artist's first release, *His Majesty the American,* he was entering into a new engagement with the American century. While Hollywood was busily reinventing itself—the major studios were achieving a vertical organization that permitted total control of picture-making, distribution and exhibition—the four members, Fairbanks, Chaplin, Pickford, and D. W. Griffith, were planning to produce, market, and distribute each of their films *individually* as handcrafted super productions.

It had only been two years since a 1917 editorial in *Photoplay* had predicted a bright future for Fairbanks. "Here he is," began the editorial, "a sane, commonplace, aggressive young fellow in his early thirties, getting a ground work of combined experience and celebrity from which no middle-age triumph can jar him. . . ."

> He is devoted to the screen, doesn't consider it a mere makeshift for the big money, but an absolute medium for the best that's in him. He is going to grow right along with camera-craft, and when, in a few years, we come to those absolutely certain sun-plays of serious life, let us hope that he will crown his career with a man of maturity who will be not only a triumph of acting but a *national expression.*[2]

A "national expression"? The prediction was not far off the mark. With the American film industry emerging unscathed from the Great War, and the dominance of foreign markets in the offing, Fairbanks—ever the personification of the Old World aristocrat and the New World self-made man, a man tied to tradition yet emancipated from history—was ready to extend his national grasp into a global reach.

Behind him were the years at Triangle and Artcraft, a time when Americans supposed themselves to suffer, in the words of historian Richard Pells, "from a deeply ingrained sense of cultural inadequacy"; and when the Old World cognoscenti regarded American culture as "derivative, provincial, second-rate, a pitiable imitation of what was going on in the arts across the Atlantic." As we have seen, Fairbanks's sharp social satires and energetic sermons had put the lie to all that. He had been energetically demonstrating that America in the new century was emerging as not just "a consumer of foreign intellectual and artistic influences," observes Pells, but as "a shaper of the world's entertainment and tastes." His American aristocrats cultivated Old World traditions and, at the same time, infused moribund class structures with a fresh and heady dose of American democratic activism. To the dismay of some foreign observers, he was "Americanizing" their imaginations and attitudes, and his agile and leaping body was a compelling metaphor for surmounting the artificial barriers separating "high" and "low" class and culture. The rub, concludes Pells, was that his and other American movies "had not been imposed or inflicted upon the populace, that the common folk were voluntarily and enthusiastically watching what their mentors told them to shun."[3]

Now, in the postwar decade of the 1920s, Fairbanks and his United Artists partners entered a golden age of the Hollywood studio film. Utilizing the full technical resources of their studios and backlots, they abjured the contemporary satires and location shooting of earlier years and instead converted Old World history and myth into studio-crafted commodities—classy exhibits of memory and nostalgia—and exported them back to foreign markets. "One of our greatest achievements has been the progress we have made in the building of sets," boasted Fairbanks in 1923. "We know that we make mistakes, but we are getting more and more of the period that we wished to recreate."[4] Consider their productions as the prototypes of the later Disney theme parks, a kind of cultural imperialism that "Americanized" the world's cultures for popular consumption. Thus, Mary Pickford created Elizabethan and Edwardian worlds in the studio (*Dorothy Vernon of Haddon Hall* and *Little Lord Fauntleroy*, respectively), Charles

Chaplin constructed his own Yukon in *The Gold Rush*, Griffith recreated the French and American revolutions for his *Orphans of the Storm* and *America*. And Fairbanks—well, Fairbanks and his designers crafted costumes and settings into lively and extravagant versions of Old California, medieval England, the Arabian Nights, and the courts of Louis XIII and Louis XIV in the Zorro films, *Robin Hood*, *The Thief of Bagdad*, *The Three Musketeers*, and *The Iron Mask*. Ultimately, in 1929, he and Pickford joined forces in their retrofitting of Shakespeare's Elizabethan world in *The Taming of the Shrew*. They were refashioning the historical past—*with advantages*, as Shakespeare's Henry V would say.

Films like these, proposes Richard Pells, were consolidating a modernist style of filmmaking that was both European in its derivation and American in its popular appeal.[5] No matter the period setting and time frame, the films were distinctly *American*. No matter the costume conception, Fairbanks was always *Fairbanks*, the go-getting apostle of American life, working on behalf of "the people" to support and restore the "people's" regimes of Spanish governors in the two Zorro films, King Richard the Lion-Heart in *Robin Hood*, Louis XIII and XIV in *The Three Musketeers* and *The Iron Mask*, while deposing a wicked Mongol usurper in *The Thief of Bagdad*, and a totalitarian South American dictator in *The Gaucho*. A review of *Robin Hood* in *Photoplay* magazine is entirely to the point: "At no time does Doug seem Robin Hood. He is always a twentieth century Fairbanks."[6]

That is true enough; and yes, Fairbanks was always Fairbanks, although sometimes even more so. But also note—*he had always been Robin Hood*. Mythic personae like these, as we have seen, had ever lain hidden, just beneath the skin of his more contemporary characters. Now in the costume films they converged in a time-slip of past and present. They emerged into the full light of day, for all to recognize. In other words, once Fairbanks put on the costumes of Señor Zorro, Robin Hood, and the others, he never took them off again. He *couldn't* take them off again. He was like the actor in a feudal pageant in the G. K. Chesterton novel who, after donning Robin Hood's Lincoln green, found himself unable to remove it. Doug's audiences loved it, of course. They recognized something lacking in their everyday lives. They found a pageant of motley and color. And, again to borrow from Chesterton, "there passed into [that pageant] much of that popular passion which at one time filled half the towns and villages with pageants; the hunger of a populace which Puritanism and Industrialism had so long starved for the feast of the eyes and the fancy."[7]

Chapter 7

"The Mark of Greatness"

The Adventures of Señor Zorro

I am the friend of the oppressed, señor, and I have come to punish you.
—**JOHNSTON McCULLEY,** *The Curse of Capistrano* (1919)

Among the varied progeny of the character of Zorro that have appeared since Fairbanks's *The Mark of Zorro* was released in 1920, we may count the Caped Crusader himself, the Dark Knight: Batman. The creator of Batman, comic book artist and entrepreneur Bob Kane, acknowledged as much in an interview with us in 1989. "When I was a kid growing up in the Bronx, I saw *The Mark of Zorro* at the movies," Kane remembered.

> Zorro was the most swashbuckling daredevil I've ever seen in my life. He gave me the idea of the dual identity . . . as a foppish bored Don Diego Vega, the son of one of the wealthiest families in Mexico around 1820 . . . and the crime fighter, Zorro. That had a profound influence on me. There had been other dual identities, like the Scarlet Pimpernel, but I got mine mainly from Zorro. So at night Zorro donned this mask, kind of a handkerchief mask with slits in the eyes; and he'd attach a trusty sword to his side and he'd exit from a cave on a black horse. I think the black horse's name was Tornado. Many years afterward the cave became the bat cave and the horse the bat mobile.[1]

Now, of course, Kane's Batman and Fairbanks's Zorro, brothers in arms, if you will, are still busily avenging injustice, in comic books, graphic novels, television, and on screen.

Difficult as it is to believe from today's vantage point, not much was initially expected of *The Mark of Zorro*. As his fourth release from the newly

The Costume Films (drawing courtesy John C. Tibbetts).

formed United Artists, it was sandwiched between his more contemporary comedies, *The Mollycoddle* and *The Nut*. His initial disinterest in the story property was purportedly changed at the behest of Mary Pickford, who enthusiastically recommended it after reading it during their recent European vacation.[2] Timid at first, Fairbanks's began to realize that adding elements of historical romance to the rather ambivalent masculinity he had performed as early as *The Lamb* and as recently as *The Mollycoddle*—counterposing the duality of "effeminate" passivity with an aggressive masculinity—might be good box office. That *Zorro* turned out to be a box-office smash was an understatement. The premiere at the Capitol Theater in New York City on November 29, 1920, broke all records, and it proved to be his most successful film to date. For the rest of the decade, Fairbanks and United Artists were wedded inseparably to escapist costume adventures.

And so we come back to Fairbanks's first entry in his historical costume cycle of the 1920s, *The Mark of Zorro*. Zorro had made his first appearance a year earlier in the magazine *All-Story Weekly* on August 9. Johnston McCulley's five-part story was called *The Curse of Capistrano*." McCulley was fascinated by the setting of Old California during the days

The Mark of Zorro (1920) launched the Fairbanks costume cycle.

of the mission empire. He began as a journalist with the *Kansas City Star* in 1913, traveled extensively throughout the country in later years, and finally settled into an apartment in New York, from which flowed his narratives of swordplay and romance. His novel *Captain Fly-by-Night*, which anticipated the events and setting of "The Curse of Capistrano," dealt with political corruption in Old California, the landed power of the blooded caballeros, and the fading empire of the missions around Reina de Los Angeles. Likewise, in *The Curse of Capistrano*, "Señor Zorro" dashes in to right injustices wrought by the corrupt political system. Disguised by a black mask and a purple cloak, he "comes and goes like a graveyard ghost," avenging wrongs all along El Camino Real. Eventually, he enlists the caballeros in his cause to overthrow the corrupt governor and his military power. Zorro is, in reality, one Don Diego Vega, son of one of the most powerful houses in Old California. Diego finds it necessary to disguise his activities by pretending to be a foppish, indifferent, trivial young man more interested in music and poetry than in justice—righting wrongs and dueling with the sword. The fame that came to Johnston McCulley, already a prolific writer of romances, also brought a "curse" of its own. McCulley became identified with the Zorro stories and ever after was called upon to provide sequel after sequel for the pulp magazines, film, and television.[3]

McCulley had his own antecedents, to be sure. The Zorro stories stand squarely in the action-romance tradition of the pulp magazines before 1920. This style of adventure story got its real impetus from the Edgar Rice Burroughs stories that began to appear in 1912. Burroughs's first "Mars" story, *Under the Two Moons of Mars* (later published as *The Princess of Mars*), appeared in *All-Story* magazine during the months of February through July of 1912 under his pseudonym of "Normal Bean." This saga of the earthling John Carter—the hero of a recent Pixar-Disney film of that name—adrift among the wild landscapes and people of "Barsoom" established the classic pattern for such adventures. Like "Curse of Capistrano," its hero is uncommonly agile and proficient with the sword. He knows not the meaning of fear, cowardice, treachery, or deceit. His sword arm wins him a place in the aristocracy of his world. The heroine, moreover, is forever being abducted by the villains, and the hero is constantly off in hot pursuit. The pattern becomes a representation of abduction-pursuit-recapture-abduction-again. If it were not for the lady fair, it seems, villains and heroes alike would have nothing to do but eat and get fat, their swords rusting in the attic.[4]

The glories of roistering, bloody combat, and camaraderie disguise only thinly a stern morality in these tales. John Carter of Mars and Zorro of Reina de Los Angeles alike act with their blades to aid the oppressed and, of course, rescue the ever-imperiled heroine. Whether hero or villain, there are always the codes of chivalry and villainy to be followed. Both pirates and heroes are worthy protagonists as long as they follow the mandate expressed by the pirate Barbados in a McCulley 1922 sequel: "If a thief, be a thief! If a pirate, be a pirate! But do not play at being an honest man and try to be thief and pirate at the same time."[5]

This sequel needs to be mentioned because it is proof-positive of the effects Fairbanks had on the development of the character of Zorro. For example, in the original novel, *The Curse of Capistrano*, there is no mention of Zorro's famous "mark"—the "Z"—carved into the foreheads of his victims. But it appears frequently throughout both Zorro films. Fairbanks apparently invented this visual trademark, the kind of identity-device he had already done in earlier films like *The Good Bad Man.* Its effectiveness is demonstrated in a scene in *The Mark of Zorro* wherein Zorro carves a "Z" into Captain Ramon's cheek and then shows Ramon its mirrored reflection in his blade. In *Don Q*, it is the "Z" that Zorro, who has just

"Warming up" in *The Mark of Zorro* (1920).

arrived on the scene in the climactic sword fight, carves into an opponent that alerts his son to his identity. In addition, there is no mention in the original edition of the novel of a bit of business also featured prominently in both films: In *The Mark of Zorro,* Don Diego's foppishness is emphasized by his foolish little parlor tricks with a handkerchief, accompanied by the words, *"Have you seen this one?"* And in *Don Q,* sure enough, both father and son perform the ritual in the final moments. As a result of all this, subsequent editions of McCulley's *Curse of Capistrano* bear Fairbanks's title; Zorro carves "Z's" all over the place; and the Don Diego persona whips out his handkerchief at every opportunity with the words, "Have you seen this one?"

But we're not done yet. So firmly was Fairbanks identified with Zorro that one can see a gradual change in the artwork that accompanied the Zorro stories from 1919 on through the 1930s. The J. P. Monahan conception adorning the cover of the 1919 *All-Story Weekly* bears no similarity to the Fairbanks image. After the film, however, subsequent drawings, particularly the Sam Cahan artwork, clearly show the Zorro character as interpreted by Fairbanks. The costumes and facial characteristics all closely resemble him.

McCulley's sequel would in turn influence later work by Fairbanks. Featured prominently on the cover of the *Argosy All-Story Weekly* issue carrying the sequel are the following words: "Which Douglas Fairbanks Will Again Play the Hero." Fairbanks, in fact, never made a Zorro film with plot elements from this story. Instead, the story appears somewhat altered in Doug's 1926 film, *The Black Pirate.* Similarities between McCulley's sequel and Fairbanks's pirate film include scenes wherein the heroine is captured by pirates, the hero scampers about the rigging of a pirate ship, and a rescue is effected by the hero's army of allies. Even the character of Barbados is echoed somewhat in Donald Crisp's portrayal of a tough but kindly old pirate. McCulley has acknowledged that his "Further Adventures of Zorro" was utilized for *The Black Pirate.*[6]

Despite the changes or additions Fairbanks brought to McCulley's story, it is nevertheless a relatively close adaptation. The sequence of events is the same, the characters are the same, details such as the boasting of Sergeant Gonzales (Noah Beery), the whipping of the Padre, the indifference of the caballeros to the governor's injustice, the rescue of Lolita from the prison, even much of the dialogue, are all almost identical.

The visualization of the story is at once clever and entirely in the spirit of the original. Already mentioned are the devices of the "Z" mark and Don Diego's handkerchief. In addition, Don Diego enjoys casting hand shadows on walls—another device that appears in *Don Q*—and manipulating his hat to emphasize his foppishness. As Zorro, by contrast, Fairbanks's acrobatics leaven the action with a dazzling airborne agility. The confrontation between Zorro and Ramon (Robert McKim) after Ramon has tried to "compromise" Lolita Pulido (Marguerite de la Motte) has Zorro literally falling from the ceiling into the frame. The chase sequence at the end of the story is considerably elaborated. With the governor's men in hot pursuit, Zorro still has time to attach a note with his sword to the bole of a tree. It advises his pursuers that this is his last weapon, that he has gone into town to have breakfast, and that he dares them to capture him! The subsequent chase reminds us of Fairbanks's most successful trajectories, taking his agile form and his bumbling pursuers over stile, walls, rooftops, and through windows. In the middle of all this frenzied action, Fairbanks takes a characteristic pause for refreshment. Reclining on a windowsill, he advises a peasant woman, "Never do anything on an empty stomach," before whirling away again back into the chase. Although none of this is

Donning the mask in *The Mark of Zorro*.

in the original, it seems entirely right and satisfactory in the film. (Again, midway in a chase sequence in *Don Q*, we see Fairbanks again taking a brief break for "the pause that refreshes.")

The conflict is resolved in the story when the caballeros band together and demand from the governor that his oppression must stop and Zorro be exonerated for his outlawry. In the film, this resolution is much more satisfactory. Don Diego confronts Captain Ramon and finally reveals his identity. They cross swords. After Ramon is bested, Zorro hurls his sword upward to the ceiling, declaring,

> *"'Till I need you again!"*

That prophecy is later fulfilled in the sequel *Don Q, the Son of Zorro*.

The story derives from the novel *Don Q's Love Story*, by Keith and Hesketh Prichard. *Don Q* was directed by Donald Crisp, who also plays the villain of the story, Don Sebastian. The action is transplanted to Spain. With a few notable exceptions, there is a remarkable consistency between the two films, even though the adventure formula in the later film is more complicated,

Fairbanks portrayed both father and son in *Don Q* (1925).

the scene design and costumes more sumptuous and detailed, and the cast numbers increased.

The events of the sequel may be summarized as follows: Don Cesar de Vega has left his father behind in California and come to Madrid to complete his education. His courage and heroic action in a series of brief skirmishes attract the attention of the queen of Spain and her visiting cousin, the archduke of Austria (Warner Oland), who befriends him. Don Cesar, meanwhile, has fallen in love (at first glance, of course!) with lovely, virginal Doloros de Muro (Mary Astor), daughter to the queen's closest advisor and, it is finally disclosed, a friend of Don Cesar's father. As a result, Don Cesar also makes a dangerous enemy, Don Sebastian of the Queen's Guard.

At a ball given in honor of the Archduke Paul, the surly Don Sebastian is inadvertently insulted by the archduke, and, losing his temper, murders him. Circumstantial evidence points to Don Cesar as the murderer, even though there is a witness, the corrupt Don Fabrique, who holds the key to the mystery, a note in which the archduke scribbles just before his death the name of his assassin. Stating his preference for death before dishonor, Don Cesar heroically feigns suicide, jumping from the casement of the castle into the sea far below. Against these impossible odds he survives, of course, to redeem the family name. Don Fabrique, meanwhile, uses the archduke's note to blackmail Don Sebastian and to insinuate himself into a government position whereby he can exploit others. Don Q summons his father from California and together, at the end, in a series of split-screen effects, they undo the villains and clear the name of de Vega.

How rarely has the sequel to a popular film lived up to the original? This is not at all the case, however, with *Don Q, The Son of Zorro*. For a number of reasons, this movie may be considered both a more entertaining and even a better film than the original *Mark of Zorro* made five years earlier. Almost all of the little tricks and touches that defined Zorro in the first film are now developed and perfected in the sequel. In addition to the aforementioned devices, there is a good deal of comic "business" with the lighting and flicking away of cigarettes—devices which Fairbanks would further embellish in *The Gaucho*.

There are some significant differences, however, in both the conception of character and setting between the two *Zorro* films. The first film was set in California, the second in Spain. The aristocratic lineage explained in the first film curves back parabolically upon itself in the second. The senior Zorro represents the New Man in the New World. His actions, bearing, and dignity harken back to an older, aristocratic tradition. His son, however, embodies the perfect synthesis of the two cultures. Zorro had brought the best traditions of aristocratic Spain—honor, courage, courtly manners, heroic style—to the New World. His son takes the best qualities of the New World—honesty, directness, vigor—back to Spain and puts them to work in Madrid, where the court itself is in danger of falling into corruption (or at least is threatened by the likes of such lowly characters as Don Fabrique). He repeatedly reminds everyone that his father is the "finest man in America," while he himself is referred to as "the Californian."

It takes father and son together, finally, to reform the court, remedy the situation, and exonerate the name of de Vega. Despite all that, *Don Q* is really an *American* story. Don Q himself is an American. New World values drive the story. For example, when Don Cesar is asked where he learned the whip, he responds,

> *"In California—my father taught me. My father is the greatest man in America."*

A bit later, as Don Cesar duels with Don Sebastian, the American casually repeats what is becoming a mantra:

> *"You know, my father is the greatest swordsman in America."*

Moreover, father and son embody the sort of moral imperative that is inherently and pragmatically American. In words that echo the motto of none other than David Crockett, Don Cesar proclaims:

> *"My father always said: 'When you are in the right, fight; when you are in the wrong, acknowledge it.'"*

Don Q is organized around a number of trials and demonstrations of courage that give Fairbanks ample opportunity to outwit and to outfight villains that appear to be more physically imposing, on the one hand, and more sophisticated and dissembling, on the other. As usual, these dangers are calculated to put Doug's cavalier recklessness on exhibit. He fights Don Sebastian, who turns out to be no worthy opponent—in swordplay or in love, as it turns out. He grapples with a maddened, rampaging bull and literally takes it by the horns. After restraining the bull, he wins the acclaim and adulation of the crowd, but he sprints and vaults away from them, partly for his own amusement (and eternally for ours) to show that he can escape the pursuing masses—a star good-naturedly fleeing his public.

This sequence, in turn, foreshadows the later escapes that are required in more serious situations. It establishes our confidence in the character, just as the character asserts and reasserts his confidence in himself. Later, for example, we see Doug expose himself to danger again when he escorts Paul to a lowly tavern in the sequence entitled "An Archduke's Night Out." This results in several encounters with local ruffians. Seemingly trapped in the café, every exit blocked, Don Q has this exchange with one of the thugs. It is classic Fairbanks.

> *"You think you leave this place, eh?"*
> *"When I am ready!"*

The film ends with that magnificent reunion between father and son. Interestingly, Fairbanks here steps into the dual role of the elder Zorro, but it is with a greater zest than when he becomes the elder d'Artagnan in

Stylish dueling in *Don Q*.

The Iron Mask. Though presumably old and visibly graying, he is still spry and happy as he retrieves the sword that was placed in that rafter in 1920 at the conclusion of *The Mark of Zorro.* He pauses for a moment, indulging us in a flashback of the climactic duel in the first film, wherein he bested his opponent and hurled his sword into the wall. Now, he proclaims:

> *"I need you again."*

He arrives in Spain in time to help the son. They fight side by side, Zorro's face momentarily concealed by a cloak. His son exclaims,

> *"I don't know who you are, but you are welcome!"*

Sandwiched between the exotically flamboyant *The Thief of Bagdad* and the virtuoso color palette of *The Black Pirate, Don Q* may at first seem a modest film by comparison. But it is lively and well paced. Fairbanks never looked more slim and trim. And, of course, the enthusiasm is there at the very beginning, as Don Cesar strides about his room, executing a variety of parlor tricks with his whip, all the while exclaiming to his servant this typical Fairbanks expostulation:

> *"It's a beautiful life, Robledo!"*

Yet, for all that, there is something . . . *missing*; something which helps explain the film's relative neglect. I believe it has to do with the construction of Fairbanks's masculinity. To review, we already know that Fairbanks translated the iconic image of his hero, Theodore Roosevelt—who had to go west to "remasculinize" himself with a hardy life, physical fitness, and acts of courage—into many of his films, as early as in the character of the clubman, Bertie, in *The Lamb* and as recently in the bespectacled wannabe aristocrat, Richard Marshall, in *The Mollycoddle*.[7] No life is worth leading, Roosevelt had preached, if it is always an easy life."[8]

While this duality had been superbly visualized in the limp handkerchief of Don Diego and the lash and steel of whip and sword of Señor Zorro in the first film, it is altogether absent in *Don Q*. Don Cesar is *always* the man of action. There is none of the needed counterpose or mystery of an alternate foppish identity. We have his father's whip but not his limp handkerchief. Thus, the tensions of an ambiguous masculinity, which Fairbanks had always thrived on, are missing; and the character from beginning to end is little more than a cardboard cutout, with no dramatic arc, no development beyond what we saw in the opening scenes. Zorro had *needed* Don Diego, as Batman later needs Bruce Wayne and Superman needs Clark Kent. This had been a Zorro with modernity's requisite gender ambivalence. Significantly, *that* Zorro is what George Hamilton had so much fun with in his own Zorro entry, *Zorro, the Gay Blade* (1981).

As Henry Jenkins notes in his remarks on the timelessness of pop culture heroes like Zorro and Batman, "There are enormous variations in the way these characters get interpreted across those various generations, dramatic shifts in styles, successive waves of revisionism, various stabs at relevance or topicality." Jenkins concludes that when our hearts cease to beat faster at the mere mention of these caped (and sometimes implicitly closeted) heroes, we have lost "something important in ourselves."[9]

Chapter 8

"A Dance of Free Men in a Forest"

Robin Hood

We who walk the greenwood do many a wild deed.
—LOCKSLEY, in Walter Scott's *Ivanhoe*

—and then from the mysterious depths of Sherwood Forest came whispers of the rise of a robber chief—
—DOUGLAS FAIRBANKS in *Robin Hood*

"We hanker after history," wrote British film critic Ernest Betts "—and then, like some new planet, *Robin Hood* swims into our ken."

In his appreciation of the newly released Douglas Fairbanks swashbuckler, Betts anoints this "nominally historical, tremendously fictitious" film as the "certain type of historical film [that] will always be popular; it is the same reason which has made and will continue to make admirers for Herodotus." Perhaps never in his most extravagant moments would Fairbanks think to align his new film with the works of the fifth century Greek "father of history," Herodotus! (And doubtless Herodotus himself would be astonished.) Yet Fairbanks's "mendacious, cheerful, and amusing" dance with history and story, concludes Betts, is "seen at its best in *Robin Hood*."[1]

Let's indulge Mr. Betts for a moment. Herodotus (480–425 BC), who was surely the godfather to Hollywood historians, fashioned his historical surveys of the ancient world without the aid of written contemporary accounts, military leaders' memoirs, and war office documentation. In contrast to his near contemporary, Thucydides, who restricted his

Robin Hood (1921) (drawing courtesy John C. Tibbetts).

historical writing to "the most careful and particular enquiry," Herodotus allowed room for historical speculation and poetic extrapolation.[2] This approach was confirmed by *Robin Hood*'s director, the redoubtable Allan Dwan, and Fairbanks himself: "The story of 'Robin Hood' is mythical," confessed Dwan. "We had little or nothing to go on. It is likely, I think, that such a character actually lived. But details regarding him are not to

The spectacular set for *Robin Hood*.

be had."[3] Fairbanks was more to the point: "*Robin Hood* was not taken from nor based upon any book. The picture was almost pure imagination, projected against the historical background of the Crusades. It was the fabrication of a dozen dim legends in a form that lent itself to the imagery of the screen."[4]

Thus, undaunted by the lack of historical documentation, Fairbanks, Dwan, and their band of Merry Men drew upon ancient legends, books by Walter Scott (*Ivanhoe*), the poetry of Tennyson (*The Foresters*), and the paintings and illustrations of Brandywine artists Howard Pyle and N. C. Wyeth to craft their own version of the Middle Ages. And *that*, to paraphrase Herodotus, is show biz.[5]

Although the story of Robin Hood had already appeared on screen many times before Fairbanks's version, the very title of his *Douglas Fairbanks in Robin Hood* suggests the highly personal agenda of the film's story and scope.[6] On the heels of the success of *The Three Musketeers*, the ambitious Fairbanks demanded more room to stretch out in, as it were. He financed the film himself at a purported $1,500,000 and purchased the former Jesse D. Hampton Studios at Santa Monica Boulevard and Formosa Avenue in West Hollywood. Christened the Pickford-Fairbanks Studios, it provided the requisite acreage and facilities for art director Wilfred

Buckland's vision of Merrie Olde England. "A great many persons would have had us go to England to film this story," said Fairbanks at the time, "but I had rather construct my castles in California. . . . One of our greatest achievements has been the progress we have made in the building of sets."[7] The preposterous size of that castle—estimated by Dwan as having massive walls over 90-feet high with an interior hall 450-feet long—was a far cry from the more modest structures of Olde England, of course, but director Dwan would have it no other way.[8] Dwan compared the fifteen weeks of shooting to a military operation: "There wasn't a single man on the lot, either in the capacity of an extra or on the technical staff, who had not had military training. . . . No man took orders from anyone but his immediate superior. And each man had his particular province inside and outside of the camera lines.[9]

Robin Hood premiered in Hollywood on October 18, 1922, at Grauman's new Egyptian Theater amid sensational press and hoopla. Robert Sherwood, who could always be counted on to deliver extravagant praise for his hero, wrote, "Here is a motion picture which is so far ahead of any spectacle that has ever gone before that it is impossible to appraise it in the same terms that have been applied to previous efforts. It represents the high-water mark of film production."[10] René Clair was charmed when he first saw it in 1923. Already a Fairbanks enthusiast, Clair called it a film that "disarms criticism." Although the French director expressed doubts that the "spirit" of the Middle Ages could accurately be revived, he nonetheless favored "the interpretation of the Middle Ages given by Fairbanks's film as much as a history book."[11]

Robin Hood begins with a romantic evocation of the past from Charles Kingsley:

> *"So fleet the works of men/ Back to their earth again/ Ancient and holy things/ Fade like a dream."*[12]

Shots of a pile of ancient ruins dissolve into the towers and battlements of a gigantic feudal castle. We are back in the Age of Chivalry, or, as the titles insist, to the "Age of Faith." A drawbridge lowers, revealing the knights of King Richard assembling for a grand tournament that is to mark their departure the following day on a Holy Crusade. We are at once overwhelmed with pageantry, spectacle, and action as Robert, the Earl of Huntingdon (Fairbanks), jousts with the devious Sir Guy of Gisbourne (Paul Dickey). Swift strokes of action immediately sketch out the main characters of this movie—Huntingdon, brave and strong, but naïve and shy; Gisbourne, spurned by Lady Marian Fitzwalter (whom he lusts after), a villain who refuses to play fair (he straps himself to his saddle). Most important here, however, is Wallace Beery's King Richard—

> *impulsive, generous, and brave—*

but also down-to-earth, blunt, honest, a king who exudes humanity and common understanding. His bluff demeanor is contrasted with the sneering, wicked brother, Prince John, who is

> *sinister, dour, his heart inflamed with an unholy desire to succeed to Richard's throne—*

And therein hangs the tale.

What follows is a complex plot which demands more than a cursory synopsis. After Huntingdon defeats Gisbourne, he is appointed second-in-command to King Richard. When Prince John promises Gisbourne his choice of maidens, Huntingdon, who is already enamored of Maid Marian, interferes and becomes her protector. Consequently, Prince John gives Gisbourne orders that neither Richard nor Huntingdon is to return from the Crusade.

These are no ordinary villains. Prince John sets his cruel, oppressive tyranny in motion almost at once as Richard disappears over the horizon. His agent in his dastardly design is the High Sheriff of Nottingham. Meanwhile, Lady Marian goes before Prince John to plead for "mercy for the people of England." Ignored, she sends word for Huntingdon to return. Prince John, sensing danger, learns too late that word has been sent. Marion takes refuge, meanwhile, in a convent. When Huntingdon's servant arrives at the Crusades to bring him the news from Lady Marian, he is torn between love and honor. He knows he must return to England, but he cannot tell Richard the reason, for the king must not be diverted from his "holy mission." Huntingdon sends word to Marian that he will come to her aid—

> *"By some pretext I shall persuade the King to allow me to return."*

But his carrier pigeon is intercepted by Gisbourne's falcon. Richard assumes Huntingdon is a cowardly deserter and throws him into prison.

Richard has his own problems, by the way, as he narrowly escapes Gisbourne's assassination plot against him. Huntingdon, meanwhile, is rescued by his loyal servant and returns to England, only to be told that Lady Marian has met with a fatal accident. In a quietly lovely interlude, he stands at the scene of her presumed death. Sword in hand, he swears vengeance:

> *"For God, to Richard, and to Her!"*

And prepares himself for a new life to come:

> *Thus it was that Huntingdon buried his yesterday—and began a life dedicated to revenge—bitter—but joyous.*

This is the last time we shall see Fairbanks as Huntingdon before the end of the film. Soon he will be reincarnated as Robin Hood, the champion of the common man, the role Fairbanks was born to play.

The second half of the film introduces us to Robin Hood and his Merry Men. Agitation against the depredations of the Prince's minions against the peasants and villagers has been brewing in the greenwood:

> *In England, sturdy men, rebellious to John's tyranny, sought refuge in Sherwood Forest.*

Who is to lead them?

> *The lusty rebels only waited for a leader to weld them into an outlaw band destined to live immortal in legend and story.*

We have waited, too. For more than an hour of screen time we have waited.

Finally, a mysterious presence: An unseen figure comes to the aid of John's victims. He leaves in his wake spent arrows, gusts of wind, and the sign of Richard the Lion-Heart.

> *A year passed—and then from the mysterious depths of Sherwood Forest came whispers of the rise of a robber chief—*

And then—suddenly, there he is, Robin Hood. Our first view sees him framed in silhouette in the high window of the castle. It is one of the great moments in all of Fairbanks's films. Impishly, he mocks the mere mortals below him. In a flash, he's gone again. For the next ten minutes of screen time, without benefit of intertitles, an ensuing chase has him eluding the sheriff's men inside and outside the castle's interiors and battlements. He dances atop a parapet, unleashes a storm of arrows, slides down a gigantic drape, and in general leaps and frolics ahead of his pursuers. Later, in Sherwood, he's *still* leaping as he joins the Merry Men, Will Scarlett, Friar Tuck, Little John. Indeed, now they are *all* leaping—*cavorting*—in the sheer hilarity of the moment. Some viewers today are understandably amused. But the rest of us are intoxicated at the sheer audacity of this innocent dance of camaraderie. Only Fairbanks could have pulled *this* off. "Thanks to Fairbanks's grace and good humor," writes Kevin Brownlow, "this evocation of the joy of freedom succeeds; had Robin Hood been played by anyone else, the response would be one of embarrassment."[13]

From this point forward, the film becomes a ballet of motion, a "fairy-pantomime" in an enchanted Sherwood Forest, or, as René Clair so aptly described it, "free men dancing in a forest."[14] Their good-natured lawlessness foils Prince John's wicked schemes:

> *"We rob the rich, relieve distressed/ On damned John to score./ We'll take a life, if sorely pressed/ 'Till Richard reign once more."*

Then—

> *A mysterious stranger invades Sherwood Forest—*

and a helmeted knight seeks out Robin Hood—

> *"Mayhap to join him—mayhap to slay him."*

We know this to be King Richard himself, who has returned from the Crusades upon hearing news of Prince John's knavery. He crosses longstaffs with Friar Tuck and defeats that formidable opponent. The narrative is true here to the spirit of medieval legend, as the enigmatic challenger tests the mettle of Robin's men. One is reminded of the coming of the Green Knight to Arthur's court, as we find in this film a pleasant visual blending of legend and chivalric myth.

Of course there is no question that Richard shall reign anon—but that is not exactly the point, even though the film does build to an exciting, fast-moving rescue and climax.

Alas, the above synopsis fails to capture the charming absurdity underlying the lavish spectacle of Fairbanks's film, with its Giant's castle, fainting ladies, luridly melodramatic plot machinery, and men flying about the greenwood like arrows loosed from Robin's bow. Best return to the perceptive and amusing commentary offered by contemporary observer Ernest Betts to better convey its fairytale charm. "The Fairbanks-Herodotus way of looking at history has the great advantage of never being tedious," Betts writes. "It is never tedious, because it is so full of surprises." The story may be "grossly untrue," but "*Robin Hood* went at such speed that the watcher had no time to pick out, even if he was conscious of them, any of its gross inaccuracies. It was speed and rhythm and, therefore, enjoyment." Everything possesses a preposterous size and energy," continues Betts. The castle set is a "man-made mountain" that seems "to out-top the pyramids. . . . Could Herodotus himself have improved on this? . . . We are not shocked, nor do we feel inclined to say, 'That's all wrong,'; or 'That's preposterous,' because it just isn't." Thus, the march to the Crusade in the first half "is reminiscent of a body of champion heavyweights setting out for the Olympic Games." No matter the subsequent brutality of battle; rather, we rejoice, as

> off goes the cavalcade, up capers Doug's horse. Marian waves from her turret, the trumpets blare, and we're off to fight for the Cross. . . . The army trails on across France, flags flying and trumpets blowing, still in the very best holiday spirit. *"Le roi s'en va-t-en guerre,"* and in those far-off days warfare was indeed a sport. No tanks, no gunpowder, no filthy gas, just strong men hacking at each other until one or the other has lost too many limbs to be able to go on hacking, the one with the majority of limbs remaining being accounted the victor!

So intoxicating and irresistible is all this, continues Betts, "that we forget the loss of life and limb, and find ourselves rejoicing with King Richard and his merry knight, swinging along with them to play our part in the great game against the Arabian infidels."

Back in England in the second half, Robin Hood's "arrows are everywhere." The Merry Men are forest elves dancing on the green. And Robin and Marian, recounts Betts, are engaged in a dance of hide-and-seek of their own:

> Marian is found, lost and found again. Doug is captured, Doug escapes, and Doug is finally tied to a stake and condemned to be shot, when out steps a knight in black armour, and catches ALL the arrows intended for Doug on his own enormous shield. Those who know their *Ivanhoe* will have little difficulty in identifying the black knight with good King Richard, and so all ends happily. King Richard is his old happy self; years of crusading, shipwreck, and prison had left no trace upon his jovial countenance. And the same applies to Doug. He is the same Doug, and ten years of outlawry have done nothing but rejuvenate him. And as for Maid Marian, she is quite definitely younger and more beautiful than she was at the beginning of the film—what an advertisement for the open-air life.[15]

Perhaps no moment in the film visually captures this spirit better than an anecdote following the climactic fight in the castle. It is little more than a grace note to what has come before, but it is pregnant with meaning. King Richard is trying to find the absent Huntingdon. "Huntingdon!" he shouts. No response. (Huntingdon and Marian are otherwise occupied.) Again he shouts, at the top of his voice—"HUNTINGDON!!!" In response, as if blown away by a mighty gust of wind, the Merry Men, sitting in a line atop the wall, tumble off their perch.

Such was the sheer force of Fairbanks's humor. Herodotus would have been proud.

A few months after the release of *Robin Hood*, the ever-restless Fairbanks was off on another, rather different quest. "*Robin Hood* embodied nothing particularly new or revolutionary," he confessed to his friend, the writer and critic Robert E. Sherwood. "There was no pleasant adventuring into the unknown, no experimentation with the screen as a medium for a new kind of expression. This is precisely what I am attempting at present."[16]

That "experiment" would prove to be Fairbanks's most ambitious scenic achievement: *The Thief of Bagdad*.

Chapter 9

"Architecture in Motion"

The Thief of Bagdad

When Shahrazad ceased speaking, Dunyazad exclaimed, "Oh, my own sister, by Allah in very sooth this a right pleasant tale and a delectable; never was heard the like of it, prithee tell me now another story to while away what yet remaineth of the waking hours of this our night." She replied, "With love and gladness if the King give me leave"; and he said, "Tell thy tale and tell it quickly." So she began, with these words.
—THE BOOK OF THE THOUSAND NIGHTS AND A NIGHT

And so we come to Douglas Fairbanks's extravagant "Arabian Nights Fantasy." He takes us to Bagdad, the "dream city of the ancient East," a brutal and magical place, where horses have wings, carpets fly, and princes, despots, and thieves alike contest for the hand of the caliph's beautiful daughter. Not just the exotic trappings of Richard Burton's *The Book of the Thousand Nights and a Night* are here, but so is its central theme, encapsulated in this quatrain:

> Seek not thy happiness to steal
> 'Tis work alone will bring thee weal
> Who seeketh bliss without toil or strife
> The impossible seeketh and wasteth life.[1]

Thief, like a handful of earlier films from the late teens and early twenties—such as imported "Orientalist" fictions of Georges Melies, Joe May's German serials, and Paul Leni's *Waxworks*—constructs an Oriental playground for white audiences on which to project their pleasures

Eluding his pursuers in *The Thief of Bagdad* (1924).

and fantasies.[2] Among the ecstatic fans and critics that greeted its New York premiere on March 18, 1924, none was more rapturous than the always reliable Robert E. Sherwood, who considered *The Thief of Bagdad* as "the farthest and most sudden advance that the movie has ever made."[3] The trick is, as Sherwood goes on to explain, that it somehow makes its wizardry seem probable. If, for example, the thief's nimble fingers can steal a merchant's purse, why can they not conjure a rope up into the air? Sherwood's judgment has, for the most part, withstood the years, and *Thief of Bagdad* remains "a feat of motion picture art which has never been equaled and one which itself will enthrall persons time and again."[4]

Today, however, as will be noted presently, in a few crucial respects, at least, we may view this exotic *caravanserai* with different eyes and sensibilities. We are prepared to regard it, one of Fairbanks's finest achievements, not just as a triumph of design and execution, but as the product of that peculiar phenomenon endemic to its time, "Orientalism." In other words, it has several stories, or "*nights*," to relate . . . so we will condense the "1001 Nights" into our own "Four Nights."

The First Night

At the outset, *The Thief of Bagdad* finds us on familiar territory, for the film's motto is:

> *Happiness must be earned.*

Whether we are in New Jersey, Arizona, Mexico, or Bagdad—as a businessman, a cowboy, an aristocrat, or a thief—Fairbanks's message remains the same, only now couched in an exotic rhetoric:

> *"O true believers, gathered in this sacred mosque, earn thy happiness in the name of the true god . . . Toil, for by toil are the sweets of human life to be found."*

Our Thief, moreover, in the best fairy tale (and Fairbanksian) tradition, will win the hand of a princess and graduate from rags to riches. The main characters of this film represent polar extremes of fairy tale society. On the one hand, we have caricatures of Asian potentates grown fat and lazy from overindulgence and luxury, such as the stout Prince of Persia (one is reminded of the indulgent rich in Fairbanks's early comedies, by the way) or slimy villains consumed by greed and political ambition, such as Cham Shang, The Great Prince of the Mongols, King of Ho Sho, and governor of Wah Hoo and the Island of Wak. At the other social extreme, we have Doug's thief, a clever, pragmatic fellow who lives by his wits and is clearly successful at his "profession." He appears as an appealing and energetic entrepreneur in baggy pants, out for himself, a rather greedy realist who states his philosophy as follows:

> *"What I want-I take. My reward is here. Paradise is a fool's dream and Allah is a myth."*

In the next sequence, at the palace at Ho Sho, this philosophy is echoed by the Mongol prince, demonstrating that cynical ambition is not limited to the lower classes. The prince proclaims that the palace at Bagdad

> *"shall be mine. What I want, I take—"*

and prepares to travel to Bagdad as suitor to the princess (Julanne Johnston). Hence, the thief thinks like a prince, or the prince thinks like a thief. Both, at any rate, shall contend later for the hand and favor of the princess.

Having bluffed his way into the palace, the thief boasts to the princess that he is

> *"Ahmed, Prince of the Isles of the Seas, and of the Seven Palaces [who] is a wretched outcast—a thief . . . I can bear a thousand tortures, endure a thousand deaths—but not thy tears."*

The palace guards take him at his word. They capture and flog him. But before they can throw him to the palace ape, the princess comes to the rescue, professes her love and gives him her ring. Transformed, in effect, from a thief to a prince, he now casts aside his pantaloons and wraps himself in silks and flowing robes.

The "test" is devised for the choosing of her proper suitor:

> *"Send them to distant lands to seek some rare treasure. At the Seventh Moon let them return. Who brings the rarest treasure I will wed."*

The "transformed" thief goes to the mosque for solace and advice. He is told there that

> *"Allah hath made thy soul to yearn for happiness, but thou must earn—"*

and the film's motto is therefore reinforced.

In no other costume film is the episodic structure so obvious as in this one. During the extended sequence of the "Seven Moons," the scenes change rapidly from one magical setting to another—from "The Valley of Fire," for example, to "The Valley of the Monsters," "The Cavern of the Enchanted Trees," "The Old Man of the Midnight Sea," or "The Abode of the Winged Horse." Equally strange and exotic are the prizes won in this "Search for Rare Treasure." All of the prizes—the prince of the Indies' magical crystal (plucked from the eye of a "forgotten idol near Kandahar at the expense of an agile servant's life"), the Persian prince's magic carpet, the Mongol prince's magic apple from the "Island of Wak"—contribute to the film's dynamic conclusion involving the rescue of the princess. The villainous Mongol prince, who has taken Bagdad with twenty thousand men, is then thwarted by the carefree and devious thief, who, having the "seeds" to power, literally sows them, conjuring up hundreds of thousands of soldiers in no time at all.

The Second Night

The film excels in its special-effects photography. The magic of its technological achievement was not missed by contemporary audiences. The *New York Times* reviewer, after seeing this film open to an appreciative audience at the Liberty Theater, wrote, on March 19, 1924, "There are some wonderfully well-worked-out double exposure photographic effects, and even to an experienced eye the illusion is in nearly every instance kept up to a state of perfection."[5] Such illusions as Fairbanks's dive into the depths of the sea and his battle with the sea monster, as well as other seemingly "magical" effects, set this film apart from his others. Obviously the production crew's ingenuity was taxed at several points in the making of this picture. How, for example, does one make a magic carpet fly convincingly? Is this the sort of trick that can be created through the camera? Raoul Walsh, the director of the film, finally found the solution to this problem while observing a group of steelworkers at a construction site in Hollywood, one of whom was riding a load of girders. Back at the studio, he found the right kind of crane, and was left only with the difficulty of lifting the carpet from the floor. Walsh remembers:

> [We] solved that problem by installing an overhead pulley and a hand winch (both off camera) and using a burly extra to wind the crank. The result [Walsh reports] was better than I had expected. The carpet had a steel frame and steel cross-strapping underneath. When the drum winch began to turn, the whole thing, with Fairbanks and Miss Johnston sitting cross-legged on it, rose before the eyes of the suitably astonished spectators and thin wires pulled it toward the window.[6]

Putting the carpet and its occupants through the window could then be done by suggestion, by cutting from the shot where the carpet reaches the window to the next shot of the carpet outside the palace on its journey over the city of Bagdad. For this outside shot, Walsh used an eighty-foot boom (and a double for Miss Johnston). The crane cables were painted white, which rendered them invisible. Beyond this, the "reality" of the effect is informed by the director's cinematic sense:

> To strengthen the illusion of flying, I made low-angle shots, added cut-ins of the people staring up from the streets—obtained by perching cameramen and

> myself on a platform at the top boom and shouting down—then resumed the slow pan showing the travelers on their way.[7]

As was often the case in these costume spectacles, cost was not spared if exactly the "right" effect had to be created. According to Walsh, *The Thief of Bagdad* was the first picture to cost a million dollars. Much of the expense, no doubt, went into the creation of the exotic costumes (designed by Mitchell Leisen) and the set designs of William Cameron Menzies. This is largely a film of architecture and atmosphere, to the extent that the Fairbanks figure is frequently subordinated to the sets as well as to the spectacle. Ornamentation becomes an end in itself, and the film becomes a spectacular and popularized masque for the millions. The Fairbanksian charm is there, to be sure, but of primary importance is the manner in which the design values excite and delight the visual sense. In conception, the art nouveau influence (as evidenced by the curving lines and the superbly decorative surface patterns) is central. It is as if a set of mobile black-and-white, pen-and-ink drawings has come to life, creating an animated *mise-en-scéne.*

The film's foremost champion was that vagabond poet and cultural prophet, Vachel Lindsay. Writing as early as 1914, in *The Art of the Moving Picture,* he had devised a theory of the film medium as "architecture-in-motion," wherein actors may be subordinated to architectural elements which, in themselves, "take on a vitality almost like that of flesh and blood."[8] Now, writing in 1926, Lindsay looks back on *Thief* as a demonstration of this phenomenon:

> Note how while on the extraordinary flying carpet which you yourself seem to ride like a flying machine, the massed buildings and streets the city pour by like real actors. This happens in no other art. Stars and clouds pile up into architecture and become actors. The stairways seem to leap like race horses from scene to scene, or pour like cataracts through the various archways . . . magnificent actors in the grand manner.[9]

However, one cannot imagine such a film being made at this particular period *without* Fairbanks in the lead, for it is his kind of picture, the perfect vehicle for his athletic versatility.

Baring the famous physique in *The Thief of Bagdad*.

The Third Night

More vividly than a work in any other medium could do, *The Thief of Bagdad* captured the American popular imagination's construction of the Middle East as, on the one hand, mysterious, alluring, and sumptuous; and, on the other, as barbaric, irrational, and despotic. Delicately scented scenes in the Princess's boudoir are juxtaposed to brutal floggings in the city square. Words from the Holy Book are corrupted by rampaging Mongols with lustful appetites. Significantly, the fair-skinned princess, and not the wicked, olive-skinned Mongol slave girl (Chinese actress Anna May Wong), is the target of their lusts. "Whiteness," or the lack of it, is an important symbolic marker here. The deep, "Oriental" tan of the profane thief contrasts with the "holy" translucent skin of the princess; yet it is to her he is drawn, not to the darker-skinned Mongol girl. We will later note a similar dichotomy in *The Gaucho*, in the instance of the swarthy Fairbanks's attraction to the white purity of the Virgin of the Shrine. Audiences were presumed to accept this, despite the anxiety of miscegenation. To recall Henry Jenkins's observation: "Though Fairbanks applies dark makeup to give himself a swarthy complexion . . . we know that he is white, just beneath the surface, thus predetermining his . . . repudiation of the disorderly woman in favor of the saintly one."[10] This ethnic sleight-of-hand is confirmed, moreover, in the ambiguity of the thief's masculinity.

For much of the first half of the film, before he meets the princess, he is an atheist, blatantly displaying his semi-naked body as he exuberantly dances about the marketplace. (It is surely not by accident that during his romp he frequently gestures aloft the phallic rope.) In the second half, he crouches in holy penitence before the princess, his body come to rest, enveloped in flowing robes, sashes, and strings of jewelry and pearls. His aggressively masculine pose gives way to a more submissive, effeminate posture, "whitening," him, in effect, as a more "acceptable" suitor to the princess. In either case, we should add, clothes make the man, coding the overall sensuality: "Whereas traditional Victorian dress had enforced rigidity in form while at the same time modestly concealing most parts of the body," notes Dr. Rosenblatt, "orientalist aesthetics allowed men and women to explore sensuality through dress."[11] (This looser form of dress became in the 1920s an important influence on Flapper fashion.) It perhaps is apposite here that in Douglas Jr.'s portrait of his father, he noted a surprisingly sensuous side to the man—that he "takes a feverish interest in his wardrobe and is an authority on styles for men" and that "he adores perfume."[12]

The motion picture in the first few decades of the New American century was exploiting the legacy of the late Victorian construction of "The Orient," that vast region of cultures and countries that included most of Asia as well as the Arab lands in the Middle East. What Edward Said famously dubbed as "Orientalism" in his classic 1978 text was, at that time, an "imaginative geography," a "Western style for dominating, restructuring, and having authority over the Orient."[13] This representation of race, nationality, and "otherness" was fueled by the historical threat that Islamic culture represented to the West. It aroused, as a result, an ambivalent attitude—the imperial West's "contempt for what is familiar and, at the same time, its shivers of delight in—or fear—of novelty."[14] Thus, the iconography and stereotypes of romance, mystery, and barbarism in *The Thief of Bagdad* derive from a wild variety of sources prevalent in the *zeitgeist* of the day—Edward Fitzgerald's "translation" of *The Rubaiyat of Omar Khayyam*, Moroccan images by "academic" painters like Delacroix, a profusion of travel literature about Arabs, the publication in 1885 of Burton's *The Book of the Thousand Nights and a Night*, the music of Rimsky-Korsakov's *Schéhérazade*, the sensuous curves of art nouveau, the Diaghilev/Leon Bakst exotic *Ballets Russes*, and the imperialist reach

In the director's chair for *The Thief of Bagdad* (1924).

of America, France, and Britain regarding their colonial possessions/interests in the Middle East.

A more immediate context for motion pictures like *Thief* was the spectacular public success of the installation of the Ottoman Pavilion at the 1893 Columbian World Exposition in Chicago. It featured a highly romanticized visual dramatization of Middle Eastern life, including belly dancers, Bedouins, camels, and donkeys. "This was the Orient brought home for the titillation and viewing pleasure of the Victorian public," says Dr. Rosenblatt. "Spectacular displays based on the color, texture, and shape of commodities engulfed sets featuring the domes and minarets of the Middle East . . . a telling example of how the Orientalist aesthetic became intimately linked with Victorian consumerism."[15]

The Fourth Night

In the final analysis, we may not be burdened over much about an "Orientalist" analysis of *The Thief of Bagdad*. That contexualization of a racist American sensibility of its time is significant and manifest, to be sure, but the film's buoyant fun and wildly extravagant fantasies speak for themselves and should be viewed on their own terms.[16] Fairbanks's extravagance is neither a critique or a confirmation of Orientalism. As G. K. Chesterton would say, "It is not the extravagance of satire, but simply the extravagance of vitality."[17] We come away with a childlike wonder, what impelled the otherwise acerbic Mark Twain to greet the Holy Land during his travels there in 1869 as a "genuine revelation of the camel trains, the bazaars, the fanciful costumes." Twain goes on in what could almost be a description of the Fairbanks film:

> The picture lacks nothing. It casts you back into your forgotten boyhood, and again you dream over the wonders of *The Arabian Nights*; again your companions are princes, your lord is the Caliph Haroun Al Raschid, and your servants are terrific giants and genii that come with smoke and lighting and thunder, and go as a storm when they depart.

The Thief of Bagdad was to have an incalculable influence on Hollywood's "Orientalist" visions to come. As historian Mathew Bernstein observes, "It would consolidate many of the narrative and visual conventions that *Arabian Nights* films would follow."[18] But such an examination requires yet another book of the *Nights*. Would that Burton had lived to write it.

Chapter 10

"A Painted Ship on a Painted Ocean"

The Black Pirate

Color is a vice, although it can be one of the finest virtues. When controlled by a firm hand, well guided by her master, Drawing, Color is then like a splendid woman with a mate worthy of her—her lover but also her master—the most magnificent mistress possible. . . . But when united with uncertainty, with a weak drawing, timid, deficient, easily satisfied, Color becomes a bold whore, makes fun of her little fellow, isn't this so?—And gallivants as she pleases, taking the thing lightly as long as everything is pleasing to her, treating her poor companion like a simpleton who is bothering her—which, moreover, is true, too. The result is visible: a chaos of drunkenness, cheats, regrets, things left unfinished! All right now, enough!
—JAMES McNEILL WHISTLER

The Black Pirate premiered simultaneously at the Tivoli Cinema in London and in New York on March 1926. Like all of Fairbanks's costume films, it offers a wide range of interests. Much has already been written about the casting, the story, and the famous acrobatics—such as the slide down the sail on the knife and the final undersea rescue. Of particular value is a two-part article by film historian Rudy Behlmer for *American Cinematographer* in 1992.[1] But *The Black Pirate* commands our attention for other reasons. It was shot in color in the relatively untried process of two-color Technicolor. The challenges involved forced the filmmakers to resort to extreme methods in the preparation and shooting, making *The Black Pirate* the most carefully controlled and executed of all Fairbanks's films. To paraphrase Gilbert and Sullivan, it was not an easy thing to be a pirate king. The results, however, attracted considerable attention. As *Photoplay* reported, "Nothing has ever been done in colors on the screen that

Action galore in *The Black Pirate* (1926), Fairbanks's Technicolor experiment.

approaches it in beauty and uniformity. . . . Mr. Fairbanks, for the first time in motion pictures, has secured the beautiful effect of mural paintings."[2]

Hue and Cry

Audiences and filmmakers alike had always been fickle about color. Hand-colored films from Pathé Frères had worn out their welcome. Mechanical processes like Kinemacolor, an early experiment in a two-color additive system, and Technicolor, a subtractive system, were condemned for either causing eyestrain or for technical shortcomings. An editorial writer for *Motion Picture Magazine* even speculated that there was a "psychological reason for their non-popularity," concluding that "color seems to cross the line between the real and the unreal and leaves too little room for the imagination."

When Fairbanks shot *The Black Pirate*, the Technicolor Corporation had already been in business since 1913. Three graduates of the Massachusetts Institute of Technology, Herbert Kalmus, Daniel F. Comstock, and W. Burton Westcott, had organized a firm of technical consultants working with a new kind of motion picture camera. Comstock had designed a camera that could photograph a scene in two colors, red and green. Two negatives, one sensitive to red, the other to green, received simultaneously the light that came through the single-lens camera. The light was "divided" by a prismatic device onto these respective negatives.[3] The two images were then superimposed onto a screen by "projecting through two apertures, each with a color filter, bringing the two components into register on the screen by means of a thin adjusting glass element."[4] This was an additive process. Thus, the Technicolor Motion Picture Corporation came into existence in 1915.

After a year of research the fledgling company decided to make its first feature film in Jacksonville, Florida, in order to take advantage of the semi-tropical sunlight. The first Technicolor lab was mounted on a remodeled railroad passenger car. It contained a laboratory with darkroom, a fireproof safe, a power plant, and an office. New colleagues were added to the staff, including Professor E. J. Wall, a veteran experimenter in color photography, and Joseph A. Ball, who later became a key director of Technicolor research. That first film was called *The Gulf Between* and was completed in the summer of 1917. Its first exhibition was a private one at Aeolian Hall in New York City on September 21. Subsequent exhibition was limited and some flaws marred its debut.

The problems Technicolor encountered with *The Gulf Between* are typical of the additive processes. The main problem was "fringing." This refers to the separation of the two colors on the image so they no longer exactly registered on the screen. Suddenly a man would have two shirts, one of red and the other of green. Another problem lay in the special equipment needed for projection. The twin-aperture kind of projector was expensive. This meant that regularly equipped movie theaters would have to install the new equipment at great expense.

Efforts were underway in 1918 to solve these problems. The result was that Technicolor began working with a *subtractive* color process. This meant that a method had to be worked out to stamp color dyes onto the film, eliminating the encumbrance of projector filters. Professor Wall had suggested as early as 1916 that the subtractive process was the answer to the color problem. Now it remained to devise an effective method of printing the color dyes onto the film.

In 1920 William Travers Jerome became chairman of Technicolor's board. It was under his guidance that Technicolor's subtractive two-strip process was further developed. Historian Rudy Behlmer describes the process:

> Separate prints were made from the red and green filter negatives on film that was thinner than regular stock. After printing, the two films were cemented together with sprocket holes in perfect registration and with both emulsion sides facing out. The side printed from the red filter negative was dyed blue-green and the side printed from the green filter was dyed red-orange.[5]

Thus, the positive filmstrip was really two strips cemented together, and the color dyes were stamped onto the filmstrips by a process called *imbibition,* wherein a dye absorbed in gelatin is transferred by contact and pressure to blank film. Each print came directly from the camera negative. The first film made in this process was *Toll of the Sea* in 1922. The film industry closely watched the progress. Rex Ingram expressed interest in reshooting his *Prisoner of Zenda* in Technicolor, and D. W. Griffith considered shooting *Faust* in it. Both projects never came to pass. Douglas Fairbanks likewise expressed interest. Plans of making a pirate picture were already forming in his mind. A few more years would pass, however, before he would do so.

With plans for extending its foothold into the film industry, Technicolor established a laboratory and photographic unit in Hollywood in 1923. The subtractive, imbibition process was expensive. The cameras used were costly and only a few were in existence. Personnel had to be specially trained to use them. Up to this point Technicolor had to finance its own ventures since it was difficult to persuade a Hollywood producer to foot the added expenses. But soon some producers, impressed by the quality of *Toll of the Sea,* began to underwrite Technicolor's services for sequences in films. The exodus of the Israelites from Egypt in DeMille's 1923 *The Ten Commandments,* for instance, was shot in the two-color process. In 1924, Technicolor had a chance to shoot some interior sequences for George Fitzmaurice's *Cytherea.* Shooting color under artificial light as opposed to natural sunlight posed more problems for the process. It was found that at least twice as much light was needed on the set than for the regular black-and-white film stock.

The next break for Technicolor came in 1924 when Zane Grey's *Wanderers of the Wasteland* was adapted for the screen for Famous Players. Grey's

Doug and director Albert Parker on the set of *The Black Pirate*.

contract stipulated that the novel be shot entirely in color.[6] The Technicolor crew worked day and night for six weeks. The negative was processed in a plant in Boston and took almost a year to produce enough prints for theatrical distribution. Technicolor actually lost money on the deal due to increased expenses. It was decided not to shoot any more features for a while. Work would be limited to sequences in a number of films spanning 1924–1925. *Wanderers of the Wasteland*, however, left no doubt in the minds of many that the two-color imbibition process was here to stay. More and more producers sought out the company and soon sequences appeared in such diverse films as *The Phantom of the Opera* and *The Merry Widow.* More importantly, the time was right for Douglas Fairbanks to realize a lifelong dream. He would make a pirate picture. It would be in color.

A Painted Ship on a Painted Ocean

The association between Fairbanks and Technicolor reveals the typical interdependence between art and business that so frequently has shaped

Hollywood's growth. Fairbanks had previously voiced doubts about making a film in natural colors:

> The film in natural colors seems to me another fetish. Every now and then someone discovers a new process for making colored photographs, but the photograph which goes on being taken and purchased the world over is not the photograph in supposedly natural colors. We have our own medium in the films, and I see no particular reason for wanting to alter it.[7]

This comment may have been influenced by the available color processes at the time. By the time *Toll of the Sea* had been produced a year later, however, he realized that such processes were steadily improving. Color was now very much on his mind:

> Pirates demand color. Stories of modern life, war stories, even romances like *Robin Hood* and *Thief of Bagdad* might be told in black and white, but what pirates needed was something more vivid. It was impossible to imagine them without color.[8]

Technicolor at that time was a struggling concern, looking for producers to foot the bills. If Fairbanks was waiting for a color process to mature, Technicolor was likewise waiting for a producer of imagination, daring, and—yes—wealth to take the risks of producing an expensive commercial feature in the still relatively untried process. Success on either hand would enhance the success of the other. The successful combination of business sense, personal artistry, and foresight is a rare one. *The Black Pirate* is an example.

With *Robin Hood* completed, Fairbanks in 1923 considered turning to a pirate subject. He hired as director Raoul Walsh and as leading lady Evelyn Brent. He let his hair grow down to his shoulders in anticipation of the role of the bold buccaneer. Plans stalled, however. One reason, previously cited, was the lack of a dependable color process. But there were other factors that plagued Fairbanks's always shrewd business sense. One was the need for assurance that Technicolor would be able to deliver the required number of prints on demand. Another was the fear that pirate pictures had already exhausted their drawing power. Everybody, it seemed, was making them. Fred Niblo was working on a picture to be called *Captain Applejack* (later titled *Strangers of the Night*), Fox was producing *Treasure Island*, and Charles Ray was sinking (!) everything he had on his super-picture, *The Courtship of Miles Standish*, which would feature some pirate sequences. Fairbanks's hesitation about flooding the market with yet another pirate picture was perhaps borne out by the failure of Ray's film, which terminally damaged his career. Fairbanks decided to postpone his own picture and waited while Edward Knoblock, the author of *Kismet*, prepared for him the storyline for the film that would become *The Thief of Bagdad*.[9] Walsh assumed the directorial helm for *Thief* instead of the pirate picture.

One result from this flurry of pirate activity was the arrival of a gentleman named Dwight Franklin, a disciple of renowned painter Howard Pyle. Producers began bidding for the services of this one-man source authority whose knowledge ranged from the life of prehistoric man to the Vikings, American Indians, Eskimo, and, or course, pirates. His miniature models of pirates had invaded the sacred precincts of staid art museums and universities. In addition, he had been for seven years connected with the New York Museum of Natural History as a wild- animal photographer, field collector, taxidermist, and sculptor.[10] This astonishing man would play a major part in the production of *The Black Pirate.* As will be seen, the film would depend heavily upon its art direction. Franklin was vital in this respect.

It is surprising, perhaps, to realize that the history of the color film has been plagued by critical reaction against the very idea of film in natural colors. As late as the release of *The Black Pirate* in 1926, *Motion Picture Magazine* published an editorial that sums up an important reason for this antagonism. "Color effects are excellent for titles, inserts, cutbacks, visions, dreams, allegories . . . but the average drama is more impressive without color." The editorial goes on to say that "color seems to cross the line between the real and the unreal and leaves too little for the imagination."[11] Writing later, in 1933, Rudolph Arnheim touches upon the objections to the color film. He, too, objects to the supposed lack of flexibility that a "natural" medium of color would impose upon the black and white film:

> The painter, who does not—as color film does—take colors ready-made from nature but creates them afresh on his palette, is able by suitable choice of tones, by distribution of color masses, and so forth, to get as far away from nature as is necessary to convey his artistic intention. Judging from what we have seen up to now, the colors in a color film are at best naturalistic—and if owing to imperfect technique they are not yet so, this lack of naturalness does not provide the artist with a potentially useful medium of expression.[12]

The point these two men make perhaps has an aesthetic validity. It is not applicable, however, to a film like *The Black Pirate*, which was made in a color process far different than those known today. Its very limitations (and there were many, including the necessity of shooting in light levels three to four times the average artificial illumination) caused the film's producers to literally alter nature and color as a painter would subordinate a painting to his available palette.[13]

A successful *three*-color process had not as yet been devised. Technicolor at this time was a *two*-color process. Two-color processes "are a compromise of the three-color systems. One film is usually sensitive to red, orange and yellow, while the other attracts blue and green. Some other colors are absent from these two-color systems and the remaining colors are not nearly so true as in full-color films."[14] The problem was that one strip attracted more red than yellow, the other more green than blue. Cameraman Hal Mohr, who shot the two-color work for *The Wedding March* and *The King of Jazz*, recalls:

> In the two-color process the blues were not true and the yellows were not true; blues were green, and the yellows were orange, but other than that, two-color Technicolor wasn't bad.[15]

Objects being photographed were not registering on film in their true colors, only insofar as they contained the reds and greens of the spectrum. Arnheim has objected that perfectly naturalistic colors merely reproduce nature, that a "lack of naturalness does not provide the artist with a potentially useful medium of expression."

By 1925, the picture was underway. The producers faced three basic problems: 1. How to restrain the color; 2. How to work with a color scheme that was virtually exclusive of blue and weak with yellow; 3. How to ensure that the color recorded on film was exactly the hue that had been desired. Technicolor had two advisers on the scene, Arthur Ball and George Cave, assisting cameraman Henry Sharp. They had with them four Technicolor cameras—four out of only eleven existing at that time. Art directors included the aforementioned Dwight Franklin and the Swedish artist Carl Oscar Borg. Borg headed his own staff of artists. These men spent six months and fifty thousand feet of color film and $125,000 before actual shooting even began on the film. In contrast to the six months of research, the production schedule lasted only ten to twelve weeks. It was the six-month period that really counted, however.

1. It might be supposed an early attempt at color would exploit bright, vivid hues. Fairbanks had different ideas. He felt it was better to *subdue* the colors, to "take the color out of color."[16] This motto underlay the entire production. Photographing with the Technicolor cameras often worked against this notion. Fairbanks himself describes this rationale:

> The color camera is remarkable. You can't feed it too much color at a time, because it will always eat up more than you give it, and instead of obtaining a natural effect . . . the exact opposite results. Nature's beauties are spread over so much landscape that the impression can never be garish. But when these same beauties of light and shade are brought to the screen, they are concentrated into so small a space that, unless precautions are taken, they become overemphasized.[17]

The paintings of Rembrandt, he realized, represented complete subordination of colors toward harmonic and compositional unity. There may be reds, blues, and greens in it—but they were cloaked in neutralizing shadow and so harmonized that it was the total *picture* and not a particular spot of color that impressed itself upon the mind. Accordingly, the filmmakers worked out a "keying" color scheme that would dominate the film's palette with green and a reddish brown. For the most part, all vivid colors were banished from the set. "If, in the hurry of outfitting a mob of extras, a scarlet bandanna was allowed to reach the set, it was immediately returned and *locked up* in a closet, never to see the light of day again!"[18]

Of course, vivid colors did have their role, albeit a secondary one. It was thought that they would tend to overstress ordinary action, but would create sufficient contrast if they were reserved for special moments. These moments might be one of great charm—as seeing the parrot in a vivid green sitting on a pirate's shoulder—or of dramatic impact—as when the galleon blows up and the screen is filled with a bright red flash. In all of this, the art directors were not only following the model of Rembrandt's subdued color, but were bowing to the more recent work of the book illustrators of the turn of the century, particularly those of the Brandywine School, including Howard Pyle, N. C. Wyeth, and Frank Schoonover. Close examination of the paintings now included in the compilation known as *Howard Pyle's Book of Pirates* reveals a number of paintings seemingly lifted right out of *The Black Pirate* (or is it the other way around?), such as a painting of a sword duel between two pirates. The composition and, above all, the muted tones of browns, reds, and greens (no blues) are astonishingly similar to the dueling scene between Fairbanks and villain Anders Randolph early in the film. The Wyeth illustrations for *Treasure Island*, moreover, reveal a mastery of muted colors, the dramatic impact coming from the judicious (and sparing) use of vivid colors. That the film was successful in this attempt to restrain colors was acknowledged by this review:

> . . . the colors themselves are always subdued, and, in fact, made so natural and inconspicuous that one soon forgets the color and retains only the feeling that what one sees is very real and very satisfying.[19]

Wishing to restrain colors is quite a different thing than doing it. The film's art staff found that a number of locations selected for shooting displayed yellows and blues that were too "violent." Catalina Island, for instance, was regarded as "all wrong" after a series of initial color tests. Many of the sets, therefore, were recreated in the studio at Formosa and Santa Monica and on the studio's backlots, under the complete control of Oscar Borg and his staff. "Borg painted what he would, secure in the knowledge that it did not matter whether nature had ever thought of the combination before him."[20] In this way "skies" were toned down, either through use of backdrops or simply letting the sky register as white. The galleons were studio-built and were placed in a giant tank that occupied most of the studio space. In fact, the vast majority of the shooting was done in the studio where color could be controlled and restrained completely.

Great care was taken that highlights, reflections of light off polished surfaces, not obtrude upon the eye:

> . . . it was found necessary to dull the surfaces of the silver and brass mountings of the pistols and cannon, and all the ironwork upon the ship, so that they would not distract the eye, nor even be noticed, until brought into use. Even the gold and jewels of the looted ships could not make these firm ascetics lose their heads![21]

Compositions of scenes were handled so that a single point of emphasis was achieved through the manipulations of color intensities. For instance, characters who were to stand out in groupings of men wore shirts keyed colors of a brighter intensity than those men standing in the background. If a light-costumed man were forced by the action to come closer to the camera, he would be dusted down with a powder of a darker hue—wig, costume, and all—to compensate for the increased emphasis his costume would entail.

2. What was to be done about photographing the color blue? "We found it impossible to do anything at all with purple, and that blue cannot be satisfactorily handled, as it takes a greenish tinge," said the film's director, Albert Parker. "This latter presented quite a difficulty—for, as perhaps you know, skies are blue."[22] Yes, and we're talking about the *deep blue* sea, too! The story of how the art directors worked around this problem is a fascinating one.

Sometimes photographing blue was inevitable. As Parker further admits, "Toward the end there is a scene where it was necessary that the sky be blue—when you see it, I think you agree with that it is far less pleasing than the others."[23] It was decided to alter the aspect of nature to get around this limitation. The blue sky, for instance, appears mostly as white with just the slightest suggestion of a warm tinge of brown. The sea had to literally be painted a particular hue of dye that enabled it to "register," according to the demands of the art director. When one pauses to reflect a moment on that last fact—staining the ocean . . . well, it is staggering. Hundreds of thousands of gallons—or is it *galleons*?—of water were treated this way.

3. In adhering to a strict color scheme of green and brown, it was necessary to alter the colors of those objects appearing in front of the camera. This formidable problem has been described in this fashion:

> Mr. Fairbanks soon found, as had others before him, that, excellent as this process is, it will not reproduce on the screen the exact color that was originally in front of the camera, and, even when it does, it fails of artistic effect. It always causes nature to take on strange and unexpected tints, and not always desirable ones.[24]

How, then, to insure that the color resulting on the film was the color that was desired? Much of the testing done in those first six months was taken up with this problem. At first, sets were built in all colors of the rainbow for test shots. Walls of the studios were painted in patches of blue, green, pink, lavender, orange, mauve, and so on. By this means it could be determined how each color would register on film and from this construct a color chart. This chart would enable the filmmaker to know what color the object to be photographed must be if it were to register as the desired hue on film. This is further complicated by the fact that colors are not the same under artificial light as when under the sky. Consequently *two* systems of charts had to be made—one indicating the color "keys" for daylight exterior shooting; the other indicating the "keys" for studio interiors. The conclusions one reaches from all this are that the Technicolor artists were artists in reverse, i.e., the painter may work for his effects directly, mixing his colors on his palette, placing them onto the canvas and manipulating their arrangement and intensity as he goes—even scraping them off if the effect is not the one desired. But the Technicolor artists, reports Albert Parker,

> must work indirectly. They first apply their colors to fabrics, to wood, to metals, to the skin of living beings, and even to landscapes. Then these colors must be mixed with light, gathered by the camera lens, transferred to celluloid, developed, and printed, and projected. Every step offers complications the painter does not encounter.[25]

Early in these experiments it was discovered that the same paint applied to different kinds of wood (or to different kinds of cloth) would register as different colors on film. By means of these charts, it might be found that paint combination no. 7 on pinewood, for instance, would yield a similar color as dye no. 103 on cotton material. In this way complete harmonic unity could be achieved on the film. "Scenes which on the screen present a harmonious whole may have looked like a crazy-quilt of clashing shades. It was necessary to make the tests first and then color the scene before the camera so that the camera would record the effect desired."[26] Again, it was important to know if the scene was to be shot in artificial light or in the sunlight. These two variables would in themselves affect the Technicolor film's registration of hue.

In effect, the whole world was painted. As a result of testing and the compilation of the color charts, and as a result of the dominant concern for muting and harmonizing each scene's color values, it was found that virtually *everything* had to be painted. Cutlasses and culverins, pistols and pieces-of-eight, gunpowder, costumes, sails, longboats, jewelry—everything suffered the artist's brush. This applied to makeup also. The actors had their own "facial color schemes" for interior and for exterior shooting. In order to maintain the same physical appearance, indoors and out, it was necessary to alter the makeup for each situation. The kind of makeup varied. The skin of some individuals was covered with a kind of oil so as "to give their skin the soft and velvet sheen of the ideal 'skin you love to

The island duel in *The Black Pirate*.

touch'—but never find."[27] Fairbanks had a very heavy beard that tended to register on film as green. It was found that by applying a reddish powder to that area of his face, the problem could be alleviated. His leading lady, Billie Dove, had to have her face toned a mellow ivory.

It is obvious that not all films shot in color would be able to take such pains as *The Black Pirate* did. It is unique. It represents a rare fusion of the filmmaking process with the art of the painter. Moreover, it represents an attempt to alter and rearrange the exterior world to match the vision of the artist.

Fairbanks himself was the dominant force in the incredible energy and effort expended on the production. Not only did he firmly believe in the possibilities of color, but he had the money and the good sense to follow through on it. Total expenses for the production amounted to a cool million dollars, no mean sum in those days. He also had the acumen to surround himself with artists/illustrators of the caliber of Carl Oscar Borg and Dwight Franklin. Their collective vision enabled the film to share in the robust vision of the N. C. Wyeth tradition. All these efforts were necessary to as complex an operation as *The Black Pirate* represented. But they alone were not enough. Fairbanks himself supplied the missing factor—he knew what he wanted. This complete trust in his own taste guided the whole film. Many times when both Borg and Franklin were satisfied with results, Fairbanks vetoed them. "Time and time again he did this," declared Ted Reed, Fairbanks's production manager. "He was determined to get the exact effect on the screen that he wanted, and he was certain from the beginning of just what that effect should be."[28]

If the film was a triumph for Fairbanks and the history of the color motion picture, the filmstrip itself presented problems in its projection. *The Black Pirate* was a two-color, subtractive, imbibition process film consisting of two strips of celluloid (one strip for the green dyes, the other for the reds) cemented together. This meant the film was twice as thick as regular film and had emulsion on both sides. A certain amount of sharpness of focus was lost on the screen and needed constant correction by the projectionist. The presence of emulsion on both sides of the filmstrip tended to make it buckle more easily in either direction, throwing the image in and out of focus. Fairbanks toyed with the idea of projecting the film with an extra-strong light. He found this would give more depth to the image, but detracted from the muted colors of the hues. Ultimately, no changes were made—the film was finally shown with regular projection apparatus. Another problem encountered was the filmstrips' propensity for incurring scratches. A scratch on a black-and-white film shows as a white line on the screen. A scratch on this Technicolor film, however, was something else again. It showed as a brilliant green or red flash—most distracting to the viewer. The two-color process doubled the cost of the film stock, the developing, the printing, and even doubled the light required on the set for interiors and exteriors. The imbibition process was a particularly troublesome headache. The matrix used to print the dyes onto the film was useful for only fifteen or twenty prints before it had to be discarded and another one made.[29]

Two-Color Technicolor: An Evaluation

Was it all worth it? The two-color process survived into the thirties, notably in two Warner Bros. horror films, *Mystery of the Wax Museum* and *Dr. X* (1932–1933), but it was replaced by 1932 with a three-strip process that would yield better focus, more reliable registration of color, and access to the primary range of blue colors. Instead of struggling with a

The Black Pirate set.

double-thickness film, a new method was devised to print all three color plates onto a single strip of film, making sure that there was exact registration of the three plates. That same year, the process was first tried by Walt Disney for his Silly Symphony, *Flowers and Trees.* By 1935, Rouben Mamoulian had made *Becky Sharp* and Richard Boleslawski *The Garden of Allah* in the three-color process. Technicolor as was known in its heyday was launched.

But what of that other world of color, that strange, beautiful half-world produced by the two-color Technicolor process? Can we ever determine what an original nitrate print *looked like*? It's a fascinating question, since recent attempts at restoring the color of *The Black Pirate* have produced questionable results. We have to measure them against what we know from contemporary accounts. Several contemporary commentators have left invaluable clues. Vachel Lindsay writes,

> Most of the sailors are . . . a brown hue. The ships, richly carved, run to this dull gold. The desert island where the treasure is buried is fortunately the

> dull gold of sand. The flesh tints vary amazingly within this general spectrum of brown. . . . There is also a good deal of it that makes one think of the days when Howard Pyle had a colored frontispiece in nearly every magazine issue, usually a pirate. . . . Winslow Homer's presence is felt in the "black-green sea" at night.[30]

Writing in *The Arts* in April 1926, Quinn Martin confirms the subdued quality of the palette:

> All [colors] were to be subdued—browns, grays, unobtrusive reds. So that while the spectator fails to find any carnival hues shooting across the canvas where this cinema is shown, still the deep, rich brown of his pirate ships is there; the faded, gray and brown clothing of the players are there; the weak, green waters of the sea are there.[31]

And Mordaunt Hall praised the "wonderful moonlight effects on the water . . . [and] glimpses of the pirates . . . are reminiscent of old masters."[32]

Attempts today to restore *The Black Pirate* are part of the ongoing Fairbanks legacy. The only time after 1926 that the film in its original color state was presented publicly was in May and June of 1940 during a major retrospective at the Museum of Modern Art. Subsequently, by the 1950s, the original Technicolor prints began to deteriorate badly and only black-and-white versions were available. A half-hour version in black-and-white appeared in the late 1950s on television on the series, *Silents Please!*, with Alan Swift's voice narration replacing the intertitles. Vera Fairbanks reports that in 1970 Douglas Jr. approached the British Film Institute National Archive about a restoration from the few surviving elements. "He was told that it would be very complicated and expensive to copy it from a 1926 negative, since that color process was long obsolete," reports Ms. Fairbanks. Subsequent costs were a reported $20,000–$25,000.[33] Unfortunately, there was only a portion of the original cut camera negative available. A negative had to be assembled primarily from extant outtakes. The reconstruction was premiered in London in 1972. A restoration like this, reports Rudy Behlmer, "was without precedent. Making a new negative from a surviving post-1928 imbibition print was one thing, but going back to the original two-color negative was quite another."[34]

Next came a home video release from Kino Video in 1996. Historian/preservationist David Shepard, of Film Preservation Associates, in an interview with this writer at that time, discussed some of the challenges in the color version.[35] "What we have on the Kino version of *The Black Pirate* is not exactly what people saw in 1926," he admits. "The British restoration on which this version is based, was partially financed by Douglas Fairbanks Jr." Four cameras had been used for the original shooting, from which one negative was assembled. All the outtakes and the second camera negative were put aside as insurance. "Unfortunately, the original cut negative is lost," adds Shepard, "and no color prints were preserved by the Museum of Modern Art. Using a black-and-white print as a guide, the British Film Institute found the second camera take of the same action that was in the original cut negative. In other instances, they went to alternate takes of the action. This kind of assembly was true of *The Passion of Joan of Arc.* Some of the greatest films we have are comprised of second takes!"

Shepard spent about a week with Paul Westerbeck, a colorist with Todd-AO:

> We painstakingly went through it to make the color as good as we could make it. With reference to our own judgment, we wanted the skin tones to be our key. Of course, the original photography was quite experimental. If there were more than one character in a given scene, like Doug and Donald Crisp, one face might turn out to be shrimp pink and the other blue. Obviously, the deficiency was in the makeup. Doug suffers the worst, because his complexion was so dark. I think they put opaque makeup all over him. He tends to be rather blue in some of the shots. But if we get him absolutely right, then the water turns red! So, we digitized those shots and paint-boxed his face. We're unable, lacking any reliable guide, to say this is absolutely what it looked like in 1926.

Shepard confirms that when blue was photographed it appeared on screen as a kind of blue-green. "In video we had more latitude, because we were able to change the chroma from shot to shot. But we didn't have an original print that preserved the color. All we could do was go for the flesh tones and see how it would work. There's no yellow, of course."

He notes that Raymond Rohauer released the Fairbanks Jr. version with altered subtitles. "This color version had Rohauer's own title cards, which placed the lettering against a yellow background. Remember, yellow is the one color that was really problematic in the two-color process!" Shepard compares Rohauer's altered titles with our best knowledge of the original titles: "We didn't have original titles, but we had the authentic texts from the black-and-white fine-grain. For the cards, I chose what

An original poster of *The Black Pirate* hanging above the music box that Fairbanks engraved and gave as a gift to Mary Pickford in 1930 (courtesy Tracey Goessel and John Tibbetts).

seemed to be the two primary Technicolor colors and used either blueish or reddish hues."

Compare the opening title cards. In the Rohauer version, we have this:

> *Having captured a ship a band of pirates prepares to make sure there are no witnesses to the foul deed.*

And in the original:

> *A page from the history and lives of the most bloodthirsty pirates who ever infested the southern seas. Being an account of buccaneers and the Spanish Main, the Jolly Roger, Golden Galleons, Bleached Skulls, Buried Treasure,*

> *the plank, dirks and cutlasses, scuttled ships, marooning, Desperate Deeds, Desperate Men, and even on this dark soil—ROMANCE. . . . It was a custom of these Pirates to subdue their prey, loot the ship, bind the captives, and BLOW THEM UP.*

Moreover, the color palette of this release ran too much to raw reds for Shepard's taste, and the focus was not as sharp. "In our version," adds Shepard, "you'll notice in the shots with sand there's no hint of yellow, which is as it should be. If you go for sand that even hints at yellow, you risk getting red water!"[36]

As an update to the quest for the "original" look of the *Black Pirate*, the British Film Institute has done a new restoration from the nitrate print. "I haven't seen it," says Shepard, "but I am told that the results are far superior to the print we had had access to years ago." He also notes there is a new Kino release on Blu-Ray. "The publicity says the new one is much better; I don't agree. But in any event, you now have a choice."[37]

After the film's release, Fairbanks was quoted as indicating more interest in color technologies. "In the course of a decade or so," he predicted, "I really believe that all pictures will be made in appropriate colors." Alas, as far as he was concerned, it was not to be. *The Black Pirate* remains as a "one-shot" in his oeuvre. It's a fascinating document in the history of a color technology that, for now at least, has vanished utterly. In any event, as we await news about future restorations, we can only hope that eventually we will see the most "authentic" version possible.

We continue to relish the prospect of sailing once again—"in a painted ship on a painted ocean."

Doug first portrayed d'Artagnan in *A Modern Musketeer* (1917).

Chapter 11

"Dumas, Douglas, and Delirium"

Fairbanks and the Musketeers

A plot based on flight and pursuit down the highway, down the street, down the lane, and across the seas and back is essentially a photoplay resource.
—VACHEL LINDSAY

"[*The Three Musketeers*] is a kind of combination of Dumas, Douglas, and delirium," enthused the *New York Herald* after the premiere on August 28, 1921, in New York City of Douglas Fairbanks's newest costumed adventure.[1] If we reverse the order to "delirium, Douglas, and Dumas," we accurately describe, in chronological order, all three of Fairbanks's adaptations of the famous musketeer stories. *A Modern Musketeer* (1917) comes first, a "delirious" satire on the spirit of chivalry run amok. Next is *The Three Musketeers* (1921), which is "Douglas" all over, and handed Douglas the signature role of his career.[2] Lastly, *The Iron* Mask (1929) is "Dumas." It carefully subordinated the Fairbanks persona to the plot and spectacle of the "Dumas" narrative.

A Modern Musketeer we already know from an earlier chapter; *The Three Musketeers* and *The Iron Mask* await us here.

The Three Musketeers

"Gentlemen," said d'Artagnan, "allow me to correct your words, if you please. You said you were but three, but it appears to me we are four."

"But you are not one of us," said Porthos.

"That's true," replied d'Artagnan; I do not wear the uniform, but I am one of you in spirit. My heart is that of a Musketeer; I feel it, monsieur, and that impels me on."

"Well, then! Athos, Porthos, Aramis, and d'Artagnan, forward!" cried Athos.

—**ALEXANDRE DUMAS,** *The Three Musketeers*

In *The Mark of Zorro*, Fairbanks had pasted on a moustache as part of his Zorro disguise, but now, a year later, in *The Three Musketeers*, the mustache was real, never to go away (save for a few scenes when Fairbanks brought a clean-shaven Zorro back to the screen in *Don Q*). Its permanence symbolized his commitment to the costume heroics to come. Prior to the Fairbanks 1921 version, Alexandre Dumas's stories of d'Artagnan and his musketeers had already inspired many screen adaptations; and there would be many more d'Artagnans to come, including, Walter Abel, Don Ameche, Warren William, Gene Kelly, Michael York, Chris O'Donnell, and Gabriel Byrne.[3]

Alexandre Dumas based the character of d'Artagnan on a real person from Gascony, Charles de Batz-Castlemore, who early in the seventeenth century had served in King Louis XIII's elite Mousquetaires de la Garde under the adopted name of "d'Artagnan." The gallant soldier died at the siege of Maastricht in 1673. Moreover, as Dumas alleged in his original "Author's Preface" to *The Three Musketeers*, the other musketeers were also based on factual history, as revealed in the memoirs of one Comte de La Fere.[4] If this is true, then it is interesting to note that among all Fairbanks's costumed adventures of the 1920s, the two musketeer films are the only ones whose characters can claim some basis in fact.

But we are keeping our characters waiting in the wings. *Hola!*

An opening title declaims:

Life knows no age nor time.
Youth will ever set out to seek fortune.
Men will ever fight for the love of Women.
Kings will threaten—Queens weep—Ministers conspire.
And so—though our story is of three hundred years ago,
It is as young as Yesterday—or To-morrow.

The scenario by Fairbanks's old friend, playwright Edward Knoblock (*Kismet*), who also supervised the scenery and costumes, reveals many differences from the Dumas stories: The episode involving Queen Anne's

"One for All and All for One!"

diamond buckle is amplified as the primary plot thread. M. Bonancieux is no longer the husband of Constance, seamstress to the queen, but Constance's uncle. The romance between d'Artagnan and Constance has been sanitized by ignoring the fact she is his mistress. She does not die in his arms, poisoned by the rapacious Lady de Winter, but is united with him at the story's conclusion by Richelieu. There is nothing of the siege of La Rochelle, or of Mme. De Chevreuse, of the murder of Buckingham, and of the execution of Milady de Winter. In sum, *The Three Musketeers*

His father's sword in *The Three Musketeers* (1921).

effectively streamlines the narrative trajectory, while paying due obeisance to the complexity of the plot.[5] And, of course, there are frequent iterations of d'Artagnan's famous motto: "One for all, and all for one."[6]

It is remarkable how easily and convincingly the thirty-eight-year-old Fairbanks portrays d'Artagnan, whose face fairly beams with provincial innocence and adolescent naivete. The more brutal aspects of d'Artagnan's nature are altered and softened to fit the Fairbanksian gallantry. Although the slightest in stature of the four comrades, when they walk together, united arm in arm, his gait has the most spring. Even in moments when danger cannot threaten him, his body is coiled for action. When it moves, it gives direction to his impetuous and constant restlessness. In this film, however, he succeeds as much by his wits as by his strength and agility. Poet and critic Vachel Lindsay applauded Fairbanks as an *actor* here, who stands equal to Chaplin: "Charlie Chaplin and Douglas Fairbanks have given complete department store examples of the method, especially Chaplin in the brilliantly constructed *Shoulder Arms*, and Fairbanks in his one great piece of acting, in *The Three Musketeers*."[7] More recently, however, we find commentaries complaining about Fairbanks's acting style. For example, biographer Jeffrey Vance objects that "it sacrifices enchanting and exhilarating action for ponderous scenes and a performance enacted

The first duel in *The Three Musketeers.*

in the traditional grand manner of silent film costume."[8] This assessment is puzzling. A recent viewing of the film confirms that with a lively music score the film moves along very nicely. Indeed, far from subordinating Fairbanks to the plot, the film is *all* Fairbanks, with the other musketeers remaining supportively in the margins.

Thus, there are moments everywhere that make the film his own. D'Artagnan's arrival in Paris is full of delightfully comic touches: Anxious to emulate the fashionable gallantries, he abandons his rude Gascon cap for an absurdly plumed chapeau with which he practices versions of bows and flourishes (he even bows to his horse!); he meets Constance when he rolls up a spool of vagrant yarn left behind by the seamstress; while being measured by a tailor for a new suit of clothes, he leaps on and off the stool, arms and legs pinwheeling as he eludes the tailor's measuring tape; and he cleverly pilfers for his comrades a huge feast of fowl, along the way skewering with his blade a collection of hats belonging to the Cardinal's Guards. At key moments during the various intrigues, he places a finger alongside his nose, as if to say, "I smell a rat!"

The swordplay, choreographed by H. J. Uyttenhove, comes at suitably frequent intervals—including the furious engagement of the Four with the Cardinal's Guard behind the Luxembourg and d'Artagnan's climactic duel with Bernajoux up and down a spiral staircase. And there is some good acrobatic stunting, notably Doug's amazing somersault with dagger and sword in hand, dispatching a fallen foe and springing upright to skewer another, as well as more frequent climbs and falls on and off more rooftops, gates, and walls, including a daredevil rescue of the beleaguered Constance.

The last third of the picture is one long, protracted trajectory that bears out Vachel Lindsay's pronouncement: "A plot based on flight and pursuit down the highway, down the street, down the lane, and across the seas and back is essentially a photoplay resource." Indeed, the pace rarely slackens as d'Artagnan fairly flies across land and sea and back again. It begins when d'Artagnan escapes the cardinal's assassination attempt, slides down a marble staircase, and flees down the broad highway with his three companions to Calais and then by sea on to England, each of his comrades falling by the wayside in turn. Once in England he confronts Buckingham, only to discover the queen's diamonds have been stolen by de Winter. Back to Calais, he catwalks along the side of de Winter's ship and slips into her cabin as she sleeps. Unable to find the buckle, he conceals himself and raps on a wooden cabinet. Milady, roused and thinking that someone is at her door, instinctively reaches for the buckle. Even though she attempts to keep it from him by depositing it within the safety of her cleavage (where *this* d'Artagnan would not think of retrieving it), the wily Gascon wrenches it from her hand by *biting* it to make her release her grip! Then he gallops back to Paris, where in the meantime Richelieu delivers the sort of delicious command we expect to find in every Fairbanks film:

> *"Guard every entrance to Paris. Line the streets. D'Artagnan must not pass!"*

Undaunted, disguised as a King's Guardsman, he invades the court. In the queen's chamber he stops short of giving the buckle to Milady de Winter when he recognizes his own teethmarks on the hand that reaches for it through the drapes. D'Artagnan, typically, makes a joke of the situation by giving Milady de Winter the empty case instead, and waiting to deliver the buckle to the queen in person. Not until Milady de Winter sees the queen advancing toward the king does she realize that she has been duped.

In a charming, appropriately theatrical epilogue, the defeated Richelieu gracefully bestows several honors upon his former foe, d'Artagnan. One by one, he pulls aside several curtains, each one revealing a reunited musketeer, until the very last one displays Constance.

In general, the story is cut from the same pattern as his earlier films. His d'Artagnan is very much the brash, gate-crashing American claiming an aristocratic heritage we have seen so many times:

"Remember, my son—"

his father advises him,

> *"—that your ancient nobility gives you the right to the best in France . . . Never forget three things—loyalty to the King—reverence for the Cardinal—devotion to the Queen."*

Thus, the upwardly mobile go-getter d'Artagnan quickly claims his rightful place at court, while deploying his "American" energies and practical ingenuity in the service of protecting the royal court against plots and intrigues. Some critics were quick to discern the film as yet another Fairbanksian parable of that peculiar institution, an American aristocracy: "[Fairbanks's Paris] looks too new and tidy, somewhat as though it were 'made in America.'" And: "Mr. Fairbanks flashes through brawls and dangers and court assemblies with the dashing assurance of a good American salesman . . . One buys, and willingly."[9]

The "*Other One*": *The Iron Mask*

> They saw him pass gravely, at six paces behind the governor, a man clothed in black and masked by a visor of polished steel soldered to a helmet of the same nature, which altogether enveloped the whole of his head.
>
> **—ALEXANDRE DUMAS,** *The Man in the Iron Mask*

The Iron Mask premiered at the Rivoli Theater in New York City on February 21, 1929. Although it was nominally adapted from Alexandre Dumas's *The Man in the Iron Mask* (1848–1850), its sources also included the two prequels, *The Three Musketeers* (1844) and *Twenty Years After* (1845). Here they are, the Four Musketeers, together again, as Dumas puts it, "venerated among all who wore a sword, as in antiquity the names of Hercules, Theseus, Castor, and Pollux were venerated."[10] The first half of the film

A courtly d'Artagnan in *The Iron Mask* (1928).

reprises elements from Dumas's first novel and Fairbanks's own 1922 *The Three Musketeers*: Against the backdrop of the court of Louis XIII (Rolfe Sedan), we have the roistering antics of the musketeers, the ambitious plots of Cardinal Richelieu (Nigel de Brulier), the conniving schemes of the Milady de Winter (Dorothy Revier), and d'Artagnan's ill-fated love for the lovely Constance (Marguerite de la Motte). The second half transpires twenty years later and finds Louis XIV (William Bakewell) on the throne, the musketeers dispersed, and the unfolding mystery of the Man in the Iron Mask languishing in a prison, his identity concealed by an iron mask.

In the care and loving detail of its production—estimated at a million-dollar budget—the Fairbanks film is arguably the most successful of the many subsequent extant film adaptations. The screenplay is officially credited to "Elton Thomas" (a pseudonym used by Fairbanks and his staff of writers). Beautifully designed by a cadre of art directors and costumiers, including Maurice Leloir, William Cameron Menzies, Ben Carré, Wilfred Buckland, and Laurence Irving; ably directed by Fairbanks's favorite director, Allan Dwan; and sensitively portrayed by Fairbanks, Léon Bary, Gino Corrado, and Stanley Sandford as the Musketeeers, it earned the praise of *Photoplay Magazine*:

> It is adroit. It is imaginative. It is resplendent. There is the characteristic Fairbanks breadth and sweep and stunts. And it is his best job of storytelling.[11]

Dwan himself, according to his biographer, Frederic Lombardi, declared that Fairbanks "seemed to be under some kind of compulsion to make this picture one of his productions. . . . In this one I think he eclipsed himself. It was as if he knew that this was his swan song."[12]

The Iron Mask is indeed "the *other* one"—to borrow a key line from the film—of Fairbanks's essays in the adventures of d'Artagnan. It is also the *last* one. That phrase, moreover, has its own tale to tell, as we shall see, among several others. We will recount them here, in order: Alexandre Dumas's further chronicles of the Four Musketeers; Fairbanks's farewell to the silent screen; the film's recent restoration; and, not least, a gallant Frenchman remembers how he came to Hollywood to design the film's sets and costumes. The latter tale is told in the Appendix of this book.

Imagine a Man in a Mask

Threading its way through both novel and film is the tale—based on historical events—of a mysterious masked prisoner who may or may not have had connections with the royal court of Louis XIV. Although this man really existed, and his face was perpetually hidden behind a mask during his incarceration in the years 1669–1703—the real-life d'Artagnan himself first escorted him to prison by royal order—his identity remains to this day a subject of endless speculation. Candidates are numerous, including a variety of Louis XIV's ministers, even Nicolas Fouquet himself. "It is the mask which fascinates and mystifies us," writes John Noone in his exhaustive study of the subject, *The Man Behind the Iron Mask* (1979), "drawing our attention to the prisoner even while rendering him anonymous, and among all the contradictions which rise to baffle us in the Iron Mask story it is this contradiction at the heart of the mystery . . . that none of the theories advanced so far has ever been able to resolve."[13]

When Dumas advanced his own solution to the identity of *The Man in the Iron Mask*, he took as his cue Voltaire's sensational attempt to solve the mystery. Writing a century earlier, in his *Siècle de Louis XIV*, Voltaire had alleged that the mystery man was someone of the highest importance, whose very existence had always been a secret, whose face bore a close resemblance to a well-known person and whose age in 1703 was about sixty years old (the age of Louis XIV). "The light of this evidence," reports John Noone, "was enough to bring the reader to the truth which Voltaire had been afraid to publish . . . [that] the prisoner was the King; or would have realized the very secret the King wished to hide: that the prisoner was his own flesh and blood, his living image—his identical twin brother."[14]

It is startling that in the original novel, as opposed to the numerous film adaptations, Dumas makes relatively little of the masked man. In the first half of the titular novel, Aramis finds the imprisoned twin, Philippe, sans mask, in the Bastille, contrives his escape, and then conspires to tutor him in replacing his brother, Louis XIV, on the throne. When the plot fails, Philippe is recaptured, masked, and returned to prison. At this point, he passes out of the story altogether, and has no more impact on subsequent events, which take the story elsewhere. Indeed, his one and only appearance in these pages wearing the iron mask occupies scarcely more than a paragraph:

> They saw him pass gravely, at six paces behind the governor, a man clothed in black and masked by a visor of polished steel soldered to a helmet of the same nature, which altogether enveloped the whole of his head. The fire of the heavens cast red reflections upon the polished surface, and these reflections, flying off capriciously, seemed to be angry looks launched by this unfortunate . . . [He] stopped for a moment to contemplate the infinite horizon . . . and to breathe a sigh resembling a smothered roar.[15]

Nothing more. The poor man is left to suffer in silence, while the story goes on without him.

Of course, as we shall see, Fairbanks and his writers will have none of *that*. . . .

Fairbanks Finds a Voice

At the outset, framed by an ornate banner on a shallow stage, d'Artagnan steps forward with a flourish of his sword and declaims—

> Out of the shadows of the past
> As from a faded tapestry
> Of Time's procession slow and vast,
> I step, to bid you bear with me
> The while your fancy I engage,
> To look upon another age.
> An age where on the human tide
> The plumed wave of chivalry

Striking a proud pose in *The Iron Mask*.

Rose to its summit,
Sweeping wide across a Nation's mighty sea.
France never shone a brighter power
Than in this high romantic hour.
So come with me to France of old,
To fiery days when hearts beat high
When blood was young, and hate was bold,
And sword crossed sword to do or die.
For love and honor gloried then,
And friendship reached its peak with men.
Friends were friends in those brave days—,
Athos, Porthos, Aramis, I—
Graved our hearts with a mystic phrase
Bound out lives with a mystic tie.
Come, stir your soul with our ringing call,
Of "All for One, and One for All."
Come on! Come on! Come on![16]

Ardent wooing in *The Iron Mask*.

The year is 1638, as an introductory title informs us—

> *In St. Germaine, public excitement ran high in anticipation of an important event . . .*

Louis XIII arrives amidst a great pomp and public display, as the whole city prepares to celebrate the imminent birth of his first child. Unbeknownst to anyone, even Louis, Queen Anne has already given birth to identical twin sons. Aware of the civil strife attendant upon rival claimants to the throne, Richelieu plans to smuggle the second twin out of the country to Spain. But the evil de Rochefort learns of the plot, kidnaps the child, and determines to groom him to usurp his brother, Louis.

Because she is party to the secret, the Queen's lady-in-waiting, Constance Bonacieux (Marguerite de La Motte), is kidnapped by de Rochefort, who has learned the secret. He lodges her at a convent under the keeping of his confederate, the wicked Milady de Winter (Dorothy Revier). News of her kidnapping reaches d'Artagnan. To horse! He gallops to her rescue but is too late to save her from being knifed by de Winter. As she lies dying in his arms, she utters a few enigmatic words about the existence of Louis's twin brother—

> *"The—Other—One!"*

But she dies before revealing the truth. D'Artagnan kneels, consumed with grief, cradling her in his arms. Meanwhile, the fleeing De Winter is seized by the other musketeers and taken to a common executioner. But Richelieu's men arrive and capture them and line them up before a firing squad. D'Artagnan gallops up and throws himself in front of his comrades. Richelieu, looking on, halts the proceedings and pardons them in an unexpected act of mercy. However—

> *"I spare your lives because I keep my bargains. I will not spare the thing you value most—your friendship."*

Whereupon he dispatches them to their respective home provinces—

> *"never to come together again on pain of death."*

D'Artagnan will remain at court to serve as friend and tutor to the young Louis. Saddened, d'Artagnan has not only lost the woman he loves but the companionship of his brave and loyal comrades-at-arms. In a beautifully staged tableau, the four are seen together in a final salute. As they depart their separate ways. D'Artagnan remains behind, his back to us, leaning against a tree in the foreground.

Back at the court, the dying Richelieu calls together d'Artagnan and the young prince to his bedside. He then does a curious thing: he breaks a coin in half and gives a half to each of them. He admonishes d'Artagnan to "keep close" to the prince. And with his dying breath, he whispers to the mystified d'Artagnan those mysterious words:

> *"The—Other—One!"*

Part Two. Twenty years have passed. D'Artagnan again faces the camera, sword in hand. This is not the same d'Artagnan we have seen. He is older now, gray at the edges, bearing the visible traces of his long and adventurous life.

Turning to the Dumas text for a moment, we recall the aging d'Artagnan's words to Louis XIV:

> "I have seen war, Sire; I have seen peace; I have served Richelieu and Mazarin, I have been scorched with your father at the fire of Rochelle, riddled with thrusts like a sieve, having made a new skin ten times, as serpents do. After affronts and injustices, I have a command which was formerly something, because it gave the bearer the right of speaking as he liked to his King."[17]

Now, on screen, d'Artagnan stands before a great tree, strides forward, and pledges that he and the musketeers will be reunited:

> "Twenty years have passed, and more
> Since Richelieu bent his iron will
> And broke the bonds that held us four.
> But Porthos, Athos, Aramis, I
> Will ride once more.
> Once more we'll heed the clarion call
> Of 'One for all, and all for one!'"

Back to the action. D'Artagnan is now Captain d'Artagnan, and the young prince is now Louis XIV. They are boon companions, even if d'Artagnan's good humor is occasionally leavened with vagrant memories of his days with the musketeers. One night, as d'Artagnan prepares to retire, a conspiracy moves swiftly at court: Unbeknownst to him, de Rochefort is carrying out his plan to place the usurping twin on the throne. He brings him to the king's bed chamber, abducts Louis, and substitutes the other in his place. Louis is taken away to a remote island prison, where he is secluded in a solitary cell behind an Iron Mask. From his tower window, Louis can only watch and wait . . . hopeful that d'Artagnan will come to his rescue. Finally, when some fishermen appear below his window, he seizes the opportunity and scratches a message for help on a pewter plate, signing it with a tracing of his half of the coin. He pitches the plate down to the fisherman, who delivers it to d'Artagnan. Bewildered and curious, the musketeer steals back into the court, where the king is behaving strangely: this is not the gentle and laughing Louis he knows. This young man *looks* like him, but he is behaving in a cruel and violent manner, as if he were an

"Till We Meet Again!" in *The Iron Mask.*

entirely different person. . . . D'Artagnan looks at the plate with the drawing of Louis's coin. He remembers those fateful words: "The Other One." Aha! He puts his finger aside his nose and exclaims—"Twins!"

Immediately he sends a servant to fetch the musketeers to aid him in rescuing the rightful king:

> *"There are three men in the world who will risk being killed with me. Fetch them—in all haste!"*

Reunited once again, they gain access to the tower through an underground passage and find their way to Louis's cell. They fight their way through stiff resistance from the guards and hurry Louis back to a waiting boat. Only Porthos, who has been wounded, is left behind to protect their retreat. Snatching up a blazing torch, he plunges it into a keg of dynamite, burying the soldiers and himself in the explosion.

On their way back to the palace, the musketeers encounter de Rochefort and his men. Athos and Aramis hold them off and kill de Rochefort, but are themselves slain in the process. D'Artagnan and Louis arrive at the palace just in time to prevent the evil twin from poisoning the Queen Mother (Belle Bennett). Louis confronts his twin and condemns him to wear the Iron Mask:

> *"Your own damnable invention will be your doom."*

No sooner does d'Artagnan attach the mask than the villain turns on him and stabs him in the back. Mortally wounded, d'Artagnan steals away alone to the courtyard and collapses. At that moment, the jolly specters of the Three Musketeers appear in the clouds and come forward to welcome the spirit of their fallen comrade. With a hearty laugh, they lift him up and exchange a salute with their upraised swords. From their immortal perspective they scornfully view below the shocked king and his retinue who are mourning d'Artagnan's corpse.

> *"Come on! There is greater adventure beyond!"*

They shout. And they march away, arm in arm, toward glory.

Dumas himself had foreshadowed such an ending. In the pages of his novel, Athos has a vision of his son, Raoul, slain on the battlefield, "where he rose into the void, still smiling, still inviting with a gesture, as he departed towards heaven."[18] We can go back even further to find a comparable moment in literature: in the conclusion of Chaucer's magnificent poem "Troilus and Criseyde," the spirit of the slain Troilus ascends to the "eighth sphere" and assumes a Boethian perspective on the pettiness of earthly things, "this spot of erthe, this wretched world":

> And in hymself he lough [laughed] right at the wo[e]
> Of [t]hem that wepten for his deth so faste.

Fairbanks's ghostly farewell is all the more affecting because it signifies his adieu to the most colorful stage of his cinema career. Never again are we to see him in the familiar costume roles, swashbuckling with the same vigor. Here was a man who had preserved his youthful image longer than most could have, and who was about to turn the corner. Technological changes in the cinema were clearly on the way, and his career and popularity would soon be eclipsed.

Enlivening the otherwise rather serious tone of much of the film are many comic and acrobatic touches. Early in the film, d'Artagnan indulges in some delightfully satiric wooing of the coyly resisting Constance—climbing her balcony, swinging her over garden walls, and slyly concealing their embrace beneath a large basket thrown over their heads by an obliging neighbor. In a hilarious barroom brawl, the roistering Four Musketeers wreak amiable havoc as they leave the joint in a shambles (d'Artagnan pausing long enough to capture thrown doughnuts on the tip of his sword). In another fracas, the tables are turned as the musketeers flee from an army of scorned females who hound, pummel, and pound them through the streets on the way to a ducking in a nearby pond. Later, there's a sly moment when a servant summons the musketeers to action and finds them sleeping in one huge bed, above which is their motto "One for All, and All for One." In the second half of the film, the plot takes over and Fairbanks's antic horseplay is replaced by a muted gentle charm, particularly in his affecting moments with the young prince.

The expected acrobatics, while fewer in number and scale than in previous films, are generally more suited to the story. Already cited is d'Artagnan's amazing leap to Constance's window during his attempted rescue. Fairbanks's dueling techniques are greatly in evidence as he gives fencing lessons to the young prince. And later, when things get desperate, there is the epic battle in the prison fortress, when the musketeers fend off superior numbers with some dazzling swordplay. It is beautifully choreographed, moving the action up and down the staircases, over balconies, and through the rooms.

It is significant that this late in his career, we find once again Fairbanks energetically doing what he always did best: deposing a wicked usurper and restoring in the name of the people their rightful leader. We've been seeing it in the pre-1920s satiric comedies and we've been seeing it throughout the cycle of costume films in the 1920s. Indeed, it mattered not whether Doug was dressed in the clothes of an American engineer in *The Americano* or garbed in the swash and buckle of a Gascon swordsman; either way, he remained an essentially "American" go-getter with the sword of the aristocrat at the ready.

In the opinion of many today, *The Iron Mask* stands at the summit of Fairbanks's films. It was also his last silent film, with the exception of those two hastily interpolated talking prologues. Reports from the set allege that Fairbanks was uncomfortable during these first sound recordings of his voice. Technician Edward Bernds, who worked with him, has left an anecdote:

> Doug . . . sprang into the foreground and delivered his prologue speech. We did the scene over and over . . . Finally, we got a complete take, and, as was the barbaric custom in those days, we played it back. Sound equipment was touchy and inefficient then. Sometimes speed would go out of control. When we made the playback for Doug, we had a "runaway" on the wax playback machine, just fast enough to give Doug a girlish falsetto . . . I think Doug never really recovered from the shock of hearing that gibberish runaway version.[19]

The film was released in two versions. The "sound" version included the two prologues, Hugo Riesenfeld's score (including a male chorus singing a "theme" song, "One for All and All for One"), and sound effects. As was customary at the time, a silent version was also released.

The Restorations

After its first release, *The Iron Mask* was consigned to the vaults of the Museum of Modern Art and was commercially unavailable for many years. Then, in 1952, Douglas Fairbanks Jr. and the Fairbanks estate came to the rescue and released a slightly abridged version by the Odyssey Pictures Corporation. Because the synchronized-sound elements (Vitaphone discs) were thought at the time to be lost, Fairbanks Jr. dubbed his own voice over his father's image in the two spoken prologues, provided a music track by Allan Gray, inserted some sound effects, stripped away the intertitles, and narrated a soundtrack commentary written by novelist Richard Llewellyn. It was packaged for Kino Films by film preservationist David Shepard in 1996. Now difficult to find, it is a worthy tribute by Douglas Jr. to his father.[20]

Now, thanks to the restoration in 1999 for Channel 4 Silents from the team of Kevin Brownlow, Patrick Stanbury, the Douris Corporation, and the Museum of Modern Art, *The Iron Mask* can be seen in its entirety, with the restored original spoken sequences by Fairbanks Sr., the intertitles reinserted, and a splendid new score by the redoubtable Carl Davis. When it was shown at the 1999 London Film Festival, critic Derek Malcom, writing in the *Guardian* on November 19, enthused, "It is tightly plotted, handsomely mounted, and full of pace and verve." A week earlier, on November 13, at the Kahn Lecture Theater, Brownlow himself described the complex restoration process, including a tribute to his frequent collaborator, Carl Davis: "Carl Davis's new score matches the film's panache and pathos—a fitting accompaniment to Fairbanks's adieu to adventure." As recently as May 20, 2012, this version was screened at the Egyptian Theater in Hollywood in a program sponsored by the Art Directors Guild. Present to introduce and discuss the film and its superb art direction and costuming were this writer, Brownlow's preservationist Patrick Stanbury, and Oscar-nominated art director Laurence Bennett (*The Artist*, 2011). Given special honors on the occasion was the French designer, Maurice Leloir, who had come to Hollywood in 1928 to supervise *The Iron Mask*'s art direction. His role in the film was recalled in his book, *Five Months in Hollywood with Douglas Fairbanks* (1929). That account is reproduced in its entirety in English translation in Appendix B of this book.

The Gaucho (1927) featured one of Doug's finest costume conceptions.

Chapter 12

"The Fall from Grace"

The Gaucho

There was a laughing Devil in his sneer,
That raised emotions both of rage and fear;
And where his frown of hatred darkly fell,
Hope withering fled—and Mercy sigh'd farewell!
—LORD BYRON, *The Corsair*

Sandwiched between *The Black Pirate* and *The Iron Mask* (1928), *The Gaucho*—its original release title was *Douglas Fairbanks as The Gaucho*—has been sadly neglected and undervalued since its premiere at Grauman's Chinese Theater on November 4, 1927. *New York Times* critic Mordaunt Hall complained it departed from Fairbanks's standard "unalloyed cheer," containing instead a "rather gruesome undertone" and a "somber strain."[1] In recent years, if it is mentioned at all, *The Gaucho* is usually curtly dismissed. Richard Schickel's complaint is typical: "*The Gaucho*, despite Fairbanks's tricks with the bola, was the flattest of his big-scale adventure-romances. Indeed, it is hard to determine just what he thought he was doing here."[2] Even Doug Jr., in his memoir, *Salad Days*, mildly noted that "it did not have the grand sweep of his earlier classics."[3] By contrast, one of the earliest and most enthusiastic commentaries appeared in our *His Majesty the American* in 1977, in which we noted, "*The Gaucho* is *not* like the other costume romances and should not be judged by the same standard."[4] Thirty years later, biographer Jeffrey Vance, agreed: "The film is an effort of unanticipated darkness in tone, setting, and character. . . . No boy scout here, Fairbanks drinks, smokes, and acts upon his carnal desires with a lascivious glee."[5]

Nowhere in his oeuvre—excepting perhaps the somber *The Half-Breed* (1916), portions of the blackly satiric *When the Clouds Roll By* (1919), and the elegiac *The Private Life of Don Juan* (1934)—did Fairbanks get down to a darker, more Byronic revelation of the self-absorption and self-destructive tendencies that were eating away at the dashing facade of the Fairbanksian hero. At the same time, *The Gaucho* was very much of its time, a reflection, in its own way, of the rampant disillusionment, greed, and corruption eating away at Hollywood in the years leading up to the Great Depression.

The opening title succinctly sets the scene:

> *This is the story of one of them who came to be known as "The Gaucho" and of the usurper Ruiz, and how these two came together at the "City of the Miracle."*

The city was so named because it had been the site of a supernatural occurrence a few years earlier when a young shepherdess (Geraine Grear) had fallen from a cliff and been healed by the apparition of the Madonna. A few years later, the girl, now grown (Eve Southern), presides over the shrine, which is visited by pilgrims who gratefully pour their gold into its coffers. Lured by tales of the shrine's wealth, an outlaw, the Gaucho (Fairbanks) invades the town, defies the local padre (Nigel de Brulier), deposes the local tyrant, Ruiz (Gustav von Seyffertitz), and, after a night of drunken revelry, attempts to seduce the virginal Girl of the Shrine. But the Gaucho's gypsy lover, The Mountain Girl (Lupe Velez), stabs him in a jealous fit of anger. Meanwhile, a leper (Albert MacQuarrie), who earlier had been banished from the town, suddenly appears and touches the Gaucho's wound. Now infected with the dreaded disease (called here "The Black Doom"), the Gaucho contemplates suicide. The Girl of the Shrine intervenes and leads him to the healing waters, where the apparition of the Madonna (Mary Pickford in a cameo role) cures him. Spiritually as well as physically healed, the Gaucho leads a climactic battle against Ruiz, who is attempting to regain control of the city.

Sin, suicide, seduction, sacrilege—this bizarre departure from the health, optimism, and virtue of the standard Fairbanks formula was inspired, he claimed at the time in *The Literary Digest*, by his recent visit to the shrine of Lourdes.[6] That may be true, but the film seems much more rooted in the turmoil and disruption at the time in his professional and private life.

On a personal level, the forty-four-year-old Fairbanks was facing some sad realities. The probabilities of age, infirmity, and neglect were lurking in ambush. He could still hurdle barriers and vault over walls with the greatest of ease; but the aging swashbuckler was stumbling on the threshold of middle age. Against his wishes, his handsome young son, Doug Jr. was making a name for himself in movies like *Stella Dallas* (1925) and in stage plays like *Young Woodley*, which premiered in Los Angeles during the filming of *The Gaucho.* Such visibly prominent reminders of Sr.'s advancing age must have galled him. (Nonetheless, he did entrust the directing of Lupe Velez's screen test and the writing of *The Gaucho's* intertitles to his son—for which Jayar made the grand sum of $250 dollars.[7]) More disturbing was the death of his elder brother John in November 1926, while the sets for *The Gaucho* were under construction. Since the desertion of the family by Doug's father, Charles Ulman, when Doug was twelve, John had been a father figure to him.

Worst of all, Doug's marriage to Mary Pickford was in trouble. Hollywood's Royal Couple had been married only seven years, but cracks were appearing in the official facade. During *The Gaucho*'s shooting, for example, the illness of Mary's mother, Charlotte, had forced Mary and Doug to leave Pickfair temporarily and move in with the ailing woman. Doug, displaced for the moment and accustomed to being the center of attention, may have nurtured a secret and growing resentment at Mary's obsessive devotion to her mother (Charlotte would die three months after *The Gaucho*'s release). Another problem was Mary's obvious attraction to Buddy Rogers, her young costar in the film she was making at the time, *My Best Girl* (in which they shared a prolonged screen kiss, unusual in a Pickford film). Doug, too, at this time, may have had his share of romantic temptations, including, hints Pickford's biographer, Scott Eyman, Lupe Velez, his costar in *The Gaucho.*[8]

Professionally, Fairbanks, one of the four founders of United Artists, was watching with increasing concern the failing fortunes of the studio. Historian Tino Balio reports that the company, for a variety of reasons had been facing a product shortage. UA was a distribution company of independent producers and had no theaters of its own. Fairbanks and his partners were making fewer and fewer pictures a year. Attempts to shore up product and exhibition revenues after 1926 were so far unsuccessful. In the midst of an industry-wide recession, UA had ended that year with a deficit of more than a million dollars. The immediate future was threatened by the impending advent of talking-picture technology—*The Jazz Singer* had created a sensation just the month before—which placed the future of the silent film in jeopardy. The development of the star system, moreover, in which Fairbanks and Pickford had played such an important part, was now finding itself under the control of the major studio executives. UA's flaw "was that those traits of independence, flamboyance, and melodramatics that characterized the owners' work as artists could not be checked in the board room, severely handicapping the management of the company."[9] In sum, as Fairbanks and the other partners produced fewer and fewer pictures, they were finding their power vested in other hands.

Thus, during the gestation of *The Gaucho*, the screen's preeminent action hero was haunted by ghosts of the past, turmoil in the present, and doubts about the future. This, of course, was intolerable for the flying figure of Doug. As Allene Talmey dryly and presciently noted in her book, *Doug and Mary and Others*, published at the time of *The Gaucho*'s release: "Everything is a situation, and [Doug] plays for the big moment, then snaps the curtain. There are no third acts for him."[10]

Clearly, the concatenation of circumstances was just right for a movie that would mark significant changes in Doug's screen character. The results, whether by intention, circumstance, or accident, bring *The Gaucho* squarely in line with that literary tradition known as the Byronic Hero, that outcast rebel increasingly marginalized by society. Jacques Barzun, in his study of the subject, explains that this new kind of heroic outlaw emerged at the dawn of the Romantic century: "Byron was simply the first, or the most successful among the first, to dramatize the attitude of the new man, the mysterious unknown who has experienced Faustian longings but who, not finding a constructive social task, risks his life for the glory of revenging mankind on society."[11] Byron's swashbuckling pirate chief Conrad, in *The Corsair*, for example, from the poem of 1814 (written when Byron himself was laboring under public scandal and private turmoil), presents the prototype: an unstable compound of criminal acts and chivalrous deeds, a renegade forced by a shadowed past to live in exile from his homeland. There are many women in his life, but there is only one he truly loves (Medorah) and she remains remote and unattainable. She was his "one virtue" opposed to his "thousand crimes." In his study of Byron, Andre Maurois commented on the obscurity of Conrad's identity: "No one knows whence he comes, nor whither he goes. He is wrapped in mystery. His past always contains a crime which is kept dark from us."[12] This enigmatic aspect establishes a kind of open end into which our imagination is funneled. It reinforces his existence outside a given system of laws and lovemaking. He becomes in effect a kind of universal symbol for man's unfulfilled broodings, longings, and frustrations. His only recourse is to live only within and for himself. As scholar Donald Sutherland put it, the Byronic Hero necessarily must be "splendidly self-propelled":

> Romanticism cannot be responsible to anything, as it cannot be justified by anything, since it will not recognize any fixed authority. But it is essentially responsive, and so all but bound to answer a challenge or put up a fight, especially in the losing game against death. . . . The game is to force death into one's own style, which the Romantics eminently do, or to rise to the style of death.[13]

The very air around such a character seems charged with the whiff of brimstone. Thus, Byron imparts to Conrad what we would regard as an infernal version of the Fairbanksian energy: "He bounds, he flies."

> There was a laughing Devil in his sneer,
> That raised emotions both of rage and fear;
> And where his frown of hatred darkly fell,
> Hope withering fled—and Mercy sigh'd farewell![14]

"I would not, if I might, be blest," declares Conrad. Barzun notes that the "crime-laden" hero can be redeemed only through the *deed*, a "daring act of revenge that condemns the corrupt society he has abjured—in a word, the Byronic hero is a noble outlaw."[15] Thus, he embodies the only resolution available: *action.* He flings away the scabbard and, at a stroke, demonstrates the power of the individual sword against entrenched injustice.

As we have seen, Fairbanks had hinted at this sort of character before. Zorro, d'Artagnan, Robin Hood, and the Thief of Bagdad—his heroes were outlaws and rebels who resolved conflicts and deposed tyrants with boundless confidence, resourcefulness, and feats of physical prowess. They were either aristocrats by direct heritage (Don Diego and Robin of Huntingdon), attachment to royalty (d'Artagnan), or connections with mysterious forces of magic (the thief).

Until *The Gaucho*, however, Fairbanks's heroes seldom displayed an ordinate degree of self-doubts and inner confusions. Their relationships with women, moreover, were wholly conventional and proper. Beyond their braggadocio, his heroes had been primarily agents of good and virtue. Not for them was the mocking rejection of religious tenets, like Manfred's defiance of a Holy Man:

> Old man! There is no power in holy men,
> Nor charm in prayer—nor purifying form of penitence. . . .[16]

The Gaucho, however, changes all that. Aided by the superb art direction of the reliable Carl Oscar Borg, which showed a South America and its people "as we think of them rather than as they are," cinematographer Tony Gaudio conjures up a sumptuous chiaroscuro that opposes the worlds of black and white, virtue and corruption, health and disease.[17] While the Gaucho moves in dark places—the robber camp, the smoky tavern, the grotto of the shrine, and the underground jail cell—the City of the Miracle lies dazzling under the sun, a polished white jewel. When the black-clad leper invades the torch-lit banquet room of the Gaucho's feast, he's a blot on a polished mirror, a serpent in the Garden, the Dark Guest come to Don Giovanni's table. The Mountain Girl's wanton sensuality and the Virgin of the Spring's spiritual chastity also embody these dualities.

The Gaucho himself is a dark figure, answering to Byron's description of Conrad, with thick, tousled black hair, sleek mustache, and a swarthy face, a crafty grin peering slyly out from under the flattened hat brim. His costume is a superb collection of dark vest, bolero pants, *botas de potro* boots, *tirador* spangled leather belt, whips, and coiled bolas. This is a man who lives only in the present and who answers to no belief or dogma other than his owns:

> *"Yesterday was yesterday. Today is today. There is no tomorrow until it's today."*

He is first introduced by the simple title,

> *Far in the North, an outlaw—*

Nothing more is needed. Or given. His chief foe, Ruiz the Usurper, is the villain of the story, apparently only because he's even a greater rascal than the Gaucho! When the Gaucho offers a toast, it is, appropriately, to himself—or, rather, to his shadow thrown against the wall.

His relationships with women are typified by his lovemaking with the Mountain Girl, which is nothing if not a series of carnal, albeit pugilistic encounters. The prompt gusto with which they literally attack each other

Defying the padre in *The Gaucho*.

may be further indicative of the Byronic tradition of camaraderie borne out of combat: like children meeting each other for the first time, they take each other's measure with an exchange of kicks in the shins. When they approach each other in the smoky, crowded tavern, the Gaucho unslings his bolas and whirls them around their waists, binding them together in a tight clinch. As they swing into a tango, he tucks his cigarette back into his mouth, kisses her lustily, pops the cigarette back out, and blows smoke into her face (a bit of business later borrowed by Gene Kelly in *The Pirate*, 1948). She in turn pummels him gratefully and enthusiastically.

But, like the Corsair, the Gaucho's real love belongs to someone else, another woman hopelessly removed from him, the Girl of the Shrine. After a night of drink and revelry, he attempts to seduce her, but discovers he cannot carry it through, that her virginal innocence thwarts him. He tells her,

> *"You're like a beautiful sunset, something I can't embrace yet I love."*

This is an echo of Byron's Childe Harold, who

> Had sighed to many, though he loved but one,
> And that loved one, alas! Could ne'er be his.[18]

The Gaucho's confrontation with the padre (Nigel de Brulier) is perhaps the most startling scene in any Fairbanks film. Audiences were accustomed to Doug's strenuous and enthusiastic support of God and His works. This is the man who, after all, as noted in these pages in an early comedy, *The Mollycoddle* (1920), stood on the rim of the Grand Canyon, lifted his arms to the heavens, and shouted "HURRAH FOR GOD!!" But here the Gaucho mocks such spiritual transports, rejects the Holy Man's pleas for mercy, and blows smoke into his face, declaring,

> *"You see, Padre, I get what I want—without the help of God and his Holy Book."*

Later, he again shows his contempt for charity and mercy when he dismisses the leper from the banquet hall:

> *"You poison the very air we breathe. Go find some hidden spot and kill yourself."*

Quite clearly, the Gaucho is a disciple of darkness, not of light. Although, unlike Byron's Manfred, he invokes no demons, he does possess extraordinary, preternatural powers. For example, when the Gypsy Girl reproaches him for not taking her along with his robber band, he orders his men to pack up her dwelling:

> *"Throw ropes around the floor beams and hitch on a hundred horses; we take this place with us."*

Sure enough, the two lovers dine merrily while the horsemen drag the girl's house down the mountain path.

The Gaucho kicks away gravity. When he escapes from the jail, he seems to fly up out of the ground. Seconds later he shinnies up a slanting palm trunk, leaps to a branch, swings out and down through space to another treetop, then to a vine, slides down to another branch, and *runs* up another steeply inclined tree trunk. In another sequence, he clambers up a series of awning railings, mounts and dismounts from a horse with flips and backflips, and hops about the village housetops as if he were treading a broad highway.

When he sits in the tavern above the jostling roisterers, he presides over the commotion like a god of the Saturnalia, his every gesture a magical invocation. When he reaches his hand behind the bar, *voila!*—he produces in his fingertips the bartender's ear, pulling it forth (the rest of his body following) as if it were a rabbit just plucked from a hat. Later, when he lifts his glass in a toast to his fellows, the camera views the action from behind his head, panning with his gaze from person to person, their faces like flowers blooming at the bidding of a dark sun. There's a particularly beautiful moment when, observing a girl on the balcony above him, he whirls his broad-brimmed hat upward to receive the tribute of her outflung rose.

Even the Gaucho's method of smoking cigarettes assumes the manner of a bizarre, choreographed ritual. Puffs of smoke precede his entrances into rooms like Mephistophelian calling cards. He can't just place the cigarette in his mouth, he has to catch it between his teeth (tossed ten feet through the air by a confederate). Nor can he simply discard the used butt without first lighting another cigarette with it, tucking it into the toe of his shoe, and kicking it away. In another piece of sleight-of-hand, he squints his eyes in one direction while flicking the cigarette from his mouth in the opposite direction. Critic/historian Alexander Walker has noted other aspects of this curious behavior:

> Every time he lights up he fights a duel with the match, subdues the cigarette before putting it between his lips and then has to reach round the back of his neck when removing the cigarette to exhale and put a wrestler's lock on it.[19]

We had seen a bit of this sort of thing before, in a few scenes in *The Mark of Zorro* and *Don Q*. Here, it's a leitmotif that threads its away along tendrils of smoke throughout the entire picture. The cigarette has now become a magician's familiar, a rebellious genie that constantly must be subdued.

Many other scenes serve solely as an excuse to exploit Doug's latest gimmick in weaponry, the bolas—a kind of Argentinian lasso consisting of a couple of yards of thong with a leather-covered leaden ball at each end. When whirled around the head and thrown, the balls spread out; upon striking the target, they wind around it and hold it fast. After many hours under the tutelage of two expert bolas throwers, Nick Milanesio and Andres Rodrigues, who had been imported from the Argentine Republic,

Celebrity group: Fairbanks, Mary Pickford, William Randolph Hearst, and Charles Chaplin.

Fairbanks acquired considerable skill. On foot, he could throw it with accuracy for twenty-five yards; on horseback, at least three times that distance. Besides using it in many scenes in the film, either to trip up an enemy or bind his lover fast to him during a breathless tango; offscreen, he also organized a band of gauchos to show it off at the World Championship Rodeo, which was held in Los Angeles that year.

As always, however, Fairbanks's best moments in the picture are those throwaway scenes when he does little more than just move about a room or pause to appraise a situation. These quiet, dance-like moments are appended to the dramatic action like gestural grace notes. The baroque curve embellishes the straight line. Decoration overwhelms the basic design. A case in point—indeed, one of the most beautiful scenes in any Fairbanks film—occurs when the Gaucho gains access to Ruiz's chambers. For the next few minutes time seems to stand still. Quite alone, the Gaucho faces the camera, backs away, holsters his pistols, and jumps midway up the shaft of an upright spear, holding himself stiffly at arm's length while he peeks over a partition. Releasing his grip, he whirls about into an adjoining room, places his pistols into his tunic, and waves his whip about him. Then, he eases back onto a tabletop, lights a cigarette, and flings the match away. After holding the cigarette aloft for a few seconds while he gazes out a window, he flicks it away and tosses a nearby mug in the opposite direction. With a sudden flutter of his legs, he twists off the table and exits the frame. The scene has no dramatic function whatsoever; it is, simply, entrancing to watch. Not even John Barrymore could have made as much of it. The poet William Blake has said that Exuberance is Beauty. Fairbanks, who probably never heard of Blake (and probably never read Byron either, for that matter), is the very personification of the notion.

For most of the film, our enterprising bandit has pursued the selfish aims and opportunities typical of the age, the rampant postwar years of boom and bust in pre-Depression America. Now the self-made man of the new century is revealed as a disillusioned, ruthless opportunist obsessed with material gain and corrupted by greed.

Admittedly, *The Gaucho* "redeems" its bandit and his story at the end—a conclusion that affirms the cynical deployment of the Hollywood commercial formula. The high hilarity and sweep of the concluding scenes of *The Gaucho* seems to leave behind the rebellious, doleful Byronic model. When Byron's Conrad comes to grief at the end of *The Corsair*, he vanishes, to be heard from no more. But when Fairbanks reverts at the last to the hearty merriment more characteristic of his earlier films, perhaps he is, ironically, evoking yet another aspect of Byron, who once wrote in a letter to a friend: "I am not one of your dolorous gentlemen; so now let us laugh again!"[20]

Part III

Doug and Mary Find Their Voices

Time hath, my lord, a wallet at his back/ Wherein he puts alms for Oblivion.

—**ULYSSES,** in Shakespeare's *Troilus & Cressida*, III.iii

Doug and Mary in 1920, at the time of their wedding.

Chapter 13

Coquette

Goodbye to the Glad Girl

If you want to see the signs of the times, watch women. Their evolution is the most important thing in modern life.
—RACHEL CROTHERS

During the production of Douglas Fairbanks's *The Iron Mask* late in 1928, Mary Pickford was busily preparing her first talking picture, *Coquette*. It premiered on April 12, 1929, just two months after her husband's film was released. In another two months, both Doug and Mary would begin their first—and only—sound film together, *The Taming of the Shrew*.

Unlike *The Iron Mask*, which was essentially a silent film, limiting Fairbanks's two spoken prologues to scant minutes of screen time, *Coquette* was *all* talking, affording curious viewers their first opportunity to hear what "America's Sweetheart" sounded like. It proved to be a box-office triumph, although today it is one of her most neglected films. Now, if *Coquette* is remembered at all, it is because it won her an Oscar for Best Actress honors in 1929—the first such award ever to be given for a talking picture. Today's viewers, unaware of the film's immediate cultural and technological contexts, will watch it with some puzzlement. How could this talky, static melodrama, this aggregate of self-conscious poses and stilted speech, ever have enjoyed any degree of acclaim? Can this really be the same Mary Pickford, who was once "the glad girl" of *Rebecca of Sunnybrook Farm* and *Pollyanna*, and the most popular and successful actress in the world?

It must be said that while *Coquette* is very much a film of its time, its use of synchronized sound is at least a considerable technical advance over *The Iron Mask* and earlier all-talking features, like Warner Bros.' *The Lights of New York*. It affords us a close-up in time of an industry and a career that, for both Doug and Mary, were at a crossroads. A reconsideration is in order.

In the late l920s, after a spectacular career that began in 1909 at American Biograph, matured in the mid-teens at Paramount-Artcraft, and soared to its greatest heights in 1919 with the formation with her husband of United Artists, Mary Pickford found herself facing an uncertain future. She had just released *My Best Girl* a few months before, and even if an isolated critic or two caviled at the obviousness of the thirty-five-year-old Mary's youthful makeup, she was still clearly a box-office draw. But change was in the air. Mary was disconsolate at the death of her beloved mother, Charlotte, on March 21, 1928. Rumors were flying that her fabled marriage with Douglas was breaking down under the pressures of his alleged extramarital pursuits. Moreover, she was growing increasingly dissatisfied with the "little-girl" image the public clung to. In August of that year she abandoned her famous curls and cut her hair into a stylish bob. "I wanted to be free of the shackles of playing little girls with curls," she recalled in 1958. "[But] I got the most indignant, insulting letters. I thought, 'If that's all it is, after a lifetime in the theater and motion pictures, if it's only eighteen curls keeping me in pictures, it's about time I retired.'"[1] Here, at least, was a challenge Mary could tackle. Despite United Artist producer Joe Schenck's declaration that UA would not make talkies, she was determined to experiment with the new technology. Drawing upon her theatrical background, she decided to adapt a popular play of the day. Allegedly, it was her friend, Lillian Gish, who first recommended George Abbott's Broadway stage play, *Coquette*.

Coquette was the big hit of the early 1927 Broadway season.[2] Helen Hayes appeared in the title role. The Jed Harris production premiered on November 8 and ran for 253 performances. Abbott is best remembered today for his hit stage productions of *Pal Joey* (1940), *The Pajama Game* (1954), *Damn Yankees* (1955), and *A Funny Thing Happened on the Way to the Forum* (1962). At the time of *Coquette*, he was very much the young man about Broadway. He had been a student of George Pierce Baker at Harvard; acted in the role of "Dynamite Jim" in John Howard Lawson's important production of *Processional* in 1924; and had staged his first successes on Broadway, *The Fall Guy*, cowritten by James Gleason (filmed by

RKO in 1930), and *Broadway*, cowritten with Philip Dunning (filmed by Universal in 1929). In the words of theater historian Howard Taubman, Abbott was extremely versatile, "for he could put his hand successfully not only to farce, at which he was a master, but to satire, melodrama, and social comment."[3]

Attracted by *Coquette*'s depiction of an independent, sensuous young woman, Mary Pickford filmed portions of the original stage production as a kind of "screen test" for her films. This was a common practice at the time. MGM, for example, shot complete sound-film records of such stage productions as Noel Coward's *Private Lives* and Eugene O'Neill's *Strange Interlude*. Such footage was not intended to be incorporated into the subsequent film adaptations but was utilized solely as a preproduction guide.[4] According to historian Alexander Walker, Pickford viewed her "tests" and pronounced the original stage cast "unsatisfactory, except for Miss Hayes, whose part she was determined to play."[5] Filming began just after Christmas in 1928, and the picture premiered in April 1929. It was a new Mary who appeared on screen, no longer the "glad girl" with long curls but a vamp with bobbed hair, silk stockings, a Southern accent, and dresses above the knee.

In the original play, Norma Besant is a beautiful, flirtatious, and conniving daughter of a gallant of the old South, Dr. John Besant. One of her admirers is young Michael Jeffery, who, because of his relative poverty and lack of social connections, incurs Dr. Besant's disapproval. Michael is ordered out of the house. He leaves reluctantly, telling Norma that in six months he will return for another talk with her father. But at their next meeting the distraught Dr. Besant shoots him dead. On trial, Besant can be saved only by Norma, whom he extorts to testify that her honor had been "soiled" by Michael and that the murder was an act of vengeance. In the meantime, unbeknownst to anyone, Norma learns she is pregnant with Michael's child. Should that fact come out in court, her father's case is weakened and her own social status would be ruined. Norma decides to save the family honor. She commits suicide.

The issues raised in *Coquette* place it in a long line of "women's" plays that marked the maturation of the American theater after the turn of the century, following the precedent of Ibsen's *A Doll's House* (1879).[6] Early examples included a series of one-act dramas by George Middleton in 1911–1914 (some of which, like *Back of the Ballot*, were avowedly pro-suffrage), Clyde Fitch's *The Climbers* (1901) and *The Truth* (1907), Eugene Walter's *The Easiest Way* (1908), William Vaughn Moody's *The Great*

Divide (1906), Charles Klein's *Maggie Pepper* (1911), and several works by Rachel Crothers—including *A Man's World* (1909) and *He and She* (1911). Crothers described their dramatic potential:

> Most of the great modern plays are studies of women. I suppose it is because women are in themselves more dramatic than men, more changing and a more significant note of the hour in which they live. If you want to see the signs of the times, watch women. Their evolution is the most important thing in modern life.[7]

Recalling the situations of Laura Murdoch and Ruth Ghent in, respectively, *The Easiest Way* and *The Great Divide*, Norma Besant is trapped midway between two contradictory conditions—that of the chaste yet coquettish Southern belle and that of a sexually fulfilled woman. For example, early in the play she's counseled by her brother Jimmy not to cause scandals by remaining out late at night. "But Jimmy," she replies, "I don't think every man wants a woman upon a pedestal like you and Daddy." Jimmy responds, "I tell you, a man wants a girl down where he can grab her, but he doesn't want every other man in sight grabbing her." Norma can only sigh at this double standard: "That must be how it is." She feels stifled and she admits to a friend later, "Sometimes when I seem to be having a good time I'm really bored to death. Didn't you ever think of that? You have to keep up the bluff, or else you won't be popular. But you get awfully sick of men!" Her declaration echoes that of Laura Murdoch's friend in *The Easiest Way*, who counsels her: "Don't you realize that you and me, and all the girls that are shoved into this life, are practically the common prey of any man who happens to come along? [But] we've got brains. That is a game, Laura, not a sentiment."[8]

Norma's problems are later compounded by the death sentence threatening her father. His defense rests upon the argument that he was protecting her chastity from Jeffery's advances. But what of the truth, asks Norma to herself, by now aware of her pregnancy—what happens if she can't lie to the jury and they learn instead of her condition? Norma's lawyer, unaware of her pregnancy, replies, "My dear, it makes all the difference between justice and murder. The fact that you are a virgin gives your father the right to defend your name." He explains further that a committee might be appointed by the court "to establish beyond any question that you are a chaste girl." Shocked at this, Norma cries out brokenly, "I guess if I were dead, the dear old chivalry wouldn't let them." She stops short when the

Mary and John Mack Brown face her stern father in *Coquette* (1929).

solution occurs to her. Act Three concludes with the offstage sound of a pistol shot, signaling her suicide.

A play like this presented considerable problems to the watchdogs of movie morality. The censorship regulations drawn up by the Hays Office after 1922—the so-called "Do's and Don'ts"—were attacked by lay leaders and Catholic clergy alike as poorly enforced and inadequate to the task. As Greg Black points out in his book, *Hollywood Censored,* one of the authors of the soon-to-be-written Motion Picture Production Code, Father Daniel Lord, S.J., argued censor restrictions should be toughened, that "the world's imperfections were the stuff of good drama, but he saw no reason why films should not show simple and direct solutions to complex moral, political, economic, and philosophical issues." A small group of producers, on the other hand, countered that with the addition of screen dialogue, actors and actresses could now "speak delicately and exactly" on sensitive subjects that could have been portrayed in silent films. The talkies should be able to use "any book, play or title which had gained wide attention."[9] The dispute was settled in February 1930 when the producers relinquished their position and agreed to accept the new Production Code. Perhaps the threats of Catholic-Protestant anti-film coalitions against the box office influenced this decision. At any rate, properties like *Coquette* were caught in the crossfire.

In order to circumvent the censor and, by no means coincidentally, to tailor the play into a suitable Mary Pickford vehicle, scenarists Sam Taylor, John Grey, and Allen McNeil had to make substantial alterations. Whereas the original Norma defied societal norms to make love with Michael, Pickford's character is essentially chaste. Her erotic scenes are restricted to a couple of cautious kisses with Michael (John Mack Brown) and tepid lines, like this declaration: "I love you more than anything in the world. I love you even more than my Daddy." After a town dance, she and Michael spend all night alone in his mother's empty house. Despite town gossip, the script goes out of its way to reassure us the encounter was strictly above board: in added dialogue between Norma and the maid, Julia (Louise Beavers), Norma confides, "He wouldn't even kiss me; he said he was afraid." Thus, there is neither the suggestion (nor the possibility) of Norma's pregnancy.

As for Norma's suicide, that fate is neatly transferred to Dr. Besant (John Sainpolis). Although suicide was a subject generally rejected by censors, Dr. Besant's self-destruction during the trial scene could be construed as an act of reparation and redemption for his murder of Michael. The richly layered complexities of Norma's personality and actions, as a consequence, are lost entirely.

Parenthetically, however, it should be noted that a *silent* version of *Coquette* was released concurrently with the talking version. This was a common practice at the time, since many European markets had not yet adopted synchronized-sound technology. According to the Department of Motion Picture Conservation of the Library of Congress, located in Dayton, Ohio, it contains additional scenes that more markedly point up Norma's sensuality, such as a seduction scene between Norma and Michael. This would support the contention that Mary did indeed originally intend *Coquette* to be a more radical departure from her previous films than is apparent in the available talking version. That this scene was not censored in the silent version suggests that restrictions were more rigorous for sound than for silence (a curious double standard that could only happen in Hollywood).

No one, either behind or in front of the camera, had previous experience with the talkies—neither cinematographer Charles Rosher, director Sam Taylor, set designer William Cameron Menzies, nor the cast. The unpredictable microphones, the claustrophobic sound stages, and the glass booth-encased cameras (designed to muffle the sound of the motors) all contribute to a static, stagy, flat-lit quality to the performances and image. Thus, with few exceptions, the visual effect closely imitates that of watching a play on a proscenium stage. Cinematographer Karl Struss (Rosher left the picture over a disagreement) shot most of the sequences from different angles with four cameras running simultaneously, permitting the actors to play out the action uninterrupted. Character groupings and the major dialogue scenes are transferred relatively intact to the film—including the opening dialogue among Norma, her brother Jimmy (William Janney), and Dr. Besant, wherein most of the back story is explicated; the long romantic exchange between Norma and Michael; the argument between Michael and Dr. Besant; and the scene where Jimmy attempts to shield Norma from her father's wrath over her late hours with Michael. The blocking is limited to a shallow-depth interior set, all entrances and exits utilizing the right and left sides of the frame, as if they were stage wings.

The only truly "cinematic" moments occur in scenes that have been added to the scenario. Struss shot the eleven-minute courtroom sequence with multiple cameras. There are several key camera moves, including a pan from the face of Dr. Besant to the loaded revolver conveniently placed on the evidence table (foreshadowing the moment when he will use it to end his life). In another added scene, Michael, instead of dying instantly from Dr. Besant's shot, languishes helplessly in his cabin while Norma rushes to his side in three brief shots of her running down a city street, across a stream, and up a hill (the only exterior locations in the movie). Locked in a passionate embrace, they affirm their love while secondary characters "frame" the action by hovering about in the background.

In its use of sound and acting techniques, *Coquette* is entirely typical of other theatrical adaptations of the day. The balance of the recorded sound is occasionally problematic, especially in the dance scene, where the orchestra drowns out the speaking voices. Incidental music is heard only briefly during the opening and closing credits. Its only other presence is strictly diegetic, i.e., it is heard only when the sound-producing source is seen,

Secrets was Mary's last film (1933), with Leslie Howard.

like the banjo-playing singer conveniently placed on the porch outside the Besant mansion, and the orchestra at the college dance. The performances are in the declamatory style characteristic of the stage. Newcomer John Mack Brown, who replaced stage actor Elliott Cabot as Michael, is the worst offender. His physical stiffness and the unrelieved monotony of his petulant, almost whiny vocal inflections are inappropriate for his role as a strong, romantic leading man. Surprisingly, Mary Pickford fares little better. Despite the fact that she had been known for her subtle acting styles in films for years, her return to theatrical material seems to have enforced a studied and forced quality to her voice and movement. Purportedly, when she listened to the playback of her first voice test, she was horrified, exclaiming, "That's not me! That's a pipsqueak voice. It's impossible. I sound like I'm twelve or thirteen." At any rate, the script doesn't help much, particularly when it calls for singularly protracted histrionics after

Michael's death, or when it calls for her to deliver lines like "Why, Michael, you look almost like you were dead!" Or when, at the end after her father's suicide, she mournfully tells Wentworth, "I've got to hurry along home now and help Jimmy with his algebra."

Coquette grossed over $1.3 million domestically, establishing it as one of Pickford's most successful pictures. Her Oscar-winning performance triumphed over the competition, including Ruth Chatterton in *Madame X*, Betty Compson in *The Barker*, Bessie Love in *Broadway Melody*, and the late Jeanne Eagels in *The Letter*. Whether or not the award was more of a "Lifetime Achievement" tribute than recognition for a single performance is an open question. But she was justly proud of it and for years kept it in the guest room at Pickfair.

Reviews were, predictably, mixed. "Mary appears too austere for the unsophisticated character she is supposed to represent," carped an English critic, "but she talks fairly well, considering she is asked to assume an affected Southern accent." Mordaunt Hall noted that her bobbed hair "improves her looks" and while she is "too grown up" for this particular role, she still retains her "pleasing child-like smile."[10] Commenting on her Oscar reception, *Photoplay* admitted that it was "a creditable first try," but complained that "few could be found who would agree with the Academicians that it was last year's outstanding labor before the microphone."[11]

"I think it has some good moments," reflects Bob Cushman, a Los Angeles–based Mary Pickford specialist, looking back with the hindsight of almost seventy years, "and for its time it was about as good as anybody could reasonably hope for. One contributing factor to its success may have been public curiosity about her voice. It was also one of the very first talkies to feature a top star."[12]

Indeed, considering that as late as 1930 there were still those, like Paul Rotha, who deeply lamented the "degenerate and misguided" talkies which "cannot be accepted as coming within the true boundaries of the cinema," Mary's determination to lend her prestige to the new medium is wholly admirable, even courageous.[13] Before the release of *Coquette* in April 1929, only a handful of prestige-level all-talking pictures had appeared, namely, *The Lights of New York* (Warner Bros.), *The Singing Fool* (Warner Bros.), *Interference* (Paramount), *In Old Arizona* (Fox), *The Broadway Melody* (MGM). Moreover, with the possible exception of Al Jolson (who was a stage personality in the first place), none of them featured a front-rank movie star. Pickford was the first of her class to gamble on the new technology. It was a seal of approval the rest of Hollywood couldn't ignore.

Within the next six months, a number of groundbreaking films would appear, like Josef von Sternberg's *Thunderbolt* (Paramount), King Vidor's *Hallelujah!* (MGM), Rouben Mamoulian's *Applause* (Paramount), and Victor Fleming's *The Virginian* (Paramount).

Meanwhile, encouraged by her own success, Mary immediately prepared for her next talking venture, which would costar her with her husband, the dashing Doug. *The Taming of the Shrew* began production in June 1929 and was released in November. Following that would be her next (and last) films, *Kiki* (1931) and *Secrets* (1933).

But *that's* another story.

Chapter 14

A Shrewd Adaptation

The Taming of the Shrew

Of all mad matches, never was the like!
—***THE TAMING OF THE SHREW,*** III. ii. 241

Consider the Fairbanks-Pickford *Taming of the Shrew* (1929) at end times—approaching the sobering end of the decadent decade of the twenties, anticipating the eventual end of the Fairbanks-Pickford celebrity marriage, portending the end of the silent film and the beginning of the talkie revolution, and redefining the theatrical roots of the cinema. A kind of logic must have drawn Fairbanks and Pickford towards a Shakespeare project at this time. This experiment would test their talents and patience. It would also result in Hollywood's first attempt to adapt a complete Shakespeare play into a synchronized-sound film.

Ironically, numerous Shakespearean adaptations of *The Taming of the Shrew* had already appeared *as silent films*. One of the first, although crude in appearance, commands our attention inasmuch as it points the way to subsequent cinematic adaptations at the time of this and other Shakespearean plays. Directed by D. W. Griffith and starring Florence Lawrence, this one-reel Biograph release in 1908 (approximately fifteen minutes) was publicized as "one of the snappiest, funniest films of the kind ever made," with a story that is "concisely told," depicting "only the stirring interesting portions of the play."[1] Shakespearean titles numbered an estimated 300 films by 1929. However, due to loss and neglect, only about 40 of that number survive today.[2] Now, with both Pickford and Fairbanks gaining some experience in sound technologies—the former with the all-talkie

"Come to Wife It Wealthily" in *The Taming of the Shrew* (1929).

Coquette and the latter with the two prologues in *The Iron Mask*—the time was right for them to bring Shakespeare's "voice" to a feature-length, synchronized-sound motion picture.

Obviously, silent films had necessarily sacrificed plot details, characterization and dialogue for the demands of pantomime, scenery, and special effects. Herbert Beerbohm Tree's description of his production of *Macbeth* in 1916 is typical: "You see," he confessed, "I thought I had reached the time in my life when I ought to be seen, and not heard!"[3] However, with sound technology, it was now feared that Shakespearean scene and action would be overwhelmed by continuous dialogue. How to balance the priorities of both silence and sound, while keeping the acting *moving*? It was a crucial challenge, declared Benjamin Glazer in March 1929. Glazer was a prominent sound supervisor for Pathé and FBO Studios, who had worked on several talkies, including Paramount's photoplay the year before, *Interference*: "I do think that the drive, the simplicity, the splendid dynamic force which the best silent pictures had, must be retained, must be absorbed by the talking picture if it is to survive at all."[4]

Released in 1929 during the summer months before *The Taming of the Shrew*, a number of talkies—including Josef von Sternberg's *Thunderbolt*, King Vidor's *Hallelujah*, Rouben Mamoulian's *Applause*—had successfully done just that, challenging the hegemony of the microphone, while privileging the pictorial beauty of set design and camera work. The prominent art director, William Cameron Menzies, who had worked on the production design of Fairbanks's *The Thief of Bagdad* and *The Iron Mask*, was preparing *The Taming of the Shrew* when he delivered a lecture at USC on April 10. While he, too, was concerned with the balance of picture and sound, he was nonetheless committed to retaining pictorial values. "As an art director, I am interested in the photoplay as a series of pictures," he said.

> When the art director receives the finished scenario he begins to transpose the written words into a series of mental pictures . . . He sketches his settings with an eye to the action that will transpire . . . Simplicity is absolutely necessary, for the audience must be able to grasp the whole scene and its meaning at a glance.[5]

And Fairbanks himself had concerns. Citing the freedom of movement in Walt Disney's first synchronized-sound cartoons, he praised "the perfect rhythm, in comedy tempo, of the little characters and the accompanying sound. It is not merely synchronization, it is a rhythmic, swinging, lilting thing."[6]

As we will demonstrate, *The Taming of the Shrew* successfully blended silent film technique with a judicious, sparing use of sound, music, and dialogue. It also brought a *sting* and *snap* of its own to a revisionist approach to marriage. The public had waited more than a decade for Fairbanks and Pickford to appear on screen together. Newsreels of their bond tours during the Great War and of their world travels in the twenties had provided only tantalizing glimpses of their partnership. In January 1929 they saw a production of *The Taming of the Shrew* in Los Angeles. "They jointly concluded," writes biographer Jeffrey Vance, "that this would make an ideal vehicle for their long-anticipated co-starring screen venture."[7] Sam Taylor, who had directed Pickford in *My Best Girl* and the all-talkie *Coquette*, was engaged as scenarist and director; Karl Struss, who had worked with Taylor on *Coquette*, signed on as cinematographer; Laurence Irving would be in charge of the costumes; and William Cameron Menzies would design the lavish sets. Filming began in late June and finished six weeks later. The

New York premiere was held at the Rivoli Theater on November 29, 1929. The *New York Times* named it one of the Ten Best Films of the Year, and *Variety* aptly pronounced it "a vastly extravagant burlesque of Bill Shakespeare's best laugh."[8]

To review briefly the main plot of Shakespeare's text . . . Katherina and her younger sister Bianca are the daughters of a well-to-do merchant, Baptista Minola. Baptista will not allow Bianca to marry until a suitable husband has been found for the cantankerous, ill-tempered, and disagreeable Kate. For obvious reasons, then, the eligible bachelors of Padia are not interested in Katherina but the beautiful and docile Bianca. Therefore, Bianca's rival suitors, Hortensio, Lucentio, and Gromio, hire a gentleman from Verona, the outspoken Petruchio, to woo Katherina in order to clear the path for their courtship of Bianca. After learning about Baptista's wealth, Petruchio seems mainly interested in Kate's dowry, and the father readily accepts Petruchio's offer of marriage. Meanwhile, Lucentio and Hortensio disguise themselves as teachers and tutors to Bianca, so as to woo her without her father's interference.

Petruchio has a few tricks up his sleeve and arrives at his wedding late, outrageously garbed in beggar's clothing, insisting that Kate marry him as he is. But this insult is merely the first phase of his plan to "tame" the wench. Throughout the next several scenes, Petruchio denies Kate food, sleep, and a suitable wardrobe, while attempting to establish himself as her "lord and master." But although he humbles and humiliates her constantly until she blindly agrees to whatever he says, Petruchio never really breaks her spirit.

The play's final scene has Petruchio, Kate, Lucentio, Bianca, Hortensio, and his new wife all celebrating their nuptials. During the wedding feast, the men wager over the obedience of their new wives. Surprisingly, Petruchio wins the wager. Kate not only shows absolute obedience to her husband's every command, but is also extremely critical of the other wives for their neglect. As Cordelia will say to her father in *King Lear*, Kate pledges her love according to her bond, on condition that Petruchio remain loving and honest. Kate proclaims Petruchio to be "her loving lord" and proves submissive to "his honest will." Consequently, Petruchio kisses Kate, proclaiming her to be his equal, not his servant.

As the first feature-length, synchronized-sound Shakespearean adaptation, *The Taming of the Shrew* outrages Shakespearean purists but nonetheless establishes a fine precedent for the melding of the Shakespearean source text to a variety of unlikely extra-texts and cinematic styles. As

Petrucchio confronts Kate in *The Taming of the Shrew*.

a satiric jab at sexual politics in a slapstick mode, it's a classic example of what cultural commentator Henry Jenkins calls "textual poaching," i.e., "an impertinent raid on [a canonical] preserve that takes away only those things that seem useful or pleasurable to the reader."[9] Thus, sight gags and comic confrontations embellish the action. Designer Laurence Irving, who was on the set, describes the process:

> Day and night [director Sam Taylor] was attended by two gagmen—rude and nonsensical after the Bard's own heart—with faces like battered bantam-weights and an inexhaustible fund of practical comicalities in the Mack Sennett tradition. Whenever dialogue that could not be cut tended to lag, or was reckoned incomprehensible to the ninepennies, they were called upon for a diversion.[10]

This is not to denigrate Taylor's intentions. Far from it. According to Pickford's biographer, Scott Eyman, Fairbanks and Pickford already had decided on a farcical tone, since seeing the Los Angeles stage production in January: "[They had] "enjoyed the manner in which the knock-about aspects of the script were emphasized."[11] Thus, Taylor was perfectly in synch. In a telegram to Irving, he had stated clearly that he "wanted to emphasize [a] light and whimsical feeling of [the] play." He further advised that in collaboration with Menzies the sets should be "intimate" rather than the typical "mountain of wood and plaster."[12]

Methods had to be devised to work around the restrictions of the clumsy camera soundproof booths and sound recording equipment, which had hitherto rendered many talkies hopelessly static and tedious. Cameraman Struss adopted the stratagem of shooting entire scenes silently so that selective sounds and a bare minimum of dialogue could be separately recorded and dubbed in later. For example, many of the dolly and tracking shots in the film are shot without sound. Freedom of movement of both camera and actors is maintained. A dynamic dolly shot frames Petruchio's initial appearance, retreating before him as he makes his swaggering way down the street. Only a quick quaff of a drink and a dally with a maid impedes his quick stride. Moments later, at the home of Hortensio, he nimbly darts up the steps, pulls his servant up over the balcony ledge, and arrogantly cracks his whip. Likewise, a powerful tracking shot prepares us for Kate's first entrance. Shouts and bumps and crashes from Kate's room are heard offscreen. A thunderstorm seems to shake the house. Servants scatter, cats and dogs flee, and a mirror cracks. We move up the broad staircase, enter through her doorway, and swivel our gaze to disclose the disordered room and a very agitated Kate, clad in black and clutching her whip. In another dynamic entrance scene, Petruchio arrives at the wedding, sitting *backwards* on an aging nag (a moment obviously borrowed from d'Artagnan's arrival in Paris in *The Three Musketeeers*), dressed in motley garb and wearing a jackboot atop his head.

The continuing tussles between Petruchio and Kate also avoid the static tedium of Shakespeare's dialogue-heavy text. They are staged as a series of "duels," both verbal and physical, if you will, in the best Fairbanksian tradition. Combats involving bandits, pirates, and musketeers in Douglas's earlier films are now translated into contests between husbands and wives. These pantomimic scenes, supplemented with a bare minimum of dialogue, successfully tease out the ambivalence in Shakespeare's play regarding the function of gender roles in courtship and marriage. Theme and technique are perfectly conjoined.

These combats begin with a Punch and Judy puppet show prologue, which replaces Shakespeare's "Sly Induction" prologue. Punch commands,

"Kiss me!" Judy responds with a sarcastic, "I'll kiss you!" and flails away at him. Punch disappears for an instant and reappears with a paddle and strikes her three times over the head, declaring, "I'll tame you!" Judy is eventually mollified, and her pained "oh's" dissolve into an ecstatic, "Oh, you're wonderful!" The camera then tracks back to reveal the puppet stage located in the middle of a Paduan street.[13]

In a nod to Fairbanks's *Don Q,* the punishing paddle of Punch is quickly replaced by the stinging whips of Petruchio and Kate. Their first encounter is indeed a veritable whip-cracking affair. "Oh, how I long to have a g-r-r-r-a-apple with her," Petruchio snarls. Let the games begin. The sequence, virtually wordless, is beautifully staged, capturing in the frame a two-shot of Petruchio, standing lower left at the base of the broad staircase, hands on hips, and Kate at the upper right on the top step. She cracks her whip. He responds with laughter and cracks *his* whip. They take each other's measure. Kate compares their respective weapons (hers is shorter). In a strikingly suggestive point-of-view shot, she regards Fairbanks in medium close-up from the waist down, his whip snaking across the floor. The two antagonists move toward each other and meet in the center of the steps. They g-r-r-a-apple and he drags her down the stairs and forcibly kisses her. She slaps him, hard, no less than four times. He's oblivious to the blows. As he speaks to her father, he endures *seven* strikes from her whip. At length he has her pinned to his lap. In a clever shot-reverse-shot sequence, Baptista approvingly sees Petruchio from the back as Kate seems nestled in his arms; but the reverse shot views Fairbanks from the front, with his hand over the mouth of the struggling Kate. The kiss is prolonged. At length, Kate relaxes, in an apparent capitulation. A close-up of Kate's face shows her breathless and (momentarily) submissive features. (Physical fatigue or sexual arousal?) When Petruchio exits, Kate declares, in words not in Shakespeare, "Katherine shall tame his haggard, for if she fails, I'll tie up her tongue and pare down her nails." His response, a little later are words verbatim from Shakespeare: "I will be master of what is mine own,/ She is my goods, my chattels . . . my horse, my ox, my anything" (3.2., 228–29; 230–31).

The next "duel," by contrast, is a wordless, ten-minute pantomimic confrontation between the two at the wedding ceremony. It is a classic bit of silent film pantomime, punctuated with a few selected sounds for comic effect. Petruchio lounges off to the side of the ceremony, scarcely noticing Kate as he munches an apple. The priest gestures for him to join the bride. "*Who, me???*" he silently mouths, pointing at himself in mock surprise. Her outraged expressions cross swords with his calculated indifference. Once he even bares his famous teeth at her with a silent "*g-r-r-r*." She seethes. The sound of the sporadic *crunch* of his apple overrides the sounds of the organ and the priest's intoned ritual. He greets the priest's request to take her hand in marriage with a shouted "AYE!" that shakes the rafters. When Kate pauses, in her turn, he stomps on her foot, eliciting her answering cry. And yes, that infernal apple, now reduced to the core, is handed off to Baptista, its subsequent progress from pocket to hand to hand is tracked by the mobile camera. The whole affair is capped off outside the church when Kate refuses to accompany Petruchio to his country house. Out comes her whip. Out comes his sword. He bounds forward, tosses her to his shoulder, leaps into the saddle, and gallops down the street. A footnote to it all is the discovery of the errant apple core in Baptista's pocket.

In a highly abridged version of Act Three, the last series of combats transpires in Petruchio's country house. After a supper scene in which Petruchio contrives to thwart the starving Kate's every attempt to down some food, she retires to the bedroom. Alone at the dining table Petruchio boasts to his dog Troilus that he'll starve her of food and deprive her of sleep: In lines verbatim from Shakespeare, he confides: "This is a way to kill a wife with kindness,/ and thus I'll curb her mad and headstrong humor" (4.1., 197–198). But Kate lurks, listening unseen on the balcony and smiles craftily at his words. Moments later, Petruchio rudely bursts into their room and loudly slams the door. She feigns sleep. In another sequence of essentially silent pantomime, he opens a window to a violent gust of wind. Kate "awakens" with a yawn and applauds. She "parries" by opening another window to another blast of air. He gazes at the moonlight and pronounces, "'tis the sun." Obligingly, Kate agrees. Increasingly bewildered and irritated, Petruchio ripostes by finding a stain on the bed sheets. Kate, in turn, takes up the mattress and hurls it to the floor. She then throws a stool at his head, connecting with an audible *crack*. Contrite now, she cradles his wounded head to her chest. Smiling all the while, in a significant gesture she tosses her whip into the fireplace. (We think of Zorro's blade, tossed aside, only to be handy when needed again.) "O Petruchio, beloved," she whispers, "there, there." Petruchio, bewildered, looks up at her. "The sun is shining bright?" he murmurs meekly, the repetition of his question no longer a demand but a beseeching inquiry. "Aye, the blessed sun," she replies softly, smiling to herself.

The next day at the breakfast table, Kate describes a wife's marital duties to her assembled guests. While she promises her (now bandaged) husband an oath to love, honor, and obey, he sits a smug smile on his face.

Mary adorns the sets of William Cameron Menzies in *The Taming of the Shrew.*

Satisfied at his "victory," he does not see what the viewer does: a cut to a close-up of Kate's broad wink (followed by a shot of sister Bianca's answering wink). Then they all sit down to eat.

In his detailed examination of these scenes, John Brett Mischo notes that "there were no stage directions regarding winks in Shakespeare." Instead, "the bit was suggested to Pickford by her former Broadway acquaintance, producer Daniel Frohman."[14]

Indeed, that knowing "wink" at the breakfast table—a sly device of gender politics to which we will allude in the next chapter regarding Fairbanks's last film, *The Private Life of Don Juan* (1934)—also signifies what has been apparent all along. From the very beginning, Fairbanks's familiar catalogue of aggressively masculine gestures, poses, and boasts has been subverted and satirized at every turn. Cutaways to Kate and the others to his boasts and declamations (even his rolling of the "rs" in "g-r-r-r-apple") reveal their amusement and friendly scorn. Fairbanks's characteristic bravado and pose wilts.

A serious reconsideration is underway of how masculinity fares in the modern era of stage and film, where feminist advances and the appearance in popular culture of the New Woman were simultaneously challenging traditional gender roles. (As discussed in the preceding chapter on Pickford's *Coquette,* since the mid-teens, many Broadway dramas were privileging female activists and attacking conventional gender roles in the marriage institution.[15]) Mary Pickford herself declared that Katherine's "meaning and knowing wink" at the end of the picture confirms this: "It is Katherine who eventually tames Petruchio . . . Katherine had the intelligence to know that both flies and husbands are better caught with syrup than with sugar."[16] In her discussion of the film's sexual politics, commentator Barbara Hodgdon agrees this is the case. She describes these scenes as "a Noel Coward-like bridal night" that offers audiences a voyeuristic glimpse" of the world's most popular couple. Hodgdon concludes that Fairbanks as the boastful but ultimately compliant Petruchio "is a son playacting the role of husband," while Pickford as the indulgent Kate "is a mother who plays a wife."[17] *The Taming of the Shrew,* in sum, prepares us in the next chapter for further meditations on love and marriage, artists and husbands, in Fairbanks's next four films.

Meanwhile, the performances of the marital duels here are not only effective metaphors for the struggles between pantomime and dialogue, male and female, husband and wife, but they may cast light on the current status of the Pickford-Fairbanks marriage. In the first place, we need to remember that their marriage was essentially one of equals. "Hipper" and "Duber," as they called each other, had survived a passionate, clandestine affair and a scandal-prone marriage to maintain their "royal" supremacy in Hollywood. By all accounts—see especially Scott Eyman's detailed description of their domestic life—Mary became "the anchor" while Douglas was the more playful, mercurial partner. Eyman quotes their mutual friend Charlie Chaplin's remark that Douglas was very much a Peter Pan to Mary's Wendy.[18] This is especially significant, in that Fairbanks, like Pan, was ultimately incapable of sharing the adoring sentiments of his "Wendy," his wife Mary Pickford. In his description of his father, Douglas Jr. aptly confirmed that late in the marriage "he loathes any sort of demonstration or show of emotion."[19] This was compounded as each began to resent the other's increasing demands for personal and professional independence. Indeed, as Eyman suggests, if either partner "was distracted by the demands of career or internal pressures that could not be controlled, the other was bound to feel abandoned."[20] For Fairbanks, particularly, the very emblem of an aggressive American masculinity, the challenges and/or constraints on that independence must have chafed, to say the least.

Domestic bliss in *The Taming of the Shrew*.

In the second place, it has been routine for biographers and on-set commentators to recite a woeful litany of incidents of professional discord on the set. Even Fairbanks's most recent biographer, Jeffrey Vance, trots out "the usual suspects"—Laurence Irving, Bruce Humberstone, and Pickford herself (in her unreliable autobiography, *Sunshine and Shadow*)—who testify to the principals' "discomfort" with shooting in sound and with each other. The production seems to have been a professional and technical disaster from beginning to end. "'Talkies' were uncomfortable, cumbersome, and awkward for Fairbanks," writes Vance. "Control had been replaced by consternation. Fairbanks decided early on that he loathed the laborious and cumbersome process of sound film production."[21]

Doubtless some of this is true. The sheer weight of testimony has to be considered. However, among the few historians who offer a more moderate view, Scott Eyman points out many qualifying testimonies regarding a more relaxed shooting schedule, absolute professionalism among the principals, even much tomfoolery with the cast and crew. [22] In an interview, Karl Struss, the film's cinematographer, objected to accusations that Fairbanks, in particular, was "difficult" on the set:

> He was never difficult. Doug was very exuberant, full of fun and Mary was concerned about the dollars and cents aspect of it all. . . . She was very serious minded. I might add that Doug was never late in the morning. . . . [He was] having a good time; nothing alcoholic, just boyish hi-jinks. As far as his acting was concerned, I thought he handled the dialogue very well.[23]

Might we also suggest that one *take a look* at the film? Seen in the Matty Kemp version that was released in 1967—the film had been unavailable in any form for many years[24]—*The Taming of the Shrew*, for all its contentiousness, is marvelous fun and a savvy blend of intelligence and slapstick pantomime; and both principals seem to be obviously enjoying themselves. Moreover, if Fairbanks's masculinity is being satirized, it is apparent to us that it is he who is leading the charge.

The Taming of the Shrew was their only foray into Shakespeare. But it set the seal on future endeavors by everybody else to bring the Bard to heel. If it was an experiment, it at least demonstrated the feasibility and utility of a Shakespeare balanced between the priorities of drama and slapstick, sight and sound. For example, the challenge of telling Shakespeare's *Shrew* entirely in visual terms remains to this day. On April Fool's Day of 2012—excellent timing, perhaps, but this is not a joke—Synetic Theatre premiered its dance version of *The Taming of the Shrew* to Washington, DC, audiences at the Lansburgh Theatre in what *Washington Post* reviewer Peter Marks described as a "hyper-aerobicized 90 minutes of disciplined mayhem." Now, that's longer than the Fairbanks/Pickford silent film, and nary a word was uttered.[25]

Moreover, this experiment by Hollywood's first celebrity couple would later be repeated by Richard Burton and Elizabeth Taylor, accustomed to over-the-top theatrical argumentation, who turned Shakespeare's shrew into a mouse that roared.[26] By contrast, Mary Pickford's shrew was a mistress of grimaces, as well she should be when her Petruchio shows up for the wedding, on the wrong end of a horse, a cocked jackboot on his head, munching on an apple that he *should* have given to the horse, neigh? Taylor's Kate the Curst is angry, nearly to the point of being hysterical. Richard Burton's Petruchio is far more boorish than the elegant Douglas Fairbanks could have made him appear. The Fairbanks Petruchio was a gentleman trickster, who is never quite convincing when he attempts to be harsh with his lady after the stormy nuptials. By contrast, Burton is physically threatening, capable of doing dastardly derring-do over the rooftops, then crashing after his ladylove into the woolstack for a tumbling tussle. Consequently, Taylor's Kate is overwhelmed, subdued rather than seduced. Or maybe she *is* seduced as well, a victim of verbal rape? Petruchio keeps his eyes on the prize, as he tells Hortensio in Act I, Scene IV: "I came to wive it wealthily in Padua;/ If wealthily, then happily in Padua."[27] Ironically, it was the release of the Zeffirelli version that encouraged Pickford to mandate the Matty Kemp rerelease of the 1929 film.

Part IV

Artists and Husbands

As for me, my arms are broken
From having clasped the clouds.
—**BAUDELAIRE,** *Les Plaintes d'un Icare*

Chapter 15

Prologue

There is a certain literary archetype, suggests the Australian historian Peter Conrad, author of *Creation: Artists, Gods, Origins* (2007), that is found in the characters of Don Quixote, Robinson Crusoe, and Don Juan. It is a compound of bruised ideals, restless wanderlust, and romantic failure. Collectively, these characters "want to go everywhere and become everyone," to migrate "through time, place and metamorphic changes of identity to declare their ambitions to experience an infinitude of possibilities." Eventually, Conrad continues, as they enter the global sphere, "they alter and contradict themselves at will: the mythic creature survives in history by mutating; eternity puts on camouflage for its descent into time."[1]

Nothing better describes the characters and trajectories of the four films, released from 1930 to 1934, that bring Douglas Fairbanks's active career to a close. *Reaching for the Moon, Around the World in Eighty Minutes, Mr. Robinson Crusoe*, and *The Private Life of Don Juan* reveal those "ambitions to experience an infinitude of possibilities." The collection of artists and husbands seen here constitute a composite of the increasingly restless private and professional Fairbanks. Crusoe-like, he forsook Hollywood for far-flung ports of call. Like Quixote, he tilted at the "windmills" of elusive ideals. And like the aging Don Juan, he sought fleshly pleasures wherever he found them.

Many critics and biographers have not been kind to these films. They point out their occasionally silly and outdated humor and their embarrassing depictions of a wealthy, middle-aged American abroad. The fine line between Fairbanks as a buoyantly optimistic young American and Fairbanks as an aging, tiresome showoff has been breached. While acknowledging the justness of this assessment, however, we hold a more moderate view. Curiosities these films undeniably are, and they are also occasionally awkward and embarrassing. They graphically reveal the cruel fate awaiting celebrities in the face of advancing age and the fickleness of audiences. That, in part, is what gives them their interest—even their relevance—to today's hyper-celebrity culture. Fairbanks, as always, made his life an open book. And he may even have come to dislike the kinds of pictures he was now making, but he made them nonetheless. We maintain, after fresh viewings, that Fairbanks gave them some of his finest moments, both as a filmmaker and an actor. If justification is needed for their inclusion here, that is it. *The Private Life of Don Juan*, in particular, is a beautiful and moving valedictory to his career. While thematically linked to the other three, we hope to demonstrate that it deserves to stand on its own as one of Fairbanks's finest films.

The years 1930–1934 saw our vagabond on the road, embarked on an ambitious travel schedule that, excepting sporadic returns to Pickfair, left Hollywood and wife Mary Pickford behind. In the opinion of the press, he was "abdicating" his Hollywood throne. While rumors would eventually fly about a "divorce" in the offing with Mary, Douglas was reported as saying, "Why don't I stay in Hollywood? Well, it probably wouldn't look well in print, but it bores me. That is the truth. Why should I spend my life in a narrow little village when there's a whole world to amuse myself in?"[2]

While Fairbanks had long expressed the desire to combine travel with moviemaking—as early as 1916–1917 he was planning to make films in Europe and South America—this new itinerary was different. It was touched with a restlessness bordering on desperation. He set sail for big-game hunting in Indochina, Siam, and India. He was in England by May for a reunion with Mary. This was the trip that would provide most of the footage for *Around the World in Eighty Minutes.* In November 1931, he left for Europe, Africa, and Asia to make another travel picture, but changed his mind while in Paris and returned to Pickfair by Christmas. By January of 1932, he was abroad again, this time in the South Sea Islands, where much of *Mr. Robinson Crusoe* was shot. He returned in May of that year, but turned right around and left in August on the SS *Chichibu Maru* to hunt longhaired tigers in Manchuria. The party was forbidden entry to Tibet to hunt the giant panda but managed to safari through Indochina. Plans for a screenplay about China never materialized. He returned to Pickfair by Christmas 1932. By February, with rumors of a divorce from Mary in the air, he was off to Europe with his son to make pictures with Alexander Korda.

We will tag along with him, first embarking on an ocean liner in *Reaching for the Moon*, continuing on to the Orient in *Around the World*, stopping off at the South Seas in *Mr. Robinson Crusoe*, and finally dipping back into the myths of Old Spain in *The Private Life of Don Juan*.

With Bebe Daniels in *Reaching for the Moon* (1930).

Chapter 16

Reaching for the Moon

Why is it that traveling Americans are always so dreadful?
—SINCLAIR LEWIS

We set sail on the ocean liner *l'Amérique* bound for England. Quixote-like, Wall Street tycoon Larry Day (Fairbanks) is in pursuit of his Dulcinea, Vivian Bennett (Bebe Daniels), a high-flying aviatrix who is hardly the saintly ideal that Larry presumes her to be. *Reaching for the Moon* (not to be confused with his silent film of that title) was the first film in which Fairbanks appeared in modern dress since *The Nut* in 1921. According to musical film historian, Miles Kreuger, the plot, originally suggested by Irving Berlin, had used the background of the 1929 Wall Street crash to test the loyalties of two shipboard lovers. Berlin planned it to be a musical and wrote several songs for it, including the title song. When producer Joseph Scheck got the project, he thought it might serve as a musical vehicle for Fairbanks! It was even suggested he might burst into the title song himself! We may never know if this did indeed occur on screen, since only one of the songs survives, and it is voiced by a youngster named Bing Crosby.[1]

The sight of a middle-aged Fairbanks with thinning hair in a business suit must have presented something of a shock to a public accustomed to the sleek and swashbuckling bandits Robin Hood and The Gaucho. Moreover, the brash businessman seen in the earlier Fairbanks satires—who really preferred climbing a tree to spending a day at the executive desk—has been replaced by a fast-talking industrialist dominating the boardroom. Putting it another way, *Reaching for the Moon* betrays the casual iconoclasm of the earlier 1917 film of that title. There we had enjoyed watching Fairbanks thumb his nose at the business world, because we knew he was only *pretending* to settle down to an office desk.

An introductory dolly shot follows Larry's swinging stride into a conference room. He is surrounded by associates hunched over banks of telephones. "Bring me some cornflakes and milk—warm," he orders. He crunches away, while talking at a breathless pace about a variety of business and patriotic topics. "One must impede this explosive urge," mutters an associate, who leaves because he is unable to get a word in edgewise.

Larry must have a sidekick, of course, and here we encounter a combination of Don Juan's Leporello and Quixote's Sancho Panza in the figure of the worldly butler, Roger (Edward Everett Horton). Roger is apparently something of a snoop or peeping Tom who habitually employs binoculars in his surveillance of prospective women for Larry. We are supposed to believe that Larry is an innocent in matters of love. Roger smirkingly informs his master that it is not idealistic romance but carnal love that will make his life "go boom." He then asks, "Do you ever dream of girls?"—to which Larry replies, "Whenever I dream, it's about horses." So much for the clever banter.

Suddenly smitten by the charms of Vivian, Larry follows her on board a ship for England. During the voyage, the ever-present Roger assists him in the art of wooing. He demonstrates the proper techniques of handholding, much to the discomfiture of an electrician arriving at just the wrong moment. To further stimulate Larry's ardor, Roger mixes him a drink he calls "Angel's Breath." Its effects on Larry, who (like Fairbanks himself) is a teetotaler, launches him into a spectacular acrobatic trajectory. He turns his stateroom into a gymnasium as he races about, grunts inarticulate sounds, leaps up the walls, and hangs from a ledge, dangling in simian style. Then, he attacks Vivian's fiance in a series of jarring flying tackles. The ship's stewards try to restrain him, but he climbs up the wall again and launches himself full upon them. We feel cheated to know that Fairbanks has to take a drink to become airborne—or that Quixote might have needed stimulants to seek his Dulcinea. The essence of either character has never needed more than a burst of exuberance.

As for Larry's wooing, his timid efforts are in striking contrast to Vivian, who cynically has placed a bet with her girl friends that she can seduce him within twenty-four hours. Meanwhile, Larry has learned that the stock market crash has wiped him out. Disconsolate, he is an easy target for her. Unaware of her plan, and bewildered by her behavior, Larry bursts into an overtly Oedipal confession: "Ever since I was a kid of ten," he tells her haltingly, "and knelt to my mother, have I felt like kneeling to anyone. But you are my idol; I worship you; and there'll never be anyone but you." Wilting under this unexpected display of romantic ardor, she admits that she returns his love. She has faith in his ability to come back from the financial ruin that recently beset him. She is, in short, Don Juan's practical Donna Anna and Quixote's fantasy Dulcinea all in one: "[A woman] is not what you pursue and love and hold," Larry tearfully tells her. "She's something that leans over and whispers in your ear what you *are* and what you can do, and what you're going to do." They melt into each other's arms. Fade out on their marriage.

With the possible exception of *Around the World in Eighty Minutes*, *Reaching for the Moon* survives today as the most difficult of Fairbanks's films for modern audiences to stomach. It comes as no surprise that it was the first time since 1916's *The Americano* that he neither produced nor financed it himself. He had been reluctant to invest in a talking picture. Moreover, without overall control, the severe cuts in Berlin's musical numbers left the film's plot exposed as thin and dull. As for the love interest, the old gusto of the comic and combative courtships that enlivened his earlier films is gone. Measured against that, the forty-seven-year-old is merely a husband now, submissive, grounded. Like Quixote, when he exchanges the mad idealism of the swain for the simple sanity of convention, he loses his forces. But whereas Quixote, finally a mildly eccentric squire known only as Alonso Quixano the Good, quietly dies, Fairbanks moves on. Apparently aware of the critical and popular disapproval to come, he sets sail for exotic ports of call on the very night of the film's premiere on December 29, 1930.

Plans for a global tour in *Around the World in Eighty Minutes* (1931).

Chapter 17

Around the World in Eighty Minutes

One thing that appeals to me about the world is that you can play around it with a mashie—good courses everywhere.
—**DOUGLAS FAIRBANKS**

Which brings us to *Around the World in Eighty Minutes,* which we rightly regard as a sequel to *Reaching for the Moon.* Shortly before its release in November 1931, Fairbanks was quoted:

> I'm not a serious artist at all. In a world such as this to-day, the new fiction is reality. No imaginary story about China is as exciting as China itself. If I can get away with it, I am going to travel.[1]

Although he was purportedly happy with the result, it was dismissed by *Variety* and garnered poor box office. It remains one of his least frequently seen films today. "Except perhaps from a sociological point of view, it is a film of no importance," sniffs Eileen Bowser in the Museum of Modern Art film notes.[2] Originally called just *Around the World with Douglas Fairbanks,* it has, for all its flaws, a great deal of ethnographic interest. He took as his model the African documentaries, notably *Simba,* that had been made in the 1920s by his friends, Osa and Martin Johnson. While on their safaris, the couple from Kansas had employed equipment like long lenses and the continuous zoom lens for a new freedom in exterior and wildlife photography.

Crusoe-like, Douglas sallies forth into the wide world. We remember that Crusoe, whatever his spiritual values were, was nothing less than an

With director/cameraman Victor Fleming in *Around the World in Eighty Minutes*.

imperialist entrepreneur who gained control over the men and goods of his island. "All the good things of this world," he says, "are no further good to us, than they are for our use; and that whatever we may heap up indeed to give others, we enjoy just as much as we can use, and no more."[3] Spoken like a true American capitalist abroad. Fairbanks intended not just to make a travelogue of exotic locales; he would seize, appropriate, and commodify for popular consumption the world's riches, pleasures, and curiosities. "This was all my own," he could have said, echoing Crusoe, "that I was king and lord of all this country indefeasibly, and had the right of possession" (80). Moreover, again like Crusoe, he regarded the whole enterprise as something of a joke: "I'd like to emphasize two things," he says at the beginning, "—first, that the world is essentially funny; it's a great place for laughs; it's also the dwelling place for magic; absolutely anything can happen."

Accompanying him is a faithful Man Friday, his cameraman Victor Fleming. In his hand is not Crusoe's rifle but the ever-ready golf club. Golf for him was no idle whim but more of an obsession. "He would give up any one or all three meals for a game of golf," wrote his son in 1930. "On the links he almost invariably loses his temper, breaks his clubs on his knee and throws them to the four winds with mumbled curses."[4]

In January 1931, he set sail on a big-game hunting expedition to Cambodia, Siam, French Indochina, and India. The trip reads like a picaresque *Innocents Abroad.* Following the newspaper headlines, we are informed that on March 27, 1931, he killed a huge panther in India and was a guest of Her Highness, Maharanee Sahiba, Regent of the State of Cooch Pehar. On April 3, he was the guest of Manarajah of Patiala, one of the delegates of the London Round Table Conference. On April 7, he was the guest of the viceroy, Lord Irwin, in Bombay, India, and so on. Back from the Orient to London, he finally returned to New York on April 29. By September, he was off on a 15,000-mile air venture into the wilds of South America and the headwaters of the Amazon for new travelogue material.

Around the World was made at a relatively modest cost of $117,866. The main complaint about it is the same one that can be directed against the Martin and Osa Johnson efforts, i.e., the sometimes insensitive narrative, supplied by Robert E. Sherwood, that does little credit to the image of the American abroad. The wisecrack, the somewhat patronizing "great white father visiting the natives" tone deflates an otherwise fascinating film with valuable documentation of the people and places visited.

The film is a highly self-conscious kind of "day book," interspacing a weird blend of trick photography, location footage, and, at the end, a film-within-a-film device. Fairbanks appears at the beginning stepping out of a photograph. He addresses the camera: "Being a travelogue lecturer I must have a pointer." He gestures with one hand and that ever-present emblem of middle-class leisure, a golf club, appears in his fist. He introduces his cameramen, Victor Fleming and Henry Sharp. Their equipage of luggage pops into the frame. Once again, we find ourselves on an ocean liner. Fairbanks loses no time converting it into his own personal gymnasium. "Now I'm going to show you a few exercises by which you can get rid of all your ailments," he says (alluding to the sort of demonstrations found in the earlier *Down to Earth*). What follows is the first of several extended athletic trajectories to come in the film. Doug cavorts all about the ship, his narration commenting as he flies along. He runs down corridors, up ladders and smokestacks, swings around poles ("now this is good for warts"), slides on his hands down stair railings, up ladders, over railings. Its clean choreography, while quite gratuitous, is beautiful to watch. Immediately thereafter, he appears dressed only in a towel, and describes the isometric style of exercise. He pantomimes lifting weights, commenting, "You pull down the Woolworth Building like this . . . and you lean way over and lift up social conditions like this." We recognize a satiric allusion to the strenuous sermons of *Habit of Happiness* and *Down to Earth.*

The first stop is Honolulu. As was his wont, he immediately seeks out the reigning champion of sport—in this case, surf boarding—and challenges him. It is "like riding Niagara rapids on a match," he says. Some stunning shots of divers off the ship's rail are interspersed with the action. We get an idea of the type of wisecrack that mars so much of the film as they cross the dateline: as he drives golf balls off the ship, he quips that some shark's going to catch them "and think it is a codfish ball."

There is an extended sequence in Yokahama, where he describes Mt. Fujiama as "the world's largest bald spot." Doug pursues the thematic line of golfing his way around the world: "One thing that appeals to me about the world is that you can play around it with a mashie—good courses everywhere." Later in a geisha house we see a geisha waking up, going through her elaborate morning toilette, including a tedious hairdressing: "No underclothes are worn," Doug comments, adding, "I'm told." After finishing her dressing, all she needs to complete her regalia is a license and a taillight. "Clever people, Japanese—they play it safe—they always make a bow *before* they do anything." A young girl runs after him to sign her autograph book. "Isn't she marvelous?" he glows, perhaps perceiving her momentarily as his Dulcinea—at which point Fleming's off-screen voice threatens to "tell Mary."

There follow more stops, including a visit to Hong Kong Harbor and a visit to China's greatest actor, Dr. Me Long Fang, and his family. About the Chinese civil war, he quips: "One day I wanted to play golf and was told that the course was being used for a battle." In the Philippines, he visits General Aguinaldo who resisted the U.S. Army under Dewey. Then Fairbanks appears with his golf club, standing on a giant floor map of the Orient. He demonstrates a "chip shot" that lands in Angkor, and the scene shifts to an ancient ruins—"These ruins are in a perfect state of preservation—like the Republican party," at which point he begins a strenuous climb to the top. Later, at the palace of the king of Siam, he dances the fox trot to a Siamese dance rhythm. Off to India and Calcutta, where a swift montage follows of harbor shots, the Ganges, the cremation of Hindus,

A tiger hunt in *Around the World in Eighty Minutes*.

the custom of "well jumping" down ninety foot shafts, and finally a big-game shoot after leopards with a Maharani. It's all for the amusement of the American tourist and amateur collector:

> Funny isn't it? We apparently assembled the entire population of Kush-Baha; we had the help of the Queen herself; she called in scientists, statesmen, generals; we set forth with innumerable followers of a battery of guns; and what did we get? Something to put on the floor for people to stumble over.

A leopard shoot is arranged. Victor Fleming wounds a beast that has broken from cover. The injured animal heads for a village, scatters the inhabitants, and drags off a victim. In the subsequent dream sequence, which is the closest thing we have to Quixote's grapple with the windmill, Fairbanks speeds after the big cat. When his rifle fails, he grits his teeth and sets off alone in pursuit, executing an exhilarating series of leaps and vaults through the jungle, including a particularly spectacular torso twist from a tree limb up and over a large boulder. But, like Quixote's delusion, this is only a dream. Fleming shakes him awake. "I dreamt I was Trader Horn," exclaims Fairbanks.

The scene changes to the Indian bazaars where a fakir puts a boy into a basket. He spears it with knives. A magic rope springs up, and the boy scrambles aloft, gathering the length from beneath him as he goes. The boy disappears. In one of the best gags in the picture, Fairbanks asks, "How did you do that?" The response: "The same way you did it in *The Thief of Bagdad!"* Doug and Fleming climb aboard a magic carpet and are whisked away to complete their trip around the world.

The most interesting part of the film is the climactic sequence after the party has arrived back at Hollywood. The camera pulls back and we realize we are in a studio at United Artists, the boom mike, camera, and rear screen behind the carpet very much in evidence. Doug and Fleming climb off the carpet and technicians swarm over the set. Fleming offers to end the picture and pulls the power switch. In the darkness a match flares and there is Doug illumined solely by the match. In offering farewell, he says he will explain the rope and carpet trick—but the match burns out.

Its detractors had no trouble pointing to the embarrassing image of the American traveler abroad. In hindsight, the film pretends to be nothing more than it is: a kind of filmic diary, a home movie, actually, of boys being boys, on holiday from wives back home. The fleet course of its trajectory, touching a country here and crossing borders there, is indicative of the course of his life that by now seemed little more than an endless golf game. Were his periodic trips back home to Mary and Pickfair merely interruptions in the larger trajectory . . . were they now just stopovers? The answer is simple. Before the film could be released on November 19, 1931, Fairbanks, like Crusoe—who no sooner came home from his adventures than he was off again—set sail, this time to China, then to Italy, and finally to Tahiti in a luxurious, two-masted schooner, where he conceived yet another travel film.

Chapter 18

Mr. Robinson Crusoe

To dig, to bake, to plant, to build—how serious these simple occupations are; hatchets, scissors, logs, axes—how beautiful these simple objects become.
—VIRGINIA WOOLF, "Robinson Crusoe"

Viewed today, even the inferior visual quality of surviving prints can't hide the great charm and visual beauty of *Mr. Robinson Crusoe.* It premiered in New York City on September 21, 1932. Despite the behind-the-scenes news of difficulties on location with unpredictable weather, and problems with equipment, and rumors of Fairbanks's own restless *amours* among the native women, it gives us our last glimpse of Fairbanks's balletic style and exuberant optimism. This is enhanced by the version available today, essentially a silent film with subtitles, a wonderful music score by Alfred Newman (including the tune that became the popular "Moon of Manakoora"), and a few post-dubbed words and sound effects.

The idea is to drop an enterprising American go-getter, Steve Drexel (Fairbanks), into a tropical island where, Crusoe-like, he can prove his mettle and conquer the wilderness with only available natural resources. Hence the opening title:

> *From the time Adam and Eve were banished from the Garden of Eden, man has vainly sought to find solace, comfort, and earthly pleasures in an artificial world of his own creation.*

On board their yacht, Steve and his friends strike a bet debating his ability to survive.

> *"I'd like to fight the battle of nature with my bare hands—just like Robinson Crusoe—"*

Steve declares, as he dives off the yacht and swims toward the island. Immediately, he sets out to reconfigure his natural environment into what he declares will be

> *"all the comforts of Park Avenue and all the joys of Broadway."*

Just as the castaway Crusoe immediately sets out "to make such necessary things as I found I most wanted, particularly a chair and a table" (56), Fairbanks first fashions rude implements, builds a lean-to, a waterway, and eventually a tree house fifty feet above the ground. There's even an aerial skyway which takes him by rope and pulleys through the trees to the beach, where a catapult has been constructed to hurl his fishing nets past the breakers. These scenes convey at least a hint of the pragmatic American ingenuity and enterprise that echoes Crusoe's subjection of every aspect of the landscape. Unlike Crusoe, however, Steve pauses (as is Fairbanks's wont), for yet another game of golf . . . not forgetting to pause for one of his apostrophes to the landscape:

> *"Isn't Nature wonderful? Isn't Nature kind?"*

By now, it's a familiar moment, a kind of secular worship. In so many of the earlier films, notably *Down to Earth* (another castaway film), we had seen nature as an important source for a re-energized Fairbanks. That, combined with the Fairbanks/Roosevelt call for a hardy life of pragmatic energies, perfectly matches the practical idealism so carefully noted by Crusoe: "As to all the disputes, wrangling, strife and contention which has happened in the world about religion, whether niceties in doctrines or schemes of church government, they were all perfectly useless to us" (175). In the end, Crusoe and Fairbanks apply a "social gospel" of their own: how to make religion *useful*. The human mind works best when it confines itself to the realm of relatively practical concerns.

The unexpected arrival of a native who at first seems to be Crusoe's Man Friday, a cannibal from a nearby island, triggers a dangerous confrontation. After a tussle, Steve kicks him off the island. Instead, a "Saturday" appears, a beautiful native girl (Maria Alba), who is fleeing from an unwanted marriage to a tribal chief.[1] This may seem to today's viewer a highly opportunistic attempt to introduce sex into the narrative. But we must remember that even before Fairbanks, in many revisionings of the castaway story, a female "Friday" was introduced. For example, when Lord Byron cast his shipwrecked Don Juan onto an island, he finds himself swept up in the loving and eager arms of the maiden Haidée.[2] However, in this case we have to all appearances a chaste marriage, as Saturday and Steve play house—or is it *treehouse*?—in a jungle paradise. (The first thing she does on board is to wash the dishes.) There is no more obvious example of the American takeover and domestication of other cultures and environments than this. It is a wholesale "makeover" that establishes the template for all the post-1933 Tarzan films, as well as the subsequent model for Walt Disney's *Swiss Family Robinson* and the related popular exhibits at the Disney theme parks.

Inevitably, the nearby cannibals arrive. They abduct Saturday and tie up Steve in preparation for dinner. But it all works out when Steve escapes, rescues her, takes to the trees, flies to the beach via his aerial skyway, and catapults himself to the waiting schooner, which has providentially arrived. He sails away, Saturday safely on board.

Back in New York, he plays impresario and introduces Saturday on Broadway as an exotic act for the *Ziegfeld Follies*. Having refashioned the native paradise in his own image, he now appropriates a bit of Tahiti—and a wife—for the applause of Broadway society. And at least one critic joined in on the appreciation. Writing in the *New York Times*, Mordaunt Hall said it was "done in Mr. Fairbanks's best vein. It is artful, jolly, and imaginative, and one never thinks that the lone man on the island was always accompanied by a camera crew."[3]

Still dashing in *The Private Life of Don Juan* (1934).

Chapter 19

The Private Life of Don Juan

The joyous Juan has left the world,
The sad Juan is his heir.
—NIKOLAUS LENAU

The Don Juan of the legend does not exist. He is more seduced than seducing. I will show you what the sort of man who gets the reputation for being a Don Juan is really like.
—W. H. AUDEN

The Private Life of Don Juan brings us to the final destination of Fairbanks's four-film odyssey—and the culmination of his meditations on the conflicts and compromises facing artists and husbands. We have now arrived at legend-haunted Old Seville. Who would blame us if by now, like Fairbanks himself, we are a bit cynical and travel-worn after our encounters with the windmill-tilting Quixote and the globe-trotting Crusoe? But now another mythic figure awaits: Don Juan.

When Fairbanks and Douglas Jr. set sail to Europe in 1933, the trip aroused a storm of controversy. Father and son were described as believing that they could get along without Hollywood. Doug Jr., moreover, was getting interested in his own career as a producer.[1] The initial purpose of the trip was to form a British film company that would produce pictures for United Artists distribution rivaling the American product. Newspapers and magazines openly rejoiced at having acquired Sr.'s services and hinted that he might become a British citizen.[2] Plans were announced for three pictures—one about Czar Peter III and Catherine of Russia, starring Doug Jr.; one called *Exit Don Juan*, starring Sr.; and a third, a Zorro story,

Douglas and his third wife, Lady Sylvia Ashley, in 1936.

costarring them both. Other rumors linked Sr.'s name with one Lady Sylvia Ashley. She was the former Sylvia Hawks, a chorus girl who married Lord Anthony Ashley, son and heir of the Earl of Shaftesbury.

Events bore out at least some of these rumors. Sr.'s business plans with Korda included discussing a partnership for him in United Artists. Korda wanted to secure American distribution for his films. United Artists had a large and costly distribution arm but could not provide a sufficient number of pictures to cover the overhead. Korda and his London Films company might supply those needed pictures. It was Sr.'s idea to sponsor Korda's entrance into UA as a partner. Then, on January 1, 1934, it was announced that Fairbanks had joined the board of London Films. From then until 1944, Korda and Sam Goldwyn attempted to buy out Fairbanks and his associates at UA, a move that was never consummated. As for the growing involvement between Fairbanks Sr. and Lady Sylvia Ashley, matters came to a head when Mary Pickford filed suit for divorce on December 8, 1934. The following February, Lord Ashley obtained a divorce from his wife, and Fairbanks and Sylvia were married on March 7, 1936.

Father and son did indeed star in two films, respectively, *Exit Don Juan* (retitled *The Private Life of Don Juan*) and *Catherine the Great*. It is very interesting, perhaps significant, that the films reveal striking parallels. Jr.

and Sr. both portrayed weak and reluctant husbands married to dominating women.[3] Both were directed by Alexander Korda—Paul Czinner got the nominal credit for *Catherine*—who the year before had directed a satire on marriage, *The Private Life of Henry VIII*; both were written by Lajos Biro; both were designed by Vincent Korda; and both were released in 1934, within a few months of each other. There were differences, of course: in the role of the wicked, doomed Grand Duke Peter of Russia, the twenty-four-year-old Fairbanks Jr. gave an acclaimed and nuanced performance that not only helped establish him as an actor independent of his father, but clearly signaled that the best years of his career lay ahead of him. By contrast, as the dashing, but aging Don Juan, the fifty-one-year-old Fairbanks Sr.'s performance was an amusing, albeit bittersweet valedictory to his own career.

The Private Life of Don Juan was made at Elstree and premiered in London on September 5, 1934. It was adapted from *L'homme a la rose* (1920), by Henri Bataille (1872–1922), and written for the screen by two writers long associated with Korda, the aforementioned Lajos Biro and Frederic Lonsdale. [4] Bataille's three-act play, according to a review at the time, was "the talk of Paris for a fortnight . . . and the Parisian public flocked in greater numbers than ever to see how one of its great men took his recreation." It depicted a Don who has grown bored with his latest intrigue and yields the conquest to another man. When the substitute is killed, the Don finds it expedient not to correct the error. He attends his own funeral, amused by the tears of the throngs of sorrowing women. He decides to retire. However, after five years of exile, he tears off his mask and resumes his philandering ways. Women now reject the aging seducer. Rebuked and humiliated, there is nothing left for him but to live out his remaining years alone, loved only for his money. "[Don Juan] is a perpetually interesting fellow," wrote Marcelle Lamasque in *La France*. "He fascinates or disgusts you, but he never leaves you indifferent." It is a sad portrait of a man "whose joys are brief," who is "always restless and never achieves happiness."[5]

The film version, as we shall see, retains the first two acts of Bataille's play relatively intact, while extensively altering events of the third act. We begin with a flurry of fans, lace, and window lattices. The night is perfumed with romance. Fainting ladies, old and young, cluster about their balconies, expectant. . . . A cloaked shadow falls across the balconies of Seville. The languishing ladies turn their hungry gaze toward the phantom figure. He tosses them a rose. . . .

Still dueling in *The Private Life of Don Juan*.

Recall the words of romantic poet Alfred de Musset in *Quoi revent les jeunes filles*:

> A girl of fifteen dreams of her lovers
> Coming in summer nights on slender ladders,
> Sword in hand, and cloak up to the eyes.

Who is casting the shadow? No, it's not Don Juan but a clumsy impersonator (Barry Mackay), a young man who by his own admission is after "the last trick—the mastery of women." When he is killed by an outraged husband, the news goes out: *Don Juan is dead*. The real Don Juan, meanwhile, who has fled from the domestic confines of marriage, hears the news and decides to attend his own funeral. He and Leporello (Melville Cooper) sardonically observe the ceremonies while the women mourn and the men celebrate The Great Lover's passing.

Debt-ridden, pursued by the wife, Dolores (Benita Hume), whom he left years ago, and glad to seize this opportunity to go into retirement at last, the weary Don flees to the country and takes up the guise of one "Captain Mariano." He is content to live the life of an anonymous bachelor.

But when a book is published purporting to be the *Private Life of Don Juan*, he scoffs at its absurd exaggerations: "If [the author] couldn't make me a hero, he wouldn't write it; if he didn't make me a cad he couldn't sell it." He decides to come out of retirement and show the public the real thing. But his attempts at a new series of seductions yield only rejections. He's too *old* to be the real Don Juan, scoff the ladies.

At this point, the film radically departs from the Bataille play. The Don decides to return to Seville, home of his greatest triumphs, where he can finally explode the myth of Don Juan's life and death. However, no one recognizes him. The only Don Juan anybody acknowledges is yet another fictional Don, this time the hero of a new stage play, *The Love and Life of Don Juan*. In a key scene, the set piece of the film, Mariano interrupts the evening performance and leaps onto the stage. Shouldering the actors aside, he proclaims to the astonished audience, "You're under the delusion Don Juan is dead. I'm the *real* Don Juan." He is hooted down and arrested for disrupting the peace. Later, released from jail, chastened, and summoned before his wife, Dolores, he admits that at last he realizes he wants nothing more than to be her husband.

Reviews were mostly negative. The derision piled on Fairbanks was just as cutting as the audience's dismissal of Juan in the film's theatrical scene. This notice by Andre Sennwald in the *New York Times* is typical:

> [There is] a lamentable air of anachronism . . . He whom we loved for his reckless swagger and airy movement now finds himself trapped and forced to play the actor. It is a poor fate for one who was once so free, and it is not always pleasant to watch.[6]

In his biography of the film's director, Alexander Korda, Paul Tabori objects to the casting of Fairbanks:

> Douglas Fairbanks, Sr. had triumphed in many swashbuckling action-packed pictures. But here he had to do a great deal more than vault over balustrades, climb balconies or fight duels. His rasping voice with the strong American accent was incongruous and unsuitable for the suave Spanish lover.[7]

Both notices are accurate in their own way, but, as we shall presently see, they miss the point.

Meanwhile, at least one contemporary critic, Otis Ferguson, applauded the film's wonderful pictorial values. While admitting that "the story is not the important thing here," he cited the stunning "funeral" scene as typical of the film's sustained mood:

> One sequence in the first part alone [makes] the picture worth seeing. A funeral in Spain, with the black figures milling slowly in all that unearthly white light. The rough stones in the walls and statues pile up into the sky, and the sky is framed boldly. Everything has a curious buoyancy and is carried along with the music.[8]

Credit George Perinal for the cinematography, Vincent Korda for the set design, and Ernst Toch for the music.

To return to the harsh critiques: Fairbanks a "suave lover" with an "American accent"? Well, Fairbanks had *never* been a suave lover, and he had *always* been an American abroad. Just so. And he bravely took on a role that all too clearly deconstructed the very youthful confidence and masculine bravado he had so effectively embodied all his life. Now, facing an uncertain future and confronted with advancing age, he was well suited to the role of a Don Juan who faced failure as an artist and domestication as a husband.

The identification was too close. The winter and spring of 1934 was an unhappy time for the aging swashbuckler. Scandalous rumors surrounded his relationship with Lady Ashley; relations with Douglas Jr. were strained; and a divorce with Mary, whose problems with alcohol were becoming more apparent, was in the offing (it became final in 1936). Although the role of a Don Juan defeated by time and marked by disillusionment would seem to be perfect for Fairbanks at this time, it proved to be very painful for him. A measure of the turmoil he was in personally and professionally can be deduced from a telegram he sent Mary as the filming began: "PASSING THROUGH WORST PERIOD I'VE EVER KNOWN. TRYING TO PULL MYSELF TOGETHER TO START PICTURE." Bravely, Fairbanks carried on, and the finished product marks the bravest, if underrated, product of his acting career.

The release in 1934 of Fairbanks's film falls midway between yet two more Don Juan plays, George Bernard Shaw's *Man and Superman* (1905) and Max Frisch's *Don Juan and the Love of Geometry* (1953).[9] It possesses a modernist irony related more to Shaw and Frisch than to Bataille. The "artistry" of his mastery of women is facing new challenges. A more independent female is less submissive to his charms. She is more than a match for him. The roles of seducer and seduced are reversed. Now he confronts something perhaps less romantic, in the poetic sense, and more conventional in the domestic sense. The Don is losing ground, as it were. And so, perhaps, is Fairbanks. In short, the artist is now a husband.

Classic, romantic, modern. . . . The Don Juan legend had endured them all. The classical version of Don Juan had delighted so much in each experience of love that he enthusiastically repeated the pleasure. His first popular incarnation appeared in the classic seventeenth century theater in Tirso di Molina's morality fable, *The Trickster of Seville* (1616?) and in the *commedia* of Moliere's *Don Juan, or the Statue at the Feast* (1665). The intervening centuries saw a more romantic sensibility in the Lorenzo da Ponte/Mozart opera, *Don Giovanni* (1787), and Lord Byron's *Don Juan* (1821). A more ironic, modernist subversion of the legend was struck in George Bernard Shaw's philosophical satire *Man and Superman* (1905) and Max Frisch's *Don Juan and the Love of Geometry* (1953).

Tirso's play was a morality fable about a hedonist, a vulgar seducer, who was thrown into the fires of hell for his transgressions. Moliere's farce was an indictment of hypocrisy. In Act Three, for example, Juan is unapologetic about his own excesses:

> "I must have freedom in love. I cannot resign myself to confining my heart within four walls. My natural propensity is to follow my fancy wherever it may lead. My heart belongs to all womankind. It is theirs to take in turn and keep as long as they can."[10]

And in Act Five, when the Infernal Statue demands his repentance, he retorts, "No, come what may, it shall never be said that I am the repenting sort."[11]

The Da Ponte/Mozart opera likewise sounds this note of unrepentant bravado. Don Giovanni proclaims:

> "It's all for the sake of love. He who serves one woman only robs every other. And such is the tenderness of my emotions that I adore them all. Unfortunately, women have no common sense and call my good nature treachery."[12]

And he hurls his final defiance with the words, "No, I don't repent. Let me go! Away![13]

The Romantic ideal held that the Don's succession of seductions was the result of his ongoing *disappointment* in each one. As a Romantic archetype, he was not only chasing a Faustian ideal, which can only fail with each encounter, but he was defying Fate at the end in a superbly Romantic, but futile gesture. As Peter Gay notes in his essay, "The Father's Revenge":

> Don Giovanni seems to have but a single purpose: to appease a nagging hunger, a hunger which no satisfaction can relieve more than momentarily. . . . The Don knows in his heart that each new conquest must fail him, yet he is compelled to try again.[14]

Now we come to the modernist irony of Don Juan, which had been prefigured in Lord Byron's *Don Juan.* He is stripped of his lustful appetites and Romantic, defiant posture, instead relegated to the role of victim of his own oedipal desires and the hapless target of women's wiles toward marriage and domesticity. The many women he loved and left were merely substitutes for the unobtainable mother he so guiltily desired. W. H. Auden points out that this Don is no "monster of depravity"; he is not even particularly promiscuous. Byron had written it as a self-defense of his own notoriety, Auden claims, as if to say, "The Don Juan of the legend does not exist. He is more seduced than seducing. I will show you what the sort of man who gets the reputation for being a Don Juan is really like."[15]

Returning to Shaw's *Man and Superman* and Frisch's *Don Juan and the Love of Geometry*, we see changes in the character that bring us much closer to Fairbanks's film. They attempt to answer the question, voiced by many: has the Don Juan myth become unacceptable to our modern day?[16] These Dons are masculine figures caught up in a new secularist century of religious skepticism and revisionist sexual and gender politics. Shaw's "John Tanner" (Don Juan) is the target of a predatory Ibsenite New Woman, Anne Whitefield. With apologies for reducing this complex play about sex, revolution, socialism, and the inexorable power of the Life Force to its barest plotline—Tanner/Juan admits that he has lived by a restless kind of code of his own: "I tell you, that as long as I can conceive something better than myself, I cannot be easy unless I am striving to bring it into existence, or clearing the way for it. That is the law of my life." But with the failure of love and artistry to "interest him permanently," Tanner/Juan reflects bitterly on the state he is in: "It was the supremacy of this purpose that reduced love for me to the mere pleasure of a moment, art for me to the mere schooling of my faculties. . . . I tell you that in the pursuit of my own failure, my own wealth, my own fortune, I have never known happiness."[17] The words are by Tanner/Shaw. But they could just as well have been a declamation by the brash young Fairbanks in full stride, on the one hand, and, on the other, the lament of a man facing the defeats of advancing age.

Finally, in Act Four, Tanner uneasily capitulates to Anne in her villa in Granada. While Anne is a really powerful woman, she also comes across as a liar and a bully. We may be convinced, points out G. K. Chesterton in his study of Shaw's play, that while Anne wishes to marry Tanner, "we lose all power of conceiving why Tanner should ever consent to marry Anne." It is a case, concludes Chesterton, "of the mousetrap running after the mouse."[18] In any event, we are reminded of the turmoil Fairbanks endured about leaving Mary and succumbing to the seductive wiles of Lady Ashley. "What we have done this afternoon," muses Tanner/Juan, "is to renounce happiness, renounce freedom, renounce tranquility, above all renounce the romantic possibilities of an unknown future, for the cares of a household and a family."[19]

The Don we see here may be best understood as a case history, observes the Austrian journalist and diplomat Henry Grunwald. The psychoanalyst, he explains, would limit the riot of Juan's libido to reasonable proportions, condemning him not to damnation or defiance, but merely to the mediocrity of the new century:

> The decline of aristocracy, the new status of women, the weakening both of convention and of religion that leaves a rebel so much less to rebel against, the fading of the supernatural, and the cult of psychology, which makes excess no longer a sin but merely a disease.[20]

Even more to the point is Max Frisch's play, *Don Juan and the Love of Geometry*. Although it was written in 1953, twenty years after Fairbanks's film, it bears a striking resemblance to its plot, whether by intent or accident. The setting is a "theatrical Seville," a city of tricks and illusion (not unlike the artifice of the studio sets of a motion picture).[21] The Don is about to celebrate his impending marriage to Donna Anna, but he realizes that he is unwilling to commit to just one woman. In seeking her in a carnival crowd, he had seen only thousands of identical masks that reflected his own image back to him. "I am in love—only—I don't know with whom," he laments."[22] He flees the city. Weary of his conquests, and tired of the public celebrity that dogs his heels, he tells Leporello that he will fake his death according to the legend handed down over the centuries. Ever the trickster, he will convert his dining hall into a magic box:

> I have a person ready to play the part of the dead Commander. The ladies will shriek the moment they hear his voice. A sneering laugh from me, an explosion at the right moment, so that the ladies hide their eyes—notice . . . this clever machine under the table—and suddenly the room stinks of sulphur and smoke. . . . All this very fast, you understand—surprise is the mother of miracles. . . . You see this cleverly concealed trapdoor? Naturally, not without an appropriate scream—one which will, according to Aristotle's recipe, arouse pity and terror." (55–56)

This accomplished, he retreats to the country, where he hopes to find his own "perfect geometry"—

> . . . the art of the earth, or the play of knowledge, measurement, what you will—the calm delight of science, which is harmonious. . . . For example, the joy of a circle, the most pure of geometrical concepts.

Indeed, the "perfect geometry" of a circle: it balances centrifugal and centripetal tensions—the "centripetal" force, in this case, that adheres to traditional masculine roles, and the "centrifugal" force that contests and breaks out of those roles. Don Juan explains it's a balance in love and life that *must* be maintained; otherwise—

> when once we take leave of the lie that shines like a glittering surface on the world and no longer see the world as the mirror of our desires—when we want to know *who* we are—ah, that's the beginning of the end, the Fall of Man. . . . Don't sink into your soul, or into anyone else's, but stay on the blue surface of the mirror, like the gnats above the water.[23]

Gone are the ringing words of Mozart/Da Ponte's Don Giovanni: "Never shall it be said that I am the repenting sort." Masculine survival in the newly gendered modern world requires capitulation to the New Woman, in this case, the Duchess of Ronda, who maintains an independent life style. The concluding scene has him married and living in her castle. He sits down with her at the breakfast table. "Here is Paradise," he says, "lying at my feet."

Now pass the bread.

The Don Juans of Shaw and Frisch have fallen from a great height. Now commodified and packaged, their artistry of seduction is now a mere bag of tricks marketed to new audiences. No longer defiant of God, society,

Man meets Myth in *The Private Life of Don Juan.*

and sexual mores, they find themselves trapped in a domestic circle that leaves them suspended between what's left of heaven and hell.

Indeed, the very survival of the mythic Don Juan is at risk. Thus, Fairbanks's *The Private Life of Don Juan* is not a portrait of the mythic Don Juan at all. Nor was it intended to be. All that is left is his shadow and a pathetic collection *of would-be pretenders.* Detached from that shadow in the first scene is only a bumbling young man who can't even woo a young lady without falling off her trellis. The Don Juan of the novel-within-the-film is only a preposterous fiction. The Don Juan of the play-within-a film is a foppish popinjay. Even Fairbanks's Don is cut down to size. "When I sit down to a quiet game with a lady, I'm no longer sure of holding the cards," he admits ruefully. His physician admonishes him to reduce his amorous pursuits and the number of balconies to be climbed each week. When he attends his own "funeral," he's unrecognized and ignored. Later, in self-exile as Captain Mariano, the local barmaid barely tolerates him. She allows his advances only because she wants him to procure some earrings for her. The aging proprietress of the inn sees him only as someone to share her old age and run the business. But hopes spring up again when a beautiful lady hidden in a coach summons Mariano to visit her that night in her turret room. In a beautiful nocturnal scene, he happily strides through the gathering dark, cape flowing behind him, a rope slung over his shoulder. Soft music attends on the soundtrack. Lithely, he unslings the rope and climbs, hand over hand, to the lady's bower. Ah! this is more like it!, he thinks. But no, she merely needs his services as a messenger and regards him only as a father figure. Indignant, he returns home in a soaking downpour with a sneezing cold.

Retreating back to Seville, Mariano visits a former girlfriend, Antonita (Merle Oberon). *She'll* recognize him. He finds that she has grown more attractive to her many suitors because of her association with the "late" Don. "No," she says, now rejecting Mariano's advances, "Don Juan is much taller and younger . . ." She pushes him out the door.

In the wonderful theater scene, Mariano arrives in a fury, an imposing figure dressed in black, with a sweeping cloak and fine, broad-brimmed hat, determined to confront the actor who is impersonating him. Fairbanks recovers some of the old bravado, eliciting critic Otis Ferguson's high praise: "He has a certain rank swagger and grace: with a cape and go-to-hell hat and a clear hip line, he is fine costume material."[24] He swirls through the lace and finery of the costumes like a dark wind tearing through curtains. He stamps his boots at the actors as they give way. He pushes his alter ego offstage and yells, "Stop this foolery! Ladies and Gentlemen, the performance is over! I bid you a good night!" He turns to the playwright: "You lied about my life!" The audience in one voice retorts, "We want to see the end of the play!" Now it's the author's turn to address the audience: "Do you care that much about Don Juan's real life and real character?"

"No!" they roar.

But Mariano reminds them that the Don Juan of the play is seen to make love to two women at once. Surely, he objects, that is impossible.

The playwright shrugs: "For *you* it is impossible, but to Don Juan . . ."

"Yes!" finishes the audience, a great open throat. One shout rises above the chorus and derides Mariano: "You couldn't even manage *one*." Then the playwright delivers the final stinging blow to Mariano: "That's how much *you* know about being Don Juan."

He departs, defeated. *He* is exposed as the ultimate imposter. As he is dragged away from the stage set, Dolores's words still ring in his ears: "No, there is a likeness . . . but my poor husband was so much bigger, and broader, and better looking . . ."

Mary Pickford and her third husband, Buddy Rogers.

There is nothing more for him but to leave the city again and return to his wife, Dolores. She has been patiently waiting for his return. She watches bemused as he goes through a travesty of the classic Don Juan wooing style. He is not seducing a maiden but his wife. Now he has to use a rope ladder she conveniently provides him to ascend her balcony.

No longer a creature of legend, like the Dons of Tirso and Da Ponte, he is now heir to the modernist ironies of Shaw and Frisch, a husband in exile from love and romance, a tired commodity confined to the cage of the New Woman's perfect geometry.

The blessings have been said. The circle closed.

We have seen in these contexts that *The Private Life of Don Juan* sums up the conflicts and uncertain compromises Fairbanks himself faced as an artist and husband in his last years. It is a fitting valedictory to his career, rejected by viewers who cannot abide any changes in the old Fairbanks spirit, but avidly embraced by those who see it as the inevitable maturation of his screen persona. Many of us who have devoted a lifetime to Fairbanks research belong to the latter camp. We have always cherished certain moments in many of his films—such as *The Half-Breed*, *The*

Man from Painted Post, He Comes Up Smiling, Mr. Fix-It, and *The Iron Mask*—where quiet nuance and charm of gesture and expression revealed an actor capable of subtlety and restraint. And in *The Private Life of Don Juan,* from first to last, he beautifully plays those qualities against the grain of his mock bravado. "Men are very weak," he tells Dolores quietly in the final scene, "very vain. During all their lives they are terribly afraid of intelligent women. They strip a man of his glory, tame the conquering male until he becomes just a husband." Now he meekly admits to her—with a saving touch of irony—that she has stripped him of his power. "Don Juan is dead," he confesses. "I don't want to be anything but your husband." She responds tenderly, "Every woman wants more than just a husband; every woman wants Don Juan, all to herself." The scene is beautifully understated, the two embracing in the darkling light, their figures partially concealed behind a transparent curtain. He reaches forward . . . and snuffs out the candle.

The Private Life of Don Juan is a wonderful, thought-provoking film. Even if the artistry of the character of the Don has failed him at the end, it is present, intact, in Fairbanks's rueful and heartbreaking performance. For a moment, at least, Fairbanks succeeds as both artist *and* husband.

EPILOGUE

"Films satisfy my desire to keep in motion in a constructive way," he had once said in 1922. "I had always been interested in stunts and in games and had always worked at them; at first because of mere energy and vitality and the desire to keep in motion, and then because I found that the work was good for me."[1] Now, his films and his youth behind him, the prospects that his high-flying, self-propelled trajectories would continue unabated—like those optimistic prophecies of speed, science, and technology that launched the American century—are in question. The years of ceaseless travel, the many stillborn movie projects, the ongoing tensions with his second wife, Mary Pickford, and the allure of a third wife, Lady Ashley, left him frustrated as an artist and unfulfilled as a husband. (See Douglas Fairbanks Jr.'s remarks about these tensions in the Appendix to this volume.) Any chance of a "perfect" geometry was gone. Life had once seemed long because his art was so. However, as William Hazlitt appositely said in his classic meditation on youth and age, we become less sanguine about these prospects as we approach the end at last: "It is not the despair of not attaining, so much as knowing that there is nothing worth obtaining, and the fear of having nothing left even to wish for." What remains "is to stagger on the few remaining paces to the end of the journey, to make perhaps one final effort."[2]

But there were to be no more films. No final effort. Less than a decade of more travels and career confusions remained to him before his death on a Sunday in early December 1939. Mary Pickford followed him in 1979, after spending her last years at Pickfair married to Buddy Rogers. The stories of the dreary last years of Doug and Mary have been recounted in detail elsewhere. It is not our intention to repeat all that here.

As we said at the beginning of this book, we are not presuming to write a biography of Douglas Fairbanks—a definitive volume still awaits. We hope to have presented instead a series of interlocking commentaries and appreciations of the Fairbanks century. Meanwhile, more details of his life and work are being disclosed; more films are coming to light. Fairbanks himself would doubtless have approved our own, ongoing, restless—certainly Quixotic—quest of the man and his work. "He opened up his life, that rich good life, to the public," wrote Richard Schickel, "and invited them to participate in it, enjoy it with him."[3]

And so we leave the Fairbanks century—and this book—*open-ended.* Ultimately, it mattered not where he was going, or why. His was the boundless choreography of a life that was most intensely *felt* in the moment. Fairbanks's art and his life were like that, caring for nothing outside itself, going its own way, rejoicing. He was the labyrinthine man—he never sought the truth, just his Ariadne.

AFTERWORD: THE MAKINGS OF A MAN 1880–1927

—Brian Faucette

The whole generation is womanized; the masculine tone is passing out of the world; it's a feminine, nervous, hysterical, chattering, canting, age, an age of hollow phrases and false delicacy and exaggerated solicitudes and coddled sensibilities, which, if we don't soon look out, will usher in the reign of mediocrity, of the feeblest and flattest and most pretentious that has ever been.
—HENRY JAMES, *The Bostonians* (1885)

We need . . . the iron qualities that must go with true manhood. We need the positive virtues of resolution, of courage, of indomitable will, of power to do without shrinking the rough work that must always be done, and to persevere through the long days of slow progress or seeming failure which always come before any final triumph, no matter how brilliant.
—THEODORE ROOSEVELT, *The Strenuous Life* (1900)

Throughout the pages of this book we have seen that Douglas Fairbanks choreographed in his films what Alistair Cooke called "athletic adventures [which] taught him to relish American pep, optimism, and cheer." Those pre-1920 satires, in particular, were breezy responses to an age wherein contemporary notions of masculinity were undergoing considerable challenge and change.

During the late nineteenth and early twentieth century, many white middle- and upper-class American men called attention to the anxiety expressed by men struggling with changes in conventional gender roles. The ideal form of manhood had to be enacted and in many cases performed through works of literature, politics, economics, and sports. In doing so, writes Michael Kimmel in *Manhood in America*, they believed it would be possible to re-energize American virility and in the process help "regenerate" a new America where manhood and the economy would work together to foster the conditions to celebrate American masculinity as aggressive, self-determined, physical, and possessing a sense of strong morality.[1]

Muscular Christianity

Fairbanks's celebration of sports and the male body, on and off the screen, brought into the new century a form of manliness and morality that linked democratic ideals with Protestant Christian values. The vision of masculinity linked to God was referred to as "muscular Christianity."[2] It found its way to America in the 1860s and took hold decades later as America was undergoing rapid industrialization, women were demanding equal rights, and waves of immigration were arriving on American shores. In his *Muscular Christianity*, Clifford Putney argues that the spread of muscular Christianity in the closing decades of the nineteenth century resulted from "a decline in the evangelical Christian antipathy toward sports, the adoption by most YMCAs of athletic programs, and the encouragement by YMCA men of character building sports such as basketball and volleyball."[3]

It was within the confines of the YMCA and its policies that a new form of American manhood was being defined. The focus was placed on a combination of Christian values that in turn were linked to notions of competitive masculinity that celebrated the male body and its larger connection to society, to the church, and most importantly to other men.

Manhood and the New Economy

As we have seen in films such as *His Picture in the Papers* and *Wild and Wooly*, images of Fairbanks in the office spaces of modern industry depicted a masculinity that was trapped and confined. Yet, like Theodore Roosevelt, the restless spirit of the *self-made man* worked to confirm those very corporate spaces. He worked *within the system*, writes Lary May, "by showing manufacturers how to capitalize on the needs of a new generation" and forge a new code of success. "Men continued to achieve in the world of production; but they now strove equally hard for the money to purchase goods and leisure pursuits to compensate for boredom on the job . . . As leisure now supplied a new frontier for male energy, mass-produced but high-class consumer goods became a reward for tolerating the modern economy."[4] As Roosevelt had done, he accepted the corporations and made them work and personified the upwardly mobile organization.

The shift in America's economy from small entrepreneurs and farmers had signaled not only a change in the economy but also a change in how American manhood was to be defined. Michael Kimmel notes that within this period many American men felt emasculated as work shifted from being self-directed to working for large corporations.[5] In fact, the number of salaried, non-propertied workers multiplied eight times between 1870 and 1910, so that by 1910, 20 percent of the male workforce were working in "white-collar jobs." These jobs were the result of an expanding bureaucratic structure in government and corporations, and to satisfy this expanding system, E. Anthony Rotundo argues that American men were confused by the new workplace where women were hired as secretaries and offices resembled parlors rather than traditional masculine spaces like bars, lodges, and men's clubs.[6]

Angel Kwolek-Folland details in the study *Engendering Business: Men and Women in the Corporate Office, 1870–1930* how, "beginning with the introduction, around 1870, of office machines (such as the typewriter), new office building types (such as the skyscraper), new forms of internal communication (such as the circular memo), and new kinds of office workers (such as typists and stenographers)" along with "the creation of management and managers, the use of welfare capitalism to deal with labor/management relations, [and] physical job segregation to denote status and gender relations" became central features of the formation of a new corporate climate that also in turn impacted American men's understanding of masculinity and its connection to occupation as a defining characteristic.[7] In the world of big business, where many men feared the influence of women on American corporate culture, employers provided "their male employees more opportunities for promotion, higher salaries, and greater authority" because it was important to make male employees feel like they were in charge of their labors and thus masculine—despite the fact that in many cases the bureaucracy of big business was designed for efficiency and to limit the economic potential of male workers.[8] Historian Elliot Gorn in *The Manly Art* discusses the changing nature of work and the workforce when he poses the following questions: "where would a sense of maleness come from for the worker who sat at a desk all day? How could one be manly without independence? Where was virility to be found in increasingly faceless bureaucracies? How might clerks or salesmen feel masculine doing 'women's work'? What became of rugged individualism inside intensively rationalized corporations? How could a man be a patriarch when his job kept him away from the home for most of his waking hours?"[9] Gorn's questions encapsulate many of the fears felt by white middle class men in America at the end of the 1880s. Along with the fears of the changing nature of the workplace and male autonomy was the increasing fear that somehow American men were becoming effeminate because of the changing makeup of the nation. There was a concern about the increasing number of immigrants and a fear that American boys were being made "female" because of the dominance of women in places such as the home, schools, and churches.[10]

National Manhood, Race, the Martial Ethic, and the Imperial Project

It will be recalled that in films like *The Americano, Reaching for the Moon,* and *His Majesty the American,* Fairbanks carried the American interests of "capital" and democracy into Europe and Latin America. Here, and arguably in the later great costume films of the 1920s, he was ever the American imperialist, shaping other cultures in his/American images. In *The Americano,* notes Lary May, "he mastered tyrants from above and revolutionaries from below who endangered foreign leaders sympathetic to the expansion of American interests."[11]

In her important study, *Manliness and Civilization,* Gail Bederman demonstrates how men of this period utilized the concept of "civilization" to advocate that white American manhood was superior to all other forms of manhood, and in so doing shows how Americans embraced a project of imperialism to "rescue" American manhood. The contemporary concept of civilization, she explains, "denoted a precise stage in human racial evolution—the one following the more primitive stages of 'savagery' and barbarism."[12] Therefore, for men at the time, "civilization" meant that American men were superior physically, spiritually, and racially compared to those men who were coming into the country from other parts of Europe. The America that Bederman locates in her study is one that is in flux and as a result seems to face contradictory impulses.

Historian Jackson Lears argues in *Rebirth of a Nation,* his history of America during the period from 1877–1920, that the ideas "rebirth" and "regeneration" formed the core of American political, cultural, economic, and social discourse. These ideas, he explains, were connected to the country's need to reinvent itself after the painful experiences of the Civil War. As the nation developed into a modern country, he notes that, "manliness, always an issue in Victorian culture, had by the 1880s become an obsession. Older elements of moral character continued to define the manly man, but a new emphasis on physical vitality began to assert itself as well."[13] These fears of American masculinity being corrupted and made "soft," Lears argues, led to the increasing acceptance of a "martial ethic" in American culture that many men believed would re-masculinize the nation and its young men during the Gilded Age, a period when American economics and imperialism merged.[14]

Kristin Hoganson, in her study of America's imperial project during the 1890s, echoes Lears's views that American politics, especially in regards to foreign policy, was often dictated by concerns of American manhood and economics. She notes that "the links between manhood, military service, and political authority led a number of political leaders to think that they would enhance their political standing if they supported martial policies."[15] The connection to gender in American politics and its relation to support for the military by men like Theodore Roosevelt is illustrative of how they used their political influence in connection with their own fears that America was becoming a "weak" nation of effeminate beings to make the case for war as an ideal tool to help sustain and regenerate American manhood. Therefore, for those men who did not support the idea of an imperial America, Hoganson argues they were constantly afraid of being labeled effeminate by their political enemies and their own constituents, which forced them to accept a vision of America that was both materialistic and martial.[16] The division of the country at the time along lines of class, race, economics, and religion, Hoganson argues, forced many politicians to attempt to create consensus by using gendered positions that were designed primarily to reify American manhood and to unify American men around the idea that the only way to protect masculinity in the nation was to protect it from the influences of women, lower-class men, African-American men, and especially the new immigrants who were flooding into the country.[17]

In *National Manhood,* historian Dana D. Nelson coined the concept of "national manhood"[18] to explain the "processes through which individual 'white' men assume the privileges and burdens of national imperatives, and how middle-class professionalization takes over and is authorized by the management of those imperatives." Nelson's idea of a "national manhood" illustrates that the changing nature of the American economic system, as well as the shifting nature of race relations, impacted the formation of American masculinities. However, it was not only questions of "whiteness" and politics that impacted American masculinity during this period.

In fact, one of the greatest challenges faced by American men was the changing nature of work, the workplace, and its composition. By the 1870s and 1880s, the notion of the ideal American male as the "self-made man" was challenged by the transformation of America from primarily an agrarian-based society into one where industrialization and urbanization became the new American economy. As a result, the old model of American manhood linked to labor, homosocial interactions, and the celebration of male prowess in activities like business, hunting, and combat was tested by the needs of the new American economy.

APPENDIX A

"His Own Man": Interviews with Douglas Fairbanks Jr.

It all goes back to my father. People sought me out in my youth because I was his son. I would shrink back, shy at one moment, then show off the next. Did I want to hide or did I want to be conspicuous? I don't think I ever decided on one or the other.

—DOUGLAS FAIRBANKS JR.[1]

We talked with Douglas Fairbanks Jr. twice before his death at age ninety on May 7, 2000. Our first encounter was in the spring of 1993 in his New York office after the appearance of two volumes of his memoirs, *The Salad Days* (1989) and *A Hell of a War* (1993);[2] the second, during which his lovely wife, Vera joined us, was on March 8, 1996, in the New York apartment of his mother-in-law, while his own apartment was being renovated. Subsequent conversations have transpired with Vera Fairbanks in New York during and after the Fairbanks Jr. estate exhibition and auction in 2011.

What follows are extracts from those occasions.

The story of Douglas Fairbanks Jr. is inextricably bound up with that of his father. About his dad, "Jayar" has always been remarkably candid. As early as 1930, when he was just twenty-one, he wrote an insightful portrait of him, to which we have alluded several times in the foregoing pages. He noted, candidly, that "he never reads a long book through"; that he is "bored with flatterers but loves flattery"; that "he is proud of his friends' accomplishments but prouder of his own"; that "he will go to any extreme to carry out a practical joke"; that "he has never had a drink in his life, yet he smokes incessantly"; that "he is exceedingly self-conscious and easily embarrassed; and that "he loathes any sort of demonstration or show of emotion." About their complicated relationship, he wrote, "His nature is such that he doesn't think he is, nor does he pretend to be a great father; but somehow or other . . . he is."[3]

Douglas Sr. and Jr. (drawing courtesy John C. Tibbetts).

Indeed, this story of father and son is complicated. The father was at times uncomfortable in the presence of a son and potential rival, yet the son not only loyally devoted much of his own life and career to his father's work, but, at the same time, courageously forged his own identity: "I made a solemn pledge to myself that somehow I would grow up to be 'my own man,' that I would make the full name, plus the 'Junior,' as individually and independently recognizable as my father's name was for him."[4] In the prologue to *The Salad Days,* he admitted that being at the bedside of his dying father, on December 12, 1939, was a decisive moment: "When my father died, I became . . . freer and more self-assured, but I had lost the one I had always wished to please."[5]

Jayar carried on Fairbanks's American century to its end, bringing it to an honorable close. Like father, like son. In several projects he clasped hands with his father across the generations. For example, in the 1952 rerelease of *The Iron Mask* (1928), he dubbed d'Artagnan's speaking voice. Since the original Vitaphone voice discs were unavailable at the time, it was only fitting that the son would step in for the father, restore the film

Doug with wife Beth and Doug Jr., approximately 1916.

with a new music track, and provide additional narration—thus insuring that the film would be saved from oblivion. Later, in the mid-1960s, he subsidized a long-needed color restoration of *The Black Pirate*, which received its premiere at the British Film Institute in 1972.

In his own way, he exhibited a set of bewildering contradictions, yet they remind us of his father. On screen, he was at once the rascal Rupert in *The Prisoner of Zenda* (1938) and the noble King Charles II in *The Exile* (1947). In person, he was the architect of the grand gesture and the sly wink. He was the common man with the soul of an aristocrat. He was an actor who deprecated his talents, a showman who pleaded modesty, and a war hero who claimed to be a coward. Although he was an avowed American patriot, he was an Anglophile who latterly spent much of his life in England (where he was made a Knight Commander by King George V in

1949). Nothing could be more telling than the fact that he kept his beautiful collection of swords in a lowly umbrella stand in his office—but the stand was decorated with his own coat-of-arms! He would say he was "embarrassed" at his success in public life and in the movies, yet he admitted with a glint of amused satisfaction that it's something he has "gotten away with" all his life.

In the conversations that follow, we will stick to the present tense—which is only appropriate, considering the very *present-ness* of the man. Surely it is merely a freak of the time continuum that he is not with us still.

Picture Douglas Jr. now, as he stands at the far end of his office suite, gazing out of the broad windows at the crowded New York City streets below. On this sunny spring afternoon the concrete vista below is not at all like the colorful, glittering metropolis he knew when he grew up here so many years ago. "When I look out on the streets now, I think, what a mess it is!" he frowns ruefully. "But at least the Algonquin Hotel is still here. I roller-skated across the lobby as a boy! And the Netherland Hotel is now the Sherry Netherland. And there's bits and pieces of the Upper West Side I still know. But how dirty it all is now. But . . . it's still exciting and it's still my home. So I'm loyal to it, in a way."

He allows himself a brief sigh as he crosses the room and sits down at his desk. Although we had corresponded years ago while we were writing our first book about his father (*His Majesty the American*, 1977), we had never met until now. He is wearing a conservative suit of a neutral gray-blue, but his crimson handkerchief proudly displays a flash of spirit. His stride has slowed down a bit after eighty-four years, and his hair is snow-white. Suddenly, he cocks his head and grins. It's the famous signature smile, a curving row of dazzling white teeth that flash like scimitars. The pale mustache draws upward at the corners and the lines around the bright blue eyes crease and tighten. It's the smile that once in Montevideo earned him the sobriquet, "El Ambajador de la Sonrise" ("The Ambassador of the Smile").

His office suite is like some extravagant dream, like Sinbad's treasure ship stuffed into a bottle. Mementoes and artifacts of his movies and wartime exploits, photos of his famous friends, and numerous plaques and awards attesting to his humanitarian activities are everywhere. A framed portrait of his third wife, Vera, whom he married in 1991, has a cherished place on his desk. Three swords protrude from an ornate umbrella stand in the corner of the room. There's a death mask of Napoleon. Along a window sill reside a naval officer's cap, shoulder boards, lieutenant's helmet, and a plaque: "To Lt. Douglas Fairbanks, Jr., USNR, a sailor good enough to be a Marine. USS Washington, Marine Detachment, 1942." It is wholly typical of Fairbanks that portraits of heads of state rub shoulders with movie celebrities.

Fairbanks escorts us to a wall where there are dozens of inscribed photographs of boon companions over the years. "This is my rogues' gallery," he smiles. He points to a dual portrait of a slim young man and a dark-haired girl. "Would you believe that's me and Kate Hepburn in *Romeo and Juliet*? We played some scenes from it in a dream sequence in *Morning Glory*. I had quite a crush on her at the time." He moves around the desk and points to another image, a beach photo from 1929 of him and his new bride, Joan Crawford. "I was pursued for years by all kinds of gossip about that marriage," he says. "Everybody said the marriage was stormy, that my stepmother snubbed her, that Joan hurt my career. I was only eighteen or nineteen when I met her, and anxious to please everybody in my family. I was not very much for myself. It was Joan who would tell me, 'Stop this nonsense! Stand up for yourself! Be independent!' It worked. She put a ramrod up my backside. I owe her a great deal."

We ask him about portraits of two other women in his early days, Marlene Dietrich and Gertrude Lawrence, about whom Fairbanks confesses in *The Salad Days* he had had affairs in the 1930s. "Did I really write those things?" he asks us in mock outrage. "Maybe I should have scratched that out! Those were caddish things to write! I don't really believe in those 'tattle-tale' kinds of books. What do you think?"

He gestures toward other photos. "Jack Barrymore—how I admired him! And Bill Wellman. 'Wild Bill' directed me in *Love Is a Racket*. He was just full of himself, always talking about the First World War." He pauses before another group of portraits. "There are several of 'Dickie' Mountbatten. I served under him in the War. I first met the Mountbattens when they came to Pickfair in the 1920s. Everybody came to Pickfair." He swivels his gaze across the wall toward a glittering, if unlikely assortment of good companions—Winston Churchill ("I have a complete set of his books, all inscribed, in the Fairbanks Archive in Boston University"); David Niven ("I first met him when he was living with Merle Oberon and they were guests at my father's house—we made *Zenda* together and later we were members of the 'Cad's Club,' a group we formed in Hollywood"); Lillian Gish ("I recently spoke at her funeral"); and many heads of state, including four American presidents (Franklin Delano Roosevelt, Harry Truman, Ronald Reagan, and George Bush) and King George VI.

The memory of King George VI is especially cherished. It was on March 28, 1949, at Buckingham Palace that he personally conferred knighthood on Fairbanks. The honorary designation was not only a recognition of Jr.'s tireless efforts during and after World War II on behalf of Anglo-American relations, but the culmination of more than two decades of friendship between the Fairbankses and the royal family.

Nearby are two of his most cherished mementoes. The first is a prized pen-and-ink set. "That was a gift from David O. Selznick," he explains. "It's many years old now, and it's been battered about. Everybody told me to accept his offer to play Rupert of Hentzau in *The Prisoner of Zenda*, but in those days I was reluctant to accept second billing—even to Ronnie Colman." He chuckles. "Nowadays when people ask me who the greatest filmmaker I ever worked with was, I surprise them. I don't answer with Henry King or George Stevens or Max Ophuls, but with David. David Selznick knew so much and was so enthusiastic. He had everything you had to have in those days—talent, taste, extravagance, and a financial backer like Jock Whitney. I don't really see anybody like him today, unless it's maybe a Steven Spielberg."

The second prized item is a large, spectacular oil painting, conceived like a mural: a rainbow arches above London Bridge; in the distance are the combined skylines of New York, London, and Paris; and in the foreground is a display of assorted elements, including a tennis racket, a reel of film, several flowers, and an Indian's headdress. "That was done by my late wife, Mary Lee. She put everything in it to represent different things in our lives. The Victorian nosegay represents our daughter, Victoria. The daffodil is for another daughter, Daphne. The skylines are our favorite cities. And there's a ship there, too, because I've always loved the sea."

Fairbanks is justifiably proud of his naval record in World War II, the subject of his second book, *A Hell of a War*. Drawn largely from his own extensive notes and journals kept at the time, it recounts his adventures in much greater detail than has hitherto been available, either in Brian Connell's 1955 biography, *Knight Errant*, or Richard Schickel's *The Fairbanks Album* (1975). As early as 1939 Fairbanks had been loudly vocal in his anti-isolationist sentiments. When he helped organize the Committee to Defend America by Aiding the Allies (otherwise known as the William Allen White Committee), he aroused the scorn of columnist Hedda Hopper, who charged him with "playing at war." He received his naval reserve commission early in 1941 and was called to active duty later that summer.

He served on several American ships, including the USS *Mississippi* and the aircraft carrier USS *Wasp*, which delivered Spitfires and Hurricanes to beleaguered Malta. A specialist in small boat operations and tactical deceptions, he became attached to Lord Mountbatten's Combined Operations staff in London. Subsequently, he distinguished himself in combat, commanding small boat actions off the Sicilian coast, Yugoslavia's Dalmatian coast, and in the South of France.

Biographer Connell claims that Fairbanks's moviemaking experiences proved to be of great value during the war. "Douglas' chief contribution was the knowledge of sound effects he had acquired during his years in films," Connell writes, "together with all the tricks of camouflage and illusion which are an integral part of the shadowy world of the cinema."[6] For example, Douglas confirms, he had the idea of using dummy parachutists manufactured in graduated sizes to fool the enemy during diversionary air drops—just the sort of thing commonly employed as filmic special effects. For his action under fire at Baie de la Ciotat, near Toulon, where he rescued a damaged landing ship and sank two German corvettes, he received the Legion of Merit with the bronze "V" for Valor. Other decorations he amassed included the British Distinguished Service Cross, the Italian War Cross for Military Valor, and the French Croix de Guerre.

As much as Fairbanks obviously is proud of these exploits—indeed, he belongs in the select company of film stars who distinguished themselves in combat, like Clark Gable and James Stewart—he laces his accounts with a certain detached irony. He admits that in combat situations he foolishly adopted some of the poses of his swashbuckling movies. "I disguised my fright with a forced show of high, good spirits," he remembers. "Usually only I knew my lighthearted banter was my particular form of hysteria." At other times, his Hollywood films proved to be embarrassing. He had to endure the jibes of shipmates when, unexpectedly, his film, *The Corsican Brothers* (1940), was shown on board his own ship. Moreover, in combat he found himself unable, as he candidly admits, to bring off feats of derring-do, like scaling a wall or parachuting out of a plane: "None of my own old movies called for this sort of maneuver," he recalls dryly.

Meanwhile, there were the other real-life adventures—the hurried visits home for the births of his first two daughters; the parties with Noel Coward, the Oliviers, David Niven, Alexander Korda; and the new friendships with the colorful figures who leap in and out of the story, like the sturdy Lieutenant "Shocker" Byerly ("a bright little chap who hopped through war like a bantam rooster"), who instructed him in commando tactics.

"That's the way it was at the time," says Fairbanks, "one minute under fire, the next at a garden party with Larry [Olivier]. It was fascinating to be in London during the Blitz. The time of the V-2 rockets was especially unpleasant. You couldn't hear them coming until just after they had arrived, if you know what I mean. Day after day. I thought, my God, no one can ever beat these people! Most of the time I was too busy to allow myself the time to think about violent death. I think I was more frightened of being wounded or being captured and tortured. Sometimes I wondered why I was there at all. Many of the people I served with confused me with my movies and thought I wanted combat action and lots of it! I wasn't brave—not at all! I knew I was a closet coward. Sometimes I thought I could have better served the cause by being a celebrity at home! I was even a little jealous of the big movie parts Errol Flynn and Duke Wayne were getting! And I remembered how my father had helped the war effort in 1918 by staying home and selling millions of dollars in Liberty Bonds."

If there is a through line, a ground bass that prevails through the bewildering eclecticism of these testaments to a long and vigorous life, it is the memory of his father, Douglas Fairbanks Sr. Haunting this office space are playbills from Sr.'s days as a Broadway juvenile, scenes and posters from his later costume films, and portraits of father and son in the mid-1930s, just a few years before his death in 1939.

As a parent, Douglas Sr. proved to be a reluctant and, in later years, an absentee father. Even though he conferred his name on his son, he seemed occasionally embarrassed and awkward in his company, and he left his upbringing largely to the boy's mother, Beth Sully, and a nurse, affectionately nicknamed "Dedie." "[My father] would come, to my secret delight, and go, to my secret regret, and rarely seemed to be more than vaguely aware of my presence," recalls his son. Indeed, Sr.'s few overt gestures at parental control seem to have been to restrict his budding ambitions to become an actor.

Douglas Jr.'s boyhood was spent in and out of a variety of military schools and private institutions. He was always in motion, as he and his mother's family shunted back and forth, from Watch Hill, Rhode Island, to Los Angeles, to New York, and across the ocean to Paris. He was precocious. He wrote poetry, sketched, discovered girls, and chatted in French with his mother's friends, Sasha Guitry, Jean Cocteau, and Gertrude Stein. He admits he grew up spoiled and indulged (although perhaps not as much as might be expected).

He had already displayed an interest in acting when, at age fourteen, he and his mother were contacted by Paramount: would he be interested in starring in a movie?

"My father discouraged my acting," Douglas says, settling back in his chair. Although he tries to seem bemused at the memory, there is no mistaking the pain and ambivalence it still arouses. "And there was a terrible row when my first movie, *Stephen Steps Out*, was announced," he continues. "I was only fourteen! I was so young a year later when I made *Stella Dallas* [1925] that I had to paste on a mustache! Obviously, people were exploiting my name, and he resented that. But acting was a necessity for me. My mother was short of money. She'd run through the settlement left her by my father after their divorce in 1918. So I had to help support her and her six or seven relatives. My father didn't know about this until later.

"By the middle 1920s we wouldn't see each other for months at a time. We were always terribly shy of each other. He'd go around the world or something, and then we'd greet each other across a room. I'd say 'hello' and he'd say 'hello' and that would be that. No emotional demonstrations at all. I was closer to his brother, my uncle Robert. He was the one I could go to, who would speak on my behalf. He could talk to my father as his brother better than I could as his son."

And yet there were memorable incidents in these early days, moments that only the son of the world's most famous movie hero could enjoy.

"I remember visiting the sets of some of his costume pictures. I'd sneak out to the *Robin Hood* set on a Sunday, when the studio was closed, and the gate man would let me in. He wasn't supposed to let anybody in, but he made an exception for me. I and some of my chums would climb around the ramparts and towers. My schoolmates were always after me to take them there. The watchman must have been nervous about that: if I had slipped and fallen, he would have gotten hell for it. Other times I'd visit my father's 'Basilica Linea Abdominalis,' as he called it, his studio gymnasium, his 'Temple Dedicated to the Waistline.' Or we'd work up a sweat playing his own game of 'Doug,' which was his version of badminton. Some of my fondest memories were when we'd spend evenings at Pickfair watching movies. It was unusual in those days to be able to watch movies at home. We'd sit on couches and chairs and the projectors would be at the back of the room. Charlie Chaplin might call up and ask what we were showing. He lived practically next door. He was a charming fellow, and became a very good friend of mine. In later years I'd keep seeing him all over the place, at Pickfair, on holiday in the south of France, in Switzerland at his own home, which was cheek-by-jowl next to Noel Coward's home. Even at the end he was amusing. He didn't dwell on things."

Throughout his long acting career in the movies, Jr. not only challenged his father on his own turf—memorably appearing in exciting prewar swashbucklers like *The Prisoner of Zenda* (1937) and *Gunga Din* (1939), and postwar thrillers such as *The Exile* and *Sinbad the Sailor* (both 1947)—but he surpassed him in the diversity of his roles, ranging from the disturbed Grand Duke Peter in *Catherine the Great* (1934); a fugitive American diplomat in *State Secret* (1950); Professor Henry Higgens in revivals in the 1960s and 1970s of *My Fair Lady*; and in a successful television career in the 1950s as producer and star in *The Douglas Fairbanks Theater*.

We ask him whether he consciously patterned his own movies after the swashbuckling style of his father.

"I always wanted to please him," he admits, rubbing his chin. "But I didn't want to copy him, to be compared to him. Especially at first. Besides, I couldn't match him, and it would be impossible to surpass him. Why bother to compete? He was much more athletic than I. He made a real fetish out of it. He worked at it every day in the gymnasium. On the other hand, I used to do decathlon and track. I don't know if my father even knew how to play baseball or football. I did. Eventually, when I started making action pictures, I decided to do them my way rather than his. That was the only way I could get away with it. I became a better swordsman, in terms of competition, but his was a more theatrical style. He could hold off dozens of villains, and I had to struggle just to hold off Ronald Colman! By the time I made *The Prisoner of Zenda* in the mid-thirties, he had become very supportive. He talked me into doing the thing, even though I had to take second billing to Ronnie Colman!"

Fairbanks seems at first to have successfully avoided direct comparisons with his father's acting style. Quickly he demonstrated a range far beyond his father's capacities. He portrayed the sympathetic gangster Joe Massara, a nightclub dancer and longtime friend of Rico Bandello (Edward G. Robinson) in the seminal *Little Caesar* (1931). He was the sweet-tempered aviator, Scott, in Howard Hawks's *The Dawn Patrol* (1931), and a gossip-mongering newspaperman in *Love Is a Racket* (1932). A particularly outstanding role was the mad Grand Duke Peter in *Catherine the Great* (1934), a neurotic conception far more subtle and complex than that of Sam Jaffe in the same role that year in Josef von Sternberg's *The Scarlet Empress*. Even his delightfully unscrupulous villain, Rupert of Hentzau, in the aforementioned *The Prisoner of Zenda* displayed a markedly different style from his father's. One can scarcely imagine Fairbanks Sr. voicing lines with the requisite nasty bravado like these when Jr. confronted Ronald Colman for the climactic duel:

RUPERT: I see you want to let the drawbridge down! I just killed a man for doing that!
RASSENDYL: An unarmed man, of course.
RUPERT: Of course!

"About the only thing I borrowed from my father in that role was the costuming concept," recalls Fairbanks. "I had approval of the costume and I remember that he always used to say to keep it simple and avoid fussy things around the neck. When I saw the elaborate, ornamented uniforms Colman and everybody else was wearing, I went the other way, to a simple black costume. I think it worked." As Mary Pickford observed at the time, Doug's flair with costumes (designed by a former colleague of Doug Sr.'s, Dwight Franklin) placed him in a class second only to his father. "It is amazing how few people can wear costumes," she observed; "most of them look like stuffed sofas." On the eve of World War II, Samuel Goldwyn pronounced Jr. "one of the best leading men in films."

"By this time our relationship had changed," continues Fairbanks. "We had begun traveling to Europe together; that must have been around 1933. I thought he was at his best when he was traveling, in motion. He loved to mix with people and dress up. He fancied himself quite a Beau Brummell. He had dozens and dozens of suits and hundreds of shirts and ties. To select the outfit of the day was quite a ceremony for him. But then later in the day he'd work up a sweat and would have to change all over again! In the early '30s we were both working at the Alexander Korda studios in London. I made *Catherine the Great* with Elizabeth Bergner, and he made his last picture, *The Private Life of Don Juan.* We loosened up; we saw each other more as comrades than as father and son. We even had different sorts of nicknames for each other than 'Dad' or 'Son.' He told me he'd like to be called 'Pete' and he started calling me 'Jayar' (for 'Jr.'). We even had plans to make pictures together. We talked about doing Alexander the Great, and a story about Lord Byron. I remember particularly one project that was going to be called *The Californian.* It was an original story of my dad's, about the life of a well-known nineteenth-century outlaw who had a brief romance with Lola Montez. None of them was filmed. One never knows if they would have been good, but they would have been fun and

Doug Jr. and Maria Montez in *The Exile* (1946).

interesting! I think he was serious about them, but other things would come along and deflect his attention. Or I'd be taken away on some other job. The enthusiasm would die out."

The outbreak of war came on the heels of the death of Fairbanks Sr., on December 12, 1939. In some of the most moving pages of *The Salad Days*, Douglas wrote poignantly about those last days with his father. "We had so seldom been demonstrative with each other. . . . But now, as he lay there, weak and dependent, it seemed as though we had exchanged relationships. I was the parent and he the child."[7] He settled down now when he married Mary Lee Epling in 1939, with whom he would have three daughters.

However, even at the end there had been still some tensions. Douglas remembers with some bitterness his relations with his father's third wife, Lady Sylvia Ashley. "She was the instrument that finally broke up my father's marriage to Mary," he says. "And I resented what I thought were her schemes to get jewels and expensive presents out of him. And there were awful jealousies there: once my father expelled me from the house because he thought I was flirting with her. I wrote in the book [*The Salad Days*] that I don't think anything in my life was so shocking as that. Later,

I learned that she had had my name removed as chief beneficiary in my father's will."

Fairbanks made a few more movies after the war. The aforementioned *The Exile* and *The Fighting O'Flynn* (1947–1948) were particularly fine costume pictures. "I was glad to get the work!" he recalls. "I had been away six years in the service and didn't know if I would get a job in pictures at all! I was even thinking of going into business or staying in the military. When RKO offered *Sinbad the Sailor*, I took it. Funny, I remember visiting the studio while still in my naval uniform. A general passed me by and I saluted him. Well, he turned out to be an extra on Stage Five! Welcome to Hollywood!"

We ask him about Max Ophuls's *The Exile*, our favorite among all of Fairbanks's films. It portrayed the exiled Charles II as a swashbuckling fugitive in Holland pursued by Puritan Roundheads. Its wonderful climactic duel in and out of a windmill between Charles and the Roundhead Ingraham (Henry Daniell) was enhanced by Ophuls's trademark virtuosic moving camera.[8] "When I did *The Exile*, I was making a bid to establish myself as an actor-producer. I organized the Fairbanks Company and released it through Universal. That remains one of my favorite pictures." He points to a photograph: he is standing on the windmill next to director Max Ophuls. "I cowrote the screenplay with Clemence Dane, which we took from a little book called *His Majesty the King*. I was so intrigued by the story, which is based in fact. Max Ophuls was on his way back to Europe. He couldn't get a job. But I thought he was awfully good. I had seen some of his pictures and wanted him to do it. He was on his way to the train station when I reached him. I was entranced with him as a person, and we made an agreement then and there to do the film. We got along wonderfully well. I believe he stayed on to do some more pictures [*Letter from an Unknown Woman*, 1948; *Caught*, 1949; *The Reckless Moment*, 1949]."

Fairbanks began devoting more and more of his time to postwar political and humanitarian ventures. His growing interest in international diplomacy had already made its mark. It was his plan to assist the recovery of Japan after the war that became the Preamble to the Potsdam Declaration on Japan. Now he became national vice-chairman of the American Association for the United Nations, helped sponsor the War Memorial Chapel of the Washington Cathedral, and supported American Relief for Korea. A particularly consuming interest was his support of the American Remittances to Europe (CARE), which sent food parcels and other goods to war-devastated countries. He has received many foreign decorations for his efforts, including Commander of the Royal Order of Orange-Nassau and the Republican Order of the Star of Italian Solidarity. In 1953, President Syngman Rhee recognized Fairbanks's efforts for Korean relief by making him an honorary citizen of Korea.

He has also continued his connections with the navy. After the war he retained his commission and rose to captain in the naval reserve. Although he retired from the active reserve in 1969, he returned temporarily to duty as a United States Naval Delegate to the SEATO Conference.

Picture him now, years later, in 1996 during our second interview. We are in an apartment in New York, where he is temporarily staying with his third wife, Vera. His daughters, Victoria and Melissa, live in Tappan, New York, and Fairfax, California, respectively. A third daughter, Daphne, currently resides in London. A grandson, Dominick, lives in London. Douglas is just getting over a cold, but he is still sharp and alert, happy to talk about his father, if not so much, typically, about his own career. He still speaks with a touch of gallant bravado, even if it is with a mild intonation and a certain amount of reticence. It is a contradiction he himself has noted all his life.

He talks about plans to release on Kino videocassette a restored version of his father's *The Iron Mask* (see that chapter for details) that he had first released in 1952 for television. A few months before, there had been a comprehensive three-week Fairbanks Festival at the Film Forum, presented by Bruce Goldstein. Douglas and Vera have just returned from Los Angeles, where they had investigated a large amount of Fairbanks material that had been in Bekins Storage since the early 1950s. "This is just a thimble, compared to what's there," declares Vera, referring to contracts, tax receipts, photographs, notes, and so on. As we speak, she brings out a very large scrapbook retrieved from storage, which contains hundreds of candid photos of two generations of Fairbankses and their respective spouses, at work and at play. "*What to do with all this?*" Fairbanks muses to himself. We spend a merry afternoon, sifting through and remarking on the wonders therein. "*Save everything*," is the unspoken voice in the room.

Asked about his work on the rerelease of *The Iron Mask* and other of his father's films, Douglas reiterates that the best of them are as good or better than anything that has been made since. "I worked on the reissue of *The Iron Mask* in 1952, voicing the narration, and adding my voice to the spoken Prologue and the midsection 'interruption.' My father's original voice tracks weren't available. You can hear his own voice on his later talkies, of course—he was trained on the Broadway stage. I think today's viewers should see these films for many reasons, particularly those aficionados of movies; and for others the sheer entertainment value is worth seeing. Properly presented and exploited, I think they would go over well today . . . except maybe for *The Nut*, which I think is a real stinker! On the other hand, *The Three Musketeers* has always been a personal favorite: I remember as a boy standing outside the theater when I was supposed to be doing something else after school, seeing it about twelve times."

There are many curious revelations during these casual afternoon hours, as he and Vera sift through the box of photographs, each eliciting a memory. Here is a copy of a poem by Noel Coward, written just hours before his death. We learn about the origins of the name of Fairbanks's terrier dog, Zorro—"It was because the dog left his 'mark' all over the house!" We find out that in the late 1920s Douglas Jr. ghostwrote intertitles for several films of his father, including *The Gaucho*. "My father wouldn't write scripts in the traditional sense, but just put down words and fragments of sentences that would be developed." What about the mysterious "Lotta Woods," whose name appears on most of Sr.'s films. "It's not a fictitious name," Jr. explains, "like some people think; she was a real person, a story editor, who was responsible for putting to paper Douglas's ideas and putting them into proper order."

More questions: what do you say to people who claim you were handsomer than your father? He quickly ripostes, "I hate to say it, but my answer comes out in *four words!*" Another question: why didn't other children of Hollywood celebrities mature, like you have, into a stable and productive adulthood? Again, a quick reply: "They didn't have a father like mine." Did he strive in later years to bring together the feuding Mary Pickford and Charlie Chaplin? "I remember Mary asking me, 'Do you ever see Charlie anymore?' I made up a story about seeing him quite often, that he always asked about her. None of that was true, I hadn't seen Charlie in ages; but she then turned to me, 'I *still* say he was a son of a bitch!'"

Is there to be a third volume of memoirs, bringing up to speed the years 1946 to the present? "Once the war was over, what could top that?" he replied with characteristic humility. "I'm not convinced it would be interesting to people; I just can't get very excited about it. It's interesting to me, yes, but probably not to others. I suppose I'll write it if I live long enough," he adds casually. "I have notes on it, but I don't know it it's exciting enough to bother with it. I also want to see how the sales go for *A Hell of a War*.[9] I have my children and grandchildren in mind all the time: I want to put my best foot forward, of course; but if my worst foot had to go forward, then I'll have to try to put the best 'shine' on it, don't you think? I'm not much of an introvert, or into self-analysis. I'm only interested in me inasmuch as I can write something that might interest other people." He pauses and looks over at Vera: "What *really* happened after the war was my being able to interest this young lady here—to marry me . . ."

Nonetheless, much remains to be chronicled about his later career. Particularly interesting is his work in television, which began in 1952 in England with a series of half-hour story films, *Douglas Fairbanks Presents*, and, later, for *Rheingold Theater*, for which he appeared in a quarter of the productions. By 1957, he had produced 160 episodes. These days, when not in his Manhattan flat or office, he is either likely to be found on the road speaking on behalf of various charitable organizations or working on the Fairbanks Archive at Boston University. It is a part of the Special Collections at the Mugar Memorial Library at Boston University.

"I began sending materials to Boston back in 1965," he explains. "Many of the things are mine, but there are lot of things of my father's and my stepmother's, too. There are things about the founding of United Artists, for example, and lots of film scripts from my television shows, and correspondence, my military things, my paintings, and such. I often go there."[10]

The preservation of memory—indeed, that of a life in films—against the slow and pitiless erosion of time can baffle even the indefatigable Fairbanks. Most of his great friends, like Lillian Gish and David Niven, are gone now. Even many of his former homes are gone or have been sold. His residence in London, The Boltons, site of so many glittering social affairs in the 1950s, was sold a few years ago. Westridge, his California Spanish-style estate in the Pacific Palisades, was sold to Steven Spielberg. Pickfair, where he spent time as a teenager in the 1920s with his father and stepmother, Mary Pickford, was sold to Pia Zadora and her husband, Meshulam Riklis, who demolished a substantial part of the structure. "It makes me grit my teeth a hell of a lot to see what has happened to it," he admits. His soft-spoken tones take on a rasping edge. "Most of it's been torn down. Isn't it sad? When I pass the spot now, it's very upsetting, very distressing. All that's left of the original is the swimming pool!"[11]

We are tempted to ask what Douglas thinks of the recent impersonations of Chaplin and his father in Richard Attenborough's film, *Chaplin*. "I thought it was pretty good and that Mr. Downey acted the part well," he replies, "but Kevin Kline didn't really look much like my father. He was much too big and less compact in his build. I wasn't keen on the

Doug Jr. in his New York City office with author John C. Tibbetts, 1993 (courtesy John C. Tibbetts).

impersonation of my stepmother [Mary Pickford], either. The references to alcohol were painful. Everyone always wanted to take care of her and protect her. Even though she's gone now, I still feel that way."

He pauses, obviously unwilling to pursue the subject.

Finally, let us flashback to our first conversation, on that long-ago spring afternoon of 1993. We are taking our leave at the end of our stay, and we can't resist asking him for a photograph. As if reading my mind, he immediately plucks one of his swords from the nearby umbrella stand. He raises the hilt to his forehead and lowers the blade in one, graceful, unbroken gesture. There is nothing arch or self-conscious about it; it seems entirely natural to the man. Something of the knight errantry he and his father made famous in their movies still survives that gesture. . . . You know he believes it. "Yes, I am a romanticist," admits this modern musketeer, without a trace of self-consciousness. "I believe in many things, even when I am disillusioned. But it really doesn't matter if there is a pot of gold at the end of the rainbow. The fun is in chasing it."

MAURICE LELOIR

CINQ MOIS A HOLLYWOOD
AVEC
DOUGLAS FAIRBANKS

FILMS MUETS
FILMS PARLANTS

par

MAX DE CUVILLON

PARIS
J. PEYRONNET & Cie, ÉDITEURS
7, RUE DE VALOIS, 7

1929

Original title page of the 1929 French edition of Leloir's *Five Months in Hollywood with Douglas Fairbanks.*

APPENDIX B

On the Set of *The Iron Mask* (1929)

—Maurice Leloir

French designer Maurice Leloir's 1929 memoir of his participation in *The Iron Mask* has never before been published in English translation. M. Leloir was a world-renowned French illustrator of the Dumas novels and an authority on French period history. To him must go much of the credit for one of the most intricately detailed, beautifully designed, and sumptuous period recreations in film history. As was customary with Fairbanks, months were spent in advance as a cadre of designers worked preparatory to the filming to bring all aspects of the period to life—not just the sets of Palace of St. Germaine, the Carmelite Convent, and the Fortress of St. Marguerite, but the props, costumes, and related paraphernalia. These designs, paintings, and architectural blueprints were then passed on to the carpenter shop, the plaster shop, the paint shop, and interior decorator.

M. Leloir was seventy-five years old when he came to Hollywood at Fairbanks's urging. His memoir, *Five Months in Hollywood with Douglas Fairbanks,* was published in French in 1929. Information is scant about the circumstances of his coming to Hollywood. Having already signed Laurence Irving (son of the famed stage actor, Sir Henry Irving) to work on the art direction, Fairbanks went to Paris to seek the services of Maurice Leloir. In the archives of the Margaret Herrick and Douglas Fairbanks Research Centers at the Motion Picture Academy in Los Angeles, we find this letter to M. Leloir, relayed by one Guy Crosswell Smith, dated May 25, 1928, on the stationery of Les Artistes Associés:

> Mr. Fairbanks asks you to go to Hollywood for a period of five months, during which time you will be the artistic director of his studios . . . You agree to leave Paris on or about June 20, 1928 and can count upon arriving back

St. Germain under construction.

> in Paris about November 20, 1928. . . . Mr. Fairbanks is certain that you will not find the ocean voyage too difficult, and one of his representative [*sic*] in New York will meet you and arrange for comfortable accommodations to Hollywood.

In another letter, dated June 15, Mr. Smith writes to Robert Fairbanks at the UA Studios on 7200 Santa Monica Boulevard, acceding to a request by Leloir:

> Mr. Leloir will be accompanied by his nephew, Mr. Maxence de Cuvillon. He [*sic*] his 75 years of age and said he could not go unless he took someone with him. Therefore, your brother [Douglas Fairbanks] agreed to pay the expenses of this gentleman from Paris to Hollywood and return. He of course receives no compensation and Mr. Leloir will pay both his own and his secretary's living expenses while there . . .

Leloir's wide-eyed amazement at life in the film colony and his canny, ofttimes whimsical observations on the day-to-day challenges of bringing the romance of the French court of Louis XIII and Louis XIV to the screen constitute one of the few contemporary accounts we have of *any* film of the day.

Leloir gives a lesson.

The Start

One fine day, at the end of May last year, Leon Bary, the dramatic actor, came to my studio and said to me, "I am here on behalf of Douglas Fairbanks, for a film that he is going to make about the French XVII century. He needs a competent person who can direct all the production from the viewpoint of technical, documentary and historical correctness. He is persuaded that you can give the production a character which will make it superior to others. He has already made a film set in this period, *The Three Musketeers* [1922], and he feels that it lacked something."

I said, "I am very flattered by the opinion Mr. Fairbanks has of my learning, but I have no illusions about the way that people would follow my advice. In the movies as in the theater, one makes a fantastic mess of the documents; and when one has produced a folly, they say, 'It is thanks to the erudition of Mr. X that we were able to realize this masterpiece,' and Mr. X becomes perfectly ridiculous."

"Mr. Fairbanks is in Paris," Bary replied. "He is going to come to see you. I am returning with him to America. Is it understood—that we can take you away?"

"What are you saying?"

"Oh, not right away; in three weeks."

"You're joking. You think that you are going to transplant me, an old man of 74, who has never been out of Paris?"

"74 years!" Bary laughed. "You say that in order to get compliments. Come on, now, think it over."

"It's all thought over, look elsewhere."

Bary went away. I was left laughing at his extravagant proposition. Nevertheless, his straightforward look, his intelligent countenance pleased me. The next day he returned to the charge.

"It's you that we need."

"Nothing doing."

But then Mr. Fairbanks arrived at my house. In person!

"I was acquainted with your illustrations of Alexandre Dumas," he said to me. "But imagine, I thought that you were his contemporary! Weren't you his friend?"

"Why, not of d'Artagnan himself," I scoffed. "But yes, I have been the friend not of Dumas, but of his son. It was my father who was the friend of the author of *The Three Musketeers*. You must have believed that I have been dead for a long time!"

"I only hoped for one of your students."

"I have never had any."

"Then you can see that it is *you* I need," Fairbanks insisted. "My representative in France, Mr. Smith, will come tomorrow to persuade you to sign an engagement. I am counting on you."

What a devil of a man with his candid and merry eyes, his captivating smile, his air so good and energetic! In short, on the 20th of June, the *Ile-de-France* cast off Le Havre and twelve days later I was going to spend five months in Hollywood in the company of Leon Bary and my godson, Max de Cuvillon.

The Arrival at Hollywood

A voyage on the *Ile-de-France* is a wonderful cruise. The extravagant luxury of this ship would be a marvel even without the decorative paintings and the ultra-modern sculptures. One look at them, in spite of the stability of the boat, is capable of provoking sea-sickness!

At New York, we only stayed two days, just enough time to visit the Museum, the beautiful parts of the City, and to ascend the Woolworth building from which one overlooks the city from the 57th floor. The

Museum is extensive and contains many very beautiful paintings of all schools. The display of arms is magnificent, and one can admire the Riggs and Reubell collections perfectly installed.

The trip across the country is less amusing. One has the time to admire the Hudson River, 5 kilometres wide, to view Lake Erie, and then a stop at Chicago on Lake Michigan, which would be able to contain the whole of England. Everywhere we were welcomed and entertained, pampered and guided by the representatives of the United Artists.

Then from Chicago to Los Angeles. One could pass the four days in the Pullman coach more cheerfully if the landscapes were less monotonous. This eternal flat desert, uniform, without water, without vegetation, of a dirty grey color, rarely showed any life. Sometimes one saw several "mole hills" of the color of the soil. It turned out to be a village of Indians. At last there appeared some mountains, resting on the desert, horizontal as bottles atop a table. In Arizona, one begins to see here and there some groups of cabins, the chimney-flue of a factory, some automobiles, the highways like black lines, covered with tar, electric wires. Then, in California came the beginning of greenery, the product of irrigation; and one is seized with admiration for those men who had the courage, the stubbornness to come here in the days of old, to these localities in wagons drawn by oxen or mules, fighting with the Indians, never stopping.

In New York, in that magnificent Pennsylvania Station, we had seen preserved the first train which crossed the desert in 1831, with its carriages shaped like "berlines," with a little locomotive with a funnel chimney. (How well it would go in our museum of vehicles and of tourism in the Chateau of Compiegne!)

Fairbanks had preceded us. He waited for us with his general staff of friends at Pasadena, the last station before Los Angeles. Pasadena seems to be a suburb of millionaires, and Douglas wanted me to make my entrance by this sumptuous road, just as, at Paris we debark people of distinction at the Station of the Bois du Boulogné.

One is bewildered by the immensity of Los Angeles, which covers an entire region—really a city populous and crowded, which, like all the American cities, bristles with buildings of the New York style that resemble immense beehives. This city stretches on in a band of greenery of over 30 or 40 kilometers as far as the Pacific Ocean. Its huge suburbs have names like Pasadena, Hollywood, Beverly Hills, Venice, Long Beach. From the port of San Pedro one can embark for Europe, going either via China or via Panama. Hollywood itself has a center of luxury, a boulevard with big

Taking a break on set.

department stores, and a few large buildings. The homes in Hollywood, except on the boulevard, are not adjoining, but in some spots are widely scattered. Most of them look like the pretty little cardboard buildings for children. This aspect is not misleading, because it is really cardboard that is the foundation of construction as it is for the sets for the cinema. It does not last more than 10 years and then only thanks to the climate. One knocks down this castle of cards and one makes another, that is all.

These bungalows are, in general, composed of the ground floor, only topped sometimes, by another floor, rarely by two. All modern comforts are installed in them, bathrooms, electricity. The red tiles, the green roofs combined with the white or colored walls, create some gay notes in the greenery, oleanders, flowers, banana trees, palms, mimosas and eucalyptus. They are always properly maintained against a background of lawns that are always green and copiously watered, to which one gives a "shave" in the morning with the lawn mower. The sidewalks are paved in cement and extend along the wide avenues or boulevards laid out in a clean checker board. As far as the eye can see, there are lines of ultra-fast autos, some busses or streetcars, and no pedestrians. Everyone, because of the spread of the town, is obliged to have his auto, from the millionaire to the workman and the domestic servant. A colored maid arrives in her car in the morning to do your house work.

There are almost as many streets, avenues, promenades and paths on Hollywood Boulevard as on our Parisian boulevards. When the shops close around 6:30, they leave their display windows well lit until late in the evening. After dinner you go for a walk along the Boulevard. Usually, when we come out of the French restaurant Musso and Frank, we walk along smoking our cigarettes and look at the shop windows.

Sometimes there would be an extraordinary excitement on the day of a movie premiere. When a new film was announced for the Egyptian Theater, the Grauman's Chinese Theater, or Warner Bros., it turned into a madness. Alongside the two sidewalks of Hollywood Boulevard from place to place the roaring electrical generators are stationed, setting in motion a host of revolving beacons that stand every 100 feet. Behind the City, the mountains are adorned with the same. The mob crowds in to see once again the stars and leading men and women in full evening dress spill out of their superb autos in front of the theater, bright with photographic and radio equipment. All is covered by the dome of a splendid starry sky. It's a land gay, stylish, neat and comfortable. Maybe a Frenchman would miss the Parisian streets, winding all askew and making the distances seem shorter. Even the occasional untidiness is picturesque!

Everything here is enormous, colossal. At Los Angeles the stadium for football is immense. Every Saturday the 80,000 seats are reserved in advance and those still in their homes remain glued to their radios during the game listening anxiously to the account of the different periods of the match and the final result.

In the mountains behind Hollywood there is held, in the summer, an extraordinary concert in the "Bowl," which is named because of the disposition of the surrounding mountains. It is located at the bottom of a depressed valley shaped as a bowl; and between three high hills there is built a stand, shaped like a half-moon, for the orchestra. From there to the top of the hill, planks form benches that can hold 250,000 spectators. At the hour ordered, 9:00 o'clock in the evening, all the lights are extinguished. Only the orchestra is lighted. Looking from above, the 150 musicians appear the size of ants. In the midst of an absolute silence, under the light of the moon, the excellent artists execute the works of which nothing is lost; the most delicate sounds of the violin or of the flute are equally heard from anywhere. Every Saturday evening thousands of autos, tramways and busses bring to this spot a multitude struggling to find places to sit.

When we think that this group of cities is the work of only a few years, the result of a gigantic effort of these chaps who have created all this out of the total desert, one is filled with admiration and respect.

In Hollywood life is very comfortable. Certainly the beauty and mildness of the climate exert an influence on the residents. One lives here very free and without embarrassment. The heat apologizes for the appearance. Clothes and shoes are made of cloth; there is no waistcoat, and often not even a jacket. One goes to and fro, very comfortably, on the boulevard, in shirt-sleeves, the collar open, the head bare. Most Californians have the top of their heads as bronzed as their faces and their arms. I do not know how their scalps can withstand a sun which is sometimes over 90° in the shade! It is a coquetry of the two sexes to be scorched by the rays of the sun. On Sundays at Long Beach at the edge of the Pacific, one sees a real ant hill of men and women, almost nude, stretched out flat on the sand and cooking all day under an implacable sun. Furthermore, however much it is considered as the utmost indecency to be seen in pajamas, it seems entirely natural that in an open car one travels the 20 miles separating Hollywood and the beach wearing at most just a tiny bathing suit. Here, in America, almost all the young women are pretty, and, thanks to sports, admirably built. It is not the artist who is going to complain!

For twenty years, fashion has made a disappearing act of clothing which from day to day becomes less and less. Will it finish by disappearing completely? Will decency be shocked? After all, it is not nudity that is indecent but *dishabille.* Certainly, at this moment the cartoonists do not lack for subjects. The American women, one knows, enjoy the greatest liberty in the United States. They do everything that they want to, and they have been accustomed to it since childhood. If they don't go "too far," no one says anything and no one is aware of anything. This is why the Americans consider themselves as being of a superior chastity and despise deeply the French who brag of terribly shocking morals.

Prohibition is conscientiously maintained by the authorities, but as soon as one is at a private party, little bottles of the forbidden fruit show up everywhere. The vineyards of California are famous and the viticulturists are the warmest partisans of Prohibition. Indeed without it, their wine could not compete with the wines of France, Spain and Italy. Now they are earning a lot of money selling their grapes very expensively. It is very innocent to buy grapes. Each family makes its own wine secretly, and one finds it excellent. As for harder spirits, bootleggers furnish plenty of it, or with the so-called denatured alcohol detoxified and with the perfumes sold by the druggists. Everyone improvises gin, whiskey, etc. There is never a dinner, never a party without a multitude of cocktails, so that often enough it finishes with drunkenness. But one does not see it, the facade is preserved.

In America, one drinks to drink. It is not like in France and in the vineyards, where one sips and one knows how to drink. I am acquainted with the anecdote of the Americans who, demanding in a restaurant the most expensive wine, saw themselves served with ceremony a *Pommard* or *Chateau-Neuf du Pape* that the Pope himself would have drunk with great respect. However, to the Americans the wine was without taste and they added Seltzer water.

My ignorance of the English language obliged me to avoid, as much as possible, all invitations. Certainly it was very nice to invite me, but this quality of deaf-muteness was very annoying to me. Nevertheless, instead of shutting myself up all alone in the Studio, on Sunday I managed with the French people, or the Americans who spoke French, to take a little freedom. My friend [the art director] Ben Carré sometimes engaged on a Sunday morning a female model in the studio of a club of artists to which he belonged; and the two of us did some sketches from life to keep our hands in practice. One time Mary Pickford and Douglas invited my godson and me to pass the day at the beach where they had a charming villa on the sand close to the waves. Beside the villa is an enormous swimming pool filled with filtered sea water. All day long, even in the evening, the masters of the house and their guests dove and splashed like porpoises. The bottom of the pool is lit at night by electricity. The most charming freedom prevailed. One ate where one wished, on the knees, on the ground; one played music, one listened to the radio, one danced. But at Mary's home, it was never to excess; one conducted oneself very well.

Another time I went with Burgess Beal almost to the border of Mexico to visit the Spanish Mission of San Juan de Capistrano. On our return we saw an enormous glow in the sky. It was a fire of the 2500 oil wells in the Santa Fe Springs region. We approached as close as possible to the fire. The flames were as high as the towers of Notre Dame. It took two months to extinguish this extraordinary fire. It was necessary to sink a sloping tunnel 180 feet deep to cut the shaft of the wells. I returned there twice with Ben Carré and passed a part of the night to make sketches by the glow of the car's headlights. The black framework of the wells resembled little Eiffel Towers standing out against the flames and the purple sky criss-crossed with black or blue smoke. It was a nightmare's vision from which one could not detach oneself.

I do not know why I wander in speaking of things which have no connection with the Cinema. That which really interests me here is not Hollywood, but the Fairbanks studio of United Artists.

The Studio of United Artists

United Artists studio occupies a large piece of rectangular ground of about 500 hectares situated at the corner of Formosa Avenue and Santa Monica Boulevard. Not all the directors of the companies of United Artists work in this studio. Charlie Chaplin's is located on La Brea Avenue. Those who make their films at United Studios are Douglas Fairbanks, Mary Pickford, Norma Talmadge, John Barrymore, D. W. Griffith, Roland West, Herbert Brenon, Samuel Goldwyn. Joseph Schenk is president of United Artists.

When one says in France that Los Angeles is an artificial town built expressly to serve as motion picture sets, that there are entire neighborhoods given over to each country and each century, that is a pleasant joke. The sets are, in reality, not inhabited but are erected in the studios and subsequently destroyed to make place for others.

Let us enter now into United Artists Studios, not by the door of Samuel Goldwyn, where a guardian dragon will not let you go through, but by that of Douglas Fairbanks on Formosa Avenue. Likewise not just anyone can enter here, either. It is at the side of a large entrance for cars, barred by a chain. There another guardian dragon, solemn and dignified, sits in his wicker armchair, dropping the chain at each passage of a car or truck. This gentleman, high in stature and in color, well placed, is flanked by a splendid dog. He distributes innumerable "good mornings" and "good nights," and calmly smokes while reading his paper.

The Studio buildings proper are enormous. These are rooms in darkness, without windows, resembling hangars for dirigibles. On all the sides are large wide doors rolling on tracks. There are three of these at United Artists, not counting the buildings for talking films, which I will describe afterwards.

I was astonished by the absence of windows. Someone explained it to me, daylight is too changeable. With windows, one is subject to the sun, grey weather, summer, winter. Whereas artificial light is placed where and how according to the situation. Its intensity is regulated at will.

The building where the film editing is done has a basement with four subterranean projection rooms. A luminous panel indicates which rooms are occupied and which company is occupying it. It is here that dailies, the "rushes"—the tests or the scenes shot the previous day—are projected. Up above is an enormous gymnasium where every day Douglas and his friends play hand ball, tennis, football, and practice lassoing. Right now there is a lot of noise coming from here, as Doug is practicing with a bull whip. His private swimming pool is beside his office.

The Art Department where I have my office, and where all the draughtsmen, designers, architects, and photo-retouchers work, is above the photographic studio.

Along Formosa Avenue in front of the stables, are sheds that abound in an accumulation of strange things, including carriages of every country, mannequins, and statues or monuments.

The studios have neither any particular style of architecture nor decoration. The Americans, always practical people, suppress anything that is superfluous. The enormous shells have, like the turtles, an internal skeleton. The interiors are adorned entirely with a framework of vertical ladders, and the ceilings are criss-crossed with a multitude of cat-walks. All this is illuminated with electric floodlights that can be adjusted at will by the apparatus of arcs, or incandescent lamps perched at a great height, which can aim their rays on the scenes being shot. The army of workers, under the direction of architect designers, work here without ceasing. It is a labyrinth of joists, planks, pipes, ropes, and wires. One can get lost amidst a torture chamber, a Louis Philippe Salon, a Chinese palace, a Louis XIV throne room, the deck of a boat, a mountain pass, a Tahitian village, the chapel of a convent, and an Alpine glacier. In other words, everything that can be shot for interiors is done inside the studio. Only sets of vast exteriors, streets, places, important landscapes are built outside in the vacant fields. All these sets are prepared with minute care by the Art Department and are erected by the intelligent and painstaking workers in a very short time. They are then just as quick to demolish them in order to make place for others. This breaking up of cardboard timbers, of plastered oakum fills up the trucks that carry this wreckage to the cemetery oven, which is an enormous furnace to which a revolving track brings the material to be burned. It seems bizarre that this quantity of wood should be sacrificed every day, when so many families would be able to use it for heating in the winter. First, in Hollywood *there is no winter*. Second, this scrap material has been offered to hospitals and to the poor.

The electric plant and the transformers furnish all the electricity. In the sites where the exterior scenes are taken, the mobile generators borrow the city current in order to transform it into direct current for the use of the floodlights. Even in full daylight there are always electric floodlights to correct the light and soften the shadows.

I amuse myself each day, when going to lunch, to watch the progress made each day on set-buildings. They go up like the magic castles of the fairy stories. All the frameworks are cut and bolted in advance with mathematical precision, interlocking one into the other like a child's plaything. An enormous expanse of wall in oakum, asbestos, a latticework of iron, wood, felt, and cardboard can become in half a day a wall in cement, thanks to a single workman furnished with a giant sprayer. An electric machine mixes the cement, and in a liquid state it is carried in a tube to the sprayer. The men direct the nozzle toward the wall and the sun dries it up. After several coats, as a painter fixes a charcoal sketch, the wall is coated in the thickness of a fine, solid cement. The high bare walls are brightened up with a uniform border of cypresses.

The Film *The Iron Mask*

It was not long during the filming that I very quickly learned what the friendship of these beautiful people was to mean to me. I am going to recount what happened to me one beautiful morning when, in order to go to the studio, I tried to catch a moving bus. I slipped, and a sudden jerk dislocated my right shoulder. Warned by telephone, Fairbanks came running with his brother Robert, and the two of them took me away to the hospital. During the time that I remained there, with my godson Max (who naturally, did not leave me for a minute), Douglas and Mary [Pickford] and everyone came without ceasing. They nursed me, brought me flowers, and tried to entertain me. At the end of eight days I was able to go back to my work at the studio. Everyone, from the actors to the most humble laborers, came to show their concern and their sympathy. If I tell you this, it is to show how the Americans are replete with heart and sensitivity. Truly, in France we do not understand them.

Before my departure from Paris, they had handed over to me a French translation of the scenario of *The Iron Mask*, in order that I would be able to assemble the portraits, costumes, furniture, exterior and interior views, etc. that I would hardly have the chance to find in Hollywood.

LE MASQUE DE FER

The Man in the Iron Mask.

The subject is borrowed from the celebrated novel of Alexandre Dumas. *The Three Musketeers* had already been made several years ago by Douglas Fairbanks. This particular film adapts the sequels *Twenty Years After* and *The Viconte of Bragelone*. The pivot of the action comes when the twin brother of Louis XIV is substituted one day for the King, who is then thrust into his prison, his face hidden by an iron mask. We begin in 1638, under Louis XIII, at the time of the birth of Louis XIV, and conclude about 1660 in the bright years of the youth of the Sun King. I put to myself the task of establishing the characteristics of all the cast members and their costumes, taking into consideration their transformation during the passage of 20 years. This resulted in the parade of actors and actresses about whom one would make tests. Each artist, costumed and standing before the camera, is required to make some movements, some gestures, and facial expressions. All these tests are projected afterward on the screen and it is up there that the artists are chosen.

The Artists

One knows that the choice of the artists is a very delicate matter. For a single part they often test as many as five or six talented artists. But it is not

Leon Bary as Athos.

Nigel de Brulier as Cardinal Richelieu.

Marguerite de la Motte as Constance.

Rolfe Sedan as Louis XIII.

Young d'Artagnan.

the talent alone that decides the choice. The notoriety of the leading star, from the point of view of publicity, represents real cash and is taken into account. Before purchasing a film and, in order to know its value, one asks what names there will be put on big letters on the marquee, what portrait will be in the newspapers. If these conditions are lacking, the film can be good and well played, but might not be a success and will not make money.

For the film of *The Iron Mask* there were several parts distributed in advance. Naturally, Douglas Fairbanks plays the part of d'Artagnan. As in *The Three Musketeers*, six years earlier, he will display his brilliant acting, his qualities of suppleness, of skill, of zest, of youth, of gaiety and of dramatic energy.

Leon Bary, who had made an excellent Athos in the first film, came expressly from Paris to take the same part again. Coming from the theater to the screen, he was a former companion of Sarah Bernhardt in the old days and travelled through all of North and South America with her. Tall, thin, distinguished, he was the Comte de la Fere, in person.

Nigel de Brulier, the perfect Richelieu in *The Three Musketeers*, naturally again took the role. If he did not resemble the Cardinal exactly, as his nose was a bit less accentuated, he had the thinness of face and of jaw, that air sometimes ecclesiastic and gentle, sometimes hard and authoritarian, that Hanotaux had described so well. His bearing, full of grandeur and of dignity, gives the impression of the portrait painted by Philippe de Champaigne. He is full of talent and his playing of the last moments of the Cardinal is truly moving.

I tried in vain with Lon Poff, the excellent artist entrusted with the part of Father Joseph, the Eminence Grise, to obtain a resemblance to the historic figure. Earlier he had played the role smooth chinned and bald. A problem for him was to be afflicted with a pair of protruding ears. He remedied it by a large ball of wax behind the ears that a headband supported until there was a complete adhesion. One day the gum did not hold and, in a pathetic moment, his two ears, giving up all constraint, suddenly opened up like a fan!

Adolphe Menjou, who was busy elsewhere, was not able to resume the part of Louis XIII. The role was entrusted to Rolfe Sedan, who acquitted himself very well. Unfortunately, Sedan is not tall and Louis XIII was, which obliged the poor actor to play all of his part perched on rubber heels on the bottom of his boots.

Charles Stevens, with his delicate face and his piercing Mexican eyes, took the role of Planchet anew. Stevens, who is a gay and charming man, is the remainder of the household.

The personage of Comte de Rochefort was awarded to Ulrich Haupt, a great artist who performed it with remarkable distinction, energy and character.

The role of Louis XIV required more research. The same performer had to perform both the twins. Douglas chose William Bakewell, a tall young man, twenty years old, who had already played several first-rate roles. His outward appearance hardly corresponded to that of the character. Bakewell certainly has the rather straight nose of the great King, but he has a larger mouth, blue eyes, blond hair, and is tall in size, while the King was of medium size with brown eyes and brown hair. One had to enlarge Louis XIII, but one could not shrink Louis XIV! But the acting talent is, after all, the essential thing. Bakewell is 20 years old with the spirit and the zest of youth. It was even necessary to moderate his spirit a little and inculcate in him the stiff dignity that etiquette demands in the Court. The Americans have no reason to be thoroughly acquainted with Saint-Simon and are not able to accomplish this rigid etiquette from which Marie Antoinette suffered so much later. This can only be learned at the Conservatory.

Stanley Sandford is a magnificent Porthos, a kind giant with a broad laugh under his bristle of mustaches. When he bites into an apple while rolling those terrible eyes, when he carries in his outstretched arms an enormous inn table, in order to crush his opponents, he was superb.

Gino Corrado puts all his Italian finesse into the part of Aramis, distinguished and secretive, pious and a pursuer of women.

The supporting parts are given to talented folk. Thus Fred Cavens, the Belgian fencing instructor, who, is in charge of the training of sword play and proper bearing, has shown so many varying aptitudes that he becomes the indispensable man to play the "background" parts of lords, peasants and bandits. I complained to him about the use of protective sheathes on the tips of the rapiers, encased in the style of Spain and not of France. "You will certainly see," answered Cavens, "that after each contest, there are many hands bleeding. What would it be if they were not protected by this sheath? I can almost teach the notions of fencing to the actors, but as for the extras, it is impossible and there is not enough time. It is because of this that each contest looks like a sharpening of knives—flic, flat, whirling their rapiers, big gestures to be skewered a hundred times! One has to be careful amid all the clattering and foot work and noise not to get the sword too close to the eyes of your opponent. When I draw swords with Bary, who knows his business well and performs coolly, everything goes well. But with Douglas, who becomes aroused, who gets excited, who believes that he is really fighting, I mistrust myself. I am obliged to parry and to defend myself!"

For the ladies, Marguerite de la Motte becomes again the Constance Bonacieux of *The Three Musketeers*. She is so pretty, so full of talent, of youth, of mischievousness, of life, that this role is one of the great delights of the film. There are love scenes with d'Artagnan that are truly delightful. But careful: In America, a kiss on the mouth cannot be longer than 3 feet of film. If it lasts longer it becomes shocking and is cut by the censor.

The thankless role of Milady de Winter, the "femme fatale," the traitoress, the murderess branded with the infamous *fleur-de-lys*, fell to the ravishing Dorothy Rivier who plays the dramatic and violent part as a finished actresss. She brings blessings on that *fleur-de-lys* that made it necessary to exhibit her wonderful shoulders! Rivier puts so much earnestness in her acting that in the struggle in the convent with Marguerite, she laid on her with great force a terrible slap that dislocated her jaw. She sustained herself many bruises.

The part of Anne of Austria gave cause for a long decision. They thought well of Belle Bennett, an actress esteemed and well known. But she was, they said, rather demanding. Her role was very short but very important. She was satisfied with $9000 for three weeks (that would be 225,000 francs) and we had an Anne of Austria flawless in charm, in distinction, in dignity, who played her part in perfection. Belle Bennett did not make gestures. Her feeling, shown in her eyes, and her play of facial expressions renders useless those titles on the screen that always come to check the action. She is a fine actress and at the same time she is a pretty woman.

An adorable little five year old boy, Gordon Thorpe, portrays in a charming fashion the double role of the young Louis XIV and his twin. A large photograph of him in his natty brocade costume resembles a reproduction of a portrait by Van Dyck.

In short, each one maintains his character very well and strives to give it characteristics of the period. Certain things, however, had the knack of irritating me. Thus, I was never able to become accustomed to seeing the actor chewing gum without showing my impatience. This mania, which has made a large fortune for its inventor, has hardly yet been introduced in France, happily. This perpetual movement of the jaws, that even tobacco chewing seems to me to be inappropriate and ridiculous. One sees the workers, having to make a big effort to stick their gum on the wall, take it back in order to lose none of it. When the flavor is exhausted, one gets rid of it at random, and there is no operation more difficult than to take it off of a shoe if one has walked over it. I said one day to the brother of the King Gaston d'Orleans, who never stopped chewing except to play his part, "Rather than relegating this ball of rubber to his cheeks, why doesn't your Highness deign to spit out his cud?!!"

Choice of the Extras

The selection of the other actors is indispensable, but the competition results in many tensions. Among all those artists of the Cinema who have come to ask for employment, and who with great effort have registered for a test, how many among them have found no work for months and await anxiously a tiny engagement in order to obtain the means to live, if only for a few days! The leading actors are the stars whose names are useful for the advertising, for the sale of the film, and to whom one concedes without flinching the high prices that they demand. These prices are spread all over the world by the newspapers, inciting all the "ham" actors who feel that they too are star material, and see in front of their eyes a stream of dollars. They collect their savings, arrive in the land of gold and cinema with a jackpot of photographs of all their roles, and a soiled collection of newspaper clippings. They arrive with their little bundles under their arms. Alas, with what indifference they are rejected and left flat. One sees them wandering, loitering, in the studio, behind each corner of the set, hoping to be

Shooting a scene.

seen. To get rid of them, they may be given bit parts. Then they disappear to offer their services and carry their miseries to other studios.

Even more laborious is the selection of "extras." For a film of the importance of *The Iron Mask*, a considerable number of them are needed—soldiers, cavaliers, gentlemen, townsmen, working people, footmen, ladies of the court, townswomen, servants, peasants, young and old, and children. Even trained dogs are needed! I had to attend the selection for the male extras. A call had been broadcast for Sunday morning at 9 o'clock. The gathering was in the immense courtyard of the Palace of St. Germain-en-Laye. There were gathered a thousand or twelve hundred people of all classes, all countries, all categories. One saw cowboys, with their immense

Allan Dwan at the helm.

felt hats, in shirt sleeves, Mexicans with swarthy skin and ink-black hair, correct gentlemen in impeccable suits, young athletes with tow blond hair, old actors with tired looks trying to present a good appearance, young elegants with flowery boutonnieres, bums in rags with bare feet, men wearing decorations, bandit types, and Negroes.

The skillful director Allan Dwan and his assistants, equipped with their megaphones, arranged in a horse-shoe shape three sides of this human herd. Then men stretched long ropes in front of this mob, pushing in their bellies in order to line up.

At the sound of a whistle, the rope is raised. Ten men step out of line.

"Advance! One, two, three, four! Bow!" They take the four steps, like automatons, then bow more or less clumsily and remain in the position. I pass in front to review them.

"Step back! One, two, three, four! Bow!"

One choses sometimes one, two or three, sometimes no one at all. The men chosen pass into another area for another test and those that have been evicted, their heads bowed, disappear. There were the sneaky fellows who, not having succeeded, slipped into the courtyard of the chosen without thinking that Dwan's sharp eyes would recognize them. At last it was necessary to make a selection among those already chosen. There was hardly a hundred remaining, who were sure to earn their five dollars a day for a little while. Yes, in France 5 dollars is 125 francs, and furthermore,

On the set.

they never make more than 25 francs. One asks oneself on seeing this deplorable and cosmopolitan throng, what they could be doing there, so many Frenchmen, Russians and Europeans of all nations? Many are deserters who cannot return their country and hope to be able to become American citizens. It is none the less true that it is a saddening spectacle at least for someone like me, who is not blasé.

The Ladies and Their Bearing

Although I did not have to busy myself with the selection of the female extras (and I was well free of it), I was responsible for their bearing and their costumes, which was not a slight job. In these days, where the style is for the ladies not to have on the body more than the equivalent of a chemise, where they have lost the practice of all clothing constraints, having them don the gowns, whalebone corsets, and heavy wigs results in their clumsy movements. It is very difficult to correct them.

Many of the scenes of *The Iron Mask* take place at the Court, either of Louis XIII or Louis XIV. Every time that the King appears, all the people of the Court must execute a deep curtsy and a low bow. To teach the ceremonious bow to the men, the famous fencing teacher Fred Cavens was a distinguished master. They must learn, as in *Le Bourgeois Gentilhomme*, the three steps, the bending on one leg, the hand on the hilt of the sword, the other grasping the hat and turning it gracefully, the bow, the three steps backward, etc. Some executed this exercise as though they had learned it as infants, others nearly fell, perspiring great drops. For the women, it was easier for they are more graceful by nature, and the charming Madame Chalif, a talented dancer, only had to show them an example. Of the remainder, many of the extras were very distinguished ladies, such as the Princess Galitzine and Baroness d'Estournelle de Constant. Having been indiscreet enough to give some advice, I was appointed on the spot as professor of curtsies. I had the perilous honor, several times, to command the squadron of the ladies of the Court and to have them do their exercise. The most difficult was the backwards curtsy, without stepping on the long trains of their skirts. A fall on their backsides would have been unfortunate. They took advantage of my efforts by filming my demonstrations. It must have been very funny to see an old man with white hair and beard showing how to curtsy to a squad of pretty women taller than me!

Scenery

Everything here is prepared methodically. Each person has his specialty and his task. Several artist designers are in charge of the same set. Laurence Irving, the great grandson of the great English tragedian, created some that were extremely clever; Ben Carré, French painter and designer, student of Amable, with a thorough knowledge of the mathematical and practical aspects of theater design, hit upon some very ingenious inventions; and other designers included Harold Miles, Carl Oscar Borg, and William Cameron Menzies. I had the role of supervisor.

Once the director, Mr. Dwan, and Mr. Fairbanks had approved a model, it passed to the draughting room where it was laid out exactly, drawn to

Setting up a dolly shot.

scale with all the mathematical precision necessary. The models of ornaments and objects, completed in full size working drawings, were given to the carpenters, cabinet makers and sculptors. I saw a forest of wooden scaffolds going up with unforgettable speed. Thus was the Chateau of St. Germain-en-Laye erected, not the one which shelters the Museum of Antiquities, but the one constructed by Henri IV, of which the only remains are a pavilion now turned into a restaurant. I must admit that despite the lack of precise documents, Irving acquitted himself marvelously. Someone had been to Paris and had found at the *Bibliotheque* the plans and the elevations desired, but even then one had to accept philosophically any inaccuracy, of either too much or too little. Large sheets of cardboard and towels soaked in plaster became the cut stones 2 centimeter thick. For the pavement of the courts or the streets, plenty of cement was poured. Facing the main entry gate of the chateau, on the other side of the court, rose the front steps giving access to the grand vestibule, or the guards' room. The doors, in carved wood carrying the arms and the mark of Henri IV, are of great height. This immense room was all in marble adorned with mural paintings and sculptures. Under construction one saw the beginning of a monumental staircase of which the upper part was supposed to give access in another set to the vestibule of the second floor.

Parenthetically, it is amusing to see made these slabs of marble for the paving, as well as those for the walls. Imagine a large flat rectangular tank full of water. Nearby are the cans of oil colors in the various tones of which one wishes to make the marble, as well as a pile of sheets of thick gray cardboard. With large brushes one sprinkles the water in the tank with the various colors. After stirring it all with a stick, they place a sheet of cardboard in the water and quickly agitate the water. All these blobs and streaks of oil color slide on the surface of the cardboard, which only absorbs the water. This gives the perfect effect of marble. This is the way, in a small scale, that book binding paper is made. Once dried and varnished, it is again very solid.

Miniatures

The sets are constructed only to a minimal height, after which one has recourse to the use of "miniatures." In my inexperience with the things of the Cinema, when someone said to me, "I am going to show you some miniatures," I believed naively that I was going to see some small portraits on ivory. I prudently kept quiet, thus hiding my ignorance.

Actually, the miniatures are sets, or parts of sets, executed at a reduced scale and matched mathematically, as seen by the camera lens, with the real set. The artists who devise and execute these miniatures must have a remarkable science and accuracy. For example, the position of the camera having been decided, a view finder is fixed just exactly where the lens will be. A gallows scaffold will support in miniature the upper floors of the houses, the top of the church, the roof of the chateau, the summit of the mountains, that have been constructed in a scale corresponding in perspective to that of the set and cut out so to "register" exactly. The painting of it is so carefully checked that even with the naked eye, in the view finder, one cannot distinguish the trickery of the two sets, one the miniature, the other full-size, well separated one from the other. Background action and scenery may consist of an entire landscape, with mountains, villages,

Informal moments on the set.

streams, railroads, viaducts, and actual vegetation composed of dwarf plants of shrubs that had been discovered by the Japanese. Electrically-driven little dolls and moving railroad trains come and go and give perfectly at a distance of several yards the illusion of scenes viewed at a great distance. At First National I saw, in front of the backdrop of a painted sky, on a lake twice as large as the *Bassin des Tuileries*, an entire 18th -century navy of ships which were at the most 10 feet long, simulating combat with perfection. When taking a similar scene, a swallow or butterfly that passes through the "take" seem as huge as antediluvian birds and insects, creating a disastrous disruption of size relationships. At Universal the publicists said the sets for *Notre Dame de Paris* [*The Hunchback of Notre Dame*, 1923) were built natural size. Having seen those sets before they were destroyed, I can say that the actual construction of Notre Dame represented only the three portals of the facade with all their ornaments, carvings and statues. But the construction stopped there. The above portion was shot separately. All the summit and the towers are represented, in miniature, and registered in the lens with the lower part. The finished film showed the real set and the miniature united, and no one was aware of the technique.

Miniatures are also necessary for the interiors and other effects, but not for the same reason. When they told us in France that in one of the great historical films they had employed 10,000 extras, we were overwhelmed with admiration. There was certainly the effect of 10,000 extras; however, only one thousand were in flesh and bones, the others were little dolls. We acknowledge that the effect is still convincing.

In a large room interiors must be fully lighted by floodlights. But where do you put them so they are not seen? Above the set, in the air. They are perched above the cornices on the scaffolds. Naturally the room will have no ceiling. In the film, however, one is seen. The fact is that the ceiling is executed in miniature, placed near the camera, lighted from below, and the perspective as well as the light and the color match exactly with the actual set. It is a spectacular achievement of precision and the illusion is complete. I was able to judge it in the wonderful set of the bedroom of the Chateau of St. Germain, executed by Ben Carré. In another example, in Fairbanks's earlier film, *The Gaucho*, one sees the illusion of thousands of heads of livestock. There is certainly a real herd in the foreground. But behind this are animated cut-outs, and behind them a painting, or enlarged photograph.

In *The Iron Mask* there is a scene where a man is hurled down into a deep well. In reality, this well is only four feet deep! To demonstrate to his victim how deep is the well, Fairbanks throws a lighted torch into it. It lights up the inner walls of the wall in its downward passage. Again, this is a miniature.

People have said to me that it would be much better to shoot films in *real* locations. First of all, that would be impossible for Americans have no architectural past or structures to speak of. It would be necessary, then, to come to Europe, but this would cost much more than to make and film reconstructions of the locations. Furthermore, the monuments and old houses of ancient Europe have long since had their appearances modified by modern life. One cannot abolish the sidewalks, the paving, the rails of tramways, the electric wires, the commercial signs, the posters, the telegraph poles. Indeed, one cannot stop the passage of an aeroplane!

No, one has to renounce reality and furnish a much better illusion with a set than with what Nature provides.

The Tricks

For many films it is necessary to contrive ingenious tricks that bring delight to the public. Many of them are well-known. Although I am amused by them, I admit that before this I knew little about them. I do not believe that it will be an indiscretion to talk about them here because to reveal them does not withdraw any merit from those who use them; rather, it shows how much work and ingenuity is necessary to amuse the audience.

At United Artists in this extraordinary property room, I caught sight of a bizarre object that resembled a height-measuring scale used by the draughting board. It was for Mary Pickford in *The Gaucho* for her miraculous apparition as the Virgin. The charming actress was standing on a little pedestal, backed against a plank trimmed to her silhouette. Two bands of leather bristling with a multitude of thin sticks of flexible metal passed through rollers following the contour of her body were moved by a crank concealed in the bottom of the stand. The silver-like sticks moved rapidly in two different directions and received the flash of the flood lights. This gave the illusion of a dazzling radiance emitted by the Lady herself.

There are so many examples of these extraordinary effects. For instance, one knows of the many tricks employed by Douglas Fairbanks in the incomparable *The Thief of Bagdad*, including the rope which he throws into the air and which becomes a climbing pole; the flying carpet carrying him and the Princess that soars above Bagdad; the invisibility cloak, the underwater battle with the sea monsters, etc. In another film, shown this summer in Hollywood at the [Grauman] Chinese Theater, *White Shadows in the South Seas* [1928] takes us down with the divers looking for pearl-bearing oysters. The camera tracks vertically downward through waters of astonishing clearness. But at the bottom of the sea, there is not enough light. It is necessary to see the divers working, prying the oysters from the shells, the struggles with suffocation, and a fight with sharks. For this purpose, under the boat a gigantic diving bell is let down, communicating by an extending tube. This diving bell contains the operator and his camera equipment. In front of him there is a window in the form of a funnel sealed hermetically by a pane of glass. An electric floodlight equipped with a large reflector sends the light onto a scene being taken. Thus, the operations of the pearl diving are taken directly on the spot. As for the shark, he goes through his evolutions in an aquarium, the diver being separated from him by a wall of glass. It must be very unpleasant for the actors to portray shipwrecked persons in a storm. They must not only receive innumerable buckets of water but they are buffeted by the frightful wind of aeroplane propellers. Such propellers created a miraculous effect in a film with John Barrymore, *The King of the Mountains* [*Eternal Love*, 1928], which was directed by that admirable director, Ernst Lubitsch. In an amazing and detailed set representing the Alps, Barrymore and his female companion are surprised by a snowstorm. Every stagehand is at his post on the scaffolding with enormous sacks of artificial snow. When the propellers begin to turn, the stagehands throw pailfuls of snow into the air, and the wind machines make the snow whirl around, blowing and stirring and fluttering the hair and clothes. Only to look at it made you feel like you were catching a cold! And think of *The Lost World* [1926] for First National. In the prop room I found an alligator, moulded in rubber, perfect but a bit shopworn. I grappled with him and made him do his little routine for me. Two levers of steel and wood made him blink his eyes, open his mouth and put out his tongue, shake his paws, puff up his sides by his breathing. Thus, they reconstituted and gave life to the antediluvian animals of which they had recovered hundreds of intact skeletons in the subterranean oil pools of the La Brea pits. (They are in a magnificent museum of Paleontology in Los Angeles.)

I speak now of several effects in *The Iron Mask*. I regarded with apprehension as Fairbanks was ready to jump through a window furnished with its panes of glass. “Don’t be afraid of anything,” he told me, “they are made of sugar!” Well, I wonder, why don’t they use that process for the windows of automobiles? That would avoid all the injuries and gashes. Unfortunately, when it is hot the “glass” gets sticky and melts. Another time on the set of *The Iron Mask* we are in a tavern where some people of evil appearance are standing around. I saw in the corners of the room and the ceiling beams some wonderful spider webs. Imagine a sort of a soldering lamp operated by electricity in front of which was a metal recipient containing liquid glue. This glue is blown with force and spurts through thin holes onto the set. There it adheres in the form of threads which resemble and can be mistaken for spider webs. It has been necessary to have explosions. Walls and buildings collapse. People are buried under the rubble. The falling stones are manufactured from a powder which mixed with water solidifies and weighs no more than a feather. Likewise, one can be hit by a cudgel, have benches, tables or chairs broken on his back without being any the worse for it. The wood used is made of yucca, a desert plant called “Adam’s Candle” of which the stalk, light as the sap of the French *sureau* and of the same consistency, can be shaped and polished. I was able to carry on one arm a dozen muskets of *Messieurs les Mousquetaires* without feeling the weight.

But it would be tiresome to describe all the ways employed to simulate reality or create the fantastic, all the more as they are continually inventing new things. Much of the remainder is owing to the talent of the cameraman, the superimpositions, the slow motion effects, the reverse motion through winding backward, etc.

Historical Accuracy

The terrible thing about Americans is that they are obsessed with depicting the periods of the past. There is always an attractiveness to those things one is not acquainted with. But the history of America is not long. Its past is very modern for us. Each one of the nations that comprise ancient Europe is rich in memories and respectful of pictorial places with religious background. Everywhere in Europe one finds monuments, works of art, furniture, jewels, arms, costumes of ancient periods. The Museums, the private collections, overflow. The libraries are mines of documents. America comes and carries away all that she can to the sound of dollars; and thanks to the exchange, we cannot fight it. But for the theater and the Cinema, she little understands how to make use of it for lack of education and experience. The errors of archeology in American films are not evident, except when the films are shown in France!

In California, for sets representing houses or exteriors, one is always tempted to veer in the direction of Spanish, Mexican, German or occasionally English styles. It depends on the nationality of the designer. When they reconstitute a European city, they permit themselves inaccuracies that some simple postal cards would have made it possible to avoid. For *The Iron Mask* I saw the *Pont Neuf* of Paris built. Look closely and you see the houses of the Place are of the 19th Century. Notre Dame stands in the Rue Dauphine. And the statue of Henri IV is in the middle of a square planted with trees facing the Institute instead of showing its back to it.

As for costumes, it is necessary to visit the big warehouse, the manufactory of Los Angeles. Colossal. Like everything here, this is an enormous building in which *La Belle Jardiniere* would be able to dance! I visited it from the basement to the top floor. In the basement are the stuffed animals, carriages, and guns. The elevator deposits you in the coach building department and the saddlery, where you find the military equipment from the prehistoric times to our day. You pass by all the tribes of the world, furniture of all periods and countries, the rags of the savages, the clothing of all epochs since the Stone Age, modern dress, religious costumes, articles from all cultures made in gold, the jewelry shop, millinery shop, shoemakers shop, dye works, laundry, dressmaking studios, the mending shop, and the manufactory of all sorts of objects. Finally on the 17th floor, is the garage for automobiles. In the vast offices there is a fine library of works and special documents. Yet, all this enormous accumulation of costumes and objects of all sorts is almost childishly inaccurate in cut and

Background music.

shape. It is nevertheless the most reliable basis of all the historical films made in Los Angeles, where each one of these carnival garments rents for at least $50.00, which would be, in France, 250 francs.

Douglas Fairbanks had asked me to direct and supervise, from the documentary viewpoint, the manufacture of the costumes and sets. But I had the misfortune of neither speaking or understanding English. I thought that my sketches would explain my thoughts better than a comic gibberish of dumb gestures. I made in water colors the models of the costumes, accompanied by technical details. But I quickly saw that the great costume designers in Los Angeles understood nothing and did things their own way. They did not even show my patterns to the workers responsible for their execution. I therefore arranged that all the principal costumes would be made at the studio. I chose the material and oversaw the cutting and the execution. I was present at the trying-ons. Miss May Hallett worked on the women's costumes, and the tailor Gilbert Clark on those for the men. The costumes, equipment included, will remain the property of United Artists. I would not know how to give enough praise to Miss Hallett and Mr. Clark for the accuracy and good will with which they followed my directions. Certainly I would have wished that all the costumes had been constructed the same way, but when you are dealing with hundreds of them, it is a good idea to close your eyes a little and persuade yourself that the camera turns so quickly that one does not have the time to see the mistakes.

When I asked that they make the tight Louis XIII boots fit closely to the ankle and not to resemble those of the sewer workers, there was consternation. They succeeded but at what price. They no longer have today the elastic leather which was used formerly, and how can you demand of the actors that they take a full hour to put on their boots? I remember the story of this commanding officer, in the XVII Century, surprised in bed by an enemy attack, wanting to put on his boots in order to jump in the saddle. He was a prisoner before he had completely put on the second one! And the linen, collars, collar bands, cuffs—it was no use to give the pattern. I wanted to make them myself, being used to work with my hands. But I was told it was undignified for a supervisor.

One thing that irritated me a little was to be obliged to leave my sketches, water colors of costumes and others behind, so I could be present at the scenes of the film that they were shooting. I well understand that is contained in my role as supervisor. It was necessary to inspect the costumes, the wigs, the linen, the footwear of each one, to touch up the appearance, to give the stage directions in order to maintain as much as possible the character of the epoch and to honor, pretty nearly, the etiquette of the Court. But often I remained seated in my folding chair for hours with nothing serious to do. Then, in order to occupy myself, I took out my sketch pad and without anyone seeing me I made quick sketches of the actors and extras.

Some of the actors often had hardly an hour of actual work in the entire day. They were bored, they sleep in all the corners and eat ice cream purchased from the ice cream vendor who slipped around everywhere in his little car. They chatter behind the sets, they gather around a radio in order to listen on Friday to the result of boxing match and on Saturday to the football games. The warm weather is bearable, thanks to a perpetual breeze, but in these hermetically closed boxes of studios, the poor performers perpetually mopped their faces, careful not to let their make-up run too much. One day I saw the Grand Cardinal, tired by his long soutane made of red cloth, and Constance Bonacieux worn out by her double wool skirt, go for a walk each of them holding their skirts tucked up as high as possible. They faced each other and did a sketchy Charleston which did not lack for picturesqueness. One day I said to venerable Father Joseph, "Oh shame! Putting your arm around the waist of the hair dresser!" "I am a monk," he answered, "I am 60 years old but I am no less a man."

Often the sleeping extras were very funny, as well as all that army of hairdressers, beauty operators and make-up people. A very amusing thing was to see them at noon, as soon as the siren whistled, mingling with all sorts of workmen and leaving the studio to pour into the neighboring cafeterias and drug stores. Even more amusing was to see them installed in a file on the high stools in front of the counter. When the extras of another film which was shooting at the same time as ours came to lunch dressed in crinolines of the Second Empire, it was wonderful and no one seemed astonished at all!

Saddles, Royal Coaches, and Cannons

A very important thing is the harnessing of the horses. I gave the model of saddles in the style of Pluvinel (the professor of horsemanship of Louis XIII, whose magnificently illustrated work is well-known), and they made up the saddles to perfection. If I was satisfied, however, the horses were less so—and the riders not at all! For example, I was never able to utilize the authentic design of the bit with the long arm. The horses flatly refused and threatened the musketeers with annoying tumbles.

Douglas said to me, "We are going to have to have a *carosse* for the King, one for Queen Anne of Austria, one for Milady de Winter, one for Cardinal Richelieu, one for Father Joseph, plus a sedan chair for Constance Bonacieux." I inspected the broken down vehicles available in the coach-house without hope, and found only a heavy machine of Henry IV or Henri someone, which, thanks to a great deal of overhauling, was awarded to Father Joseph. A monk, above all, must have simple tastes. But for the other royal carriages it was necessary to create them from the beginning.

I put myself to the task and made the necessary working drawings with all the details of construction. The Art Department enlarged all these to full-size drawings, but I was a little apprehensive. I, myself, had had to make up a series of small models of ancient carriages for the museum of carriages and tourism at Compregne, because I could not find in Paris a single workman who could or would undertake it; but now to allow them to be made by American workmen, who understood not a word that I was saying, became another matter. I had been dumbfounded by the cabinet makers that I had to train. In this immense hall of the carpenter shop with all the improved machinery and the connecting belts in movement, among an army of workers, there were presented to me two men, one an old fellow of my age, Pop Schreider, and one young, Paul Wilduska. They

A royal carriage.

understood immediately what I wanted and constructed a royal carriage for Louis XIII, with an exactness, rapidity, and perfection of the undercarriage, wheels and body. It was a little large, a little heavy because it was necessary to give enough strength; these vehicles had a hard test ahead of them and the wood was only Alaska white wood. I had to accept the doors and the roof in wood because solidity was necessary. In one scene Douglas had to climb aboard one of the carriages, and it was necessary to devise a brake to prevent serious accidents. The other carriages followed and the craftsmen, painstaking and disciplined, liking and respecting a boss like Douglas who is as good, fair and affable with the smallest as with the most important, thanked me for having taught them something. And I find myself wondering if on my return to France I would have a good deal of difficulty finding workmen like them.

It was afterward the work of the painters who very cleverly reproduced the arabesques and coats of arms for which I had given them the patterns; the carvers who made all the relief motifs; and the upholsterers, adorning three vehicles with leather, with satin, with velvet with fancy braids of gold.

It was the same when, for the prologue of the film, I had to have some cannons constructed. This prologue is presented like an ancient tapestry with its ornamental border and a central subject under the title "The Iron Mask." In a fortified stronghold, the four musketeers are depicted taking an oath of mutual assistance while crossing their swords. This tapestry is from a water color that I executed. At the end of a moment the central subject comes to life and, always framed by the border, the characters become animated, become alive. D'Artagnan taking two steps forward recites a prologue in verse that the Vitaphone makes heard. The cannons of the stronghold executed to actual size; at the side of the "gabions," cannon balls and "fascines" were so perfect that one would have believed them to be genuine.

The Furniture

All the carriages in *The Iron Mask* are colorfully painted, gilded, and richly decorated in order to come out well in the photography. They seem to us, perhaps, as gaudy as a merry-go-round of wooden horses. We must remember, however, that in the period of time of their original construction, they had been just as shocking. On the other hand, by contrast, too many artists and designers today do not hesitate to depict a scene of the Middle Ages with houses in a tumbledown condition, with sagging, wavy roofs—whereas in the past they had just been freshly built. Similarly, too many times in interior scenes, we see actors in front of tapestries that have been faded as we see them today, whereas they were originally brilliant, high in tone, and bright in colors, as one can perceive from viewing the sides which have survived the centuries sheltered from the light. Likewise, ancient furniture is made to seem of a uniformly chocolate color, the way they appear today, whereas formerly they possessed the fine color of the species of wood of which they were made. And this chocolate tone that the centuries have induced was exaggerated by the walnut stain of which every antiquarian or maker of antiques coats the wood in order to sell his junk, thinking to imitate in this way the patina of time. Apropos of imitation, what I have seen of the antique furniture at United Artists is excellent, because an army of antique dealers lives in Los Angeles. I have frequently accompanied on his visits my friend Burgess Beall, an American artist of much taste, whose delicate duty for this film was to decorate, furnish and adorn all the sets by pilfering all the stores in the region. The massive silver throne that appears in a painting of Versailles had to be reconstructed, as well as the tall vases, the pedestal tables and the silver candelabrum. As to the consumption of materials to which I assisted, it was frightening. The brocades, the damasks, the cloth of gold, the velvets, the satins, the trimming braids arrived at the studio by the hundreds of yards. For the Throne Room of Louis XIV, to be hung with crimson velvet and blue velvet with *fleur-de-lys* on gold, the cloth came in 150 yards at a time.

When one has seen with what toil, what art, what cleverness of craftsmanship an interior set is mounted, one regrets seeing it pass on the screen so swiftly, like an arrow, without time enough for the spectators to admire the perfection and the detail. Above all, I have to admit that it is unfortunate in a black-and-white film *not to see the color*. When I saw on the set the marvelous bed of Anne of Austria, behind the delicately carved balustrade, the bed of the 20-year old Louis XIV, and the bed of the Queen Mother in a wonderful harmony of color, I would have liked to paint these marvelous ensembles and make some good studies to keep. A particularly beautiful scene perfect for a painting was the poignant scene in the bed chamber when Richelieu was dying.

No, the movie set is not like the theater where the set is a painted canvas. Here, it is built, it is tangible, with real wainscoting, real sculptures, real material and real furniture. The carvings are made of plaster which has been transformed into the illusion of species of wood. All the tapestries, copied on canvas from a documentary collection of photographs, were perfect enlargements, four or five meters high. Just think that all these beautiful things are destroyed in the rotation from film to film; that tomorrow these sumptuous palaces, will be in the crematory oven!

Exterior Sets

Laurence Irving created a very interesting exterior set, a Square at St. Germain-en-Laye. It is unnecessary to say that Irving did not try to make an exact reconstitution. That would have been impossible. It was all for the sake of the camera's view.

The wide Square was paved with irregular stones; in the center, a fountain with the muzzles of lions; to the left, an inn; then, a church of the 15th Century, behind which one viewed a winding street. To the right are old houses in wood, their plaster roofs covered with tiles, the ground floors occupied by the signboards of old shops and various stalls for the baker, shoemaker, old clothes seller, barber, etc. Closer to the foreground occupied by the Musketeers was the hostelry with its court, its wells and its stables. When all was built and painted with the spray gun; when the shops were trimmed—some with casks, others with loaves of bread—with boots, with old clogs, with old clothes and hats; when the vine and the glycine covered the walls and framed the windows with their small panes; when the heads of the lions in the fountain were spitting water;

when one saw the court of the hostelry alive with sheep, hogs, fowl and the pigeons on the roofs; when the housewives at the windows spread out their linens; and when the people were coming and going—one truly had the illusion of reality! Then there appeared, coming down the street, the company of Musketeers led by Treville, preceding the drummers and the trumpeters on horseback, waving their banner and surrounding the luxurious *carosse* of Louis XIII pulled by six richly decked out horses. This had great style, viewed from the platform of the cameraman, for it was necessary to be at the exact point of the lens for the sake of the complete illusion. As I have already said, it is only from this vantage point that set and miniature match exactly. Anywhere else, the houses and church appear to have had their upper stories amputated. The hill in the background and the old chateau of St. Germain are only silhouetted in the miniature. And, by the way, I recall that a painter on his double ladder, busy lightening the top of the church, was inadvertently photographed. Nothing is funnier than this church, which seemed to be in one single piece, being repainted by a man the size of Gargantua! The unchanging blue sky of California becomes white in photography. So to avoid this white surface, they camouflaged it like the houses. Above the miniature, placed about 15 feet from the lens, they stretch a gauze that fits the forms of the set. This gauze is dusted with black, in order to obtain the grey value desired.

For another scene they transformed an old set with a German-Alsacian character, which had been used before, into some streets, a Square, old houses, and a little stream where the water ran with continuous currents. This brook, into which a man was going to fall, was a circular ditch lined with tar, where an electric machine imparted to the water a rapid and continuous movement, which gave a perfect imitation of running water. Beside it, in a clearing, was erected a rustic cottage serving as the house of the hangman who was going to execute Milady de Winter. How many trees I watched them bring to furnish all the necessary vegetation! All of them, of medium sizes, were stripped of their branches and replaced with artificial trunks covered with a rough bark made of tow and plaster. They were painted green, because in the California sun, the leaves of cut branches would quickly turn yellow. One exited from the woods by a country road bordered by walls made of big stones piled on each other, and leading to a miniature village that stood against a painted canvas sky. Further on was a little chateau in the Pyrenees where the little twin brother of Louis XIV, the future Man in the Iron Mask, had been confined. In the background was a beautifully accurate silhouette of mountains. It was an enlarged photograph of the Pyrenees cut out and hung before the camera.

A set which was particularly difficult to build was the fortified Chateau erected on a rock in the middle of the river. It was built on pilings in an artificial basin. A bridge with ogival arches led there. But there wasn't enough space to show the water and the opposite bank, because the carpenter shop was too close by. Therefore, they hanged some painted drops measuring at least 150 to 180 feet on which were painted the banks, the hills, and the sky. For the real water in the foreground four boat propellers that were hidden under the pilings and moved by dynamos, made the waves splash strongly—so strongly that one would have said that a steamboat had just passed by! In the background, on each side of the Chateau, it was necessary to have an artificial river taking up the same movement at a reduced perspective. Two slanting platforms were set up on which a green cloth embroidered with particles of mica was stretched rather loosely. A shaft, inside of which was inserted a series of pulleys becoming progressively smaller, received most of the cords that were on top of and underneath the platforms. To these little cords bags of sand were sewn. The green cloth covered everything. The shaft revolved by electricity, which made the pulleys turn and the cords and the bags of sand move under the cloth which rippled and thereby made the particles of mica shimmer. The movement gave an impression of perspective, thanks to the difference in the size of the pulleys.

At the base of the rock on which the chateau was erected was the entry to an underground passage by which d'Artagnan, one stormy night, by the glow of the lightning flashes, entered by boat to rescue the real Louis XIV. Further on were built the underground galleries. This constituted the stage for a heroic struggle where Porthos, putting the flame to a powder cask, was buried with his pursuers under the rubble of rocks. Happily for Porthos, the rocks had only the weight of a package of fritters. I was more anxious that the camera would not register the breathing movement of the dead man's chest!

Locations

I have already said that sometimes scenes were shot in the country outside of the studio. The scenario states that when Constance Bonacieux is kidnapped by Rochefort, she is bound and taken away by Milady de Winter and confined in a convent at Rueil. It is there that d'Artagnan, who has discovered the hiding place of the young girl, came with his friends to tear her away from that prison. They chose a spot on the "Riviera of California," rather far from Hollywood, near the ocean. I went there a few times. The convent, or at least its facade, was constructed from a sketch from Irving. It was necessary to create an alley of large trees, a row of clipped junipers. The bedroom occupied by Constance Bonacieux was situated on the fourth floor, the window protected with iron railings. D'Artagnan, seeing Constance waving to him through the window bars, climbed from branch to branch to the top of a tall tree until he reaches the level of her window. From the tree he made a stupendous leap across the open space, landed with his feet on the window ledge, and seized the bars. Milady, who was in Constance's bedroom, knocked the girl over and hurled herself toward the window to stab d'Artagnan. He fell backward on top of the trees below and from there into the arms of his three friends. All the construction needed for his acrobatic prowess, as well as for the installation of the camera equipment on a scaffold, was very curious and called for some very ingenious processes, although one can detect nothing of that on the screen.

Nothing is more amusing in these locations than what is happening beyond the camera. There might be a long caravan of trucks, some carrying the material for the meals, others the floodlights, the horses, and the carriages. Following are the busses of the stagehands and the electricians. The artists arrive in their own autos, all in costume and make up. The busses bring the hair dressers, the make-up people, secretaries, extras. And what a picturesque spectacle, that of an autobus filled with Musketeers with hooked mustaches, ladies of the Court in low-cut gowns, bandits in rags, and veiled nuns conducted by an abbess who is wearing a cross and smoking cigarettes!

In this site there was to be a terrible attack by the bandits against the Cardinal's carriage. The guards are killed or put to flight, the coachman falls from his seat, and the six horses bolt and race away. D'Artagnan comes to the Cardinal's rescue, jumps on the back of the vehicle, climbs up, takes the place of the coachman, and subdues the horses. It is true that in this case the horses were not seen, and d'Artagnan's climb was onto a motionless vehicle, shaken by stagehands. Behind it all is a painted forest which, mounted on revolving drums, seems to rapidly pass by.

Oh! those beautiful horses of the *carosse*, what training they had to submit to! Every day, from my office, I saw the painted and gilded vehicles, harnessed to their six horses, with the postillion, coachman, and cowboys in short sleeves and big felt hats, going off to make their tour of the city. In Hollywood one is accustomed to this perpetual Mardi Gras, and one hardly pays attention to it. I remember, nevertheless, that one evening, at the Place St. Germain, the carriage of Father Joseph executed a *saraband,* hardly a common-place. The crowd frightened the horses who in turn frightened the crowd as they started off at full speed.

These scenes, shot at night, achieved a very pictorial effect. Male and female extras seated on the drums and benches in the gloom awaited their turn. The floodlights, throwing a blinding light, made a cloud of giant moths dance in front of them. One heard the scream of women brought on by the appearance of enormous tarantulas. And the Cardinal's guards went bravely to hunt the spiders. Sometimes this extended until well after midnight.

The End of the Picture and the Return

I am unable to give an account of the final assemblage of the film as I am not familiar with the process myself. But I did see *The Iron Mask* shot from day to day, the scenes photographed out of sequence, with each scene projected the next day at the "rushes." They had printed 300,000 feet of film, which would have lasted for many hours if uncut. This necessitated the cutting, or editing, an indispensable and tricky art for which it is necessary to have a feeling and expertness in dramatic art that few people possess. In short, since I am the public, I will not know this film on which I have cooperated until I go, like everyone else, to see it in the theater. I hope it will be a pleasing experience to the audiences of both the old and the new continents.

Finally, December drew near. I had been in Hollywood for five months. Some important works were waiting for me in Paris, including the position of Curator of a Museum and Academy of Costume. I had carried out my tasks on *The Iron Mask* with pleasure, and as conscientiously as possible. Now I had to return home.

The actors left the studio as their parts were finished. The designers departed. No more could you see the plumed hats, the swords, and the gowns with trains occupying the little neighboring restaurants. It was the final curtain, although the liveliness of the studio was undiminished. Other companies were shooting other films there. Mary Pickford was beginning to make her first talkie [*Coquette*, 1929], which will probably take several months of work.

After having said good-bye to Douglas Fairbanks and all my friends in California, on my way to the station I wanted to take one last glance at the studio where I had passed so many good moments. They were shooting one of the last scenes of *The Iron Mask*. Everyone, actors and extras in costume, cameramen, electricians, surrounded me to shake my hand while the orchestra played the *Marseillaise*. This could have been very funny and yet I was deeply moved, almost as much as when, to celebrate my birthday and my 75 years, everyone gathered in order to offer me a magnificent memento. Except for Douglas and Mary Pickford, maybe one or two other friends who will come to France, I will never see these kind people again who have shown me so much friendship.

Several friends accompanied me to the railroad station. Among them was Laurence Irving, who said to me, "You have made the conquest of California. To the conquerors one gives the keys of the cities. Here is the key to Los Angeles." And he gave me an enormous gold key on which, around a medallion representing the City Hall of Los Angeles, is inscribed "Key to California."

I was no longer going to see the bright sun of Hollywood. The next morning I was on the plateau of the Colorado River, at 2500 meters altitude, at the edge of the Grand Canyon. This fantastic precipice is a crevasse 20 kilometers (14 miles) wide, 1500 to 1800 meters deep, bristling with peaks, actual mountains, rocks blood red, black, grey, yellow or bluish. One perceives at the bottom, between these cliffs of black granite, the Colorado River, which is wider than the Seine. I could not descend because of the weather. All along its 300 kilometers (nearly 200 miles) there are only three paths to take you down there. One rents mules, one carries provisions and water. One must not be subject to dizziness. After having skirted these steep cliffs by the narrow path that borders them for an entire day, and after contemplating the sunset on this implausible stage setting, we resumed our course across the desert to Chicago.

In passing through New York before re-embarking on the *Ile de France*, I passed anew four or five hours at the Metropolitan Museum. Museums attract painters like me like liquor stores attract drunkards.

Americans all the time were saying to me, "Your eyes will get so accustomed to the immensity, the size beyond measure that everything takes in America—the untamed plains, the beaches, farms, rivers, lakes, towns, constructions—that when you return to France, everything will seem to you poor, small, and shabby." Oh well. I must believe that my stay in the New World must have been insufficient, because in the train from Le Havre to Paris, in spite of the winter season, I found the Normandie landscapes that marched past my eyes, still charming.

Upon arriving back in Paris, people asked me what was the most outstanding thing that I had seen in California? I listed the Grand Canyon of the Colorado, the burning of the oil wells, the beauty of the women, and the height of the buildings. Above all, there was the science and the perfection of execution of the crafts of the Cinema, the excellent spirit and the affection for the work. These things should be envied by us. I loved the delightful mentality of the Americans who welcomed me as a friend and who showed, with perfect tact, an affection for which, I must admit, I was not prepared.

When I first left France someone had said to me, "The American is only a businessman. He values only appearance and bluff. You must take this into account; you must flabbergast him in order for him to hold you in esteem." But it is only due to our ignorance that the Americans are slandered. I can only speak of those whom I saw, the people who surrounded me. I must report that the truth is quite different. One has seen so many bragging, tricky Frenchmen that one is on one's guard. But the Americans are very shrewd, and as soon as they see that they are dealing with an honest man who doesn't boast, who isn't trying to pass for that which he is not, without pretension or subterfuge, his arms open, and with the enthusiasm of grown up children, they receive you in a touching fashion, with all their youthful and good heart. Moreover, I believe that if many Frenchmen of open and simple character were to come to America, their prejudices would fall, and one would soon be able to say, without repeating a ready-made phrase, that the two nations are sisters; and wouldn't it be beautiful to see the two peoples mingling their qualities—America with its vigor, its boldness, its energy, its willingness; and we with our traditions, our experience of the past, our artistic taste and our good humor. Our hearts are the same. Are we not made to understand each other?

NOTES

Foreword

1. Charles Stevens was an authentic Indian who played in every Fairbanks film; he had something like nine parts in *The Black Pirate.* He was invariably cast as villain—sometimes a gut-eating savage—but Fairbanks loved him and he was one of his closest friends. Studio publicity did what it could for him—even describing him as the son of Geronimo!—but he never became an important actor.

Introduction

1. Vachel Lindsay, "The Great Douglas Fairbanks," *Ladies Home Journal*, August 1916, 12.

2. Robert E. Sherwood, "Robin Hood Rides upon the Screen," *Literary Digest*, November 18, 1922, 32–33.

3. Douglas Fairbanks Jr., "Dad," *Theater*, May 1930, 75.

4. "How Can Doug Stay Away from Hollywood?" *Motion Picture Magazine*, February 1934, 82.

5. Allene Talmey, *Doug and Mary and Others* (New York: Macy-Masius, 1927), 39.

6. Booten Herndon, *Mary Pickford and Douglas Fairbanks* (New York: W. W. Norton & Company, 1977), 302.

7. Herndon, 302.

8. Gary Carey, *Doug & Mary* (New York: E. P. Dutton, 1977), vi.

9. Richard Schickel, *His Picture in the Papers* (New York: Charterhouse, 1973), 7, 90.

10. Gaylyn Studlar, *This Mad Masquerade: Stardom and Masculinity in the Jazz Age* (New York: Columbia University Press, 1996).

11. Jeffrey Vance, *Douglas Fairbanks* (Los Angeles: University of California Press and The Academy of Motion Picture Arts and Sciences, 2008).

12. Frederic Lombardi, *Allan Dwan and the Rise and Decline of the Hollywood Studios* (Jefferson, NC: McFarland & Company, 2013).

13. John C. Tibbetts and James M. Welsh, *His Majesty the American: The Films of Douglas Fairbanks, Sr.* (Cranbury, NJ: A. S. Barnes, 1977).

14. Quoted in Tibbetts and Welsh, *His Majesty the American*, 9.

15. For accounts of the activities of the National Film Society and its journal, see the trilogy of books *American Classic Screen*, edited and written by Tibbetts and Welsh (Lanham, MD: Scarecrow Press, 2010). "What attracted me so much about *American Classic Screen*," writes Kevin Brownlow in the foreword to volume one (*Interviews*), "was that it did not regard the silent cinema as something primitive and peculiar . . . *ACS* was enthusiastic and spread the word about how extraordinary these pictures could be. In fact, enthusiasm was its watchword and I have missed that quality ever since" (ix). See also the profile by silent-film authority Anthony Slide in *International Film, Radio, and Television Journals* (Westport, CT: Greenwood Press, 1985), 12–16.

16. Alistair Cooke, *Douglas Fairbanks: The Making of a Screen Character* (New York: The Museum of Modern Art, 1940), 31.

17. Geoff Brown, *Alistair Cooke at the Movies* (New York: Allen Lane, 2009), 292.

18. Schickel, *His Picture in the Papers*, 163–64.

19. As influential as Cooke's study has been, it is very strange that, although a handful of brief excerpts from Cooke continue to be quoted by almost everyone who has subsequently written about Fairbanks, no one has bothered to probe into the circumstances of how it came to be written, and how an English journalist, who is known today primarily as the host for the PBS *Masterpiece Theatre* series, was in a position to write such an insightful study. Geoff Brown's new book, *Alistair Cooke at the Movies* (2009), from which the following quotations appear, provides a most welcome context. Long before he settled in his mid-twenties in America in 1937, Alistair Cooke (1908–2004) was already a veteran film critic. Just in his mid-twenties and fresh from a university career on both side of the Atlantic, at Cambridge, Yale, and Harvard, he began broadcasting movie commentaries for the BBC on October 8, 1934, and continued for the next three years. In his "Critic's Testament," he wrote, "I declare that I am a critic trying to interest a lot of people into seeing, a few ambitious people into making, interesting films. I have no personal interest in any company. As a critic I am without politics and without class . . . My malice extends only to those who have a dull talent and continue to exploit it" (11). Selected for praise, for example, are those comic masterpieces *The Thin Man* and *Design for Living*; and for scorn John Cromwell's wartime weepie, *The Fountain*. During that time he also wrote film columns for *Sight and Sound*, published by the newly formed British Film Institute.

In 1937, Cooke moved permanently to America, where he settled in New York and took U.S. citizenship in 1941. Immediately upon arriving, he edited a volume of film essays by himself and others, *Garbo and the Night Watchmen*. He broadcast reviews on WQXR and continued broadcasting back to Britain until the outbreak of the war. In 1939, he began delivering lectures at the Film Study extension course of Columbia University, organized in conjunction with the Museum of Modern Art. The connection with Iris Barry, the curator of MoMA's film library's curator, led to Cooke's organization shortly after Fairbanks's death of a landmark Fairbanks film retrospective, from May 6 to June 30, 1940, the first such retrospective of a film star (the bulk of surviving materials had been deposited at MoMA two years before). The opportunity culminated what had already been Cooke's lifelong enthusiasm for Fairbanks. Growing up in northwest England, in Salford and Blackpool, Cooke had come to relish, as historian Geoff Brown notes, "Douglas Fairbanks' athletic adventures [which had] taught him to relish American pep, optimism, and cheer" (xix). Cooke himself recalled in a broadcast on December 20, 1939, "I spent a lot of time, between the ages of nine and twelve, in a gymnasium . . . I did learn to do some tricks, and it became a pleasure for anybody who had some training to identify the things he could do with what Fairbanks was doing" (292).

In his program notes for MoMA, Cooke acknowledged that "the charm of Fairbanks was the trajectory of his private life and that the movies were already the only known art which might catch it on the wing." The early comedies, moreover, "parodied, with no discernable time-lag, the pattern of a rapidly changing social scene; and the Fairbanks screen character flattered the average American's ability to meet and conquer every puzzling fad and affectation of the day: at one time or another he briskly demolished the Eastern clubman, pacifists, blue-bloods, ouija boards, slumming parties, pictorial journalism, nervous breakdowns, bobbed hair, and Couéism." About the later costume epics of the 1920s, Cooke wittily noted that his physical prowess had prepared his audiences for the sights of Robin Hood and d'Artagnan "playing Douglas Fairbanks for awhile." Cooke concludes, in general, that the sight of Fairbanks in motion "is a kind of spiritual grace; and it is as surely an indigenous gift of the movies as the flying feet of Fred Astaire, as Disney, or the skimming shore-bird of *The Song of Ceylon*." These program notes led to the extended essay we know as *Douglas Fairbanks: The Making of a Screen Character.*

20. See Chapters Four and Five of *His Majesty the American*, 53–102.

21. G. K. Chesterton, *What I Saw in America* (London: Hodder and Stoughton, 1932), 277.

22. Cooke, *Douglas Fairbanks*, 20.

23. G. K. Chesterton, *Manalive* (London and New York: Thomas Nelson and Sons, 1912), 30–34; 368.

24. Quoted in Alma Guillermoprieto, "Merce Cunningham & the Impossible," *New York Review*, February 9, 2012, 29.

25. This anecdote was first reported in Hancock, 275. Vance repeats it in his biography, 306.

26. The words are uttered by the character of Tommy Sandys in James M. Barrie's *Tommy and Grizel* (1900). He was Barrie's "adult" Peter Pan—and he just as well stands in for Douglas Fairbanks. The full quote is singularly apt: "I was given wings, I think, but I am never to know that I have left the earth until I come flop upon it, with an arrow through them. . . . and yet, I believe I am rather a fine fellow when I am flying" (New York: The Readers Club, 1943, 240).

Chapter 1

1. Vance, *Douglas Fairbanks*, 32.

2. Douglas Fairbanks, "Let Me Say This for the Films," *Ladies Home Journal* 39, no. 5 (1922), 13.

3. John C. Tibbetts, *The American Theatrical Film: Stages in Development* (Bowling Green, OH: Popular Press, 1985). See the chapter, "Feature Attractions: Theater/ Collaborations, 1912–1915," 53–111.

4. George Creel, "A 'Close-Up' of Douglas Fairbanks," *Everybody's*, December 1916, 732.

5. Los Angeles historian and Fairbanks authority Dr. Tracey Goessel is hard at work documenting these years of transition. We hope her book will be published soon.

6. Studlar, *This Mad Masquerade*, 13.

7. Patricia King Hanson, ed., *The American Film Institute Catalogue, Feature Films, 1911–1920* (Berkeley, Los Angeles: University of California Press), 498.

8. Ralph Hancock and Letitia Fairbanks, *Douglas Fairbanks: The Fourth Musketeer* (New York: Henry Holt, 1953), 120.

9. Fairbanks, "Let Me Say This for the Films," 14.

10. Montrose Moses, *The American Dramatist* (Boston: Little, Brown and Company, 1925), 203–204.

11. *Bookman*, February 1914, 611–12.

12. *Blue Book Magazine*, April 1914, 1044–45.

13. "The New Henrietta," *Theater Magazine*, February 1914, 62.

14. For a true adaptation of *The New Henrietta*, see Buster Keaton's first feature film, *The Saphead*, released in 1920.

15. Unidentified press clipping from a collection of clippings, New York Public Library, Lincoln Center, New York City.

16. "Knickerbocker Opening," *Motography*, October 2, 1915, 663.

17. Studlar, *This Mad Masquerade*, 10.

18. Ibid., 30.

19. *Variety*, October 1, 1915, 18.

20. For a discussion of this film, see Siegfried Kracauer, *From Caligari to Hitler* (New Jersey: Princeton University Press, 1969), 34.

21. Studlar, *This Mad Masquerade*, 35.

Chapter 2

1. Anthony Slide, ed., *Before, In and After Hollywood: The Autobiography of Joseph E. Henabery* (Lanham, MD & London: Scarecrow Press, 1997), 153–54

2. Heretofore, only two studies have considered these pre-1920 films in any detail, the authors' *His Majesty the American*; and Gaylyn Studlar's chapter, "Building Mr. Pep:

Boy Culture and the Construction of Douglas Fairbanks," in *This Mad Masquerade*, 10–89.

3. Quoted in Paul F. Boller Jr., *American Thought in Transition* (Lanham, MD: University Press of America, 1982), 227.

4. Cooke, *Douglas Fairbanks*, 17.

5. Studlar, *This Mad Masquerade*, 25.

6. "The Shadow Stage," *Photoplay*, March 1917, 117.

7. Henri Bergson, "Laughter," in *Comedy* (New York: Doubleday Anchor Books, 1956), 62.

8. Gary Carey, "Written on the Screen," *Film Comment*, Winter 1970, 51, 71.

9. Ibid., 313.

10. Anita Loos, *A Girl Like I* (New York: Viking Press, 1966), 154.

11. G. K. Chesterton, *Charles Dickens, The Last of the Great Men* (New York: The Readers Club, 1942), 158–59.

12. Loos, *A Girl*, 221.

13. Ibid., 273.

14. Ibid., 215.

15. Ibid., 253–54.

16. Anita Loos in *Picture-Play*, October 1918, 251.

17. G. K. Chesterton, *The Defendant* (London: J. M. Dent and Sons, 1901), 125–26.

18. Studlar, *This Mad Masquerade*, 50.

19. Quoted in Terry Teachout, *The Skeptic: A Life of H. L. Mencken* (New York: Harper/Collins, 2002), 143.

20. Carey, "Written," 51.

21. *Flirting with Fate* was released on July 1916, directed by Christy Cabanne, and written by Robert M. Baker. A rather somber affair with a few flashes of obligatory climbing and vaulting confined to the final reel, it tells the story of penniless artist Augy Holliday who, disconsolate by a series of misfortunes, contracts with an assassin, one "Automatic Joe," to kill him. The titles are a pretty tiresome lot, imposing on the viewer with an unwonted familiarity, like the boorish guest who won't leave the party.

22. Karl Schmidt in *Everybody's*, May 1917, 622.

23. John Emerson and Anita Loos, *How to Write Photoplays* (Philadelphia: George W. Jacobs and Co., 1923), 39.

24. *Photoplay*, July 1918, 88–89.

25. *Everybody's*, May 1917, 622.

26. Loos, *A Girl*, 98–99.

27. Paul Grant, "John, Anita, and the Giftie," *Photoplay*, December 1917, 50.

28. After 1919, Emerson lost interest in directing and turned to producing some of Loos's later films, notably *San Francisco*. After a long illness, including mental instability, Emerson died in 1956. They were never divorced.

29. "The Shadow Stage, *Photoplay*, March 17, 1917, 109.

30. Lary May, *Screening out the Past: The Birth of Mass Culture and the Motion Picture Industry* (New York: Oxford University Press, 1980), 116–17.

31. "His Picture in the Papers," *Variety*, February 4, 1916, 24.

32. "The Matrimaniac," *Variety*, December 4, 1916, 11.

33. Chesterton, *Charles Dickens*, 154.

34. Henry Jenkins, *What Made Pistachio Nuts?* (New York: Oxford University Press, 1992), 216–19.

35. Cooke, *Douglas Fairbanks*, 18.

36. Peter Bogdanovich, *Allan Dwan: The Last Pioneer* (New York: Praeger, 1971), 25.

37. *Theater*, January 1927, 38.

38. Bogdanovich, *Allan Dwan*, 109.

39. Ibid.

40. Quoted in Lombardi, *Allan Dwan*, 85.

41. "Fred," "The Habit of Happiness," *Variety*, March 13, 1916, 5.

42. *New York Times*, March 13, 1916, 5.

43. "Reggie Mixes In," *New York Times*, May 29, 1916, 9.

44. "Reggie Mixes In," *Variety*, June 2, 1916, 16.

45. "D.P.: "Dramatic Dynamo," *Motion Picture Classic*, February 17, 1917, n.p.

46. Studlar, *This Mad Masquerade*, 43.

47. The loss of so many Artcraft films—including some of Fairbanks's films released at the height of his career—is one of the tragedies of film history. Kevin Brownlow reports that of a reported 1,014 features, only 37 have been preserved. "Fairbanks offered his films to MoMA, but they didn't take very good care of them. It is very sad." (Brownlow letter to authors, April 21, 2013.)

48. *Mr. Fix-It* has been restored from a negative in the Eastman House collection and brought to the San Francisco Film Festival in 2011 by that indefatigable Fairbanks enthusiast and scholar, Dr. Tracey Goessel. "I suspect that parts of the print are missing, as it runs short, and was an Italian print. Our family foundation funded the restoration of English titles, and a couple of prints for the archives." (Correspondence with the authors.)

49. Lombardi, *Allan Dwan*, 43.

50. "Mr. Fix-It," *Variety*, April 5, 1918, 42.

51. http://article.archive.nytimes.com/1918/09/97026263.

52. For details on Roosevelt's own physical regimen, see David McCullough, *Mornings on Horseback* (New York: Simon and Schuster, 1981), 110–14.

53. Lary May, *Screening the Past*, 114–16.

54. Douglas Fairbanks, *Laugh and Live* (New York: Britton Publishing Co., 1917), 12.

55. For a discussion of the "New Nationalism," see Aida D. Donald, *Lion in the White House* (New York: Basic Books, 2007), 250–60.

56. William Allen White, "Roosevelt: A Force for Righteousness," *McClure's*, February 1907, 389.

57. Henry F. May, *The End of American Innocence* (Chicago: Quandrangle Books, 1964), 18.

58. Ibid.

59. Allen, *The Big Change*, 98.

60. Douglas Fairbanks, "How I Keep Running on High," *American Magazine*, August 1922, 37.

61. Quoted in McGloughlin, *Billy Sunday Was His Real Name* (University of Chicago Press, 1955), 45.

62. Ibid., 224.

63. Booth Tarkington's classic comment is here quoted in full: "Fairbanks is a faun who has been to Sunday School. He has a pagan body which yields instantly to any heathen or gypsy impulse—as an impulse to balance a chair on its nose while hanging from the club chandelier by one of its knees—but he has a mind reliably furnished with a full set of morals and proprieties: he would be a sympathetic companion for anybody's aunt. I don't know his age; I think he hasn't any. Certainly he will never be older—unless quicksilver can get old." See Booth Tarkington, "Booth Tarkington Sends Us This Word about Douglas Fairbanks," insert in Fairbanks, "Combining Play with Work," *American Magazine*, July 1917, 33.

64. Quoted in Richard Hofstadter, *Anti-Intellectualism in American Life* (New York: Alfred A. Knopf, 1966), 115.

65. Ibid., 119.

66. See a useful discussion of the Social Gospel in Paul F. Boller, *American Thought in Transition*, 120–122.

67. Sinclair Lewis, *Elmer Gantry* (New York: Harcourt, Brace, and Co., 1927), 358.

68. McLoughlin, *Billy Sunday*, xx.

69. Ibid., 159–60.

70. William T. Ellis, *Billy Sunday: The Man and His Message* (New York: F. W. Mead Publishing Co., 1936), 26.

71. Ibid., 138.

72. Bogdanovich, *Allan Dwan*, 40.

73. McLoughlin, *Billy Sunday*, 163.

74. Ibid., 73.

75. Bogdanovich, *Allan Dwan*, 40–42.

76. *Photoplay*, August 1920, 57.

77. As quoted by Cleveland Amory, *Who Killed Society?* (New York: Harpers, 1960), 64.

78. As quoted by Henry Nash Smith, *Virgin Land* (New York: Vintage Books, 1950), 144.

79. Amory, *Society*, 9.

80. Henry James, *Hawthorne* (New York: St. Martin's Press, 1967), 57.

81. G. Edward White, *The Eastern Establishment and the Western Experience* (New Haven: Yale University Press, 1968), 6.

82. E. Digby Baltzell, as quoted by White, *The Eastern Establishment and the Western Experience*, 17–18.

83. Loos, *A Girl*, 73.

84. “American Aristocracy,” *Variety*, November 6, 1916, 9.

85. For an account of the stage play and film, see Tibbetts, *The American Theatrical Fllm*, 65–69.

86. Lombardi, *Allan Dwan*, 86.

87. Jack G. Shaheen, *Reel Bad Arabs: How Hollywood Vilifies a People* (New York: Olive Branch Press, 2001), 2.

88. “His Majesty the American,” *Variety*, October 31, 1919; Julian Johnson, “His Majesty the American,” *Photoplay*, December 1919, 117.

89. “A Defence of Heraldry,” in Chesterton, *The Defendant*, 109.

90. Ibid., 62.

91. Lary May, *Screening the Past*, 117.

92. A book-length study of Disney’s European sources is Robin Allan, *Walt Disney and Europe* (Bloomington, Indiana: Indiana University Press, 1999).

93. P. F. Reniers, “The Three Musketeers,” *New York Evening Post*, August 19, 1921, in *American Film Criticism*, ed. Stanley Kauffmann (New York: Liveright, 1972), 126.

94. Siegfried Kracauer, *The Mass Ornament: Weimar Essays* (Cambridge, MA: Harvard University Press, 1995), 293

95. Chesterton, *What I Saw in America*, 277.

Chapter 3

1. It will be recalled that the character of M. Lange imagines himself in a highly successful series of magazine articles as the redoubtable “Arizona Jim,” hero of a thousand scrapes and tussles, in Jean Renoir’s *Le Crime de M. Lange* (1937). Lange/“Jim” keeps a map of America on his wall, where a crudely inscribed circle marks Arizona’s boundaries.

2. Douglas Fairbanks, “Why I Left the Stage,” *Motion Picture Classic*, September 1917, 46.

3. William K. Everson, *The Western* (New York: Bonanza Books, 1962), 125.

4. See Richard Slotkin’s invaluable study of these and related issues, *Gunfighter Nation* (Norman, OK: University of Oklahoma Press, 1998).

5. Ibid., 61.

6. White, *The Eastern Establishment and the Western Experience*, 4.

7. Edwin Fussell, *Frontier: American Literature and the American* West (Princeton: Princeton University Press, 1965), 4.

8. Henry Nash Smith, *Virgin Land: The American West as Symbol and Myth* (Hew York: Vintage Books, 1950), 143.

9. Fussell, *Frontier*, 211.

10. Leslie Fiedler, *Love and Death in the American Novel* (New York: Stein and Day, 1966), 196.

11. Quoted in Smith, *Virgin Land*, 111.

12. Joe Frantz and Julian Choate Jr., *The American Cowboy: The Myth and the Reality* (Norman, OK: University of Oklahoma Press, 1955), 121.

13. Smith, *Virgin Land*, 124–25.

14. George Creel, "A 'Close-Up' of Douglas Fairbanks," *Everybody's*, December 1916, 729–38.

15. See two essential histories of this subject: Richard Abel, *Red Rooster Scare: Making Cinema American, 1900–1910* (Los Angeles: University of California, 1999), 14–25; Abel, *Americanizing the Movies, and "Movie-Mad" Audiences, 1910–1914* (Los Angeles: University of California Press, 2006), 61–84.

16. Loos, *A Girl*, 154.

17. Michael Sragow, *Victor Fleming* (New York: Pantheon, Books, 2008), 10.

18. Ibid., 53.

19. John C. Tibbetts, "Glen MacWilliams: Following the Sun with a Veteran Hollywood Cameraman," *American Classic Screen* 3, no. 3 (1979), 32–39. All subsequent quotes from MacWilliams come from this article.

20. Authors' correspondence with Tracey Goessel, April 14, 2013. Earlier, truncated and altered versions demonstrate the mutilations that all too often have damaged silent films. For example, all the characters in the Grapevine version have different names on the title cards. Lo Dorman is "Dave Carson," a "Wilderness Man." All we know about him is that he has fled from "civilization with its stifling restraints." The silly city girl "Nellie" is now "Peggy," and the dance hall girl "Teresa" is now "Dolores of the Faro Palace." The early scenes with the naturalist are missing, as is the famous bathing scene in the forest with the half-nude Fairbanks. Also missing are any references to scandal regarding his relationships with Nellie/Peggy. There are a few scenes of drunken Indians whooping it up in the forest and starting a forest fire. (A title card describes these Indians as debauched "children of nature" living in a "blighted" forest.) We also see Fairbanks rescuing the dance-hall girl who is fleeing her boss. He takes her to his tree-home. And there's a scene when the city girl comes to the forest. He shows her the way out, but not before she embraces him and moves to kiss him (but he turns away). In one of the rewritten titles, she says:

> *"What a strange man you are! Is it living apart from the world that has made you like this? . . . It seems that I understand the secret of your life here, far from the petty world I live in."*

The last scenes in the fragment have Fairbanks saying farewell to the forest—

> *"Civilization has overtaken me; farewell, my wilderness"*

And, in a radical reversal of the original plot, he returns to civilization to take up with the city girl, rather than with the dance hall girl! There's an interesting intertitle card here:

The last frontier is always vanishing. Civilization, unhindered, marches on—with the conquest of each Wilderness Man.

That scene is followed by Fairbanks lifting the city girl over a fence, followed by a "The End" title card. (This sequence transpires midway through the original film.)

Historian Kevin Brownlow suggests that these fragments are "a reissue from the 1920s when the distributor was trying to feather up the old Triangle pictures to appeal to the flappers." Some of the names, he speculates, must have been changed because they seemed "old-fashioned, too staid." Or: "The change in character names sometimes happened between foreign and domestic releases—they were always messing about with foreign releases, and I have never seen a foreign release which was on a par with the American original." Moreover, perhaps the fear of censorship necessitated dropping the nude sequence. (Letter to authors from Kevin Brownlow, December 21, 2012.)

21. Lombardi, *Allan Dwan*, 63.

22. Quoted in ibid.

23. Bret Harte, *In the Carquinez Woods* (Forgotten Books; originally published in 1884 by Houghton Mifflin).

24. Slide, ed., *Before, In and After Hollywood*, 153, 162–67.

25. David Dary, *Cowboy Culture* (New York: Alfred A. Knopf, 1981), 325–26.

26. For an overview of the various incarnations of *The Virginian*, see John C. Tibbetts, "The Stage Goes West: Routes to *The Virginian*," *Indiana Social Studies Quarterly* 34:2 (Autumn 1981), 26–39.

27. Owen Wister, *The Virginian: A Horseman of the Plains* (New York: Bantam Books, 1985), 286.

28. Slotkin, *Gunfighter Nation*, 180–81.

29. Lombardi, *Allan Dwan*, 82. Dwan's 1938 *The Three Musketeers* was a strange mixture of drama and musical farce. Don Ameche was the d'Artagnan to the Ritz Brothers' musketeers.

30. Slotkin, *Gunfighter Nation*, 52.

31. Quoted in Sragow, *Victor Fleming*, 85.

32. Studlar, *This Mad Masquerade*, 351.

33. "Wild and Woolly," *Variety*, July 13, 1917, 27.

34. Vance, *Douglas Fairbanks*, 47.

35. Slotkin, *Gunfighter Nation*, 56.

36. Douglas Branch, *The Cowboy and His Interpretors* (New York: Cooper Square Publishers, Inc., 1926), 17.

37. R. W. B. Lewis, *The American Adam* (University of Chicago Press, 1955), 7–10. He cites Emerson's vision of the divisions of the American experience into a "party of the Past and the Party of the Future," or Memory and Hope. Lewis adds a third component, i.e., the party of *irony*, the sense of ironic detachment regarding the collision of Memory and Hope, innocence and experience. In Fairbanks's westerns, that irony achieves a particularly comic ambivalence.

38. Henabery, *Before, In and After Hollywood*, 158–59.

39. Quoted in Lombardi, *Allan Dwan*, 61–62.

40. *The House that Shadows Built* was a fifty-five-minute anthology film released in 1931 made to celebrate the twentieth anniversary of the studio that became Paramount. In addition to an excerpt from *Headin South*, it also included clips from two Mary Pickford films, *The Good Little Devil* (1913) and *The Little American* (1917). The film was a promotional film for exhibitors and never had a regular theatrical release.

41. Lombardi, *Allan Dwan*, 87.

42. Frank Thompson, *Lost Films: Important Movies That Have Disappeared* (New York: Citadel Press, 1996), 86–94.

43. Wister, *The Virginian*, 262.

44. Ibid., 96.

45. See John C. Tibbetts, "Splendidly Self-Propelled: Douglas Fairbanks' *The Gaucho*," *Films in Review* XLVII, no. 718 (July-August 1996): 96–101.

46. For an amusing account of these escapades, see Ralph Hancock and Letitia Fairbanks, *Douglas Fairbanks: The Fourth Musketeer*, 1–11.

Chapter 4

1. Lary May, *Screening the Past*, 109.

2. Ibid., 119–42.

3. It is misleading to infer that the majority of Mary Pickford's films featured little-girl protagonists. Pickford played a little girl in only seven of her fifty-two feature films, and in only three did she remain a child throughout (*The Poor Little Rich Girl*, *Rebecca of Sunnybrook Farm*, and *The Little Princess*). Unjustly neglected and now forgotten are a variety of "mature" roles Pickford essayed in the numerous short films and twenty-three feature films she made before and after *The Poor Little Rich Girl*. In the years at Biograph for Griffith, she had played criminals and prostitutes. In her pre-1917 features she played a deposed Bosnian queen in *Such a Little Queen* (1914), the mother of an illegitimate child in *Hearts Adrift* (1914), a rebellious wife in *Behind the Scenes* (1914), an Alaskan Inuit in *Little Pal* (1915), a cross-dressing spy in *Nell Gwynn* (1915), a factory worker who protested sweatshop labor in *The Eternal Grind* (1916), and suicidal mothers in *Hearts Adrift* (1914) and *Madame Butterfly* (1915), to cite just a few. In later films she played a woman secretly married to a German spy in *The Love Light* (1921), a Spanish street singer in *Rosita* (1923), a southern belle accused of murder in *Coquette* (1929), the headstrong Kate in *The Taming of the Shrew* (1929), and a sexy chorus girl in *Kiki* (1931).

4. Robert Windeler, *Sweetheart: The Story of Mary Pickford* (New York: Praeger, 1973), 96.

5. Mary Pickford, *Sunshine and Shadow* (Garden City, NY: Doubleday & Company, Inc., 1955), 46.

6. In 1901, the nine-year-old Pickford portrayed Evangeline St. Clare, "Little Eva," in a Canadian production of Uncle Tom's Cabin. "[She] was the ubiquitous, everyday, wonderful girl about whom thousands of popular songs and movies have been made," writes Ann Douglas in *The Feminization of American Culture* (New York: Alfred A. Knopf, 1977): "Like her descendants, she flatters the possibilities of her audience; she does not quicken their aspirations" (4). Her primary achievement was to die a lingering death of consumption, which subsequently canonized her as the very epitome of the saintly child. Her last words are a plea for her father to free his slaves and to become a serious Christian. "We are meant to bestow on her that fondness we reserve for the contemplation of our own softer emotions," writes Douglas. "Her only real demand on her readers is for self-indulgence" (4).

Later, in 1913, after achieving a measure of screen fame with Biograph, Pickford returned to the stage as Juliet, the blind girl in David Belasco's production of Austin Strong's adaptation of *The Good Little Devil*, a fairy play by Rosemonde Gerard and Maurice Rostand. Although the play is forgotten—the original playscript has never been translated into English and Pickford's subsequent 1914 screen version is unavailable for screening—it was enormously popular in its day. Juliet, like Little Eva, was a damaged creature whose inner faith in spiritual values lift her above her infirmities. Critics applauded what movie audiences had already been quick to notice: "Miss Pickford not only looks the little Juliet to perfection—a beautiful picture child—but acts the role with abundant grace and feeling and real childish spirit." (*New York Times*, January 9, 1913, 9).

7. Pickford, *Sunshine and Shadow*, 46. Pickford expounded on this several times in articles and interviews in the late teens and early twenties. For example, in "The Greatest Business in the World," which appeared under her byline in *Colliers*, June 10, 1922, she wrote: "One deep-seated grudge I held against the world [was] that it had cheated me out of my youth. [After] the death of my father made it necessary for the rest of the family to make a living, life had been merely a procession of jobs. I had never really played; I had never been a real child, with toys and games and time to enjoy them. . . . What I wanted was a real childhood with all the candy I wanted to eat and all the things that other children had. I was becoming a little bitter about it" (22–23).

8. Scott Eyman, *Mary Pickford, America's Sweetheart* (New York: Donald I. Fine, 1990), 91. Pickford's biographers all agree that *The Poor Little Rich Girl* was one of the major turning points in her screen career. See Eyman, 91; Herndon, 156; Windeler, 98. Commentator Edward Wagenknecht flatly pronounced the year of its release, 1917, "possibly the greatest in Mary's career" (150).

9. Only once before had Pickford experimented with a little-girl role on screen, in a brief flashback sequence in *The Foundling* (1916), scripted by her longtime collaborator, scenarist Frances Marion.

10. *Exhibitor's Trade Review*, March 10, 1917, 976.

11. Bert D. Essex, "Poor Little Rich Girl," *Photoplay Journal*, April 1917, 33.

12. Douglas, *The Feminization of American Culture*, 3–4.

13. Pickford, *Sunshine and Shadow*, 252.

14. In *Popcorn Venus* (Coward-McCann, 1973), Marjorie Rosen singles out the "growing girl" films for a vigorous attack that can only be based on ignorance of the films themselves: "Her specialty was the winsome waif, the sweet and sturdy ragamuffin who would not disturb the status quo, flirt with immorality, or exude sexuality. Who would not, in short, emerge a woman" (37–38).

15. Mary's wish to destroy her films lacks specific documentation, although it has been alleged in numerous biographies and memoirs dating back to 1931. The most reliable confirmation of this comes from Pickford herself, as quoted by Kevin Brownlow in *Mary Pickford Rediscovered.* When asked by Brownlow if she had ever ordered her films to be incinerated, Pickford purportedly replied, "Definitely. Well, frankly, I didn't want to be compared with the modern trend" (64). Robert Cushman, photographic curator at the Margaret Herrick Library of the Academy of Motion Picture Arts and Sciences, likewise explains that the unavailability of Pickford films has been no accident: "[I]t was Mary herself who had been hesitant to permit screenings, fearing to suffer by comparison to the films of later generations" (in Brownlow, 18). Moreover, she made no provisions in her will for the distribution after her death of her immense collection of stills, papers, and memorabilia crated in boxes at her Pickfair home. Worse, there are lamentable gaps in this collection. According to Cushman, the bulk of her papers from her active years as a star and producer remain a mystery. His detailed account of the eventual installation of this collection at the Academy can be found in pages 46–51.

16. Lynne Vallone, *Disciplines of Virtue: Girls' Culture in the Eighteenth and Nineteenth Centuries* (New Haven: Yale University Press, 1995), 4.

17. Beverly Lyon Clark, "Fairy Godmothers or Wicked Stepmothers?: The Uneasy Relationship of Feminist Theory and Children's Criticism, 1993–1994," *Children's Literature Association Quarterly* 18: 172.

18. Vallone, *Disciplines of Virtue*, 157.

19. Anne Lundin, "Secret Gardens: The Literature of Childhood," *Childhood Education* (Summer 1991), 215.

20. Alfred Habegger, *Gender, Fantasy, and Realism in American Literature* (New York: Columbia University Press, 1982), 159. For discussions and definitions of the Cult of the True Woman, see Alice S. Rossi, ed., *The Feminist Papers: From Adams to de Beauvoir* (New York and London: Columbia University Press, 1973), 252–53. Rossi notes that whereas colonial women had shared many of the productive work skills of her husband, the expanding era of Jacksonian democracy saw women increasingly separated from "the significant work of their society." As her "real" contributions declined in worth, the "Cult of True Womanhood" emerged: "What mattered for a woman by the late 1820s were four qualities: piety, purity, submissiveness, and domesticity. The new prevalent values in the larger Jacksonian society—education, success at work, and political participation—were denied to women" (252). See also Barbara Welter, "The Cult of True Womanhood: 1820–1860," *American Quarterly* XVIII, no. 2 (Summer 1966), 151–174.

By contrast, the emerging "Ideal of the Real Woman" in the second half of the nineteenth century, as advocated by advice books and described by Francis Cogan in *All-American Girl: The Ideal of Real Womanhood in Mid-Nineteenth-Century America* (Athens: University of Georgia Press, 1989), described a woman who was solid, down-to-earth, and productive—"a popular, middle-of-the-road image that recognized the disparities and the dangers protested by early feminists but tried to deal with those ugly realities in what it saw as a 'female' way'" (4). Moreover, Vallone notes that one of the most striking differences between the "True Woman" and the emerging "Real Girl/Woman" was the advocacy of physical fitness and health: "For the girls who were to become pillars of their homes, maintaining a healthy body and mind was considered a moral duty" (114).

21. A particularly cogent examination of this dichotomy is Mark Spilka's "On the Enrichment of Poor Monkeys by Myth and Dream; or, How Dickens Rousseauized and Pre-Freudianized Victorian Views of Childhood," in Don Richard Cox, ed., *Sexuality and Victorian Literature* (Knoxville: University of Tennessee Press, 1985), 161–79.

22. Catherine Maria Sedgwick is a particularly interesting writer from the antebellum period. Her work ranged from advice pamphlets to gothic romances like *Hope Leslie* (1827). Her young heroines, while decidedly "womanly," exhibited a degree of liberality and activism that would have shocked her repressive New England forebears. In *Women's Gothic and Romantic Fiction: A Reference Guide* (Westport, CT: Greenwood Press, 1981), Kay Mussell notes: "Sedgwick's novels are sometimes adventurous, set in historical periods, with elements that some critics defined as gothic. She also, however, seems to have been consciously writing against the sentimental tradition by attempting to construct models of behavior for women who marry only after their character is formed and who can be valued by the men around them for their qualities of integrity and maturity" (9).

23. Vallone, *Disciplines of Virtue*, 114

24. Ibid.

25. Beatrice K. Hofstadter, "Popular Culture and the Romantic Heroine," *The American Scholar* 30, no. 1 (Winter 1961), 102.

26. Until Jo March appeared in 1868, the most popular model for the young heroine in nineteenth century children's fiction was Little Eva. Joe broke the rules of ladylike conduct, displayed a temper, indulged in strong language, and refused a marriage proposal in favor of a career. According to Linda Levstik, "Jo and the other tomboys of children's fiction protested against the restriction inherent in the traditional lifestyle of an American 'lady'" (14). Writing in *Children's Literature in Education* 11, no. 1 (1980), Jill P. May reminds us that Jo is not the only adventurous one of the March sisters. "Jo, Amy and Meg all come to grips with their roles as wives and women by the end of [*Little Women*], and each makes a subtle statement on the right of women to think and act as individuals" (14). Prior to the writing of *Little Women*, Alcott cast a tomboy, Sylvia Yule, as the heroine of her one serious adult novel, *Moods* (1864).

27. This study necessarily excludes the series books featuring girls and young women that appeared after the turn of the century, like the "Dorothy Dale" books; the many

volumes of *The Motor Girls, The Ranch Girls,* and *The Outdoor Girls*; and, later, the "Nancy Drew" books. Although these heroines were adventurous and physically fit, like their Real Girl forebears, they were not, strictly speaking, *growing* girls. Unlike the characters examined here, like Rebecca (of Sunnybrook Farm) and Pollyanna, who mark the transition from girlhood to young adult maturity, a girl like Nancy Drew seemed suspended in time, always sixteen years old, forever "poised, capable, self-sufficient"; someone "who can take care of herself and who needs neither guidance nor exhortation." (See Nye, Russel, *The Unembarrassed Muse: The Popular Arts in America* [New York: The Dial Press, 1970], 87; see also Kismaric, Carole and Marvin Heiferman, *The Mysterious Case of Nancy Drew & the Hardy Boys* [New York: Simon and Schuster, 1997]; and Deborah Felder, "Nancy Drew: Then and Now," *Publishers Weekly,* May 30 1986, 30–34.)

28. Grant M. Overton, *The Women Who Make Our Novels* (New York: Moffat, Yard & Company, 1922), 125.

29. Kate Douglas Wiggin, *Rebecca of Sunnybrook Farm.* (St. Petersburg, FL: Worthington Press, 1993), 129. All quotations from this edition.

30. Kate Douglas Wiggin (1856–1923) was born of New England stock. Her interests in educational reform surface in her popular books. Under the influence of suffragist and progressive educator Carolina M. Severance, she became actively interested in the kindergarten method, which held that instruction could take place through active and amusing play. She supported her educational projects—which included establishing the first free kindergartens in California—with her writing. *The Story of Patsy* (1889) reflects her philosophies as a teacher to abused and neglected children. *Timothy's Quest* (1890) is about two orphan children who narrowly escape incarceration in an orphans' asylum and eventually win over the hard hearts of two selfish spinsters. *Rebecca of Sunnybrook Farm,* which chronicles Rebecca's education as a writer, appeared in 1903, while Wiggin was convalescing from an illness in a New York hospital. The book was hailed by Mark Twain, Sarah Orne Jewett, Jack London, and Frances Hodgson Burnett. See Anita Moss, "Kate Douglas Wiggin," in Glenn E. Estes, ed, *Dictionary of Literary Biography* 42 (Detroit, MI: Gale Research Company, 1985), 381–93.

31. Douglas, *The Feminization of American Culture,* 76.

32. Jean Webster (1875–1916) was educated at Vassar College, where she began what would be a lifelong concern for the plight of children in orphanages and other institutions. She also served on committees for prison reform. Thus, after describing the "soul-crushing" conditions in the John Grier orphanage in *Daddy-Long-Legs,* she tells of the reformation of the place in the sequel, *Dear Enemy.* She died one day after giving birth to a daughter.

33. Jean Webster, *Daddy-Long-Legs* (New York: Alfred A. Knopf, 1993), 200. Lynne Vallone in *Disciplines of Virtue* compares the structure and thematic content of Webster's story of a teenager's "rise in the world" to another novel written in epistolary form, Samuel Richardson's *Pamela* (1740–1741): "Pygmalion stories such as these, created from the 'frisson' of class and gender conflict, continue to interest us with their fairy tale marriages and happy endings" (155).

34. Frances Hodgson Burnett, *A Little Princess* (New York: Platt & Munk, 1967), 1.

35. Marian E. Brown, "Three Versions of *A Little Princess*: How the Story Developed," *Children's Literature in Education* 19, no. 4 (1988): 199–210. Most of the books of Frances Hodgson Burnett (1849–1923) reflect the straitened circumstances of her youth and upbringing. She was born Frances Eliza Hodgson in the industrial city of Manchester, England. Most of her books reflect the circumstances of her upbringing. Her father died of a stroke when she was only three, and she and her four siblings grew up in a poor factory neighborhood. Sensitive to the blight all around her, she sought escape in writing thrilling stories. At Miss Hadfield's School, she quickly grew popular through her ability to entertain the other girls with her stories. In 1865, she and her impoverished family sought fresh opportunities in America. From her log cabin home, Frances pursued her storytelling and began selling stories to publications like *Peterson's Ladies' Magazine* and *Godey's Lady's Book.* After the loss of her mother in 1870, Frances assumed control of the family. Her stories shifted from melodramatic morality fables to more realistic tales, like *Surly Tim's Trouble* (1871) and *Seth* (1872), which drew upon her childhood memories of life in the English mill towns. In 1873, she married a childhood friend, Dr. Swan Burnett. The publication of *Little Lord Fauntleroy* (1885), *A Little Princess* (1903), and *The Secret Garden* (1911) established her worldwide fame. She died in 1924.

36. Rosemary Threadgold, "The Secret Garden: An Appreciation of Frances Hodgson Burnett As a Novelist for Children," *Children's Literature in Education* 10, no. 3 (1979), 116.

37. Lawrence Ferlinghetti and Nancy J. Peters, *Literary San Francisco* (San Francisco: Harper and Row, 1980), 36. Tomboy characters like the orphaned M'liss stem from Bret Harte's experiences in the rough-and-ready wilds of the mining camps of Sonora, California. Harte (1836–1902) was just a boy when he and his mother left Albany, New York, and migrated to California. He was a sensitive youth, uprooted from a gentle, domestic environment and set down at a rough outpost of civilization. His most creative period, which produced "The Luck of Roaring Camp" and "M'liss," stems from the latter 1860s, when he was the editor of the *Overland Monthly* in San Francisco. Although he relocated to New York City after 1871 and published forty-four volumes of prose and verse, he never forgot the stimulus of his years in California: "It was to California, to the very last, that he always looked backward when his literary energy and invention flagged—looked backward in the hope that by imitating himself he could duplicate his earliest successes." See Ben Ray Redman, Introduction, *The Works of Bret Harte* (Roslyn NY: Black's Readers Service Co., 1932), x.

38. Bret Harte, "M'liss," in Redman, *The Works of Bret Harte*, 78–79.

39. Habegger, *Gender, Fantasy, and Realism in American Literature*, 159.

40. Eleanor Hodgman Porter (1868–1920) was something of a tomboy herself, with interests in social reform. She was born in Littleton, New Hampshire, and grew up more interested in outdoor life than books. After studying music at the New England Conservatory, she turned to writing in 1907 and published her first book,

Cross Currents, and its sequel, *The Turn of the Tide*. They were studies of the wretched conditions of child labor in the big city. Her "Miss Billy" series explored the impact a free-spirited woman makes in the home life of three bachelors. Her most popular works were the two "Pollyanna" books. After her death, a number of other writers produced more Pollyanna books.

41. Jerry Griswold, "Pollyanna; Ex-Bubblehead," *New York Times Book Review* 25 (October 1987), 51.

42. In ibid.

43. In ibid.

44. Henry F. May, *The End of American Innocence: A Study of the First Years of Our Own Time, 1912–1917* (Chicago: Quadrangle Books, 1964).

45. Although William John Locke (1863–1930) was a popular novelist at the turn of the century, he is virtually forgotten today, and information concerning him is difficult to obtain. He was born in Demerara, British Guiana, the elder son of a Barbados banker. He was sent to England at age three, where he remained for nine years. After completing prep school at Queen's Royal College, Trinidad, he matriculated from St. John's College, Cambridge, specializing in mathematics. After spending thirteen years as a teacher, a profession he thoroughly detested, he became secretary to the Royal Institute of British Architects in 1897. His novels in the next fifteen years included *The White Dove* (1900), *The Morals of Marcus Ordeyne* (1905), *The Beloved Vagabond* (1906), and *Stella Maris* (1913). Critics in his time applauded his idiosyncratic characters and exotic situations. "Their appeal is compounded of delicate and unobtrusive humor and a gentle irony, as well as of the gifts of imagination and language," wrote G. W. Harris in "W. J.Locke, An Apostle of Cheerfulness in Fiction," *Review of Reviews* 41 (March 1910): 376–77. See also "William J. Locke," *Current Literature* 53 (December 1912): 700.

46. William J. Locke, *Stella Maris* (New York: Dodd, Mead Co., 1929), 92.

47. As of this writing, we have been unable to unearth any background information about Belle K. Maniates and her "Amarilly" series of books.

48. Belle K. Maniates, *Amarilly of Clothes-Line Alley* (New York: Grosset and Dunlap, 1915), 1.

49. For a survey of the roles the Real Girl's older sisters were playing on Broadway at this time, see John C. Tibbetts, "The 'New Woman' on Stage: Women's Issues in American Drama, 1890–1915," *Helicon Nine: The Journal of Women's Arts and Letters*, no. 7 (1982), 6–19,

50. Clayton Hamilton, "The Players," *Everybody's Magazine*, April 1913, 512.

51. Ibid., 512.

52. Leon Edel, Preface, in Henry James, *What Maisie Knew* (London: The Bodley Head, 1969), 6.

53. Ibid., 8.

54. Maxwell Geismar, *Henry James and the Jacobites* (New York: Hill & Wang, 1975), 148.

55. Edel, *What Maisie Knew*, 7.

56. Eleanor Gates, *The Poor Little Rich Girl* (New York: Grosset and Dunlap, 1940), 62.

57. Eleanor Gates (1875–1951) is completely forgotten today. Beyond the facts that she wrote the novel and play version of the highly successful *The Poor Little Rich Girl* (1912), an autobiography, *A Biography of a Prairie Girl* (1902), and a series of articles and stories in *Cosmopolitan* from 1906–1907 on girls' topics—"The Girl Who Travels Alone" (November 1906, 2–13) and "Making Her Way in the World" (January 1907, 308–315)—there is no extant information available.

58. Hamilton, "The Players," 51.

59. Eleanor Gates, *The Poor Little Rich Girl: A Play of Fact and Fancy in Three Acts* (New York: Arrow Publishing Company, 1916), 294.

60. "Poor Little Rich Girl," *Theatre*, March 1913, 71.

61. "Poor Little Rich Girl—Something New in the Drama," *Current Opinion* LIV, no. 3 (March 1913), 291.

62. Hamilton, "The Players," 513–15.

63. Richard Corliss, "Queen of the Movies," *Film Comment*, March–April 1998, 59.

64. Cari Beauchamp's *Without Lying Down* (New York: Scribner's, 1996), 45, is the first thorough examination of Frances Marion and her circle of female associates and friends. Prior to this, aside from a useful overview of her life in DeWitt Bodeen's *More from Hollywood* (South Brunswick and New York: A. S. Barnes, 1977), the record of research on this important figure in American screen writing is dismal. She is nowhere to be found in Richard Corliss's pioneering study of screenwriters, *Talking Pictures* (Woodstock, NY: Overlook Press, 1974). For some of the writers who have bothered to notice her at all, she has been dismissed with a sexist sneer. "She had a tough exterior, a gravelly voice from too many cigarettes and too much Scotch," wrote Fred Lawrence Guiles in *Hanging on in Paradise* (New York: McGraw Hill, 1975), "It is said that she thought like a man and, indeed, from personal observation, I found her to have very few obvious feminine traits" (11). (In fact, the opposite was true, as the sleek, darkly handsome Frances wryly observed in response to similar cheap shots received in her lifetime: "Everybody expects to find a great big mannish woman with spectacles and perhaps a tailored suit. . . . And then they find me.") In a blatant charge of sexual politicking, Nancy Lynn Schwartz in *The Hollywood Writers' Wars* (New York: Alfred A. Knopf, 1982) not only falsely accuses Frances of being "the darling of L. B. Mayer [in fact, Marion despised him], but goes on to label her friend, writer Anita Loos as "another producer's darling" (19). Even when the tone is more respectful, as in the token page or two accorded Marion in Marjorie Rosen's *Popcorn Venus* and Molly Haskell's *Reverence to Rape* (New York: Holt, Rinehart, and Winston, 1973), they are fraught with errors. Marion's autobiography, *Off With Their Heads!*, which appeared in 1966, does not help matters, since it frequently substitutes humorous anecdotes for the historical record.

65. Lizzie Francke, *Script Girls: Women Screenwriters in Hollywood* (London: British Film Institute, 1994), 6.

66. Beauchamp, *Without Lying Down*, 45.

67. Several of Pickford's other films were based on properties by Frances Hodgson Burnett. In addition to *A Little Princess*, for example, *The Dawn of a Tomorrow* (1915), in which she played a waif of the London slums, was based on Burnett's 1906 novel (dramatized in 1909); and *Esmeralda* (1915), in which she played the daughter of a farming family, was based on Burnett's 1881 play.

68. Kevin Brownlow, *Mary Pickford Rediscovered* (New York: Abrams, 1999), 50.

69. Quoted in ibid., 30, 32.

70. Robert Cushman, program notes for the AFI Mary Pickford Retrospective, 1971, American Film Institute, Washington, D.C. Maurice Tourneur (1876–1961) was highly acclaimed for his pictorially beautiful and "artistic" productions, such as *The Wishing Ring* (1914), *The Poor Little Rich Girl* (1917), *The Blue Bird* (1918), and *The Last of the Mohicans* (1920). Director Clarence Brown, who worked with Tourneur, has left this description of his method in Kevin Brownlow's *The Parade's Gone By*: "Tourneur was an artist. He had been a painter, and although he did little painting while he was making pictures, he painted on the screen. Many of the tricks they use in the picture business today were originated by Tourneur, with his cameraman, John van der Broek. . . . Whenever we saw a painting with an interesting lighting effect, we'd copy it. We had a library of pictures. . . . Tourneur was great on tinting and toning. We never made a picture unless every scene was colored. . . . The most beautiful shots I ever saw on the screen were in Tourneur's pictures. He was more on the ball photographically than any other director." See Brownlow, *The Parade's Gone By*, 140–41.

71. Frances Marion, *Off With Their Heads!* (New York: Macmillan, 1972), 43–44.

72. Phyllis Bixler and Lucien Agosta, "Formula Fiction and Children's Literature: Thornton Waldo Burgess and Frances Hodgson Burnett," *Children's Literature in Education* 15 no. 2 (1984), 65.

73. Athene Farnsworth, "How Mary Pickford Stays Young," *Everybody's Magazine*, May 1926, 37.

74. Mary Pickford Correspondence, Number 461, Scenario File Number 19, Margaret Herrick Library, Academy of Motion Pictures Arts and Sciences, Los Angeles.

75. Corliss, "Queen of the Movies," 62.

76. The fullest account of Pickford's retirement years can be found in Whitfield, 337–64. She died on May 29, 1979.

Chapter 5

1. G. K. Chesterton, "A Fairy Tale," in *Lunacy and Letters* (New York: Sheed and Ward, 1958), 103.

2. Vance, *Douglas Fairbanks*, 36.

3. Kevin Brownlow links it to a series of drug-related films, beginning in 1912 with D. W. Griffith's *For His Son*, and including Lubin's *The Cocaine Traffic* (1914) and Famous

Players' *The Secret Sin* (1915). He reports they had become "a glut on the market" by the time the Loos-Emerson satire was released in 1916. The film was disowned by Triangle-Fine Arts and by Fairbanks himself. "What makes it of interest today is the fact that anyone could fine anything funny in the subject of drug addiction" (102). See *Behind the Mask of Innocence* (New York: Knopf, 1990), 96–119.

4. Cooke, *Douglas Fairbanks,* 18.

5. Henabery, *Before, In and After Hollywood,* 177–78.

6. Edward Weltzel, "Say Young Fellow!," *Moving Picture World,* July 6, 1918, 109; and "The Shadow Stage," *Photoplay,* July 1918, 79.

7. Vance, *Douglas Fairbanks,* 86.

8. Ibid., 87, 89.

9. Jeffrey Vance argues that "despite the claims of many film historians," the figure of Chaplin is "clearly a Chaplin imitator" (91).

10. "Technical Effects for *When The Clouds Roll By,*" *Literary Digest,* July 3, 1920, 75.

11. Quoted in Celia McGerr, *René Clair* (Boston: Twayne Publishers, 1980), 10. Clair frequently voiced his enthusiasms for the freedom and movement of Fairbanks's films. See especially his autobiography, *Cinema, Yesterday and Today,* ed. R. C. Dale, trans. Stanley Appelbaum (New York: Dover Publications, Inc., 1972), 60–62.

Chapter 6

1. See Tibbetts and Welsh, *His Majesty the American,* 102–109. See also Tino Balio, *United Artists: The Company that Changed the Film Industry* (University of Wisconsin Press, 1987); and Gertrude Jobes, *Motion Picture Empire* (Hamden, CT: Archon Books, 1966).

2. "Editorial," *Photoplay,* March 1917, 109.

3. Richard Pells, *Modernist America* (New Haven and London: Yale University Press, 2011), 207–210.

4. Fairbanks, "Let Me Say This for the Films," 156.

5. Pells, *Modernist America,* 209.

6. "Robin Hood," *Photoplay,* January 1923, 64.

7. See G. K. Chesterton, *The Return of Don Quixote* (London: Chatto & Windus, 1927). When the character of Michael Herne dons a costume of Robin Hood-like lincoln green for a feudal pageant, he discovers at the conclusion of the play that not only is he unable to discard the costume, but that he has been transformed for the rest of his life into a character from the Age of Chivalry. Moreover, "he had forced all his commonplace companions back into their masquerade clothes and compelled them to play the masque until they died" (208).

Chapter 7

1. Portions of this interview with Bob Kane at the Registry Hotel in North Hollywood, June 14, 1989, were published by Tibbetts in an essay, "High-Pressure Hype Surrounds '*Batman*,'" *Christian Science Monitor*, June 29, 1989, 10–11.

2. Vance, *Douglas Fairbanks*, 94.

3. For details, see Robert Sampson, *Yesterday's Faces: Violent Lives* (Bowling Green, OH: Bowling Green State University Press, 1993), 30–45.

4. For details about the "John Carter" stories, see Richard A. Lupoff, *Barsoom: Edgar Rice Burroughs and the Martian Vision* (Baltimore, MD: Mirage Press, 1976). Also the chapter "Destination Mars," in John C. Tibbetts, *The Gothic Imagination* (New York: Palgrave Macmillan, 2012), 177–92.

5. *Argosy All-Story Weekly*, May 6, 1922.

6. Acknowledgment from a letter dated April 2, 1946, from McCulley to Vernell Coriell of Kansas City, Missouri.

7. Sarah Watts, *Rough Rider in the White House: Theodore Roosevelt and the Politics of Desire* (Chicago: University of Chicago Press, 2003). Watts explores how a psychological reading of Roosevelt's character, fascination with American masculinity and his policies can help explain the development of the U.S. into an imperial nation.

8. E. Anthony Rotundo, *American Manhood: Transformations in Masculinity from the Revolution to the Modern Era* (New York: Basic Books, 1993), 226.

9. Jenkins, *What Made Pistachio Nuts?*, 67.

Chapter 8

1. Betts, *This Film Business*, 204.

2. Daniel J. Boorstin, *The Discoverers* (New York: Random House, 1983), 564–66.

3. Quoted in Adele Whitely Fletcher, "The Man Who Made Robin Hood," *Motion Picture Magazine*, February 1923, 25.

4. Quoted in Robert Sherwood, "The Best Moving Pictures of 1922–1923," in *Selected Film Criticism, 1921–1930*, ed. Anthony Slide (Metuchen, NJ: Scarecrow Press, 1982), 240.

5. Indeed, the origins of Robin Hood are shrouded in the mists of history and legend. In his book, *Robin Hood: A Mythic Biography* (1982), J. C. Holt goes so far as to cite the contention of *The Dictionary of National Biography* that the character never existed at all. Or . . . could he have been from Nottinghamshire, where one might now expect to find a Sherwood Forest theme park? Or from Barnsdale in South Yorkshire at a site called "the Sayles," overlooking the Great North Road, now called, less Romantically, the A-1 dual-carriageway? And where might screenwriters turn for a possible authoritative source text? The "rymes of Robyn Hood" are mentioned in passing by William Langland in his satire, *Piers Plowman*, dating to 1377. But there is no trace of Friar Tuck or Maid Marian until the end of the fifteenth century, and Robin's king in the medieval legend is

Edward (who assumed the throne in 1272), *not* Richard Coeur de Lion (who makes his legendary appearance much later, in the sixteenth century). Was Robin the same person as Robert of Huntington, or a yeoman archer, or merely a forest elf? In 1598, playwright Anthony Munday presented Robin as the Earl of Huntington in disguise. And, of course, he is "Locksley" in 12th century England in Walter Scott's *Ivanhoe* (1820).

6. For a survey of Robin Hood films, see Rudy Behlmer's Introduction to *The Adventures of Robin Hood*, Wisconsin/Warner Bros. screenplay series (Madison, WI: Wisconsin Center for Film and Theater Research, 1979), 11–53.

7. Fairbanks, "Let Me Say This for the Films," 15.

8. Lombardi, *Allan Dwan*, 89.

9. Quoted in Fletcher, "The Man Who Made Robin Hood," 25. For production details, see Brownlow, *The Parade's Gone By*, 246–257; and Vance, *Douglas Fairbanks*, 125–151.

10. Sherwood, "Robin Hood Rides upon the Screen," 32.

11. Clair, *Cinema, Yesterday and Today*, 60.

12. Bogdanovich, *Allan Dwan*, 63.

13. Brownlow, *The Parade's Gone By*, 257.

14. Clair, *Cinema*, 61.

15. Betts, *This Film Business*, 205–207.

16. Quoted in Sherwood, "The Best Moving Pictures of 1922–1923," 341.

Chapter 9

1. Richard F. Burton, ed. and annotated, *The Book of the Thousand Nights and a Night*, vols. 1 and 2 (New York: The Heritage Press 1934), 232. In his 1885 English translation, Burton introduces us to storyteller Sharazad (Sheherazade), the daughter of King Shahryar's Wazir. In the first tale, "The Story of King Shahryar and his Brother," we learn that she was a seductive storyteller who dared to marry the king, whose madness at the infidelity of his former wife led him exorcise his demons by marrying a new wife every morning and slaying her that same night. Sharazad succeeded not only in avoiding her fate with her many tales, but she bore Shahryar three children, as well! Burton's extensive introduction to the original edition (i–xvii) details the many sources from which he derived his own translation.

2. For detailed accounts of Hollywood "orientalism," see Matthew Bernstein and Gaylyn Studlar, *Visions of the East: Orientalism in Film* (New Brunswick, NJ: Rutgers University Press, 1997).

3. Writing in *Life*, April 3, 1924, 32, as quoted in *Spellbound in Darkness*, 298.

4. As quoted in George C. Pratt, *Spellbound in Darkness: A History of the Silent Film* (Greenwich: New York Graphic Society, Ltd., 1973),

5. Ibid., 298.

6. Raoul Walsh, *Each Man in His Time: The Life Story of a Director* (New York: Farrar, Straus, Giroux, 1974), 168.

7. Ibid.

8. Vachel Lindsay, *The Art of the Moving Picture* (New York: Liveright Publishing Corp., 1970), 161–62.

9. Lindsay, "The Great Douglas Fairbanks," 12–13, 114.

10. Henry Jenkins, *The Wow Climax* (New York University Press, 2007), 146.

11. Naomi Rosenblatt, "Orientalism in American Popular Culture," *Penn History Review* 16, no. 2 (Spring 2009): 9.

12. Fairbanks Jr., "Dad," 75.

13. Edward Said, *Orientalism* (New York: Vintage Books, 1978), 2.

14. Ibid., 59.

15. Rosenblatt, "Orientalism in American Popular Culture," 58–59.

16. For a detailed examination of the production history of the film and its special effects, see Vance, *Douglas Fairbanks*, 2008.

17. Chesterton, *The Defendant*, 118.

18. Bernstein and Studlar, *Visions of the East*, 4.

Chapter 10

1. Rudy Behlmer, "High Style on the High Seas," *American Cinematographer*, April 1992, 34–40; Behlmer, "*The Black Pirate* Weighs Anchor," *American Cinematographer*, May 1992, 34–40. For a summary of those articles and an update, see also Vance, *Douglas Fairbanks*, 202–225.

2. "The Black Pirate," *Photoplay*, May 1926, 48. Before the appearance of our *His Majesty the American* in 1977, references to the Technicolor processes employed in *The Black Pirate* were scant. The material from that book has been expanded and updated in the present volume.

3. Behlmer, "Technicolor," *Films in Review*, June-July, 1964, 334.

4. James L. Limbacher, "Four Aspects," 26.

5. Behlmer, "The Black Pirate Weighs Anchor," 38.

6. Behlmer, "Technicolor," 340.

7. Fairbanks, "Let Me Say This About Films," 120.

8. Schallert, "Yo Ho and a Bottle of Rum," *Picture-Play Magazine*, February 1926, 17.

9. Schallert, "Doug Rubs the Magic Lamp," *Picture- Play Magazine*, September 1923, 87.

10. Barbara Little, "The Pirates are Coming," *Picture-Play Magazine*, March 1923, 47.

11. Eugene V. Brewster, "Why Color Pictures and Talking Movies Can Never Be Universal," *Motion Picture Magazine*, June 1926, 5.

12. Rudolph Arnheim, *Film as Art* (Berkeley and Los Angeles: University of California Press, 1957), 66.

13. According to Rudy Behlmer, in "High Style on the High Seas," another problem was that the film had to be hand-cranked at 48 frames per second, twice the normal

crank speed. "The reason for the 48 frames was that two standard-size frames were exposed simultaneously through the use of a beam-splitter prism; one frame through a red filter and one through a green filter (35).

14. Limbacher, "Four Aspects," 14.

15. Leonard Maltin, *Behind the Camera* (New York: Signet, 1971), 112.

16. Dunham Thorp, "How Fairbanks Took the Color out of Color," *Motion Picture Classic*, May 1926, 29.

17. Schallert, "Yo Ho and a Bottle of Rum," 108.

18. Thorp, "How Fairbanks Took the Color out of Color," 87.

19. "Doug Gets Away With It," *Outlook*, April 14, 1926, 561.

20. Quoted in "Swashbuckling with Doug on a Painted Ocean," *Literary Digest*, April 10, 1926, 42.

21. Thorp, "How Fairbanks Took the Color out of Color," 89.

22. Ibid., 87.

23. Ibid.

24. "Doug Gets Away With It," 561.

25. "Swashbuckling with Doug on a Painted Ocean," 35.

26. Ibid.

27. Thorp, "How Fairbanks," 87.

28. Schallert, "Yo Ho and a Bottle of Rum," 17.

29. Maltin, *Behind the Camera*, 116.

30. Lindsay, "The Great Douglas Fairbanks," 114–15.

31. Quinn Martin, "The Black Pirate," *The Arts*, quoted in *American Film Criticism*, ed. Kauffmann, 173.

32. "Swashbuckling with Doug on a Painted Ocean," 36.

33. Letter from Vera Fairbanks, June 5, 2012.

34. Behlmer, "*The Black Pirate* Weighs Anchor," 40.

35. These and other remarks from David Shepard were gathered in the preparation of John C. Tibbetts, "The Choreography of Hope," *Film Comment*, May-June 1996, 51–55.

36. Authors' interview with David Shepard, Los Angeles, March 2, 1996.

37. Letter from David Shepard, June 4, 2012.

Chapter 11

1. "Fairbanks Makes D'Artagnan into a French Cowboy," quoted in *Literary Digest*, September 17, 1921, 28.

2. Entirely appropriate here is Robert E. Sherwood's critical note in *Life* magazine, September 22, 1921: "D'Artagnan lives in Fairbanks. Fairbanks lives in D'Artagnan," in *American Film Criticism*, ed. Kauffmann, 127.

3. Prior to the Fairbanks version, there were at least five screen versions, including a French serial, *Les Trois Mousequetaires* (1921–22), directed by Henri Diamant-Bergerk,

and a Max Linder satire, *The Three Must-Get-Theres* (1922). The former led to a ban in France of the Fairbanks film. The latter brought the fencing master, Fred Cavens to Fairbanks's attention. For a detailed account of Dumas's novel and its many adaptations, see Tibbetts and Welsh, eds., *The Encyclopedia of Novels into Film* (New York: Facts on File, 2005), 449–52.

4. Alexandre Dumas, "Author's Preface," in *The Three Musketeeers* (New York: The Heritage Press, 1953), vi.

5. Details can be found in F. Reniers, "The Three Musketeers," *New York Evening Post*, August 19, 1921, in *American Film Criticism*, ed. Kauffmann, 125–26.

6. For the record, d'Artagnan first voices the motto in Chapter IX: "'And now, gentlemen,' said d'Artagnan, without stopping to explain his conduct to Porthos—'all for one, one for all, that is our device, is it not?' . . . and the four friends repeated with one voice the formula dictated by d'Artagnan—'All for one, one for all.'" Dumas, *The Three Musketeers*, 65.

7. Lindsay, *The Art of the Moving Picture*, 44.

8. Vance, *Douglas Fairbanks*, 122.

9. F. Reniers, "The Three Musketeers," 126.

10. Dumas, *The Man in the Iron Mask* (New York: The Heritage Press, 1964), 368.

11. "The Iron Mask," *Photoplay*, February 1929, 53.

12. Lombardi, *Allan Dwan*, 163.

13. John Noone, *The Man Behind the Iron Mask* (New York: St. Martin's Press, 1988), 252.

14. Ibid., 4–5. Noone goes on to advance a far more mundane theory of the Iron Mask's identity: he was one d'Angers, a lowly valet whose knowledge of a State Secret (unknown to this day) caused him to be imprisoned at Ste. Marguerite and later at the Bastile under the charge of the gaoler Saint-Mars, a former musketeer. Out of vanity and a measure of diplomacy, Saint-Mars stage-managed a colossal hoax involving a real iron mask "to bamboozle the public" that his prisoner was a significant figure. "The idea of masking the prisoner was a ploy thought up by Saint-Mars to advertise the supposed secret of his prisoner's identity, and he chose to do it in such a theatrical way because he knew a steel mask would have greater impact on those who saw it than would a normal mask . . . [He] conducted his campaign with all the flash and flair of a modern promotor" (265). In short, concludes Noone, "The Iron Mask was a nonentity who became famous precisely because he was a nonentity" (275).

15. Dumas, *The Man in the Iron Mask*, 294.

16. The words are a reworking of a speech Edward Knoblock wrote for the earlier *The Three Musketeers* (1921).

17. Dumas, *The Man in the Iron Mask*, 388.

18. Ibid., 404.

19. Edward Bernds, *Mr. Bernds Goes to Hollywood* (Lanham, MD: Scarecrow Press, 1999), 72–73.

20. The 1952 version was repackaged by film preservationist David Shepard and released on Kino Video in 1996. In an interview with the author, Shepard noted: "This

has the music score by Allan Gray, which I think is beautiful. It was especially written for it and performed by the Philharmonia Orchestra, a seventy-five-piece orchestra. Douglas Jr. dubbed the talking sequences and narrated the silent sequences. I really admire the intelligence with which it was adapted. It represents the best attempt I've seen to put a soundtrack on a silent film. We really wanted to get the original 1929 talking version, with Fairbanks Sr.'s own voice, but it was at the Museum of Modern Art and they would not cough it up. Douglas Jr. is pleased about it. It is clear that he reveres his father's accomplishments" (interview with John C. Tibbetts, Los Angeles, March 2, 1996).

Chapter 12

1. Mordaunt Hall, "An Argentine Cowboy," *New York Times*, November 22, 1927, 32:2.
2. Schickel, *His Picture in the Papers*, 112.
3. Douglas Fairbanks Jr., *Salad Days* (New York: Doubleday, 1988), 119.
4. Tibbetts and Welsh, *His Majesty the American*, 155.
5. Vance, *Douglas Fairbanks*, 227.
6. "When 'Doug,' the Gaucho, Hurls His Trusty Bolas," *Literary Digest*, December 31, 1927, 30–32.
7. Authors' interview with Douglas Fairbanks Jr., New York City, March 8, 1996.
8. For accounts of this troubled period in Fairbanks's life, see Gary Carey, *Doug & Mary* (New York: E. P. Dutton, l977), 177–80; Brian Connell, *Knight, Errant: A Biography of Douglas Fairbanks, Jr.* (New York: Doubleday & Co., l955), 50–54; Eyman, *Mary Pickford*, 168–80; Booton Herndon, *Mary Pickford and Douglas Fairbanks* (New York: W. W. Norton & Co., l977), 262–68.
9. Tino Balio, *United Artists: The Company that Changed the Film Industry* (University of Wisconsin Press, 1990), 13.
10. Allene Talmey, *Doug and Mary and Others* (New York: Macy-Masius, 1927), 37.
11. Jacques Barzun is careful to distinguish between the "Byronic personae" of his early poems—with their protagonists of "agitation and recklessness"—and the "corrective effect" of his letters, which reveal the man himself as possessing a "unique discharge of intellectual vitality"—a "concentrated mind and high spirits, wit, daylight good sense, and a passion for truth." See "Byron and the Byronic in History," in Jacques Barzun, *The Energies of Art* (New York: Harper & Brothers, 1956), 49–80.
12. Andre Maurois, *Byron* (New York: D. Appleton and Co., l930), 24l.
13. Donald Sutherland, *On Romanticism* (New York: New York University Press, 1971), 255–56.
14. Lord Byron, *The Corsair*, in *Byron's Poetical Works*, ed. Paul Elmer More (Boston and New York: Houghton and Mifflin), lines 224–27.
15. Barzun, *The Energies of Art*, 53.
16. Lord Byron, *Manfred*, in *Byron's Poetical Works*, ed. More, act III, scene I, lines 65–68.
17. Fairbanks quoted in Vance, 232.

18. Lord Byron, "Childe Harold's Pilgrimage," in *Byron's Poetical Works*, ed. More, canto one, V, lines 37–40.

19. Alexander Walker, *Stardom* (London: Michael Joseph, 1970), 115.

20. Letter from Lord Byron to William Harness, December 15, 1811, in *The Selected Letters of Lord Byron*, ed. Barzun (New York: Farrar, Straus and Cudahy, 1953), 38–40.

Chapter 13

1. Quoted in Eyman, *Mary Pickford, America's Sweetheart*, 184–85.

2. George Abbott and Ann Preston Bridgers, *Coquette* (New York: Samuel French, 192). All quotations from the play are taken from this edition.

3. Howard Taubman, *The Making of the American Theatre* (New York: Coward-McCann, Inc., 1965), 185

4. Musical film historian Miles Kreuger has noted that the practice of filming stage shows directly from the stage was a common practice at the time. These filmed records were used as guides for subsequent film adaptations. The casts of the stage shows were paid by the film studio for these recordings. It was never the intention to use any of this footage in the movie versions (authors' interviews with Miles Kreuger, May 26, 1979, and March 3, 1980, in Los Angeles, California).

5. Alexander Walker, *The Shattered Silents* (New York: William Morrow, 1979), 92.

6. For an overview, see Emma Goldman, *The Social Significance of the Modern Drama* (Boston: Richard Badger, 1914); and Tibbetts, "The New Woman on Stage: Women's Issues in American Drama, 1890–1915," *Helicon Nine: The Journal of Women's Arts and Letters*, no. 7 (Winter 1982), 6–19.

7. Quoted in Lois Gottlieb, "Obstacles to Feminism in the Early Plays of Rachel Crothers," *Papers in Women's Studies* II, no. 2, 71.

8. Eugene Walter, *The Easiest Way*, in *Best Plays of the Early American Theatre*, ed. John Gassner (New York: Crown Publishers, Inc., 1967), 660.

9. Gregory Black, *Hollywood Censored: Morality Codes, Catholics, and the Movies* (Cambridge University Press, 1994), 41–42.

10. Quoted in Walker, *The Shattered Silents*, 148.

11. Quoted in Eyman, *Mary Pickford, America's Sweetheart*, 191.

12. Authors' interview with Robert Cushman, September 6, 1996.

13. For an overview of the negative reactions to the talking picture technology, see the preface to Tibbetts, ed., *Introduction to the Photoplay* (Los Angeles and Kansas City: The National Film Society, 1977), xi–xviii.

Chapter 14

1. See Robert Hamilton Ball, *Shakespeare on Silent Film* (London: George Allan & Unwin, 1968), 63.

2. See also Judith Buchanan, *Shakespeare on Silent Screen: An Excellent Dumb Discourse* (Cambridge, UK: Cambridge University Press), 2009.

3. Quoted in Ball, 235. *Macbeth* as adapted by Fairbanks's old friends, scenarist Anita Loos and director John Emerson. For details on the production, see John C. Tibbetts, *The American Theatrical Film*, 103–105.

4. Benjamin Glazer, "The Photoplay with Sound and Voice," in Tibbetts, ed., *Introduction to the Photoplay*.

5. William Cameron Menzies, "Pictorial Beauty in the Photoplay," in Tibbetts, ed., *Introduction to the Photoplay*.

6. Quoted in Schickel, *His Picture in the Papers*, 125–26.

7. Vance, *Douglas Fairbanks*, 270.

8. Sime Silverman, "Taming of the Shrew," *Variety*, December 4, 1919, 15.

9. Henry Jenkins, "*Star Trek* Rerun, Reread, Rewritten: Fan Writing as Textual Poaching," *Critical Studies in Mass Communication* 5 (1988), 86.

10. Quoted in Eyman, *Mary Pickford, America's Sweetheart*, 195.

11. Ibid., 192.

12. Ibid.

13. Although Punch and Judy shows did not emerge as popular entertainment until after the Restoration, it is significant that Kate does utter this line to Petruchio in the play: "Belike you mean to make a puppet of me" (4.3.103).

14. For detailed examinations of these sparring sequences, see John Brett Mischo, "The Screening of the Shrews," in Lisa S. Starks and Courtney Lehmann, eds., *The Reel Shakespeare* (Madison, WI: Fairleigh Dickinson University Press, 2002), 212–28.

15. For details about the appearance of "The New Woman" on the American stage at this time, see Tibbetts, "The New Woman on Stage: Women's Issues in American Drama, 1890–1915," 6–19.

16. Quoted in Eyman, *Mary Pickford, America's Sweetheart*, 193.

17. Barbara Hogdon, "Play(K)ating the strictures of Everyday Life," in *Shakespeare on Film*, ed. Robert Shaughnessy (New York: St. Martin's Press, 1998), 164.

18. See Eyman, *Mary Pickford, America's Sweetheart*, 164–76.

19. Fairbanks, "Dad," 75.

20. Eyman, *Mary Pickford, America's Sweetheart*, 176.

21. See Vance, *Douglas Fairbanks*, 274–78.

22. See Eyman, *Mary Pickford, America's Sweetheart*, 194–95.

23. Scott Eyman, "An Interview with Karl Struss," *Journal of Popular Film* 4, no. 4 (1975): 318.

24. The film purportedly became the victim of the unfounded allegation that the original release contained this credit: "By William Shakespeare; with additional dialogue by Sam Taylor." Not true. As the script, the pressbook, and the print of the original version of the film preserved at the Museum Modern Art attest, the credit was, simply, "Adapted and Directed by Sam Taylor."

25. *Shrew* was the eighth Synetic attempt to adapt Shakespeare without words—following, for example, *Antony and Cleopatra* and *King Lear*, and *A Midsummer Night's*

Dream—all adapted by director Paata Tsikurisvili, whose wife, Irina, played and danced the role of Kate. The challenge here, as in any silent film, is to transform emotion into "powerful, plot-driven action" in such a way that "movement becomes an expression of character." Of course, the medium of dance is quite different from cinema, and achievement and success must be gauged by different standards. But Synetic's success would seem to suggest that Washingtonians have been satisfied.

26. Franco Zeffirelli's film is like a Punch and Judy spectacle of ill temper and abuse. His actors had been in training. Burton started preparing for the role with his "angry" portrayal of Jimmy Porter in John Osborne's *Look Back in Anger*; then Burton and Taylor rehearsed for the *Shrew* in their edgy and bitchy adaptation of Edward Albee's *Who's Afraid of Virginia Woolf?* In that one, Taylor seemed to strip Burton of his manhood, setting his Petruchio up to get his revenge. But while this spectacle of boorishness and shrewishness may be amusing for some, it's not an especially "shrewd" adaptation, as Jim Welsh found when he was privileged to discuss the play and film with a group of Kuwati women graduate students near the Persian Gulf in 2011 at Kuwait University. They seemed to have an immediate understanding of Katherine's ploy. Kate's final speech concerning obedience made more sense to them than it might do for a more fiercely feminist Western audience. During the 1990s, a production of this now dated Renaissance comedy at Stratford-upon-Avon that its best to emasculate the play and overcompensate for feminist fury.

27. Quoted from the Yale Shakespeare edition, Thomas G. Bergin, ed., *The Taming of the Shrew* (New Haven: Yale University Press, 1954). Trial runs of this chapter were read and presented at Kuwait University in December of 2011, by the kind invitation of Dr. Yasur W. Al-Madani and the department of English there, then, later, at the national Popluar Culture.

Chapter 15

1. Peter Conrad, "The Libertine's Progress," in *Don Giovanni: Myths of Seduction and Betrayal*, ed. Jonathan Miller (New York: Schocken Books, 1990), 81.

2. "How Can Doug Stay Away from Hollywood?" *Motion Picture Classic*, March 1933, 68.

Chapter 16

1. The original conception was for the film to have been a musical, but all the numbers, save the "Lowdown" routine with Bing Crosby and Daniels, were cut out. Even Irving Berlin's theme music, "Reaching for the Moon," is heard only in the background. The original running time was ninety-one minutes, not the seventy-four-minute version commercially available today (authors' interview with Miles Kreuger, Los Angeles, California, October 6, 1978).

Chapter 17

1. "The Headline Career of Mary and Doug," *Motion Picture Classic*, March 1933, 68.

2. Eileen Bowser, ed., *Film Notes* (New York: Museum of Modern Art, 1969), 80.

3. Daniel Defoe, *Robinson Crusoe*, ed.John Richetti (New York: Penguin Books, 2001), 103.

4. Douglas Fairbanks Jr., "Dad," *Theater*, May 1930, 75.

Chapter 18

1. Maria Alba was not a Tahitian but of Spanish-American descent who, before appearing at age twenty-two as "Saturday" in 1932, made her film debut in *Road House* four years before. She made her last film in 1946.

2. See Byron, *Don Juan* (canto 2, stanza 202).

3. Mordaunt Hall, "On a Desert Island," *New York Times*, September 22, 1932, 25.

Chapter 19

1. For details, see Brian Connell, *Knight Errant* (Garden City, NY: Doubleday & Company, 1955), 64–66.

2. "How Can Doug Stay Away from Hollywood?"

3. The portrayal of strong women in *Catherine the Great* could be usefully compared to the scheming women trying to dominate Don Juan. Early in the film, for example, Catherine, on the eve of her marriage to the grand duke, is counseled by the empress: "There's only way for a poor, defenseless woman to treat a husband, and that's to get the upper hand of him in the first five minutes and then to rule him. . . . Women can rule, men can't."

4. Henri Bataille's three-act play, *L'homme as la rose*, opened in Paris in 1920. M. André Brulé portrayed Don Juan de Marana. The American version was entitled simply *Don Juan* and was adapted by Lawrence Langner. The Broadway League production opened on September 5, 1921, and closed after fourteen performances. Lou Tellegen portrayed Don Juan.

5. Marcelle Lamasque, "A Don Juan Character Study: Henry Bataille's New Play Entertains While Analysing," *La France* 5 (February 1921), 207.

6. Andre Sennwald, "The Private Life of Don Juan," *New York Times*, December 10, 1934, 16.

7. Paul Tabori, *Alexander Korda* (New York: Living Books, 1966), 156.

8. See Robert Wilson, ed., *The Film Criticism of Otis Ferguson* (Philadelphia: Temple University Press, 1971), 63–64.

9. Max Frisch's play opened in the Zurich Schauspielhaus in 1953. For the historical and cultural contexts of the play, see Michael Butler, *The Plays of Max Frisch* (New York: St. Martin's Press, 1985), 47–60.

10. Moliere, *Don Juan, or The Statue at the Feast* (Baltimore: Penguin Books, 1966), 230.

11. Ibid., 247.

12. Lorenzo Da Ponte, "The Punished Libertine," in *The Theatre of Don Juan*, ed. Oscar Mandel (Lincoln, NE: University of Nebraska Press, 1963), 303.

13. Ibid., 314.

14. Peter Gay, "The Father's Revenge," in *Giovanni*, ed. Miller, 76.

15. W. H. Auden, "Don Juan," in *The Dyer's Hand* (New York: Random House, 1962), 392

16. V. S. Pritchett asks the question in his essay, "The Supreme Fairy Tale" (909). He claims that whereas Don Quixote has become a "universal myth," Don Juan has failed under the brunt of modernism. See *V. S. Prichett: Collected Complete Essays* (New York: Random House, 1991), 909.

17. Stanley Weintraub, ed., "Don Juan in Hell," *The Portable Bernard Shaw* (New York: Penguin Books, 1986), 286.

18. G. K. Chesterton, *George Bernard Shaw* (New York: John Lane, 1909), 207.

19. George Bernard Shaw, *Man and Superman: A Comedy and a Philosophy* (London: Penguin, 1965), 208.

20. Henry Anatole Grunwald, "The Disappearance of Don Juan," *Horizon* IV, no. 3 (January 1962), 58.

21. Frisch's play opened in the Zurich Schauspielhaus in 1953. For the historical and cultural contexts of the play, see Michael Butler, *The Plays of Max Frisch* (New York: St. Martin's Press, 1985), 47–60.

22. Max Frisch, *Don Juan and the Love of Geometry*, in *Three Plays*, trans. James L. Rosenberg (New York: Hill & Wang, 1967), 61. All quotations are taken from this edition.

23. Ibid., 37–39.

24. Ferguson, *The Film Criticism of Otis Ferguson*, 64.

Epilogue

1. Fairbanks, "Let Me Say This for the Films," 13.

2. Quoted in Duncan Wu, *William Hazlitt: The First Modern Man* (New York: Oxford University Press, 2008), 280.

3. Schickel, *His Picture in the Papers*, 158.

Afterword

1. Michael Kimmel, *Manhood in America: A Cultural History* (New York: Free Press, 1997), 119.

2. Clifford Putney, *Muscular Christianity: Manhood and Sports in Protestant America, 1880–1920* (Cambridge: Harvard University Press), 2001.

3. Ibid., 3.

4. Lary May, *Screening the Past,* 116–17.

5. Kimmel, *Manhood in America,* 118–21.

6. E. Anthony Rotundo, *American Manhood: Transformations in Masculinity from the Revolution to the Modern Era* (New York: Basic Books, 1993), 248–50.

7. Angel Kwolek-Folland's study *Engendering Business* provides a historical analysis of the creation of American business bureaucracy and policies from the late 19th century into the 1930s. In the study, Folland shows how men resisted what they perceived as the "feminization" of the American workplace through the usage of specialized language and hiring practices that would place men in positions that were superior to the growing number of women working in these offices.

8. Clark Davis's study, *Company Men: White-Collar Life and Corporate Cultures in Los Angeles, 1892–1941,* uses Los Angeles and its changing status to explore how masculinity and the needs of big business found themselves in competition at times, and at others in-sync. Davis's book offers a historical understanding of how corporate culture was organized and how men functioned within that system and in the process illustrates how American notions of masculinity were being redefined as a result of the new form of American economy.

9. Elliot J. Gorn, *The Manly Art: Bare-Knuckle Prize Fighting in America* (New York: Cornell University Press, 1986), 192.

10. Kimmel, *Manhood in America,* 120–21.

11. Lary May, *Screening the Past,* 117.

12. Gail Bederman, *Manliness and Civilization: A Cultural History of Gender and Race in the United States, 1880–1917* (Chicago: University of Chicago Press, 1995), 23–25.

13. Jackson Lears, *Rebirth of a Nation: The Making of Modern America, 1877–1920* (New York: Harper Perennial, 2009), 29.

14. Ibid., 29–34.

15. Kristin L. Hoganson, *Fighting for American Manhood: How Gender Politics Provoked the Spanish-American and Philippine-American Wars* (New Haven: Yale University Press, 1998), 10.

16. Ibid., 3.

17. Ibid., 22.

18. Dana D. Nelson, *National Manhood: Capitalist Citizenship and the Imagined Fraternity of White Men* (Durham: Duke University Press, 1998), x.

Appendix A

1. Fairbanks Jr., *The Salad Days*, 73.

2. *The Salad Days* was published by Doubleday in 1988; *A Hell of a War* was published by St. Martin's Press in 1993.

3. Fairbanks Jr., "Dad," 75.

4. Fairbanks Jr., *The Salad Days*, 87.

5. Ibid., 3.

6. Connell, *Knight Errant*, 155.

7. Fairbanks Jr., *The Salad Days*, 1.

8. For an account of the production of *The Exile* and Max Ophuls's Hollywood films, see Susan M. White, *The Cinema of Max Ophuls* (New York: Columbia University Press, 1995), 334–36.

9. To date, no posthumous third volume has appeared.

10. The Howard Gottlieb Archival Research Center, at the Mugar Memorial Library, is located in the heart of the campus of Boston University. Gottlieb dedicated the lobby of the Mugar Library to Douglas Jr., and a large portrait of Douglas Jr. in his naval uniform hangs alongside a descriptive bronze plaque in his name. According to Vera Fairbanks, the Fairbanks collection there is the second largest collection amongst 2,200 collectees. The largest is devoted to Martin Luther King Jr. (letter from Vera Fairbanks to the authors, May 26, 2012). Presently in charge is Vita Palladino, former assistant to Gottlieb. The materials there are primarily those of Douglas Jr., although there are also many items relating to his father and stepmother, Mary Pickford Among the holdings are many film script from Jr.'s movies and television shows, a collection of military decorations and swords, and many of his paintings and sculpture pieces. Our thanks to Ryan Henderson, assistant director for manuscripts, for his assistance in identifying the holdings.

11. The Pickfair property was purchased from Zadora by Unicom for $15 million in 2005. As it now stands, the extensively renovated mansion and grounds sits on 2.25 acres and has seventeen bedrooms, elevators, a ballroom-sized living room, an indoor glass dome spa, a gym, a swimming pool, a disco, and parking for thirty cars. It is currently listed on the market for a purported $60 million. www.bergproperties.com/blog/legendary-picfkfair-mansion (accessed May 26, 2012).

INDEX